MUSIC FOR ELEMENTARY
CLASSROOM TEACHERS

YO-EFL-660

Also by Patricia Shehan Campbell

Free to Be Musical: Group Improvisation in Music (coauthor)

Global Music (series coeditor)

Lessons from the World: A Cross-Cultural Guide to Music Teaching and Learning

Multicultural Perspectives in Music Education (coeditor)

Music in Childhood: From Preschool through the Elementary Years (coauthor)

Music in Cultural Context: Eight Views on World Music Education

Musician and Teacher: An Orientation to Music Education

The Oxford Handbook of Children's Musical Cultures (coeditor)

Redefining Music Studies in an Age of Change: Creativity, Diversity, and Integration (coauthor)

Songs in Their Heads: Music and Its Meaning in Children's Lives

Teaching Music Globally: Experiencing Music, Expressing Culture

Also by Carol Scott-Kassner

The Magic of Music (coauthor)

The Music Connection (coauthor)

Music in Childhood: From Preschool through the Elementary Years (coauthor)

The World of Music (coauthor)

MUSIC FOR ELEMENTARY CLASSROOM TEACHERS

Patricia Shehan Campbell
University of Washington

Carol Scott-Kassner

Kirk Kassner

W. W. Norton & Company
NEW YORK · LONDON

W. W. Norton & Company has been independent since its founding in 1923, when William Warder Norton and Mary D. Herter Norton first published lectures delivered at the People's Institute, the adult education division of New York City's Cooper Union. The Nortons soon expanded their program beyond the Institute, publishing books by celebrated academics from America and abroad. By mid-century, the two major pillars of Norton's publishing program—trade books and college texts—were firmly established. In the 1950s, the Norton family transferred control of the company to its employees, and today—with a staff of four hundred and a comparable number of trade, college, and professional titles published each year—W. W. Norton & Company stands as the largest and oldest publishing house owned wholly by its employees.

Copyright © 2017 by W. W. Norton & Company, Inc.
All rights reserved
Printed in the United States of America

First Edition

Editor: Maribeth Payne
Editorial assistants: Grant Phelps, Julie Kocsis
Managing editor, College: Marian Johnson
Associate project editor: Michael Fauver
Media project editor: Meg Wilhoite
Media editor: Steve Hoge
Media assistant editor: Stephanie Eads
Production manager: Eric Pier-Hocking
Photo researcher: Travis Carr
Permissions manager: Megan Schindel
Copyeditor: Courtney Hirschey
Proofreader: Barbara Curialle
Indexer: Marilyn Bliss
Design director: Rubina Yeh
Designers: Anna Reich, Lissi Sigillo
Composition and layout: GraphicWorld
Manufacturing: LSC Communications, Inc.
Marketing manager: Trevor Penland

Library of Congress Cataloging-in-Publication Data

Campbell, Patricia Shehan, author. | Scott-Kassner, Carol, author. |
  Kassner, Kirk, author.
Music for elementary classroom teachers : creating the musically
  vibrant classroom / Patricia Shehan Campbell, Carol Scott-Kassner,
  Kirk Kassner.
First edition. | New York : W. W. Norton & Company, [2018] |
  Includes bibliographical references and index.
LCCN 2017027567 | ISBN 9780393284119 (spiral)
LCSH: Music--Instruction and study. | Education, Elementary.
LCC MT1 .C225 2018 | DDC 372.8/044—dc23
LC record available at https://lccn.loc.gov/2017027567

W. W. Norton & Company, Inc., 500 Fifth Avenue, New York, NY 10110
www.wwnorton.com

W. W. Norton & Company, Ltd., 15 Carlisle Street, London W1D 3BS

1 2 3 4 5 6 7 8 9 0

We dedicate this book to the memory of four inspiring music educators who left us too soon. They lovingly taught music to children as well as to teachers who would one day teach music: Patricia Costa Kim, Rita Klinger, Linda Leubke, Liz Wing

Brief Contents

Preface xv

About the Authors xix

PART I

THE MUSICAL LIVES OF CHILDREN AND TEACHERS ... 3

1 Music and Children: Then, Now, and Evermore ... 4

2 Teachers as Facilitators of Music and the Arts ... 16

3 The Musical Growth of Children ... 37

PART II

THE MUSICAL MAKEUP OF CHILDREN ... 55

4 Their Singing Voices ... 56

5 Their Ears: Listening to Music ... 74

6 Their Moving Bodies ... 103

7 The Instruments They Play ... 119

8 Their Creative Imaginations ... 139

PART III

MUSIC THROUGHOUT THE DAY ... 161

9 Music for the Joy of It ... 162

10 Music and Language Arts ... 183

11 Music and Social Studies ... 210

12 Music and Math ... 240

13 Music and Science ... 261

14 All of the Arts ... 276

Appendix 1 Music Fundamentals ... A1

Appendix 2 Three Common Methods of Teaching Music to Children ... A13

Appendix 3 Resources for Listening ... A19

Appendix 4 National Standards for Music Education, Pre-K through Grade 8 ... A31

Bibliography ... A41

Classroom Resources for Children ... A45

End Notes ... A49

Credits ... A53

Index ... A55

vii

Contents

Preface xv
About the Authors xix

PART I

THE MUSICAL LIVES OF CHILDREN AND TEACHERS 3

CHAPTER 1

Music and Children: Then, Now, and Evermore 4

In the Classroom 5
Vignette One • Vignette Two • Vignette Three 5

Music in the Lives of Children 6

Music in School 7

Music's Many Functions 7

Their Brains on Music 9
Brain Research on Music 9
Brain-Based Learning 10

Justifying Musical Study and Integration 12

Standards in School Music 14

Summary, Review, Critical Thinking, and Projects 14
Additional Resources for Teaching 15

CHAPTER 2

Teachers as Facilitators of Music and the Arts 16

In the Classroom 17
Vignette One • Vignette Two • Vignette Three 17

The Musical Importance of Classroom Teachers 18

Finding Your Own Musicianship 19

Structuring the Classroom for Musical Experiences 19
Informal Uses of Music 19
Creating Music Centers 20

Designing Arts-Integrated Curricula 21
The Value of Arts Integration 21
Integration versus Infusion 22
Individual Planning 22

Collaborative Planning 24
Models of Multidisciplinary Projects 25
Models of Interdisciplinary Projects 28

Connecting the Classroom to the Community 28
Bringing Artists into Schools 28
Parents as Resources 31
Connecting to the Larger Arts Community 31
Taking Children into the Community 32
Bringing the Community into the School 32

Models and Resources for Teacher Training in Arts Integration 33

Summary, Review, Critical Thinking, and Projects 34
Additional Resources for Teaching 36

CHAPTER 3

The Musical Growth of Children 37

In the Classroom 38
Vignette One • Vignette Two 38

Matters of Child Development 39

Stages of Musical Development 41

Musical Skill Development 42
Vocal Development: Singing Skills 43
Kinesthetic Development: Movement and Dance 46
Perceptual Motor Skills: Playing Musical Instruments 46
The Evolution of Listening 48
Developing Creative Musical Thinking 49

Simple to Complex Phases of Learning 50

Summary, Review, Critical Thinking, and Projects 52
Additional Resources for Teaching 53

x Contents

PART II
THE MUSICAL MAKEUP OF CHILDREN 55

CHAPTER 4
Their Singing Voices 56

In the Classroom 57
Vignette One • Vignette Two • Vignette Three •
Vignette Four 57

Children's Singing Selves 58

Singing as a Healthy Endeavor 60

The Voice as a Personal Instrument 60
The Adult Voice 61
The Child Voice 62

Songs Children Sing 64
Songs by Children 64
Songs for Children 65
Other Songs: Patriotic, Popular, and All the Rest 66

Leading the Musical Classroom 66

Tips for Song Leading 66

Singing with Young Children 67

Singing with Children in the Intermediate Grades 69

Song-Based Lessons 70

Summary, Review, Critical Thinking, and Projects 72
Additional Resources for Teaching 73

CHAPTER 5
Their Ears: Listening to Music 74

Children as Listeners to Music 75

In the Classroom 75
Vignette One • Vignette Two • Vignette Three 75

Developing Listening Skills 76

Occasions for Listening 78

Listening to Music in the Background 79

Listening to Music in the Foreground 80
Classical Music 81
Orchestral Music 81
Ballet 82
Opera 82
Jazz 88
Popular Music 90
Folk and American Roots Music 90
World Music 91

Listening to Music in Live Performances 93
Concert Etiquette 94
Preparing Children to Understand the Music 94

Listening Responses through Other Arts 95
Drawing or Painting in Response to Listening 95
Writing in Response to Listening 96

Summary, Review, Critical Thinking, and Projects 98
Additional Resources for Teaching 99

CHAPTER 6
Their Moving Bodies 103

In the Classroom 104
Vignette One • Vignette Two • Vignette Three •
Vignette Four 104

Children, Rhythm, and Movement 106

Rhythmic Movement in Development 107

Exploring Movement 107

Safe Movement Activities 109

Components of Rhythm in Movement 109

Moving Rhythmically in Early and Middle
Childhood 110

Rhythmic Movement in Speech and Song 111
Rhythm in Speech 111
Songs That Move 112

Movement in Manageable Dance
Experiences 113
Folk and Other Pattern Dances 115
Popular Dances 116

Singing Songs, Signing Songs 116

Summary, Review, Critical Thinking, and Projects 117
Additional Resources for Teaching 118
Additional Songs for Singing 118

CHAPTER 7
The Instruments They Play 119

Children and Instruments 120

In the Classroom 120
Vignette One • Vignette Two • Vignette Three 120

Sound Exploration and Discovery 121

Sources of Sound and Kinds of Instruments 122
Found Sounds 123
Body Sounds 123
Invented and Constructed Instruments 124
Standard Classroom Instruments 125

Occasions for Play 133
Performing Rhythm Patterns 133
Accompanying Chants 133
Accompanying Story Readings 134
Accompanying Songs 134

Instruments and the Teacher 135
Keyboard 135
Guitar 135
Autoharp 136
Recorder 136
Percussion and Other Instruments 137

Summary, Review, Critical Thinking, and Projects 137
Additional Resources for Teaching 138

CHAPTER 8
Their Creative Imaginations 139

Children as Creators of Music 140

In the Classroom 140
Vignette One • Vignette Two • Vignette Three 140

Composing Music in the Classroom 141
Developing the Musical Imagination 142
Using the Body and the Voice 142
Creating Musical Instruments 145
Percussion Instruments 145
Wind Instruments 146
String Instruments 146

Improvising and Composing 147
Inventing Chants and Raps 150
Composing Songs 153
Other Arts and Composing 154
Music for Plays and Videos 154
Music for Operas and Musicals 155
Music and Poetry 155
Visual Arts and Composing 156

Summary, Review, Critical Thinking, and Projects 157
Additional Resources for Teaching 158

PART III

MUSIC THROUGHOUT THE DAY

161

CHAPTER 9
Music for the Joy of It 162

In the Classroom 163
Vignette One • Vignette Two • Vignette Three •
Vignette Four 163

Musical Openers and Closers 165
Musical Ways to Start the Day 165
Musical Ways to End the Day 166
Signals and Attention-Getters 167
Musical Breaks and Transitions between
Subjects 167

Music at Classroom Listening Centers 168
Music at Camp and on Field Trips 168
Music for Holidays, the Seasons, and Special
Events 170
Autumn Holidays: September–November 170
Winter Holidays: November–December 173
Winter into Spring Holidays: January–May 175

Summary, Review, Critical Thinking, and Projects 181
Additional Resources for Teaching 182
Additional Songs for Teaching 182

xii   Contents

CHAPTER 10
Music and Language Arts 183

In the Classroom 184
  Vignette One • Vignette Two • Vignette Three 184

Relationships between Language Arts and Music 184

Music Helps Children Learn Language Arts 185

Integrating with Integrity: Engaging the National Standards for Music Education 185

The National Standards in This Chapter's Vignettes 187

Music and Children's Literature 187
  Musical Play 187
  Creating Soundscapes 190
  Songs and Literature 191
  Adding Songs and Other Art Forms into Stories 193

Developing Reading and Thinking Skills through Music 195
  Basic Reading Skills 195

Phonological (Phonemic) Awareness 195
  Initial Sounds 196
  Middle Vowel Sounds 198
  Rhyming Sounds 198

Building Comprehension 200
  Adding Movement 200
  Using American Sign Language 200
  Sequencing and Cumulative Songs 202
  Using Chants and Choral Reading to Build Fluency and Inflection 203

Writing About Music 205
  Creative Writing About Music 206
  Narrative Writing About Music 206
  Descriptive Writing About Music 206
  Expository Writing About Music 207
  Persuasive Writing About Music 207
  Technical Writing About Music 207

Summary, Review, Critical Thinking, and Projects 208
Additional Resources for Teachers 209

CHAPTER 11
Music and Social Studies 210

In the Classroom 211
  Vignette One • Vignette Two • Vignette Three 211

Musical Connections to Time and Place 213

Illuminating History through Music and the Arts 213
  Music in Ancient Greece 214
  Music in Ancient Rome 214
  Music in Medieval Europe 215
  Music in the Age of Discovery 217
  Music of the American Revolution 218
  Music of the Industrial Age 219
  Music in the Twentieth Century 220

Sample Lessons for Music and Social Studies 221

Valuing Culture through Music and the Arts 227

Summary, Review, Critical Thinking, and Projects 237
Additional Resources for Teaching 238
Additional Songs for Teaching 239

CHAPTER 12
Music and Math 240

In the Classroom 241
  Vignette One • Vignette Two 241

Getting in the Music Groove with Basic Math 242

NCTM Goal #1: Understand Numbers, Ways of Representing Numbers, Relationships among Numbers, and Number Systems 243
  Count with Understanding 243
  Understanding Place Value and Number Order in the Base Ten System 243
  Connect Number Words and Numerals to the Amounts They Represent 248
  Recognize "How Many" in a Set 248
  Understand and Represent Commonly Used Fractions 249

NCTM Goal #2: Understand Meanings of Operations and How They Relate to One Another 251
  Understand Various Meanings of Addition and Subtraction of Whole Numbers and the Relationship between the Two Operations 252
  Understand the Effects of Adding and Subtracting Whole Numbers 252
  Understand the Effects of Multiplying and Dividing Whole Numbers 253

NCTM Goal #3: Compute Fluently and Make Reasonable Estimates 255
  Compute Fluently 255
  Develop and Use Strategies to Estimate the Results of Whole-Number Computations and Judge the Reasonableness of the Results 256

Algebra, Geometry, and Music 258

Summary, Review, Critical Thinking, and Projects 259
Additional Resources for Teaching 260

CHAPTER 13
Music and Science 261

In the Classroom 262
    Vignette One • Vignette Two 262

The Science of Sound 262

Basic Concepts and Experiments in the Science of Sound 263
    Vibration 263
    Resonance 266
    Pitch 268

Other Intersections of Music and Science 270
    Whale Communication 270
    Planets 273

Summary, Review, Critical Thinking, and Projects 274
Additional Resources for Teaching 275
Additional Resources for Listening 275

CHAPTER 14
All of the Arts 276

Considering the Arts 277

In the Classroom 277
    Vignette One • Vignette Two • Vignette Three • Vignette Four 277

Roles of the Arts 279

The Arts in Learning 279

What Makes Something Artistic? 280

Music and Other Arts 280
    Music and Dance 281
    Music and Visual Arts 283
    Music and Media Arts 285

    Music and Theater 285
    Music and Literature 286

Connecting the Arts 288

Summary, Review, Critical Thinking, and Projects 291
Additional Resources for Teaching 292

Appendix 1: Music Fundamentals A1
    Visualizing Sounds with Symbols and Icons A2
    Musical Elements A2
    Notating the Element of Pitch A3
    Notating the Element of Time A6
    Notating the Element of Timbre A10
    Notating the Element of Intensity A10

Review, Critical Thinking, and Projects A11
Suggestions for Further Reading A11

Appendix 2: Three Common Methods of Teaching Music to Children A13
    Dalcroze: Movement with a Mission A13
    Kodály: Inner Hearing and Music Literacy A14
    Orff: Schulwerk A15
    Personal Method A17

Suggestions for Further Reading A17

Appendix 3: Resources for Listening A19

Appendix 4: National Standards for Music Education A31

Bibliography A41

Classroom Resources for Children A45

End Notes A49

Credits A53

Index A55

Preface

We have dreamed of this book for many years, in recognition that elementary classroom teachers need a guide for integrating music across the curriculum. We come from the premise that every child is musical and that teachers can help children engage with music throughout the day. We recognize that classroom teachers are under tremendous pressure to teach the basics, and we hope that this book may persuade them that music is basic to the lives of children and can be woven into the classroom curriculum to enliven language, math, the sciences and the social sciences. We acknowledge that classroom teachers frequently advocate music and the arts as fundamental to the holistic education of every child, and that research attests to the power of music to enrich and enhance the intellectual and social-emotional lives of children.

Earlier approaches to elementary classroom methods have emphasized developing a vast (and somewhat unrealistic) array of musical skills. In this book, we aim to help prospective and practicing elementary teachers understand the many ways that children spontaneously express their musical ideas. We believe that teachers, like children, have musical propensities all their own, and that they can rediscover their own musical nature even as they weave live and recorded melodies and rhythms into their curricular activity. We see classroom teachers as facilitators of children's discovery of knowledge and skills, and thoroughly capable of using music to teach language arts, math and science, and social studies, to celebrate holidays, and to enable everyday classroom routines, exchanges, and interactions. We hope that *Music for Elementary Classroom Teachers* will give teachers tools for developing children's natural musicality through singing, moving, creating, listening, and playing simple instruments.

PART I: THE MUSICAL LIVES OF CHILDREN AND TEACHERS

We introduce the world of music and children to future teachers of preschool through grade six.

Chapter 1, Music and Children: Then, Now, and Evermore, touches on brain research in music, how children learn music, and the musical world of the child, including the cultural influences of families, neighborhoods, and other social communities.

Chapter 2, Teachers as Facilitators of Music and the Arts, shows teachers how to engage children musically and how to structure experiences to help children express musical ideas. Here we place the teacher in the role of "guide on the side," leading children into myriad interactions with music.

Chapter 3, The Musical Growth of Children, focuses on how children develop their vocal, kinesthetic, and aural abilities, as well as how children develop creatively. These ideas are drawn from child development from preschool through the elementary years.

PART II: THE MUSICAL MAKEUP OF CHILDREN

We help teachers to understand how children naturally express themselves musically.

Chapter 4, Their Singing Voices, shows teachers how to promote vocal development in young children and share age-appropriate songs with children. It is our hope that through singing these songs, teachers will gain confidence not only in their own singing abilities, but also to lead songs with children. As the book unfolds, teachers will find a wide range of folk songs, children's songs, and heritage songs from American and world cultures that fit the need and interests of elementary school children.

Chapter 5, Their Ears: Listening to Music, introduces many ways to bring recorded music into the classroom. Ideas for informal classroom use of recordings are provided alongside ideas for formal lessons to acquaint and engage elementary school children with music of many styles, genres, and cultures. We offer a range of strategies to help build children's perceptive music listening, including combining listening with expression in the visual arts. Finally, the chapter shows how to prepare children to attend live performances of music, whether in class, at school assemblies, or during field trips into the broader community.

Chapter 6, Their Moving Bodies, emphasizes the crucial importance of having children move to rhythms and melodies throughout the day for their brain health as well as to release energy and build coordination. Featured are simple singing games appropriate for young children as well as strategies for enhancing creative movement and learning folk and popular dances.

Chapter 7, The Instruments They Play, introduces traditional classroom instruments used at the elementary school level as well as correct techniques for playing them and suggestions for using them throughout the rest of the curriculum. Elemental techniques to help teachers play classroom-friendly instruments such as guitar, recorder, and autoharp are provided.

Chapter 8, Their Creative Imaginations, contains a wealth of ideas for how to invite children to create music in response to literature, images, sounds, and themes. Many of these ideas relate directly to curriculum content in other areas, allowing children to make connections through their own compositions. Many potential sound sources and ideas for having children build their own instruments are included.

PART III: MUSIC THROUGHOUT THE DAY

We help teachers integrate music into the daily lives of their classrooms, connecting music in significant ways to each aspect of the elementary school curriculum.

Chapter 9, Music for the Joy of It, offers myriad ways to use music informally throughout the day. Techniques are presented for using music or musical sounds to get children's attention, to change pace, to calm or energize children, to celebrate seasons and special events, and to create community through group music-making.

Chapter 10, Music and Language Arts, connects key standards in language arts with key standards in music, and advises formulating lessons that integrate the curricula of these two subject areas. The chapter also offers suggestions for using music to enhance basic reading skills such as fluency, inflection, and comprehension, and to help children learn to write for different purposes with music as the stimulus.

Chapter 11, Music and Social Studies, offers music as a launch for understanding people in local and global communities. This chapter is a treasure trove of music from ancient to contemporary historical periods and in various cultural contexts.

Chapter 12, Music and Math, employs music to develop basic mathematical understandings and skills, emphasizing mathematical competence in the elementary years.

Chapter 13, Music and Science, provides extensive resources to explore the science of sound with children and ideas for multidisciplinary lessons featuring science and music.

Chapter 14, All of the Arts, is a guide to core understandings in visual arts, drama, dance, media arts, and literature and how they can be combined with each other and with music. This chapter helps teachers understand how to bring all of the arts to children in single or sequential lessons, thus tapping into children's varied artistic-expressive traits.

Appendix 1, Music Fundamentals, provides basic skills for reading music notation and understanding key concepts about music.

Appendix 2, Three Common Methods of Teaching Music to Children, briefly articulates the essential philosophies and principles of Orff-Schulwerk, Dalcroze, and Kodály methodologies as well as techniques for using each with children.

Appendix 3, Resources for Listening, provides full information for key recordings and artists whose works are cited throughout the book.

Appendix 4, National Standards for Music Education, provides guidance developed by the Music Educators National Conference in 1994, with a focus on specific musical processes.

ONLINE RESOURCES

In addition to the many helpful materials provided in the printed volume, we offer two resources online:

A Song Book of the nearly two hundred songs mentioned in the text—with both notation and recordings—giving teachers of all levels the tools they need to bring music into the classroom.

A Recorder Manual gives teachers a crash course in playing this common classroom instrument.

To access these resources, go to digital.wwnorton.com/classroom

ACKNOWLEDGMENTS

We have been professionally committed to teaching prospective teachers (both music teachers and classroom teachers) for decades, and have recognized how music enlightens, energizes, and empowers children to learn. We are fully aware that moving music into the scope of elementary education students and classroom teachers is a complicated enterprise. We are grateful to a long list of educators (as well as children themselves) for their contributions and insights, as they have helped to clarify and consolidate the pathways we are providing here. We are grateful for the shared ideas of colleagues in music and education who have contributed to our vision for this volume, with sincere appreciation especially to Katalin Forrai, Virginia Mead, Julia Schnebly-Black, and Jim Scholten. We celebrate the founders and participants of the Mountain Lake Colloquium in General Music Education who, since 1991, have consistently wrestled with questions of how to make elementary music methods classes more relevant to future elementary school classroom teachers. We extend our deep appreciation to Maribeth Anderson Payne, our editor and friend, who believed in the value of this project to bring more children and their teachers into the remarkable and unique phenomenon of music. In bringing this book to its full flowering, we deeply appreciate the expert editorial attention of Michael Fauver, who worked with us through every detail of text, table, figure, and photo, and provided the necessary cohesion and polish to the voices of three authors.

Seattle 2017

About the Authors

Patricia Shehan Campbell is Donald E. Peterson Professor of Music at the University of Washington, where she teaches courses at the interface of education and ethnomusicology. She has lectured on the pedagogy of world music and children's musical cultures throughout the United States, in much of Europe and Asia, and in Australia, New Zealand, South America, and eastern and southern Africa. She is the author of *Lessons from the World* (1991), *Music in Cultural Context* (1996), *Songs in Their Heads* (1998, 2010), *Teaching Music Globally* (2004), and *Musician and Teacher* (2008); coauthor of *Music in Childhood: From Preschool through the Elementary Years* (2013); and coeditor of *The Global Music Series* and *The Oxford Handbook on Children's Musical Cultures* (2013). Campbell was designated the MENC Senior Researcher in Music Education in 2002, was the recipient of the 2012 Taiji Award for the preservation of traditional music, and was awarded the Koizumi Fumio Prize in Ethnomusicology in 2017. She is chair of the Smithsonian Folkways advisory board and a consultant in repatriation efforts for the recordings of Alan Lomax to communities in the American South.

Carol Scott-Kassner is a retired Professor of Music Education specializing in elementary general music and musical development in young children. She began her career as a first-grade teacher and then as an elementary music specialist working with children from kindergarten through sixth grade. Working with future elementary classroom teachers has been at the heart of her teaching at the university level. Carol codirected a Master's in Arts Education for nine years and is a recipient of the Kennedy Center Award for Leadership in Arts Education. This book is a realization of much of her thinking and experience over 40 years. She is coauthor with Patricia Campbell of *Music in Childhood: From Preschool through the Elementary Years* and author of chapters in two editions of *The Handbook of Research in Teaching and Learning in Music*. She cofounded and chaired the Early Childhood Commission of the International Society of Music Education and chaired the Society for Research in Music Education and the Society for General Music Education.

Kirk Kassner, Ph.D., Nationally Certified Music Educator, is a writer, lecturer, and consultant in music education. His 40-year career included teaching music in public schools at all age levels and as an adjunct instructor at Portland State University and the University of Central Florida. He supervised over 50 intern teachers and mentored in-service teachers for many years. His eclectic teaching methods include principles and techniques of Jacques-Dalcroze, Orff, Kodály, Comprehensive Musicianship, Computer-Assisted Instruction in Music, Cooperative Learning, and Mastery Learning. He has served the profession in many capacities, including as a member of the Editorial Committee for the *Music Educators Journal*. He has written many articles for *MEJ* and other journals, contributed to several MENC publications and Silver Burdett textbooks, and lectured across the United States and in Great Britain, Italy, Greece, China, and Brazil.

MUSIC FOR ELEMENTARY CLASSROOM TEACHERS

PART I
THE MUSICAL LIVES OF CHILDREN AND TEACHERS

Music is fundamental to human life. Even as our capacities for language define us, so too are we defined by our human need to express something beautiful through music. In fact, we become more human through music. Children and adults are naturally drawn to sing, play, and dance, and to enjoy music as thoughtful listeners. As the saying goes, "If you can talk, you can sing, and if you can walk, you can dance," and children demonstrate this in their playful ways.

Because music is alive in children's play, music in the classroom can advance the way children think musically and employ musical thinking in other intellectual endeavors, social-emotional expressions, and physical-motoric skill development. Classroom teachers further the development of children as listeners, singers, dancers, players, and creators of music. They nurture children's natural musical interests for life-long experiences, and they enrich learning by pairing music with various subjects, topics, and concepts.

The three chapters in Part I explore the nature of music, how it functions in the lives of children and adults, how it informs children's experiences in the arts generally, and how children's understanding and use of music develop in fairly predictable patterns as they grow. Together, these chapters explore music's role in communication, in the expression of ideas that often cannot be verbalized, and in enhancing social cohesion and cooperation. Part I clarifies the important role and responsibility of classroom teachers to make music more meaningful to children in their daily work and play. We hope these chapters will convey to teachers that music is alive in them and just waiting to transform the school day.

The joy of singing begins early.

IN THIS CHAPTER

In the Classroom

Music in the Lives of Children

Music in School

Music's Many Functions

Their Brains on Music

Justifying Musical Study and Integration

Standards in School Music

Summary

Review

Critical Thinking

Projects

Additional Resources for Teaching

1

MUSIC AND CHILDREN: THEN, NOW, AND EVERMORE

Music may be the activity that prepared our pre-human ancestors for speech communication and for the very cognitive, presentational flexibility necessary to become humans.

—Daniel J. Levitin, *This is Your Brain on Music: The Science of a Human Obsession*[1]

A teacher and students engage in musical activity.

The way toward a more musically expressive, community-oriented society is grounded in what schools and their teachers provide for children. Thoughtful classroom teachers who weave music into the curriculum have the power to make music part of the everyday experiences of their students.

IN THE CLASSROOM

Everyone has memories of elementary school classroom experiences. In some classrooms, the second hand on the clock dragged along so slowly that it seemed to move backward. But in other classrooms, teachers presented lessons in fascinating ways that kept each student focused and involved in the joy and wonder of learning. The most memorable experiences were facilitated by teachers who carefully wove in moments of amusement, allowed for children's natural rhythmic energy, and incorporated singing, chanting, listening to music, and dancing. The following vignettes provide glimpses into school settings in which outstanding classroom teachers use music to keep children motivated and on track so that they can learn joyfully.

VIGNETTE ONE

Mrs. McConnell finds that her kindergarten children respond enthusiastically to musical activities. "It's like water off a duck's back," she explains, and follows with a flood of ways in which music surfaces in her classroom. "We sing, we dance, we play," she offers, and she describes the music-making that comes from children who independently rhyme words rhythmically, sing their conversations at snack time, and dance their way to recess. She purposefully weaves music into her classroom by providing an ever-changing playlist of "entrance music" at arrival time, converting circle time to singing-circle and storytelling time, inviting student members of the school orchestra to visit her classroom, making time for children to build their own musical instruments from natural and household items, and turning poems into percussion pieces. In Mrs. McConnell's kindergarten, children participate in a curriculum alive with musical experiences and are encouraged to express themselves musically.

VIGNETTE TWO

Mr. Howard knows what his third-grade children need: plenty of straightforward goal-directed activity, a good measure of individual time to quietly contemplate a math or writing assignment, and group work for learning from one another and testing out knowledge and skills. He finds that music is useful for setting the mood of his students' learning, for releasing energy between concentrated periods of study, and for motivating them to meet the challenges of new material in all subjects taught in his classroom. He chooses soft and subtle music to signal quiet working time. During brain breaks, he turns up the volume on a salsa number and models a basic side-by-side stepping pattern for his students, and they join with enthusiasm. He features a student-selected tune (with school-appropriate lyrics) and allows free time for the students to listen. Mr. Howard arranges for visiting artists at school assemblies and in his own classroom so that his students can

---

You Will Learn

- about children's inherent musicality

- about music's role in school and community

- about how music affects children's brains

- about the National Standards for Music Education

Ask Yourself

- How was music important in your childhood?

- How did your teachers use music in their classrooms?

- What role does music play in your life today?

- How are children naturally musical?

- How can music motivate and enhance learning in language arts, math, social studies, science, foreign languages, art, technology, physical education, history, and geography?

learn about music in real time and develop respect for—and sometimes a rapport with—practicing musicians. In his words, "music enhances the subjects I teach too much to be relegated to the once-a-week music class at the end of the hall."

VIGNETTE THREE

Ms. Washington's students excel in her classroom, even if they have a history of failure in other classes. She encourages students to come to her study center when they first arrive at school, and she provides another 20 minutes in the late morning and in midafternoon for children to do homework in an environment with calm background music instead of distracting TV, Internet, family, or neighborhood noise. Year after year, her students' test scores are significantly higher than those of other students in the district. Ms. Washington is also known for her love of music, and she recognizes that children respond well to musical activities that channel their expressive tendencies. She schedules daily singing for her students, in which she leads and then selects students to lead traditional Anglo- and African-American songs, patriotic songs, and heritage songs of other cultures that she has found online. For 10 minutes every morning, and for another 10 minutes immediately after lunch, Ms. Washington and her children sing their hearts out. Their principal refers to the fifth grade "singing scholars," and Ms. Washington has discovered that singing and calm study time help children master their environment as well as improve their academic performance.

MUSIC IN THE LIVES OF CHILDREN

Listen to children and their music. Intentionally or not, it springs spontaneously from them as they sing, play, and dance. Consider their speech as it unfolds in melodic contours of high and low pitches, in rhythms both fast and slow. Children talk softly or loudly, and their words flow smoothly or as detached sound bites. They sing, hum, whistle, and chant. They invent and play hand-jive games, they clap, stamp, and snap their fingers, and they find surfaces on which to pound, pat, slap, or tap. Let them within arm's reach of instruments, and the wild rumpus starts. Children are drawn to the music-making potential of pianos, electronic keyboards, trumpets, drums, violins, flutes, xylophones, accordions, harps, and clarinets. They will pluck, press, toot, and tap out all the sounds they can muster. They create sounds and patterns from drums, wooden sticks, cymbals, and shakers, and they find joy in making their own music from pots, pans, household items, and garage "junk." At times exploratory and free, at other times surging into repeating or sequential patterns, the music of children is evidence of their innate musicality and expressive abilities.

In fact, children are *musicking*, that is, engaged in the process of producing sounds that are meaningful to them, from their earliest days.[2] Making music is part of their personal drive and social being. Children babble melodiously during their first year of life, and they experiment with the possibilities of their voices in the earliest stages of their language development. Vowel and consonant sounds emerge from infants, sometimes in rhythmic patterns or in roller–coaster rises and falls. Children sing spontaneously and expressively at ages two and three. Prior to beginning formal schooling, children have already amassed their own repertoire of songs to sing.[3]

While children's voices sing, their bodies dance in musical ways. From their earliest age, children move rhythmically to music and to speech. They do not sit or lie still when they hear patterned sounds, and sometimes they are compelled to move to the music in their own heads. They rock and bounce, then jump, then turn and twirl to music from toddlerhood onward, realizing through dance the musical rhythms and melodies they hear or imagine. This, too, is musicking, as they engage their bodies in response to the music and sound patterns of their environment. Musicality is an inherently human characteristic, evident from birth, growing strong in preschool years, and waiting to flourish when nurtured through childhood, adolescence, and adulthood.

Responding to music is an inherently human characteristic.

MUSIC IN SCHOOL

When children enter school, they are ready to grow their musical knowledge and skills. They need teachers to guide them, expanding what they have learned from family, community, and media. Teachers who shape children's knowledge, skills, and values across all subjects can and should further children's musicality. Teachers attuned to children's expressive development provide time and space in their classrooms for children to sing and chant, and to listen and respond to music. They make all learning more musical, and thus enhance their children's overall intellectual, emotional, social, and physical growth.[4]

Historically, music has been valued in school curricula as a way of thinking, a means of expressing, and an avenue of creativity. Europeans over the centuries have viewed music as part science (in its theoretical analysis) and part art (in its performance practice). Across the world, music has served both as a highly technical and expressive art form performed by talented specialists, and as a common activity in which all can engage, be it in song, dance, or instrumental play. Music preserves cultural heritage and enhances quality of life. It gives pleasure to the performer as well as to the listener. When taught by certified music specialists and by classroom teachers who value music as part of the holistic education of their children, music takes its rightful place as a subject for experience and study by children from preschool onward.

MUSIC'S MANY FUNCTIONS

An anthropological view of music in human culture suggests that music can feature throughout the school day. Alan P. Merriam described music's various functions in daily life across cultures and societies, and likewise music's presence

TABLE 1.1 HOW MUSIC FUNCTIONS IN CHILDREN'S LIVES

FUNCTION	MEANING	EXAMPLE
Emotional expression	The release of emotions and the expression of feelings	Children release a range of emotions, from joy to sorrow, in their songs and dances.
Aesthetic enjoyment	The experience of music for its artistic beauty and its deeply emotional expression of life's beauty	Children experience music and, while they may not be able to articulate their responses, they feel the music's message.
Entertainment	The use of music as diversion and amusement	Children are attracted to the music of DVDs, television shows, electronic games, and the Internet.
Communication	The capacity of music to convey ideas and feelings	Children understand music as meaningful within their family and community.
Symbolic representation	The expression of symbols in song lyrics and the cultural meaning of musical sounds	Children are attuned to melodic and rhythmic qualities that are meaningful within their musical cultures.
Physical response	The use of music for dancing and other movement activities	Children naturally respond to music with a wide range of movements.
Social structure	The use of music to provide instruction or warnings	Children learn safety and appropriate social etiquette through songs and rhymes.
Institutional and religious rituals	The presence of music in religious services and state occasions	Children's identities are woven into the patriotic, sacred, and seasonal songs they sing.
Cultural continuity and stability	The use of music as an expression of cultural values	Children learn aspects of history, literature, and social mores through music, which bring them cultural understanding.

Source: Merriam, Alan P. (1964). *The Anthropology of Music*. Evanston, IL: Northwestern University Press.

in the everyday life of the classroom can enhance children's intellectual, physical, social, and personal growth. As in the aesthetic principle of art for art's sake, music stands on its own merits as a uniquely human experience that is deeply moving and personally meaningful. Yet music can also teach children how to live according to the fundamental values of a culture. Further, music amuses and entertains, provides a socially appropriate means of releasing emotional and physical energy, and creates pathways of communication. Music is at home in the hands of teachers who use it in varied ways to improve the classroom climate and to enrich children's lives.

People of all ages have the capacity to organize sound, to harness it and shape it into beautiful, effective, and heartfelt musical expression. They do this as they sing and play musical instruments, and as they create new music from an array of sonic possibilities. Listeners, too, organize sound, making perceptual sense of live musical performances and recordings. People welcome music into their lives for stimulation, relaxation, and the feeling of being fully immersed in sound. For this reason and many others, music belongs at the core of day-to-day learning in schools.

Although culture-specific preferences exist, music has universal characteristics. People from all cultures sing, and their songs convey meanings and emotions.

Young children are eager to be sung to. Singing to infants and with children of all ages nurtures and builds human bonds, which are crucial to healthy child development. Holding and rocking a child provides a sense of security and love. No matter where they live, or how they have been raised, children enjoy music. They are born to listen, born to sing, and born to groove.[5]

THEIR BRAINS ON MUSIC

Recent developments in neuroscience link music to the growth of children's skills and understandings, and to their moods and social dispositions. Active music-making appears to be associated with the development of language discrimination, mathematical ability, and problem-solving skills. A consensus is emerging that not only is music a fundamental human characteristic, children who participate in music can enhance the rapid physical development of their brains. Further, brain research has clarified music's role in enhancing how children think, reason, and create.

BRAIN RESEARCH ON MUSIC

Infants are mentally stimulated by the music they hear.[6] Ears begin functioning four months before birth, but the brain requires many months to gain full capacity for auditory processing. Infants recognize songs and notice changes in pitch and meter, which indicates that they are capable of processing musical relationships. Within a year of birth, children recognize and prefer the music they heard in the womb.[7] Across many cultures, young children learn music the same way they learn language—by interacting with their parents, who sing, chant, rock, and dance their little ones to the music they make and value. Further, infants learn that music and art make mundane and everyday experiences special. They express themselves and bond socially when they participate as singers, players, dancers, and makers of poems, stories, and works that integrate their various artistic capacities.[8]

Most children internalize their culture's musical style in early childhood, long before they begin formal schooling. They listen and grasp what makes sense melodically, rhythmically, and harmonically, and they can detect errors or deviations from the standard musical gestures of their culture's musical style. By the time they enter kindergarten, their keen perceptual sensitivity is so finely tuned to familiar music that other musical styles, while interesting, are more difficult for them to grasp.[9] As with language, the neural synaptic connections involved in recognizing musical events strengthen with repeated use.

Researchers have found neural firing patterns that suggest music may be a key to higher brain function.[10] Young children who take piano lessons score higher on tests of general and spatial cognitive reasoning, which is also required for math and engineering.[11] Children who play a musical instrument strengthen their eye–hand coordination and fine motor skills, and they develop discipline through regular practice that focuses their attention on discrete tasks. Their practice leads to musical accomplishment and they learn that there are rewards for hard work. Research shows that 10,000 hours of attentive practice leads to high-level performance skills.[12] Further, there appears to be a relationship between making music and getting along with others, such that children who make music together—working to make something beautiful in the company of others—learn to regulate their emotions and to become more aware of other people's feelings.[13] Music plays an important role in childhood, informing and shaping children's thought processes and social interactions.[14]

Neuroscientists have debunked the myth of talent, arguing that the role of innate talent is highly exaggerated.[15] On the one hand, some are born with the physiology necessary for a pleasant-sounding voice, and there could be a natural propensity for motor coordination necessary for playing a particular instrument. Still, this is no guarantee of high-level accomplishment or a professional career as a singer or instrumentalist. There is no music gene, nor is there evidence that talented musicians have a different brain structure than nonmusicians; however, the experience of making music does change the brain. Frequent musical activity creates a circuitry that strengthens neural synapses and makes music-making more efficient. While further research may clarify the genetic components of musicianship, the environmental components are strong, including motivation, personality, and the dynamics of family, neighborhood, and culture, and the social value of music in children's education. More certainly, while children are born into the world well equipped for learning, caring teachers develop children's capacities to think and achieve in various ways, including about music.[16]

Research on music and the brain indicates that both music-making and music listening are sophisticated neural processes, and that specific areas of the brain are involved in emotion, timing, perception, and the production of sequences.[17] Musical ability is more likely a set of abilities that includes aural acuity, tonal and rhythmic memory, pattern recognition, eye–hand coordination, and the intelligence to weave sensory information into one's own web of knowledge in a meaningful way. Studies of human evolution have contributed theories as to why humans developed music, including music as an evolutionary accident, with humans exploiting and extending language to invent music for sonic pleasure. A Darwinian theory suggests that music was selected early in human evolution because it signals intellectual, physical, and sexual fitness to a potential mate. Still another theory argues that music supported cognitive development; because of its complex activity, music assisted our early ancestors in the development of speech.

BRAIN-BASED LEARNING

Over the years, neuroscientists have learned much about how the brain learns and remembers. Emotional learning appears to take place in the amygdala, deep in the temporal lobe of the cerebrum, which automatically triggers and strengthens neural connections in several other memory areas of the brain.[18] This supports the commonly held belief that learning is strengthened when accompanied by emotional stimuli. John Medina, a molecular biologist, applied studies of human brain development to devise a set of rules for teachers and their students.[19] These rules pertain to how children learn concepts and skills in all school subjects, including music (see Table 1.2).

TABLE 1.2 BRAIN RULES WITH LEARNING IMPLICATIONS

1. Exercise	Exercise boosts brain power.
2. Survival	The human brain evolved, too.
3. Wiring	Every brain is wired differently.
4. Attention	We don't pay attention to boring things.
5. Short-term memory	Repeat to remember.
6. Long-term memory	Remember to repeat.
7. Sleep	Sleep well, think well.
8. Stress	Stressed brains don't learn well.
9. Sensory integration	Stimulate more of the senses.
10. Vision	Vision trumps all other senses.
11. Gender	Male and female brains are different.
12. Exploration	We are powerful and natural explorers.

Source: Medina, John. (2014). *Brain Rules*. Seattle, WA: Pear Press.

These rules seem obvious, but now there is scientific evidence, with detailed explanations in a growing body of literature, that these rules apply to complexities of the human brain. Several rules are particularly important for understanding music's impact on learning.

Regular exercise (Brain Rule #1) is good not only for the body's heart, lungs, and muscles, but also for the brain, and children require playful periods of exercise throughout the day. With a hearty set of sit-ups, a good jog around the perimeter of the playground, or a vigorous dance, the brain receives oxygen-rich blood to increase alertness. Neurotransmitters such as dopamine and serotonin are released, increasing energy and concentration necessary for learning. Music is a remarkably effective way of awakening the brain, and children who sing and chant rhythmically, move to the rhythm of a recording, or clap, pat, tap, bend, stretch, and play drums, sticks, and shakers in patterns set by a leader are charging themselves up for their academic studies.

Because learning takes energy, only so much information can be received before the brain overloads. Attention wanes and distractions become harder to ignore, or boredom sets in. Children do not pay attention to boring things (Brain Rule #4), so every teacher needs to gain and maintain children's attention with interesting content delivered emotionally. The hippocampus, which processes new sensory information, can receive a steady stream of stimulation for 15 minutes before it begins to ignore further input. This is the time to reflect, to rehearse, and to apply the learning in various ways. It is the point at which children can be led to "repeat to remember" (Brain Rule #5) and to "remember to repeat" (Brain Rule #6). Musicians know that practice makes perfect, and music, through rhythmic or sung chants, can be an appealing emotional way to enhance the review of vocabulary,

Music can reduce anxiety and make learning more efficient.

math concepts, state capitols, and a variety of other topics, until they become ingrained. Adding rhythm, pitch, dynamics, and timbral variety to information can avert boredom, stave off distractions, and encourage the information to stick in the brain.

Stressed brains do not receive new information well (Brain Rule #8), and learning is least likely when the emotional center of the brain is focused on neglected basic needs. Continued stress releases cortisol, a hormone that interferes with one's ability to retain information; it goes in one ear and out the other and cannot be integrated into the individual's knowledge base. Children feel stress in disruptive households, or when they fear unrealistic expectations or punishment. Counseling may be best for stress relief, but the presence of music in school can be a less intrusive way to reduce the stress of children's concerns. Music—through listening, singing, playing, and dancing—can help reduce anxiety and make learning more efficient.

Because our senses work together, learning happens best when our experiences are multisensory (Brain Rule #9). Vision is processed in the occipital region at the back of the brain, while hearing happens in the temporal lobe on each side of the brain. Yet there are also convergence locations where information from the various senses comes together. This argues for sensory integration as an effective approach to teaching and learning. Children may need to see, hear, and experience a concept, even through touch, taste, or smell, in order to understand it. In music, children can be guided to hear, see, feel, and move to a rhythm. Likewise, they can learn about other subjects and concepts through a multisensory approach that combines musically inspired aural and kinesthetic experiences with visual presentation.

Children learn naturally through exploration and play (Brain Rule #12). In the earliest days of life, infants probe their environment, looking at, listening to, feeling, and tasting everything they can. They are curious, and curiosity is a classic and continuing human trait. Because parts of the brain remain malleable, exploration of the new and unfamiliar continues through childhood and adolescence into adulthood. In the classroom, children deserve time to explore topics of interest and seek their own discoveries in their own ways. Play is children's exploratory work. Children play with rhyming words to create poetry and with sounds, colors, shapes, and textures to create art.

JUSTIFYING MUSICAL STUDY AND INTEGRATION

There are cherished beliefs about music, including the idea that musical exposure begets mathematical ability. Parents in particular embraced the notion that music makes you smarter, especially the classical music of the late-eighteenth-century

Viennese wunderkind, Wolfgang Amadeus Mozart. This "Mozart effect,"[20] as the popular press has referred to it, led Disney to release an explosion of Baby Mozart videos, DVDs, CDs, toys, and even interactive websites on music for children and parents. Yet people do not necessarily become smarter because they make music. Children with Williams Syndrome are a case in point, as they tend to have high levels of musical interest and ability and low intelligence in other areas. They may sing in many languages, or play memorized music on piano or violin with tremendous verve, yet they often cannot draw a picture of a horse or count a stack of coins. Regardless of their IQs or the potential of music to increase their intelligence, people engage in musical experience because they are drawn to music. They enjoy music and its many benefits, and they do not "do music" because of the unfounded belief that it may raise their scores on an intelligence test.

Music may not make you smarter, but it is another way of being intelligent. Psychologist Howard Gardner's theory of multiple intelligences posits the existence of 10 intelligences (musical–rhythmic, visual–spatial, verbal–linguistic, logical–mathematical, bodily–kinesthetic, interpersonal, intrapersonal, naturalistic, existential, and moral), one or several of which determine how an individual learner processes the world.[21] Gardner theorized that everyone has some measure of each of these intelligences, but that some individuals are closely tuned to one or another intelligence in particular. It follows, then, that all children possess potential across the spectrum of intelligences, including the capacity to know music and to be musically expressive. Like logical–mathematical and verbal–linguistic intelligence, musical–rhythmic intelligence is nurtured through instruction, and society and its schools should value it highly enough to ensure that all children have the opportunity to learn music. Of course some children will show greater musical competence than others, just as some will do better in math or reading than others. But, just as we teach math and reading to all students, regardless of their "talent," so should all children learn music.

Music performance involves cognition, perception, and motor control. These skills apply to different kinds of intellectual activities and academic subjects. Cognitive components of musical study include deciphering notation, learning a song by ear, developing muscle control for playing an instrument, and assembling the building blocks of pitch and rhythm. When a child reads music notation, her eye moves sequentially from note to note as she translates iconic representations of sound into musical sound itself, just as her eye moves and her brain translates when she reads words. Likewise, learning a song by ear sharpens the listening skills for other orally-presented material and develops phonemic awareness in language. Instrumental facility, with its complex coordinated movements of arms, hands, and fingers, not only provides physical exercise to these body parts but also energizes the brain for other tasks to come. Finally, the creative act of building pitches and rhythms into an original musical expression is an exercise in constructing a coherent whole from individual parts, as well as in problem-solving—two processes crucial to making sense of math.

Classroom teachers who integrate music into their teaching find that it supports learning in other subjects. When children sing a counting song in a math session or play a beat while reciting new vocabulary words, there is more joy than struggle. Teachers use music to set the desired classroom mood, be it quiet and calm or lively. Music promotes social engagement during holidays, birthdays, or just

NATIONAL STANDARDS FOR MUSIC EDUCATION

1. Singing, alone and with others, a varied repertoire of music

2. Performing on instruments, alone and with others, a varied repertoire of music

3. Improvising melodies, variations, and accompaniments

4. Composing and arranging music within specified guidelines

5. Reading and notating music

6. Listening to, analyzing, and describing music

7. Evaluating music and music performances

8. Understanding relationships between music, the other arts, and disciplines outside the arts

9. Understanding music in relation to history and culture

Source: Music Educators National Conference. (1994). *National Standards for Arts Education*. Reston, VA: Rowman and Littlefield.

indoor recess time. Music partners with countless units in other subjects, from the social history of African-Americans to the scientific principles of sound vibration and parallel electrical vibration.

STANDARDS IN SCHOOL MUSIC

As an academic subject, music is a crucial component of curricula designed for the holistic development of children. The U.S. Department of Education lists the arts as a core academic subject, along with English, reading or language arts, mathematics, science, foreign languages, civics and government, economics, history, and geography.

The Department issued a national policy on standards in the arts in 1994 to assist teachers in organizing instruction in music, the visual arts, dance, and drama. The policy on music was developed by the Music Educators National Conference (MENC), now known as the National Association for Music Education (NAfME). While no specific repertoire of songs or rhymes is prescribed, nor particular works for listening, the national music standards offer voluntary guidelines for teachers who want to teach musical skills and competency. These standards form the basis for musical goals at the state and local levels, with minor modifications and variations. They encompass what teachers and administrators believe every child should be challenged to learn in music. These standards are used throughout this text as a framework for identifying key dimensions of musical development and for ways to integrate music throughout the entire classroom curriculum.

Summary

Music is in the very nature of childhood; children are drawn to engage in music. This music-making enriches and advances children's language development, logic and reasoning, and social-emotional interactions. Integrating music into the school day ensures that learning occurs, and that it is enjoyable. Some of the most successful (and enjoyable) learning to transpire in an elementary school is geared toward musical goals, threading music through a lesson on any subject or topic only to make it that much more palatable to children. Music's constant place in the classroom complements its prominent place in children's everyday lives.

Review

1. Define *musicking* and explain its relationship to children's development.

2. What are the functions of music in children's lives? Which functions are constant, occasional, or rare in the everyday activities of childhood?

3. List the brain rules that emanate from neuroscience research and their relevance to practicing teachers.

4. Name the nine national standards for music education.

Critical Thinking

1. What is the evidence that all children are musical, particularly as defined by both receptive and expressive musical encounters?

2. What neuroscience research informs an understanding of children's musicality?

3. Which brain rules apply to music as a tool to enhance learning of other subject matter?

Projects

1. Watch children at play or interacting with one another. Take 30 minutes to notice how their speech inflections rise and fall in melodic patterns and their bodies move in rhythmic patterns. Listen for rhymes and rhythms that are chanted or sung, and watch the footwork that appears in patterns that resemble dance. Note ways in which children use everyday objects, including pencils, erasers, cups, and utensils, to create vaguely musical expressions. Share a short report of children's natural musicking behaviors.

2. Talk with children of a particular age about the music they prefer, and to which they give their attention in their free time. Note their favorite musical (and dance) forms, song titles, and artists. Discuss the varied responses to questions of preference depending upon children's age.

3. Search the Internet for new brain research that supports the importance of music and the arts in children's daily lives.

4. Choose one national standard for music education, and brainstorm the possibilities for classroom experiences that are attuned to that standard.

Additional Resources for Teaching

Keil, Charles and Steven Feld. (1994). *Music Grooves.* Chicago, IL: University of Chicago Press.

Koelsch, Stefan. (2012). *Brain and Music.* Chichester, UK: John Wiley & Sons, Ltd.

MacDonald, Raymond and Gunter Kreutz. (2012). *Music, Health, and Wellbeing.* Oxford, UK: Oxford University Press.

Margullis, Elizabeth Hellmuth. (2014). *On Repeat: How Music Plays the Mind.* New York, NY: Oxford University Press.

Medina, John J. (2014). *Brain Rules.* Seattle, WA: Pear Press.

Patel, Aniruddh D. (2008). *Music, Language, and the Brain.* New York, NY: Oxford University Press.

Peretz, Isabelle and Robert J. Zatorre (Eds). (2003). *The Cognitive Neuroscience of Music.* New York, NY: Oxford University Press.

Online Resources: Audio and Songbook

digital.wwnorton.com/classroom

2
TEACHERS AS FACILITATORS OF MUSIC AND THE ARTS

You are the music while the music lasts.

—T. S. Eliot, *The Dry Salvages*

IN THIS CHAPTER

In the Classroom

The Musical Importance of Classroom Teachers

Finding Your Own Musicianship

Structuring the Classroom for Musical Experiences

Designing Arts-Integrated Curricula

Connecting the Classroom to the Community

Models and Resources for Teacher Training in Arts Integration

Summary

Review

Critical Thinking

Projects

Additional Resources for Teaching

The arts captivate children's senses and imaginations.

The world is alive with words, colors, images, textures, sounds, and the pulse of rhythms. Children are drawn to all of this energy, particularly as it is represented in the arts. Teachers seeking to engage students in exciting ways use the arts and arts processes to help convey meaning.

IN THE CLASSROOM

Music and the arts can be woven into the daily life of elementary school classrooms in numerous ways. How they are used depends on the intent of each teacher, their understanding of how the arts can positively impact all learning, and their creativity in planning lessons that require children to use all of their senses as well as their imaginations. Just like children, teachers have innate musical and artistic qualities, at times in full bloom and at other times hidden and untapped, waiting to be revealed. The incorporation of music and the arts into formal lessons, transitions between lessons, and the classroom climate are all critical to children's overall growth as thoughtful students and contributing members of society.

VIGNETTE ONE

Mr. Hong is a first grade teacher who values the arts deeply, and he wants to pass on those values to the children he teaches. His room is full of bright colors. He has a wall with art prints that he rotates throughout the year. Children read about the artists and listen to stories that Mr. Hong tells them. They also draw or paint their own works in the styles of the various artists. In one corner is a music listening center with recordings of a range of composers and children's picture books about those composers. Mr. Hong highlights various works throughout the year, playing the pieces multiple times until children can name the pieces and the composers. He and the other first-grade teachers bring to the school artists in residence to teach all of the first graders about their art form. By teaching in several classrooms, each artist is guaranteed a longer residency. Teachers acquire funds for this residency from the parent-teacher association and their local arts commission. Once a year, Mr. Hong takes children on a field trip to visit the local art museum. He also serves on the school assembly committee, where he advocates for at least one assembly each year that features a woodwind quintet or a string quartet from the local symphony. He uses the symphony's educational materials to prepare his students for their visit and always offers follow-up lessons to reinforce the art and music concepts and the musical works presented in the concert.

VIGNETTE TWO

Ms. Graham teaches third grade. She is deeply committed to infusing the arts throughout her curricula. On any given day her children might be singing a song to help them memorize the times tables; listening to two sets of rhythm patterns she claps and then adding, subtracting, multiplying, or dividing the beats in each pattern; using graph paper to create designs out of various numbers and their constituent parts; chanting their spelling words; or singing a goodbye song at the end of the day. She knows that children need to move regularly to get oxygen to their brains, so

You Will Learn

- how to structure a classroom for music and arts integration

- how to plan lessons that integrate the arts

- how to involve the greater community in a classroom

- where to receive training for integrated lessons

Ask Yourself

- How confident are you using music with children in the daily life of your classroom?

- What factors contribute to your feelings?

- What would make you more confident?

- How is a classroom teacher's role similar to or different from that of a music specialist in engaging children with music?

- What are some advantages to having teachers collaborate on projects that integrate music and the arts into their classrooms?

- What are some informal ways you might use music throughout the day?

she guides movement activities for the children's regular movement breaks every day. She has also developed other patterned movements for the children's regular movement breaks, and she supplies recorded music to help them move with energy.

VIGNETTE THREE

Ms. R. is a fifth grade teacher who knows that Halloween is an exciting time for children. She uses that excitement to encourage creative writing employing imagery and descriptive language. She teaches children about establishing a story structure that leads to a climax and then a resolution, highlighting the important artistic concepts of tension and release. Children take two weeks to write their first drafts, critique each other's work in small groups of peers, and then revise their stories until they meet all of the criteria for effective story writing. Once children have written their stories, Ms. R. invites them to think about creating soundscapes for their stories to make their story presentations more exciting. (See Chapter 8, "Their Creative Imaginations," for ideas.) The children use body sounds, found sounds, and homemade instruments as sound sources. They work in teams to set their writing to music, recording the results. Finally, Ms. R. works with the children on ideas for telling their stories expressively, emphasizing the use of dynamic shaping, pauses, and other devices that make storytelling interesting. Children share their completed stories and soundscapes with each other and with students in the other fifth grade classes.

These scenarios illustrate three completely different ways teachers might choose to include music and other arts in their curricular designs. With Mr. Hong, students learn about art for art's sake, deeply experiencing visual arts and music throughout the year by encountering important works of art, internalizing them in various ways, and developing an artistic vocabulary. Mr. Wong is helping to develop artistic literacy. Ms. Graham incorporates music and movement into every day, using aspects of the arts to help children learn a variety of subjects. She understands that children are more likely to learn if they are experiencing material not only visually but also aurally and kinesthetically. She also knows that being actively engaged in singing, chanting, and moving helps children to remember as well as to understand. Finally, Ms. R. is integrating music and other arts into her teaching with creative writing. Her children learn significant content in each aspect of their projects, producing a whole that is greater than any of the pieces by themselves.

THE MUSICAL IMPORTANCE OF CLASSROOM TEACHERS

Classroom teachers sometimes question their role in weaving music into the daily routines of their classrooms, especially if their students are already receiving music lessons from a music specialist. Many classroom teachers are not confident about making music in front of others while others have studied music for years and feel highly confident including it in the curriculum. Regardless of confidence levels, classroom teachers are absolutely central to engaging their students with music and must find ways of using music throughout the school day. Classroom teachers are vital to the exposure, experience, and education of children in and through music, and they have advantages that music specialists usually do not.

Classroom teachers are:

- ▶ with their children most of each day.
- ▶ aware of the needs, interests, and abilities of individual students and can quickly adjust to meet those needs, as well as planning lessons and strategies that build on those needs and interests.
- ▶ knowledgeable about their entire curriculum and able to determine key places where integrating music and the other arts would enhance their students' learning.
- ▶ aware of shifts in energy in the classroom and know when children need a music or movement break, or when recorded music might calm them down or activate them.
- ▶ able to create an environment in which the music that is already in children can emerge spontaneously from them without criticism or reprimand.

FINDING YOUR OWN MUSICIANSHIP

Teachers' attitudes toward music and what it can do for children are more important than their music-making skills. Musicality goes beyond performing (singing and playing instruments). Humans engage with music when listening to songs and instrumental music, dancing, reading a musical score, improvising and composing music, and learning about music in history and culture. All teachers can draw from the music in their lives, their family, and their communities, and find ways to value music and model that valuing to their students. Teachers do not need extraordinary performance skills to lead music activities or incorporate music in significant ways in their classrooms.

STRUCTURING THE CLASSROOM FOR MUSICAL EXPERIENCES

This book offers myriad ways for teachers to use music meaningfully with children. This chapter provides an overview of how the classroom can be structured for experiences in music and the arts, and refers to later chapters in which specific techniques are discussed in more depth. Both aspiring and practicing teachers can become more confident by developing a deeper understanding of how music and the arts are incorporated into classroom culture and all-subject curricula, making every classroom a musically vibrant classroom.

INFORMAL USES OF MUSIC

One way teachers can make classrooms come alive is to intersperse musical activities throughout the day to help with transitions and to create a positive learning environment. The goal of these activities is not necessarily to teach music or to practice musical skills but to harness the power of music to gain children's attention, to get their wiggles out, and to create a musical environment. Chapter 9, "Music for the

Joy of It," will fill in details with specific materials and strategies, but the following ideas briefly illustrate informal ways of incorporating music into the school day.

1. Using a simple musical instrument, such as a bell, has long been an effective way to gain children's attention, whether on the playground or in the classroom. A musical sound cuts through chatter and activity in ways that a teacher's voice does not. Clapping a simple rhythm pattern, which children know to imitate, will also draw children's attention and help them focus on what the teacher's words.

2. Playing recorded music in the classroom can calm or excite, depending on the energy, flow, and tempo of the music and whether or not there are lyrics.

3. All children need to move regularly. It is painful for most children to sit still for long periods of time. With action songs, hand-clapping songs, and singing games, children experience a change of pace when they need to get out of their seats to gain energy and focus. These activities meet children's needs to get more oxygen to their brains and muscles and to move their bodies, and also help with classroom management and motivation.

4. Finally, learning songs together as a class to sing at the opening or closing of the day creates a sense of community and provides structure for the day. See Chapter 4, "Their Singing Voices," to build confidence in song leading.

CREATING MUSIC CENTERS

Teachers understand the power children have to learn on their own or in small groups, provided they have stimulating materials to explore and to guide them. Music centers are places where children can go alone or in pairs to engage with a wide variety of recorded music. A center is most effective when the materials in it change throughout the year. Following are a few introductory ideas for music centers, with more possibilities developed in Chapter 9, "Music for the Joy of It."

Computer music programs can engage small groups in a learning center or the whole class.

1. For young children, create a "sound box" out of a refrigerator box. Decorate it with images of musical instruments. Place carpet squares on the floor and put a few small musical instruments in it that children can use. Include a CD player or mp3 player and headphones so children can listen to some of their favorite music and play along. Change the instruments and recordings over time. Books that illustrate children's songs could also be displayed. See Chapter 10, "Music and Language Arts," for age-appropriate books.

2. For older children, set up a table with a digital recorder, microphone, and headphones. Encourage children to record their original songs over time. See Chapter 8, "Their Creative Imaginations," for more details.

3. Set up a science-of-sound table with a diagram of the ear and how sound moves through the ear. Provide instruments that children can use to explore the relationship between the length of a vibrating surface and its pitch (longer is lower, shorter is higher) or other science-of-sound concepts. See Chapter 13, "Music and Science," for more ideas.

4. Use classroom computers with headphones to help children learn various musical skills on their own. Students can also use computers to create multimedia reports on music and musicians. See Chapter 10, "Music and Language Arts," for writing projects.

DESIGNING ARTS-INTEGRATED CURRICULA

The Association for Supervision and Curriculum Development (ASCD) defines integrating curricula as making connections across multiple disciplines and making connections to real life.[1] Integrating curricula helps children learn the standards of each discipline and connect common ideas across disciplines. Three main approaches for curricular integration have evolved over many years: multidisciplinary, interdisciplinary, and transdisciplinary. The difference between these approaches is the degree to which the various disciplines are separated, and these distinctions often become blurred. The multidisciplinary approach organizes lessons on a common theme taught from the perspectives of distinct disciplines.

The interdisciplinary approach is similar in organization to multidisciplinary, but it emphasizes the overarching skills and concepts rather than discrete skills and concepts of each discipline. The transdisciplinary approach organizes lessons around student questions and concerns and challenges students to develop life skills in real-life contexts. The transdisciplinary approach works well for more independent learners, typically adolescents.

THE VALUE OF ARTS INTEGRATION

Integrating music and the other arts throughout school curricula makes all learning vibrant and exciting for children, because:

1. The arts are multisensory, thereby reaching children who have various learning-style needs. They invite hands-on engagement, providing concrete experiences to enhance learning.

2. The arts allow children to develop skills on their own, but they also build social skills for collaborating with others.

3. The arts are unique ways of knowing or of being intelligent, as defined in Howard Gardner's Theory of Multiple Intelligences (MI). Integrating the arts into non-arts lessons helps children exercise their personal intelligences and develop those ways of knowing that are not as strong.

> "The arts should be supported not only because research supports their value but also because they are as dynamic and broad-based as more widely accepted disciplines. They contribute to the development and enhancement of multiple neurobiological systems, including cognition, emotional, immune, circulatory, and perceptual motor systems. Ultimately, the arts can help make us better people."
>
> —ERIC JENSEN, teacher, scholar, and member of the Society for Neuroscience and New York Academy of Science

4. The arts are nonverbal forms of literacy readily accessible to speakers of all languages. Arts are especially useful in culturally diverse classrooms, especially where many children do not speak English as a first language.

5. The arts touch people emotionally and spiritually, helping them develop nonverbal ways of being and knowing the world. They encourage children to use imagination and metaphor, creating symbolic meanings beyond the discursive or mathematical.

6. The arts invite creativity, developing the important abilities to imagine possibilities and to solve problems in numerous ways.

INTEGRATION VERSUS INFUSION

When planning an integrated lesson, teachers need to keep in mind the difference between integration and infusion. Infusion uses activities of one discipline to enhance and reinforce learning in another discipline, but does not further students' understanding in both. Infusion is a valuable and useful technique, but not as powerful for helping students understand the interconnectedness of ideas across various disciplines.

Integration, on the other hand, leads students to greater understanding of each subject involved and shows equal respect for the value of all disciplines. Integration involves more of the children's senses and creative imaginations and thus stimulates more areas of the brain, which helps children see the connections between subjects and remember the learning more deeply. Singing a song about long division is arts infusion, a pleasant and highly effective way to ease the drudgery of memorizing math facts. A lesson that teaches division of numbers in math as it relates to divisions of rhythm notes in music is integration, a powerful way to help children remember important learning in both subjects.

To achieve full integration, teachers need to plan consciously for the achievement of important learning outcomes in every discipline they integrate. Lessons whose stated goals for each discipline can be found in national, state, or district learning standards are much more likely to be integrated. Lessons using techniques of infusion and of integration will be found throughout this book. Lesson Plan 2.1 offers both infused and integrated approaches to the same material. In the integrated approach, significant concepts are taught through each subject and tied to a common theme.

INDIVIDUAL PLANNING

Individual classroom teachers can plan and teach by themselves activities, lessons, or entire units that integrate the arts. They can also write grants to hire artists in residence to come to their classrooms and teach specific art skills that enhance and expand upon what the classroom teacher is able to teach. (For ideas for bringing artists into the classroom, see pp. 28–31.)

LESSON PLAN 2.1

A Unit on Arts in Northwest Coastal Indian Culture, Arts-Infused vs. Integrated Arts Approaches

ARTS-INFUSED APPROACH

Sing Lummi "Paddling Song" and pretend to paddle the canoe while you sing.

Read and discuss the legend of how Mt. Rainier came to be.

Color in the images on a predrawn totem. Cut out the totem and paste it onto a milk carton.

INTEGRATED ARTS APPROACH

Learn the "Paddling Song" by singing with the vocal style typical of Lummi culture, dropping the pitch at the end of the song like a sigh. Decide the purpose of your journey by canoe. Map out your route on a map of Puget Sound. With a group, form the shape of a Lummi canoe. How can you create the height and shape of its bow? Pretend to paddle through the waters of Puget Sound, singing your song as you go. Is the weather calm or stormy? How do you know? (It is calm because the song glides along smoothly.) Keep your paddles synchronized to the beat. When you get to your destination, show through movement or drama where you were going and what your purpose was.

Discuss the purpose of legends. How does this legend differ from scientific knowledge of how Mt. Rainier came to be? Research the meaning Mt. Rainier holds for the native peoples. Learn to tell the legend in a dramatic style that conveys some of that sacred meaning. Accompany the telling with motions and the sounds of drums and rattles. Later, write your own legend about how a landmark in your community came to be.

Study various totems and the images on them. Learn what each figure means and why each totem is unique. Notice common aspects of each figure: bold, symmetrical, curved lines; outlined shapes; red, black, and white dyes. Why was cedar used to make totems? Design a totem for your family or school, selecting figures that have symbolic meaning for them. Create images in the style of traditional totems. Carve your totem out of foam and add colors. Or, for a school totem, hire a native carver to instruct children, and all design and carve a totem.

Continued on next page

| Learn a salmon dance and accompany it with drums and shakers. | Research different kinds of dances and the occasions on which they were used. View videos of the dances and ceremonies. Note the style of dancing and the instruments used to accompany them. What makes a salmon dance different from other dances? Build some of the instruments, decorate them, and play them to accompany dancing. |

Music and other arts bring to life the study of Northwest Coastal Indians.

COLLABORATIVE PLANNING

Most models of arts integration are planned collaboratively, because two or more teachers bring to the process a much richer body of knowledge, skills, and experience than one teacher planning alone. Collaborative planning can be done by two teachers; a grade-level team working with specialists; or a large team involving classroom teachers, administrators, specialists, community artists or arts organizations, parents, and university experts. Some schools have one early-release day each week during which teachers can gather to plan curricular units. Grants are often available for teachers to work collaboratively over the summer on incorporating the arts into the study of language, math, science, or the social sciences.

This kind of planning requires deep commitment. A well-planned integrated unit typically takes about twenty hours of planning. Ultimately, the effort is worth the expanded knowledge, creativity, and competency gained by teachers and students, and it makes teaching and learning more interesting for everyone. A process[2] for successful collaborations is outlined below, transpiring across several collegial meetings.

1. Gather a team of classroom teachers and arts specialists. This may involve teachers from one grade level or teachers from across the grades depending on the scope of the project.

2. Choose a central focus for curriculum development: a theme, specific subject area, event, issue, or problem. The best themes will cross several disciplines, such as transportation, the solar system, prehistory, a certain country, or heroes and heroines.

3. Brainstorm topics that relate to the chosen theme, reserving judgment of ideas through the process. Allow plenty of time. Record all of the ideas. If possible, invite students to respond to the possibilities.

4. Select major themes and identify any motifs that underlie the themes. Critique their educational validity within each discipline: Is it important content for each discipline? Will combining disciplines enhance student learning? What methods of inquiry will students use? Will reflective practices be involved?

5. Evaluate in terms of practical criteria: Is there a budget to support staff development and acquire resources and materials as needed? Will there be political support from parents, principal, school boards, and so on?

6. Develop the theme and its specific learning experiences. Key concepts and skills must drive each unit of study. Integrate various disciplines including the arts into content and processes.

7. Develop methods of assessment, including portfolio assessment, journals, and rubrics for performance assessment. Establish benchmarks against which to evaluate student work. These benchmarks can represent key content in the various subjects being combined as well as the affective component of children's work.

Collaborative planning draws ideas from a richer body of knowledge, skills, and experience than one person planning alone.

MODELS OF MULTIDISCIPLINARY PROJECTS

The goals of multidisciplinary curriculum design are not only learning significant content in each subject, but also gaining understandings that transcend individual subjects (metaunderstandings). Synthesis activities at the end of a unit can help draw out metaunderstandings. Multidisciplinary design is commonly used at the elementary level by a team of two or more classroom teachers, and sometimes includes specialists. Team members plan together, each contributing suggestions for learning about a central organizing theme in each of the curricular areas. Teachers sometimes trade classes, so that each instructs in only one or two subjects.

Lesson Plan 2.2 is an example of the multidisciplinary webbed model using rain as the theme. Significant content is taught in each subject. Depending on the length of time available for the unit, more content and activities could be developed in each subject area, making it even richer.

A multidisciplinary curricular plan can be a modest, short-term connection of two or three subjects, or a gigantic, whole-school project lasting four to six weeks or the entire school year. Planning such a project is exciting and engaging. Teams of teachers, specialists, and administrators, come together with community artists, arts organizations, and other community experts to determine an entire school

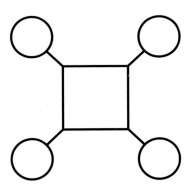

Multidisciplinary (webbed) curriculum model. Each circle represents a subject area. The square represents the common theme.

LESSON PLAN 2.2

Rain as a Theme in the Multidisciplinary (Webbed) Curriculum Model

MUSIC
Experiment with rain sounds, using body or instruments to convey different kinds of rain. Create a storm. Learn songs about rain and discuss different qualities of those songs. Add rain sounds to accompany. Listen to recorded works about rain. What images are created and how?

VISUAL ARTS
Learn to use various watercolor techniques, including wash, to create a rain scene. Discuss how rain mutes colors and obscures objects, and reflect these phenomena in the painting. Consider how other artists depict rain.

CREATIVE DRAMA
Dramatize settings in which rain, or lack thereof, plays an important role.
- A young child in a mud puddle
- A couple caught in a downpour in the park
- The first rain after a drought
- A flood that threatens property
- A dog coming in after the rain

Dramatize stories about rain.

DANCE
How would you move if you were:
- a raindrop
- a storm
- lightning
- water going down a drain
- dripping

Discuss using dance terms. Learn or create a rain dance.

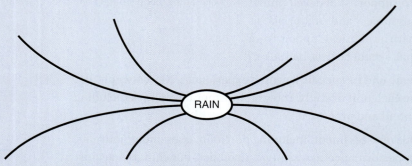

SCIENCE
Learn about the water cycle. Create one in the classroom. Study what causes rain to fall and which kinds of clouds generate which kinds of rain. Watch a weather report. Interview a meteorologist. How do they predict the weather?

MATHEMATICS
Construct a rain gauge. Collect and measure rainfall over a period of several weeks. Chart the daily and weekly totals. Compare your totals with a weather website's monthly report for your town. Research and chart average annual rainfall in your community over the past ten years.

LANGUAGE ARTS
Read various poems about rain. How do the poets create a sense of rain? Do they use onomatopoeia or alliteration? Write your own rain poem using at least five words to describe rain. Read books about rain. How does rain affect people, animals, the environment? Write a story about how rain affects a family.

SOCIAL STUDIES
Study a map of weather patterns. Learn about the lives of people who live with heavy rains, and with little or no rain. Learn traditions for asking for rain. Consider the importance of rain to different populations around the world.

---

curriculum through this theme. Something of this magnitude requires commitment from the entire school community and the support of a school leadership that understands the value of this kind of education (see the Arts Impact model, p. 33). Such projects require a theme broad enough to touch all areas of the curriculum at all grade levels. For example, a theme for a short project might be the circus, which invites playful ways of learning through the lenses of various disciplines. Year-long themes might include Native American studies from a particular region of the country, the medieval period in Europe, or sub-Saharan Africa. Cultural and historical themes are broad enough to allow perspectives from every discipline to add knowledge. Scientific, literary, and artistic themes are also possible, as well as skill-based themes, such as writing across the curriculum.

LESSON PLAN 2.3

Comets as a Theme in the Threaded Curriculum Model, Based on Theory of Multiple Intelligences

Main Lesson: Comets
The teacher provides students with pictures and diagrams describing comets and their size, composition, and orbits.

Centers
Martha Graham Center: Students make their own comets out of toothpicks and marshmallows, adding streamers for comet tails. Some children form the sun, and other children move as comets in an elliptical orbit, keeping their tails pointed away from the sun. Children demonstrate what happens to a comet as it moves closer to the sun (bodily–kinesthetic intelligence).

Diego Rivera Center: Using glue and glitter, students create comets on colored paper, correctly labeling all the parts (visual–spatial intelligence).

William Shakespeare Center: Students read about comets in science textbooks, astronomy books, encyclopedias, and poetry, and answer questions about their reading (verbal–linguistic intelligence).

Kitarō Center: Using the melody of "Twinkle, Twinkle Little Star," students in small groups compose lyrics that include several facts about comets. Children perform their songs for each other (musical–rhythmic intelligence).

Emily Dickinson Center: Individually, students write about how they are similar to or different from comets (intrapersonal intelligence).

Albert Einstein Center: Using graph paper and rulers, students draw a series of comets to different scales with the tail 10 times as long as the head, 50 times as long, 100 times as long, and 500 times as long (logical–mathematical intelligence).

Rachel Carson Center: Using the Internet, students research the possible relations among comets, asteroids, and meteoroids (naturalistic intelligence).

Paul Tillich Center: Students listen to "Halley Came to Jackson," by Mary Chapin Carpenter, or read her book by the same name, and consider: How did it make the people of Jackson feel to see Halley's Comet? Why did they make a wish and say "amen"? Think about how it would make you feel to see a comet (existential intelligence).

Mahatma Gandhi Center: In groups, students create a game show about outer space that includes visuals and fact cards. Questions presented to the contestants must call upon higher-level thinking skills (interpersonal intelligence).

Webbed multidisciplinary curricular lessons can be presented in any order, without regard to sequence of material. In contrast, in threaded delivery, children progress sequentially or linearly through a series of interrelated lessons. Threaded delivery is necessary for lessons in which information learned in one subject provides fundamental understanding needed for subsequent lessons. All students receive the lessons in the same order. Threaded delivery is also useful when information does not need to be presented sequentially but groups of students must progress orderly through several learning stations. Groups start learning at one of several stations and continue sequentially until they have learned what each station provides.

Lesson Plan 2.3 is an example of threaded delivery with learning stations, teaching about comets using all of Howard Gardner's multiple intelligences. It doesn't matter where students enter the cycle, but once they start, they continue sequentially through all nine stations, exploring a theme using different intelligences. This delivery allows each child to work in his or her preferred intelligence(s), as well as strengthen learning in other intelligences. Not all lessons require children to experience all of the intelligences.[3, 4] Lesson Plan 2.3 names each learning station after a famous representative of that intelligence.

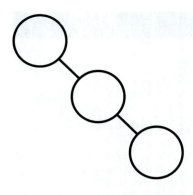

Threaded curriculum model. Significant content is taught in each subject.

MODELS OF INTERDISCIPLINARY PROJECTS

The interdisciplinary approach is similar in organization to multidisciplinary, but emphasizes overarching skills and concepts over discrete skills and concepts of each discipline. Children are immersed in many connected ideas and resources; for this reason, the interdisciplinary approach is sometimes referred to as "immersed." As with multidisciplinary design, interdisciplinary lessons can be presented in random (webbed) order, or sequential (threaded) order.

Lesson Plan 2.4 is an example of an interdisciplinary (immersed) approach to the study of insects. The disciplines of science, math, reading and language arts, music, art, and theater have been integrated with important skills of thinking, writing, numeracy, collaboration, creating, and presenting throughout these learning experiences. All the subjects overlap and add to the children's understanding of the theme in different ways. Boundaries between subjects begin to disappear as ideas and resources are networked. In the immersed curriculum, both affective and cognitive growth is stimulated, and a group synthesis occurs as members derive personal and shared meaning from their experiences. The culminating performance becomes an authentic assessment of the learning.

Interdisciplinary lesson plans can also be designed to build on a specific skill rather than on a theme, such as the example on writing across the curriculum described in Box 2.1.

CONNECTING THE CLASSROOM TO THE COMMUNITY

BRINGING ARTISTS INTO SCHOOLS

Most states, counties, cities, and towns throughout the United States have arts commissions that play various roles, from promoting the development and employment of local artists, to selecting art works for the community and artists to work in the schools. The National Endowment for the Arts (NEA) website offers current connections to regional, state, and local arts organizations as well as pertinent information on the arts in education. View the arts education site to find out what is happening in many locations. This is also a source for grants. Their publications often give important information about the value of the arts in education. Often state arts commissions will provide a variety of programs and resources to generate more arts and artists in the schools of their region.

Most arts commissions publish annually the names of approved artists for schools and descriptions of what each teaches children. Individual classroom teachers, groups of teachers, or whole schools can apply to employ an artist in residence for a period of time. The arts commission pays most of the cost and the school pays a smaller amount. Often parent-teacher associations provide funds for these grants.

Rather than for one performance, artists in residence come for several weeks so that children can have deeper arts experiences. In some places, residencies last from 20 to 100 days. State law requires teachers to stay in the room and supervise while artists teach, because most artists are not certified teachers, even though they have worked with children and feel comfortable in the classroom.

LESSON PLAN 2.4

Interdisciplinary (Immersed) Grade-Level Lesson about Insects

A team of four second-grade teachers wants to do a month-long study of insects for their science curriculum. They invite the music and art specialist to collaborate with them. They design a unit of study in which all second-grade children delve into the insect world. Children learn how to identify and classify insects; where they belong in the food chain and what their natural enemies are; their ecological functions; and about their habitats and how those habitats influence what they eat. They also learn how insects fit into the broader biological world. The classroom teachers teach all the science content, integrating math, reading, and writing into the study. Children create graphs and charts to show what they've learned about insects. They demonstrate reading comprehension by writing reports about their insects.

After the children learn many facts about insects in general, each classroom chooses one insect to study in greater depth. The children list facts about their chosen insect. Then the teacher introduces the idea of writing poetry that fits a rhyming and metrical scheme. Once children understand the scheme, the class writes a group poem, synthesizing what they learn.

Children take their poems to music class and work with the music and art specialist to turn their poems into songs (see Chapter 8, "Their Creative Imaginations," for how to write songs with children). They practice their song until they can sing it confidently. Then they add instrumental accompaniment and dance movements. The movements reflect what they have learned from watching films of how their particular insect moves. The music and art specialist asks children to bring photographs of their insect to her class, and, using paper bags, pipe cleaners, and shiny paper and glitter, they create simple costumes based on the insect's size, color, shape, and markings.

Once all of this is accomplished in each classroom, all of the teachers collaborate to help the children put on a show about insects for the rest of the students in the school and for the parents. Children write a script to tie the songs and dances together and assume the speaking roles for their insect drama. Teachers coach them on presentation and acting skills. All the children are completely engaged in the learning process, synthesizing all they learn through these creative activities.

BOX 2.1 INTERDISCIPLINARY (IMMERSED) GRADE-LEVEL LESSON ON WRITING SKILLS

An elementary school in a community in Massachusetts committed to a project of writing across the curriculum. Children wrote about something they learned in every subject. Once a week each class voted on the best writing samples, which were fed through a mail slot in a giant Gumby's tummy next to the principal's office. Each Friday, a representative team of students from various classrooms and grade levels read all entries and selected the top writing for that week. Friday afternoon, the entire school assembled to hear the top writing read and celebrated. Sometimes, a local jazz trio would come to accompany the readings, improvising in the background. Parents were welcome to attend these assemblies.

The school committed to hiring specialists in music, dance, art, and drama to work with all of the children every week. Often, the written pieces were turned into dance, theater, or song, or illustrated to become actual collections in books that were then placed in the library for all to read.

Not surprisingly, reading and writing test scores for these children rose from the 25th percentile to the 95th percentile over the years this program was in place. And, interestingly, scores in other content areas also rose into the 90th percentile range. Year after year, students from this community in Massachusetts won national poetry-writing awards. Committing to an interdisciplinary immersed curriculum in which the arts were central transformed this school.

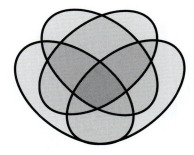

Interdisciplinary (immersed) curriculum model. All the subjects overlap and add to the children's understanding of the theme in different ways.

While supervising, teachers can learn first-hand new ways of using the arts with their children.

Here are several examples of typical residencies:

Music: A musician from a particular culture teaches a musical tradition to a class or group of classes. A rock musician, singer-songwriter, country musician, or hip hop artist helps children write a class song or a rap on a current event or

Artists in residence bring enriched learning resources from the community into schools.

a topic they're studying in a non-music subject. An instrumentalist teaches them Japanese Taiko drumming or a percussion tradition from West Africa. A folk musician strums a three-string dulcimer while singing an Ozark folk song, then teaches children to make and play a one-string monochord that can be plucked to sound a range of pitches.

Visual Arts: A weaver teaches children how to build simple looms and weave patterns typical of a particular weaving culture (African Americans, the Mixtec of southern Mexico, or Bhutanese immigrants, for example). A mosaic artist teaches children in several classrooms to create mosaics of small, brightly colored ceramic tiles that later become part of a permanent installation in a school courtyard. A muralist helps the entire school collaborate to create a large mural in the foyer that reflects the multicultural makeup of that school. A mask maker from Indonesia or Nigeria teaches children to construct masks for a story they wish to dramatize. An illustrator teaches children how to illustrate stories they've written in their writing program. A Haida woodcarver works with children throughout the school year to carve a Northwest coastal Indian–style totem pole that is installed at the school's entrance.

Dance and Movement: A dancer from Cambodia, Croatia, Samoa, or Senegal teaches children traditional dances from a culture they are studying. A dancer of contemporary styles, such as modern or jazz, helps children learn to move their bodies in various shapes and forms that relate to what they're learning in mathematics. A choreographer teaches children how to design their own dances to selected music.

Literary Arts: A storyteller weaves her magic by telling stories from the Appalachian Mountains and then inviting children to tell their own stories about where they live. A local award-winning poet shares his own poetry and teaches children how to write and critique their own poetry. A writer of children's books helps children learn how to write, critique, and revise their own stories or poems.

Theater Arts: A playwright from the community theater teaches children how to write and produce short plays. A makeup artist helps children learn to create effective makeup for a drama they are producing. An actor teaches them core principles of movement, focus, character, and delivery. A puppeteer teaches children to make simple puppets and use them to dramatize stories they've been learning to tell in their reading program. A musician guides children in composing music to accompany their play.

Media Arts: A videographer teaches children to plan a series of scenes, create a storyboard, and film their ideas. A photographer teaches children concepts of framing and shooting effective pictures, how to transfer them to the computer, and then how to manipulate the images using software. Students demonstrate their understanding of scenes and photos in reports they make on important places in their community. They support their show with recorded sounds from various locations in their community.

PARENTS AS RESOURCES

Teachers have long welcomed the help of parents in their classrooms. Parents can be wonderful resources, but the wise teacher will establish clear invitations, directions, and boundaries to guard against the small handful of parents who may try to change or redirect projects. One successful effort to tap into parent power comes from the Center for Arts Education of New York City, which has an entire branch called Parents as Arts Partners (PAAP), a model of ways for teachers and parents to work together so that children can learn in captivating ways.

Once teachers have planned the year's major curricular units of study, they can survey parents to determine their expertise or connections in certain subjects and their availability. Some parents may have particular training in certain arts and be willing to help with arts-related projects. For example, a mother might be a weaver or a quilter who would help fifth graders with a project related to colonial arts during the early settlement of the United States. A father might be a musician or dancer, a violinist, flutist, or player of lute from a particular culture being studied. Mothers and fathers may also wish to accompany children on field trips to community arts events.

CONNECTING TO THE LARGER ARTS COMMUNITY

In addition to the artist-in-residence programs described earlier, communities both large and small have numerous ways for children to be involved with the arts and arts organizations. In larger cities with major performing and visual arts organizations, it is possible to tap into those resources in a number of ways. Museums and galleries, theater programs, ballet and modern dance companies, and civic symphonies and opera companies may have ongoing educational programs that teachers can use for their own skill development and that of their students. By contacting various organizations, teachers can learn of education programs in the arts, many of them outstanding for their capacity to enhance arts experiences for children. Some arts organizations regularly put on programs for schoolchildren, too, and provide ancillary material in support of these programs.

Even in smaller towns, there may be galleries, performing artists, museums, or cultural groups with resources for teachers. Look for event listings in towns and cities of all sizes to see what offerings might connect with the classroom curriculum.

TAKING CHILDREN INTO THE COMMUNITY

Many cities with symphony orchestras have a tradition of field trips by fourth-, fifth-, or sixth-grade students to an orchestra concert. The concert may be funded by the orchestra and transportation provided by the school district or by a grant. Theaters, particularly children's theaters, offer morning matinees for schoolchildren, and may provide tours of the studios or on-stage exchanges with the actors. Art museums often have lively programs for children in conjunction with particular exhibits, including spaces for exploring the music, dance, and drama of the artist's era, or even stand-alone programs for literacy in the visual arts.

Classroom teachers assume many responsibilities when taking children out into the community:

- ▶ Identifying or responding to community-based programs
- ▶ Preparing children in terms of behavior, attitude, attire, and decorum
- ▶ Preparing children in terms of what they will be listening for or looking for, such as by providing questions ahead of time that they will need to answer upon their return to school. Most arts organizations provide excellent educational materials to help prepare children to attend their events.
- ▶ Communicating details of the field trip to the administrator and to parents, including obtaining permission slips from parents
- ▶ Arranging for transportation and for parent chaperones
- ▶ Conducting follow-up activities to secure the experience in the children's minds

BRINGING THE COMMUNITY INTO THE SCHOOL

Most arts organizations have educational programs or performances that they bring to schools for a reasonable fee or free of charge. Some will provide concerts and assemblies for all the children; some will send artists into the schools to work in individual classrooms. Some have programs that train teachers to work with children more effectively through the arts (particularly the Metropolitan Opera, the National Opera, and the National Symphony, along with local and regional arts organizations). At the national level, various museums of the Smithsonian Institution as well as the Metropolitan Museum of Art provide online resources to teachers. At the local or regional level, art museums, science museums, and history museums can help enlarge children's experiences in the wider world of art (as well as the humanities and sciences).

Parent-teacher associations (PTA, PTSA, or PTO) often raise money annually to provide assemblies for children in their schools. Typically, they have access to musicians, artists, actors, dancers, storytellers, and poets who are willing to offer assemblies. Teachers should be involved in deciding assembly content along with a representative from the PTA. (An assembly led by a professional storyteller is educational and helps children engage with an art form; a clown parachuting from a helicopter might be entertaining, but has questionable educational value.)

The national PTA sponsors an annual arts program for children called Reflections. It supplements arts education programs in the schools and invites children to submit original writing, visual arts, musical compositions, and other art forms for judging at the district, regional, and national levels. This program motivates children to develop their artistic expressions, but also joins together teachers and parents in guiding children through the process of creating art and packaging it for submission to a jury.

Teachers may also connect with various cultural groups in their city or town. Resources from these groups enrich social studies, culture, and history curricula. Some national-level cultural centers may have local organizations, such as the Filipino Cultural Association, the Japanese Cultural Center, the Polish-American Cultural Center, the Irish Heritage Club, or the Samoan Center. Often members of these organizations will come to classrooms to teach children about their culture. Typically, they bring music, dance, visual arts, theater, and stories to create cultural understanding. Children can experience these art forms and may even be invited to learn the songs, stories, instrumental music, dance, or art styles of that culture. Elementary children particularly enjoy watching performances by similar-age children from different cultures.

MODELS AND RESOURCES FOR TEACHER TRAINING IN ARTS INTEGRATION

As teachers consider how to integrate the arts effectively into their classrooms, they may feel overwhelmed by the number of possibilities or wonder where they can continue their own growth in the arts. Many resources are available nationally and locally, and all maintain an online presence (see Table 2.1).

Washington State has launched the Arts Impact model for training classroom teachers to work collaboratively and integrate the arts throughout their curriculum.[5] In this model, school districts or individual schools obtain grants to train all classroom teachers and administrators in a given school to use the arts on a daily basis to enhance children's learning. Artists in music, dance, visual arts, and drama devote two summers to training educators, and later spend time working alongside teachers in their schools as the teachers learn to integrate the arts. Community-based artists and arts organizations partner in this work.

In Arts Impact, teachers learn to identify concepts that exist in at least two disciplines—for example, symmetry, which exists in both visual art and math—and then to incorporate the concepts of art into the rest of the curriculum. Teachers who learn to use the Arts Impact approach are transformed, and the social climate of the entire school is enlightened when the arts are placed daily in the academic subjects.[6]

The Tennessee Arts Academy trains arts specialists from Tennessee and beyond to teach music, visual arts, dance, or theater more effectively in the schools, often by connecting with the entire curriculum. The Florida Alliance for Arts Education (FAAE) has many publications and online lesson plans, and trains teachers

TABLE 2.1 RESOURCES FOR TRAINING TEACHERS TO USE THE ARTS WITH CHILDREN

ORGANIZATION	WHAT IT OFFERS
Arts Impact	A model for teacher training and online lessons
Tennessee Arts Academy	Training for arts specialists to teach the arts more effectively
Florida Alliance for Arts Education (FAAE)	Teacher training and publications
The Center for Arts Education (CAE)	Grants, parent programs, advocacy, a model program, and research
Lesley University	Regional summer masters programs to train teachers to use the arts in education
New Horizons for Learning (now affiliated with Johns Hopkins University College of Education)	Online support for developing brain-based learning including the arts in education
Waldorf schools	Private schools based on the work of Rudolph Steiner in which engagement with the arts is central
Reggio Emilia schools	An approach to early childhood education in which children learn through their "natural" languages of the arts
The Total Learning Institute	An arts-integrative approach to elementary curriculum that includes teacher training, with a focus on multimodal instruction

throughout that state to use the arts in education. The Center for Arts Education is committed to quality arts education in all of New York City's public schools, kindergarten through 12th grade. The CAE funds grants and programs and includes a research arm at Columbia University. The Creative Advantage is a collaboration by the Seattle Foundation, Seattle public schools, private non-profits, and the Seattle Office of Arts & Culture to restore access to the arts for all students in the public schools by 2020. Their website contains information about their program and the value of the arts in education. More ideas and resources can be found in Table 2.1; each organization maintains an online presence.

Summary

Teachers who incorporate music and the other arts in their classrooms can expect many rewards for their efforts. Their classrooms will feel more alive, their children will be more excited about school and more engaged in learning, absences will likely decrease, test scores will likely increase across the curriculum, and they themselves will become more excited about teaching.[7] Many community, national, and online resources are available to help teachers become more confident and competent in integrating the arts into their classrooms. Formal education and training in the arts and how to integrate them are offered through many universities (some accessible online from anywhere). Teachers who turn their students loose to exercise their innate creativity will be richly rewarded.

Review

1. List several reasons why the classroom teacher is central in bringing music and the other arts into the classroom.

2. What are some ways that music can be used informally in the classroom?

3. What do the arts do for children's learning that seems to be unique to the arts?

4. What is the difference between arts integration and arts infusion?

5. Name one model for planning an arts-integrated curriculum.

6. Describe two ways to link your class to community-based artists or arts organizations.

Critical Thinking

1. Why might teachers struggle to implement artistically rich curricula on the elementary level? How might you overcome those struggles?

2. What are the advantages of collaborating to plan and implement arts-integrated units of study? What are the advantages to children of such study?

3. What other community-based resources might you use to bring the arts to your students that are not suggested in this chapter?

4. What unit of study would you would want to do with your students that would be enhanced by an artist in residence? How might you use that person's gifts in your classroom?

5. How did you feel when reading Vignettes 1, 2, and 3? Could you imagine yourself involved in such programs? What do you think that kind of learning would do for your students?

Projects

1. Write your musical autobiography. Begin with your earliest memories of being comforted or stimulated by music as a very young child. Include your experiences in community and school music programs and choices you've made in listening to recorded or live music. Finally, consider the ways you are engaged with music now. Reflect on how these experiences have made you the person you are. Imagine yourself as a person who would incorporate music into your classroom. State what you would feel comfortable doing and why.

2. Collaborate with a small group of your classmates to select a topic of study that would be appropriate for elementary-age children. Designate the age level or range for this unit of study. Use a webbed curriculum design to plan your unit. Brainstorm age-appropriate activities to include in each element of your web. Work to make sure children will gain understanding and skill in the arts as well as in the various content areas of the curriculum.

3. Create an activity to be used independently in a music center by children of a particular grade level or age range.

4. Search the Internet for a community arts resource that can support you in incorporating the arts in your classroom. Name the various ways that resource could be used in your program. Develop a project that incorporates at least one aspect of that resource.

5. Search the Internet for one of the models for teacher education and student development in the arts listed in this chapter. Summarize their philosophy, and identify and list the ways the arts are at its core. Read any research they have used to support their beliefs, and write a short summary of the findings.

6. Find several online lessons that use the arts to teach another subject area. Analyze how the arts are used. Is it arts integration or arts infusion? Justify your decision.

Additional Resources for Teaching

Campbell, Patricia Shehan and Carol Scott-Kassner. (2014). *Music in Childhood: From Preschool through the Elementary Grades* (4th ed.). Boston, MA: Schirmer/Cengage.

Gilbert, Anne Green (Producer). (2003). *Brain Dance* [motion picture]. (Available from the Creative Dance Center, AGG Productions, 7327 46th Ave NE, Seattle, WA 98115)

Jazz at Lincoln Center: www.jazz.org

Jensen, Eric. (2005). *Teaching with the Brain in Mind* (rev. 2nd ed.). Alexandria, VA: Association for Supervision and Curriculum Development.

Phillips, Lisa. (2012). *The Artistic Edge: 7 Skills Children Need to Succeed in an Increasingly Right Brain World.* Toronto, ON: The Artistic Edge.

Online Resources: Audio and Songbook

digital.wwnorton.com/classroom

readiness to learn, and may set expectations too high (or too low) for children of a particular age and stage. Just as learning in literacy and numeracy is best facilitated by teachers attuned to children's linguistic and cognitive development, learning in music is similarly advanced when teachers are aware of how musical understanding develops within the context of students' intellectual, social-emotional, and physical growth.

STAGES OF MUSICAL DEVELOPMENT

Research of children's development through various intellectual stages has led to stage theories, which assert that children pass from simple to increasingly complex stages as they mature. Jean Piaget, a twentieth-century Swiss biologist, postulated an early, influential stage theory that identifies approximate ages at which children typically develop through stages of thinking. The specifics of his work are somewhat Eurocentric; they disregard the cultural priorities that accelerate learning in some settings. Still, basic principles remain: [Children construct their learning through interaction, they need to be respected in their various stages of development] (and not treated like adults), and they should be viewed as individuals with different rates of development rather than as groups. Piaget identified four stages:

1. sensorimotor (birth to two years), involving learning through direct sensory experience within the immediate environment;

2. preoperational (ages two to seven years), involving learning through the manipulation of objects—noting the consequences and internalizing them for the future, thus transforming stimuli into symbols;

3. concrete operations (ages seven to 11 years), involving viewing objects in concrete, tangible, and systematic ways but not abstractly; and

4. formal operations (ages 11 through adolescence and adulthood), involving learning abstractly using logic and deductive reasoning.[6]

In the sensorimotor stage, infants enjoy exploring the sight, taste, feel, and sounds of objects, including simple instruments (such as rattles, jingle bells, drums, and toy pianos), books embedded with musical sounds, and other musical toys like the jack-in-the-box. Finger plays with associated chants and songs, action songs with gestures, and musical patty-cake interactions are perfectly suited to children in this earliest period of development. Infants and toddlers in their early pre-language period learn the sounds of objects and thus acquire fundamental musical understandings.

As children move into the preoperational stage in preschool, kindergarten, and first grade, they engage in play that is frequently rhythmic and melodic in nature. Children respond well to active and participatory learning activities that take place seated, so teachers in early childhood programs often bring songs into circle time and create listening and music-making learning stations, thereby encouraging foundational understandings to emerge naturally from experience. In this stage, children develop meanings from concrete experiences, which form foundations critical for understanding abstract symbols, including words, figures, and written musical notation. Kindergarten and first-grade teachers recognize that musical concepts like tempo (fast–slow), pitch (high–low), and

Children respond well to learning activities that take place on the floor, that are active and participatory.

dynamics (loud–soft) are best understood through musical experiences, and that only afterward do terms and symbols become meaningful to children.

From age seven, when children enter Piaget's third stage of concrete operations, until age 11, they acquire substantial musical skills as singers and instrumentalists. They are able to read musical notation and to write it, based upon earlier years spent listening and doing. Children of this age gradually become more able to order and classify objects, to remember and recall objects and events that are not physically present, to "conserve" or recognize stimuli and situations that may be slightly altered (such as a melody sung twice as fast as it originally was), and to reverse actions, such as backtracking the steps of a math problem or playing the notes of a melody from end to beginning. Children are ready to sing in tune and on tempo, and from second grade onward they gradually develop the motor skills to play musical instruments such as recorders, xylophones, drums, pianos, guitars, and instruments of the band and orchestra. They are able learn by listening and by reading notation that symbolizes the melodies and rhythms they sing and play. Given their growing cognitive capacities in this stage of concrete operations, children can triumph over many intellectual and musical challenges.

By the time children leave elementary school, typically in the fifth or sixth grade, they have reached Piaget's fourth stage, formal operations, in which they can think in abstract and sophisticated ways as they listen to, perform, and create music. They can understand symbols that represent experiences, understand and form ideas about objects that are not concretely present, and analyze their own ideas and those of others. They can read musical notation, listen analytically, sing and play with dynamic expression, and articulate similarities and differences in the music they know. They can also compose and improvise music thoughtfully according to the conventions they have experienced and learned, and enjoy making new and innovative musical sounds. Of course, children do not achieve these skills without a sequential program of instruction; these accomplishments require a teacher's guidance. Classroom teachers can engage children in musical experiences in their classrooms, support the work of the music specialist teacher, or team with the specialist to reinforce and encourage musical learning.

MUSICAL SKILL DEVELOPMENT

Many researchers in music, psychology, and neuroscience have observed, measured, and documented children's development from infancy to adolescence in different cultural contexts, with and without various handicapping conditions.

VOCAL DEVELOPMENT: SINGING SKILLS

Their findings have added to our understanding, and several stage theories for music learning have evolved, a handful of which are provided here as abbreviated descriptions of children's musical maturation in vocal skills (singing), kinesthetic skills (playing instruments, moving musically, dancing to music), aural skills (discrete listening), and creative thinking skills (music composition and improvisation).

VOCAL DEVELOPMENT: SINGING SKILLS

Children are vocally active from birth, and in their infancy are discovering the expressive possibilities of their voices. They draw out their vowels, sputter and babble their consonants, and join the phonemes they have heard in ways that make sense to them and communicate to others. They prolong some sounds, babble at high and low pitches, and find patterns that please them to repeat hours on end. As their expressive language begins to evolve, so, too, do their voices begin to shape sounds that are musical by anyone's definition: melodic, rhythmic, and with a formal organization of repeated and contrasting segments. They learn to sing from the vocalizations they explore, and from the singing, chanting, and instrumental music that surrounds them (see Table 3.1).

Toddlers of two to three years play with vocal sounds, imitating spoken and sung segments, stringing syllables together on stepwise pitches, or skipping one to two pitches at a time. Regular rhythms seep into their spontaneous songs, and they begin to reproduce nursery songs, childhood chants, and folk songs of short repeating melodic patterns. By kindergarten, children of four to five years are capable of singing solidly within a range of five pitches, from D4 to A5. They distinguish between their speaking and singing voices and can shift from a light and airy quality to the timbre of an outdoor voice for animated songs. They learn words, rhythm, phrases, and melodic shapes of rising and falling pitches. They imitate the quality of the teacher's voice, the voices of their friends and family members, and the voices of recordings that are played for them.

Children sing for the joy of it, and to release a spectrum of emotions. As they enter first grade, they develop a fuller vocal sound and more expressive control of their voice. Their vocal range and tessitura (the smaller range in which they are most comfortable) increases yearly, so that they grow from a vocal range of C4 up to B4 (with a smaller tessitura, D4–B4) in first grade to a vocal range of G3 to G5 (with smaller tessitura, B3–D5) by sixth grade (see Example 3.1).

Elementary school–aged children are more apt to sing in tune than younger children, and by second grade (eight years old) their sense of key stabilizes and remains intact from one phrase to the next within a song. They can learn longer and more complex songs as their musical memories increase. By third grade (nine years old), they are able to sing simple harmony parts, such as rounds, partner songs, and vocal ostinatos (a short recurring pattern under a tune) against a melody. Their perceptual awareness is fine-tuned by this age, and they are able to blend their voices in an ensemble of singers.

As children mature through the intermediate grades, they develop increasing range and resonance and become capable of singing progressively more involved harmonies—canons, rounds, descants, countermelodies, and even two- and three-part songs. They begin to experience physiological and psychological changes

TABLE 3.1 CHILDREN'S VOCAL DEVELOPMENT

AGE	DEVELOPMENTAL ACTIVITY
Less than one	Vocalizes (babbles) vowels and consonants
One to two	Babbles in irregular rhythmic patterns
	Imitates the contour of songs' melodic phrases, but not discrete pitches
Two	Babbles in extended melodic phrases
	Babbles in small intervals of seconds, thirds
	Imitates occasional discrete pitches of songs
Three	Invents spontaneous songs with discrete pitches and recurring rhythmic and melodic patterns
	Reproduces nursery rhymes and childhood chants
Four to five (kindergarten)	Discovers differences between speaking and singing voices
	Shifts song qualities from light and airy to the playground yell for lively songs
	Sings spontaneous songs spanning two octaves
	Sings in tune within range of five pitches, D4 to A4
Six to seven (first grade)	Sings in tune in range of C4 to B4, with smaller tessitura
	Can begin to develop head voice, with guidance
	Begins to have expressive control of voice
Seven to eight (second grade)	Sings in tune in range of octave, about C4 to C5 or D4 to D5, with smaller tessitura
Eight to nine (third grade)	Sings in tune in range of B♭3 to E♭5, with smaller tessitura
	Can perform fundamental harmony songs such as melody over vocal ostinato or sustained pitch
Nine to ten (fourth grade)	Sings in tune in range of A3 to E5, with smaller tessitura
	Sings with increasing resonance (grades four, five, and six)
	May experience first vocal change (boys, beginning age ten)
	Can perform canons, rounds, descants, countermelodies
	Can sing with appropriate phrasing, with guidance
Ten to eleven (fifth grade)	Sings in tune in range of A♭3 to F5, with C4 to C5 octave tessitura
	Is increasingly selective of song repertoire
	Prefers songs in middle range
	Prefers songs without sentimental or babyish texts
	Can perform two-part songs
Eleven to twelve (sixth grade)	Sings in tune in range of G3 to G5, with C4 to C5 octave tessitura
	Can perform three-part songs

Note: C4 = middle C; C3 = one octave lower; C5 = one octave higher

EXAMPLE 3.1

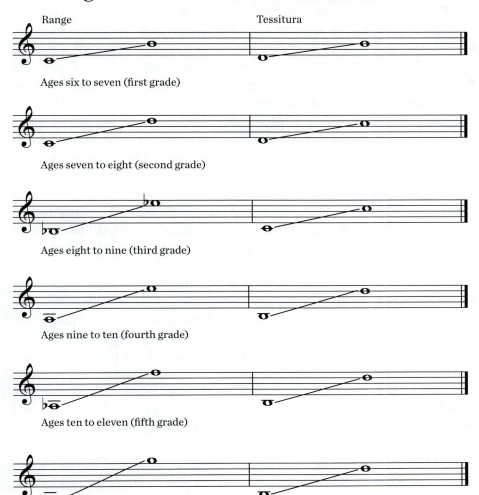

typical of preadolescence, and by age 10 or 11 their voices may change: Girls may sing more lightly than before, while boys may develop a deeper quality to their speaking and singing voices. Furthermore, some children may become less interested in singing, particularly if they are not singing regularly, and some may be self-conscious about singing, especially boys whose voices become unpredictable. As adolescence creeps up, girls may become embarrassed to sing in front of boys, and boys may perceive singing as a feminine activity. Such is not the case in the culture of British boy choirs in the churches, chapels, and cathedrals of England, for example, or in far-flung countries and cultures across the continents. In much of the world, male singing is a prized activity. The frequency and fervor of children's singing exercises their ears and voices, so that children in classrooms where singing is valued as a regular activity—whether for the sake of singing together or as a tool for learning language or math concepts—tend to sing easily and accurately, and with confidence.

KINESTHETIC DEVELOPMENT: MOVEMENT AND DANCE

Children's kinesthetic and motoric capacities unfold gradually. By the age of six months, infants begin to coordinate their heads, arms, chest, and legs. Their movement is definitively rhythmic, whether they are sucking, kicking, or thrusting their arms into the air. By two years, they are rocking rhythmically from side to side, bouncing up and down to their own internal beat, and moving rhythmically to music with a strong beat. The exploratory movements that may appear haphazard in the nursery become well controlled as children of ages three to four practice and perfect particular movements they already know. Children can run before they can walk (by age two), they can jump before they can hop on one leg (age three to four), and they can gallop before they can skip (age five to seven). They clap their hands early on, in patty-cake games with parents at age two, and typically can alternate between clapping and patting their laps at age five to six (see Table 3.2).

By kindergarten, children are physically coordinated enough to move accurately to the pulse of the music they hear. As they attain beat competence, usually by six or seven years, they can perform singing games and simple folk dances in rhythmically accurate ways. They clap, pat, and tap to the beat, and they can keep the beat on drum and rhythm sticks.

As their small-muscle coordination develops, they become increasingly accurate in their ability to color, draw, print numbers and letters, and play xylophones (beginning in first grade), piano or keyboard (second grade), recorder (third grade), and wind and brass instruments (fourth or fifth grade). They continue to fine-tune small muscles and shape larger motor behaviors through the elementary grades and into the middle grades. They also grow their athletic capacities to dance, run, jump, swing, kick, maneuver soccer balls, and interact in physically coordinated ways with their teammates. This greater coordination of the torso, arms, and legs allows them to express themselves musically and respond quickly to music's changes in tempo, rhythmic patterns, and textures.

When teachers feature time for children to listen to music, march or gently step to music, and pat the beat—on laps, shoulders, heads, chests, desks, and tables— children improve the connections among their ears, brains, and bodies. They can perceive, think, and respond kinesthetically, almost simultaneously. It's a small leap from patting the beat to conducting meters—feeling and showing the grouping of pulses in twos, threes, and fours—especially when children have had extensive experience listening and moving with purpose to music's elemental components.

PERCEPTUAL MOTOR SKILLS: PLAYING MUSICAL INSTRUMENTS

As children's kinesthetic and perceptual motor skills develop, their muscular control increases and their capacity to play musical instruments improves. They gradually develop the fine motor coordination necessary to grasp and hold musical instruments in good playing positions, to transfer their sense of rhythm to the instruments, and to decode musical notation and apply its symbols to their playing. Their physical maturation, musical perception, and cognitive understanding combine to prepare them for playing instruments of various complexities, at various ages and stages of their development.

CHAPTER 3 | The Musical Growth of Children **47**

TABLE 3.2 CHILDREN'S MOVEMENT DEVELOPMENT

AGE	DEVELOPMENTAL SKILL
Less than six months	Responds to music through generalized body movement; movement not yet synchronized to rhythm
Two years	Responds by rocking, bouncing, waving arms to rhythm
	Develops walking and running skills
	Attempts to imitate clapping and patty-cake movements
Three to four	Practices known movements by repeating them
	Invents and imitates new movements
	Begins to develop large-muscle coordination for jumping, hopping
	Can perform simple action songs and game songs
Five to six (kindergarten)	Begins to develop rhythmic clapping and patting
	Begins to develop skills for galloping (one-sided skip) and jumping rope
	Can perform simple folk dances in circles and lines
	Begins to develop small-muscle coordination for drawing and printing (writing)
Six to seven (first and second grades)	Begins to develop skipping skills
	Responds (frequently) to music through hand clapping; achievement of beat competence
	Can follow the pulse and dynamics of music and respond to gradual changes through movement
	Can perform beat on drum, rhythm sticks; can play sustained bourdons on xylophone (but requires prepatory movement to precede performance)
Eight to nine (third grade)	Can maintain a steady beat while tapping, patting, clapping
	Can accurately reproduce rhythms by chanting, tapping, patting, clapping, or stepping
	Can perform ostinatos on xylophones (but requires preparatory movement to precede performance)
	Develops small-muscle coordination for playing recorder, keyboard
	Can respond quickly and accurately to musical changes (in tempo, rhythmic patterns, texture) through movement; can have quick reactions
	Can perform more complex folk dances in circles, lines, squares, and partners
	Can conduct meters with rhythmic accuracy
Ten to twelve (fourth through sixth grades)	Develops small-muscle coordination (and dual coordination of breathing and fingers) for performing wind and brass instruments
	Enjoys active physical involvement; may prefer sports to dance
	Can perform rhythmic canons by moving to music that is previously sounded (four beats earlier) while listening to other music
	Can respond to two distinctive features of music through simultaneous movement (stepping the rhythm while conducting the pulse)

In their earliest years, infants and toddlers develop muscular capacities to rock, nod, and sway, first freely and then in a regular rhythm. Voluntarily gripping, grasping, and starting and stopping their hands in a shaking movement paves the way toward playing instruments. Children can shake rattles and jingle bells while yet in the crib, and by age two to three they enjoy tapping a drum or clicking a pair of wooden sticks together. By three to four years, children's sensitivity to pulse and their perceptual motor skill development equip them to rub sand blocks together or glide a stick across the ridges of a guiro (see Figure 8.3). Their basic eye–hand coordination at three to five years prepares them to strike triangles, tambourines, and cymbals.

As children develop their perceptual motor skills, they become ready to tackle many non-pitched and pitched percussion instruments. By kindergarten, they can alternate hands in playing a conga, bongo, timpani, or hand drum. In the primary grades, they have developed the eye–hand coordination necessary to play simple drones and short, recurring ostinato patterns on xylophones. They are typically ready to play one-hand melodies on the keyboard by age six, and two hands in melody plus chord arrangements by age seven or eight. Such a two-handed task is more involved than it seems; the eyes, ears, and multiple muscles of the fingers, hand, and forearm all must work together.

By second or third grade, children are capable of playing a chording instrument, such as the autoharp. They typically achieve the coordination to play two or three chords on the ukulele by third or fourth grade, but the size and strength of their fingers won't fit most guitar chords until they reach age ten. As they learn to control their breathing, children in the intermediate grades can learn to play recorder and then wind and brass instruments of the band and orchestra. By age ten, all children can play musical instruments, provided that schools offer children opportunities for training and repeated practice to develop aural, motor, and visual skills (the last for the purpose of note reading). The special case of Suzuki violin study, which has spread from the use of 1/8- or 1/10-sized violins for young children to a listening and performance pedagogy for full-sized violin, cello, flute, piano, and other instruments, emphasizes parental involvement in individual and group lessons and in children's practice of previously learned music.

THE EVOLUTION OF LISTENING

As their aural skills sharpen from infancy onward, children discern the sounds, and the music, of their environments. Long before they develop language, infants show their sensitivity to music by turning toward the sounds of music, or their parents' voices, or new and unexpected sounds. They delight in imitating the sounds they hear, begin repeating words in the language of their parents, and sing songs they've heard with stylistic nuances intact. Children of all ages enjoy listening to songs, bedtime stories, soothing music for inducing sleep, and stimulating music of rhythmic intensity and speed for moving to. They learn to listen with focus and insight, especially when guided by questions and reinforced for the aural perceptive abilities they are developing.

Since children's auditory systems begin developing prior to birth, they are launched as newborns into a world of sounds they can already identify and sort. This head start in listening is sharpened and refined through experience and training, and they gradually learn a vocabulary to describe what they hear: loud-soft, high-low, fast-slow (three paired comparisons that children often find confusing at first). Through directed instruction in school, children learn to identify a vast musical repertoire aurally, and can discern details of the music such as instrumental timbre or metric organization, whether sections are identical or different, and even the music's historical time and culture. They find serenity and stability, deeply expressive qualities, and great value in the music they listen to, and can be challenged by teachers to listen to complex music from beyond their home, family, and community. In fact, teachers can open new worlds for their children's listening pleasure, with songs and selections that become increasingly meaningful to children through study and experience.

DEVELOPING CREATIVE MUSICAL THINKING

Children have a natural capacity to invent personal ways to express themselves, and teachers can guide them to create their own music. Much of the learning sought in school is convergent; that is, children are expected to arrive thoughtfully at a single, correct answer. Creative musical thinking is a divergent process that allows children to make choices, manipulate sounds, and to express what feels to them like a day at the park, a dreary day, and so on. Musical creativity develops conceptually and practically, and is influenced by environmental factors, human musical thought, and individual understandings and personalities. Children's original songs and instrumental pieces result from their musical nature and the encouragement and time they are given to play with the possibilities.

Like all musical skills, creativity is developmental (see Table 3.3). Driven by their own motor energy, infants, toddlers, and young children explore and express themselves in sputters and spurts that are at times rhythmic, either repeating or free-ranging, vocally and on instruments (any object is potentially a sound source worthy of exploration). Parents and teachers enrich the creative musical potential of children by providing varied music listening experiences, sound sources, and musical instruments, so that children may experiment with music-making possibilities. As children enter school, they make up songs and instrumental pieces that reflect the music they know, featuring melodic and rhythmic conventions to which they have become accustomed. From the primary grades on into preadolescence, children understand music's organization according to customary, cultural rules. They learn the uses of repetition, and when it is reasonable to build in a contrasting melody or rhythm, and by the intermediate grades they start to understand how to develop a musical idea. With careful questioning by teachers (who must avoid becoming overly critical), children learn to evaluate the structure and expression of their original music. Some of the best of children's creative musical thinking offers unusual or unique musical ideas within a discernible form, and a dynamic expression that reflects their own aesthetic sensitivity.

50 PART I | The Musical Lives of Children and Teachers

TABLE 3.3 DEVELOPMENT OF CREATIVITY

AGE	FLOHR (1985); KRATUS (1985, 1991)	TILLMAN AND SWANICK (1989)	TEACHER ACTION
Birth to four or five years	Driven by motor energy. Highly individualistic in approaches and patterns. Lacking musical syntax.	Mastery of materials and range of sounds through sensing and manipulating.	Provide age-appropriate instruments to explore. Encourage and reinforce discovery and respect individuality.
Four or five to nine (kindergarten to fourth grade)	Predictable rhythmic and tonal patterns, influenced by familiar music. Changing meters and emerging sense of tonality, but no strong sense of phrase structure or cadence.	Imitation of both personal and vernacular ideas occurs with greater expressive quality. Meter emerges; greater use of dynamic expression, ostinati.	Encourage growth of ideas and craftsmanship. Build musical concepts and awareness of many conventions. Build skills of self-evaluation.
Ten to twelve (fourth through sixth grades)	Music becomes organized according to cultural rules or structures. Use of melodic and rhythmic motives. Increased use of sounds and patterns of familiar music. Often less original.	Imaginative play in which surprise is an element but using more references to popular music idioms. Concern for form and structure; use of harmony emerges.	Keep expanding the repertoire of conventions for structuring music. Help students to avoid becoming too critical of their or others' works. Encourage self-expression.

Sources: Flohr, J. (1985). Young children's improvisations: Emerging creative thought. *The Creative Child and Adult Quarterly, 10*(2), 79–83.
Kratus, J. (1985). The use of melodic and rhythmic motives in the original songs of children aged 5 to 13. *Contributions to Music Education, 12*, 1–8.
Kratus, J. (1991). Growing with improvisation. *Music Educators Journal, 78*(4), 35–40.
Tillman, J. and K. Swanick. (1989). Towards a model of development of children's musical creativity. *Canadian Music Educator, 30*(2), 169–174.

SIMPLE TO COMPLEX PHASES OF LEARNING

A host of theories has arisen on the nature of learning and instruction across all curricula, and many of them apply to music learning as much as learning in other subjects.[7] While these theories are not "developmental" in the sense of the day-by-day and year-by-year steps of children's gradual maturation, they encourage teachers to consider particular instructional precepts, principles, and sequences. These theories, which teachers have probably already encountered in other classes, show the merits of reinforcing children's appropriate social and academic behaviors:

▶ Skinner's behaviorism, on the roles of positive and negative reinforcement.
▶ Johnson and Johnson's cooperative learning, on motivating by fulfilling the need for social belonging.
▶ Maslow's hierarchy of needs as attunement to the needs of children relative to their well-being and sense of accomplishment.
▶ Vygotsky's socialization, on the merits of expert–novice interaction that socializes children through adult intervention and guidance to acquire cultural knowledge.
▶ Gardner's theory of multiple intelligences, on the importance of knowing students' individual strengths and interests when designing and delivering instruction to them.
▶ Barbe and Swassing's learning modalities: visual, auditory, and kinesthetic.

Jerome Bruner, a widely influential educational psychologist, suggested a type of stage progression, known as modes of representation, that depends somewhat upon children's development, but that can also be applied to students of all ages and experiences, including adults. His modes are:

Enactive: learning through a set of actions;

Iconic: learning through images, figures, and other visual depictions; and

Symbolic: learning through abstract symbols beyond what is immediately perceptible in the environment.

In learning to read notation, for example, students can apply an enactive strategy by which arm and body movements represent melodic contours, an iconic strategy by which students draw and then trace line graphs while they listen to or sing the melody, and a symbolic approach that is the actual reading and writing of music with staff notation. The modes of representation are developmentally oriented in that the youngest children will require enactive learning, children of seven to ten years do well with iconic examples of ideas, and preadolescent children of 11 years become able to learn concepts abstractly, such as through symbols. Older children (and even adolescent and adult learners) may also delight in learning from enactive or iconic experiences, proceeding in phases to an understanding of a rhythmic phrase or the formal architecture of a concerto, a salsa number, or a Native American pow wow song.

The anthropologist Gregory Bateson described three broad phases of learning that appear relevant to children's intellectual development but that, like Bruner's modes of representation, can also be applied to students of various ages. From early and informal encounters with ideas (the first phase, or Learning I) to conscious attention to learning (the second phase, or Learning II), the ultimate third phase (Learning III) is one of mastery and perfection of a concept or skill. Catherine Ellis applied Bateson's phases to music, noting that Learning I occurs effortlessly as a musical idea becomes enculturated, familial, or familiar through everyday experience and playful exploration. Learning II is exemplified in children's commitment to practice, when they become seriously interested in developing coordination, strength, ability, and speed on an instrument or in singing. Learning III, musical mastery, is seldom attained by students, and it represents the leap past technical skills to music as a deeply personal and aesthetic experience. There is a developmental tinge to this three-phase theory, certainly, and children cannot move easily to the second phase without those first playful encounters that spark their interest in, and love for, music, which then motivate their study of singing or playing—when they are developmentally ready.

Music can be notated with invented icons or standard music notation symbols.

Each of these theories presents a simple-to-complex sequence of instruction that fits well the teacher's intention to reach and teach children where they happen to be developmentally. As children grow to master understandings and skills that are increasingly complex, their musical abilities can be shaped through graduated tasks that they can accomplish at the stage or phase at which they are operating.

Summary

Classroom teachers care about developmentally appropriate practice, and they monitor the changing levels and layers of children's strengths, interests, and needs. They understand that there are optimal periods for development and learning, and they tailor their classroom activities to match what they have observed of their children's learning capacities. They know that development proceeds differently for each child, and they know that learning is influenced by many factors, including children's personalities, their families and communities, and their experiences outside of school. Teachers sensitive to typical development schedules as well as the needs of individuals are able to slip in musical activities that delight and motivate their children, pique their interest, raise their energy, and offer them an outlet of expression.

Review

1. What are the developmental characteristics of five-, eight-, and 11-year-old children?

2. Describe the stage theory of Jean Piaget. At what approximate ages do children develop through the four stages of thinking?

3. How can music exercise children's divergent thinking?

Critical Thinking

1. Discuss why it is important for classroom teachers to know the motoric, cognitive, social, physical, and musical capacities of typically developing children.

2. What happens musically to children at Piaget's four stage levels? How do teachers ensure that this development is in motion?

3. Give examples of ways teachers can enhance children's listening skills.

Projects

1. Using key words and phrases such as "musical children," "music and children," "young singers" ("dancers," "pianists," "violinists," "drummers"), and "elementary school music programs," search the Internet for examples of children's musical capacities. Note the approximate ages and grade levels of these musical children.

2. Study this chapter's tables of children's vocal development, motoric development, and developmental sequence for playing instruments. Draw up a list of skills and knowledge domains with consideration for those that can be taught, reviewed, or enriched by classroom teachers.

Additional Resources for Teaching

Barrett, Margaret S. (2011). *A Cultural Psychology of Music Education*. New York, NY: Oxford University Press.

Hallam, Susan, Ian Cross, and Michael Thaut, eds. (2008). *The Oxford Handbook of Music Psychology*. Oxford, UK: Oxford University Press.

MacDonald, Raymond R., David Hargreaves, and Dorothy Miell, eds. (2002). *Musical Identities*. Oxford, UK: Oxford University Press.

MacPherson, Gary, ed. (2016). *The Child as Musician* (2nd ed.). New York, NY: Oxford University Press.

Online Resources: Audio and Songbook

digital.wwnorton.com/classroom

PART II
THE MUSICAL MAKEUP OF CHILDREN

Music fascinates children long before they enter school, and they continue to experience music at home and in their neighborhoods all through their childhoods. Their formal musical education begins with teachers who know what musical experiences children bring with them to school, and who implement music regularly and consistently throughout the school day. Teachers can use their children's repertoire of songs, dances, rhymes, and chants, to shape their expressive, creative musical skills and understandings. Children's natural musical makeup is the origin from which a full-fledged education in and through music can take off. All that's needed is sequential instruction and the curricular presence of music in formal lessons and informal class activities.

> Teachers can tap into their children's natural music-making, using their songs, dances, rhymes, and chants.

4
THEIR SINGING VOICES

IN THIS CHAPTER

In the Classroom

Children's Singing Selves

Singing as a Healthy Endeavor

The Voice as a Personal Instrument

Songs Children Sing

Leading the Musical Classroom

Tips for Song Leading

Singing with Young Children

Singing with Children in Intermediate Grades

Song-Based Lessons

Summary

Review

Critical Thinking

Projects

Additional Resources for Teaching

We sing because we must.

—Keri Kaa, Māori writer and educator[1]

Children love to sing songs with motions.

Imagine a singing classroom, a place where children are seen and heard as they sing their ABCs and chant their counting sequences by twos, fives, and tens. Voices joined in an inclusive community, children sing as they prepare for lunch, transition from individual study projects to whole-class activities, or celebrate a coming holiday. Consider how teachers fit singing into their classrooms, and how they make the most of children's expressive voices.

IN THE CLASSROOM

VIGNETTE ONE

Mrs. Quevedo's kindergarteners enjoy circle time because it means songs, stories, rhymes, and show-and-tell. Mrs. Quevedo draws children to the group by singing a favorite song they know well. Their little bodies hop eagerly toward the circle to the sounds of "Hey, Betty Martin," "Mighty Pretty Motion," and "Skip to My Lou." Once they are in a circle, Mrs. Quevedo quietly welcomes them, takes roll by singing their names (to which the children sing back, "I'm here") and introduces them to the activities they will experience that day. She talks about the weather, presents the word of the week, and leads children in rhythmically chanting their numbers from one to ten in English and Spanish. She starts children singing Happy Birthday to Darnell. She reads the classic story of *The Little Engine That Could*, challenging children to recognize and chant the repeated words "I think I can" and "I thought I could" while patting and clapping a steady beat. When circle time comes to an end, Mrs. Quevedo leads the children in singing "This Old Man," and off they bounce to their learning pods. Through the mixing of music into the exchanges that occur in a sharing circle, Mrs. Quevedo's children have experienced the natural flow between speaking and singing.

VIGNETTE TWO

The children in Ms. Miller's second grade class enjoy hand-clapping songs at recess. They sing with enthusiasm their own renditions of "I Went to California," "Little Sally Walker," and countless other songs. Ms. Miller understands that children have different learning styles. Some children quietly listen to a song five or six times until they create a map in their heads, then feel safe singing it aloud (and perfectly). Other more spontaneous and extroverted children jump into a song before they have even heard it through once. With several repetitions, they too learn to sing songs well. Ms. Miller schedules ten minutes before the end-of-school bell every Tuesday and Thursday for groups of children to perform these songs and chants with their classmates in a semiformal sharing. The children feel validated by Ms. Miller's attention to their own songs, and they work together to develop a class-approved repertoire of songs they all know and perform on cue.

VIGNETTE THREE

Ms. Leone keeps a set of rhythm instruments in her fourth-grade classroom to teach math facts and operations. She pulls them out from time to time, distributing sticks, shakers, and drums to the children. She establishes a beat and then

You Will Learn

- how singing is natural for all humans, especially children, and how singing is good for one's health

- more about children's voices and vocal ranges, and how they differ from men's and women's

- diverse songs for different age groups

- tips, techniques, and strategies for teaching songs in the classroom

Ask Yourself

- Do you enjoy singing?

- Do you sing alone, in a group, or with recordings?

- Did you sing as a child? Where and when did you sing?

- As a child, what were some of your favorite songs to sing?

- What songs do you enjoy singing now?

- Do you do other things while singing—like working, exercising, dancing, or playing games?

- What do you notice when you hear children singing?

invites small groups of children to play different rhythm patterns on the instruments, layering the patterns for a full-energy sound. Over the beat, she chants a sentence containing a math fact, which the children echo back to her. After a while, children are called upon to make up their own sentences and chant them rhythmically over the beat, and the other children echo. The chants and percussion parts add a palpable joy to the children's learning. Further, Ms. Leone's children score consistently higher than others on the standardized math exams. The children in Ms. Leone's class are getting the best of two worlds, as they learn math while engaging together rhythmically in a collective musical groove. Their voices chant in a style somewhere between speaking and singing.

VIGNETTE FOUR

The children in Mr. Morrison's sixth-grade class are studying the unequal treatment of people throughout history and around the world—in France, India, South Africa, and the United States. Sheridan searches the Internet for the word *freedom*, and the category of freedom songs emerges. When Mr. Morrison passes by her station, he suggests that she team up with Lisa to research freedom song lyrics. Together they collect a set of lyrics and discover the expressions of oppressed peoples struggling for equal rights. Mr. Morrison encourages them to listen to some of the songs online, and learn one that they can teach to the class. Sheridan and Lisa find two African American slave songs particularly powerful: "Gonna Sing When the Spirit Says Sing" and "Swing Low, Sweet Chariot." The following week, they present recorded selections of freedom songs and teach their classmates to sing "Oh Freedom." Mr. Morrison has successfully facilitated a social studies project that fully integrates musical study, and by motivating students to learn music that they can then teach to their classmates, he has taken them to a new level of understanding, empowerment, and accomplishment.

CHILDREN'S SINGING SELVES

Children sing because they must. Singing is a core activity, particularly for young children who have few inhibitions, but also in later childhood, when singing comes as readily as speaking. Children sing with wide-eyed enthusiasm or softly under their breath, and they chant and hum and whistle the melodies that come to them spontaneously. They sing as they work on school projects, as they ride their bikes, and as they play with blocks, cars, trucks, trains, action figures, and dolls. They can hardly help it. When a song comes to them, they sing it out loud to express joy, quiet

Songs help children make sense of the world as they grow.

contentment, love, and sometimes sadness. They sing what they have heard before, and they also create new songs. They sing for fun in the games they play, and they often dance the songs they sing—bouncing, rocking, and nodding along to the feel of the song. It is a part of who they are to be songful, and the songs they know carry them through their childhoods and help them make sense of the world at large.

The National Standards for Arts Education[2] names the first of its nine content standards as: "Singing, alone and with others, a varied repertoire of music." While music teachers work to develop children's singing techniques, classroom teachers use singing to exercise children's lungs and give them a natural vent for their energy and expression. The National Standards for Music Education affirm that even children as young as two to four years can speak, chant, and sing expressively, and they can sing alone and together many simple songs in various keys, meters, and genres. Expectations of the National Standards increase as children move into their school years. By fourth grade, children should be able to sing independently, on pitch and in rhythm, and with appropriate timbre, tempo, dynamics, phrasing, and interpretation. Throughout their elementary years, children sing songs representing various styles and cultures, but by the third or fourth grade they are capable of singing rounds and canons as well. By their last years of elementary school, children with continuous singing experience can blend their voices and create two- and three-part harmonies.

Children will sing, with or without formal singing activities in school, because it is their natural penchant to do so. When nurtured by teachers who value cultivating the voice for its greater resonance and range, children sing even better. They

SINGING SONGS TO MEET MUSIC STANDARDS

1. Singing. Offer children ample opportunity to sing together in large and small groups, in solos, duos, and trios, with live song leaders and recorded sources, throughout the day and year—because there's always a good reason to sing.

2. Playing. Children can accompany their songs on a variety of pitched and non-pitched instruments. They can sing while playing harmonies on guitar, keyboard, or barred xylophones, and to the sound of countermelodies or sustained pitches on recorders. They can also sing to the rhythms they play on drums, shakers, claves, woodblocks, and other percussion instruments.

3. Improvising. Allow children to change the songs they know, to personalize them or vary them spontaneously, giving new flavors to the melody's pitches, rhythms, or lyrics (without, of course, losing the song altogether).

4. Composing and arranging. Young children frequently make up their own songs, and they should be able to have their songs heard. Songwriting is useful for exploring language, including poetry, and is an important expressive avenue for children of any age.

5. Reading and notating. Teach children to learn songs by reading notation, beginning with simple melodies with few pitch changes and gradually shifting to

songs with larger ranges and stepwise melodies with occasional skips. Challenge them to notate a familiar song (or a composed song) using standard western staff notation or their own iconic notation.

6. Listening. Children learn to sing by listening to models—adult singers as well as children who sing solo and in groups. Provide plenty of occasions for listening to songs, many of which—as with folk and traditional songs—have been learned orally for generations.

7. Evaluating. Direct children to listen to recordings of their own singing, or for half the class to listen to the other half sing. Lead them to evaluate constructively what's good and what needs work in terms of singing in tune and in time, accurately and expressively.

8. Connecting to other arts and curricular areas. Consider how songs and singing are frequently integrated with movement, dance, and dramatic expression. Direct children to depict their song visually in a panel-by-panel story text, or in another visual representation of the song's meaning to them personally.

9. Connecting to culture and history. Songs foster understanding across time and distance. Support children's explorations of songs as cultural and historical expressions, and incorporate singing into lessons about people, places, and times.

add to their repertoire of familiar songs as they experience making something beautiful together, wherein singing both energizes and relaxes them. Because singing is physical, emotional, and social, song activity plays into children's holistic development. Classroom life becomes more vibrant when children sing songs to open and close the school day; to learn history, culture, math, and science; to build community; and to value each other and work together. Singing enhances learning, even as it builds on children's songful nature. Children sing because they must, and they sing better over time and with practice.

SINGING AS A HEALTHY ENDEAVOR

Research has drawn attention to the health benefits of singing. The evidence for singing as a healthy endeavor, as a way to wellness, is overwhelming. Singing releases endorphins[3] and makes the singer feel energized and uplifted.[4] It exercises the lungs, tones the abdominal and intercostal (between the ribs) muscles and the diaphragm, and stimulates circulation. Because singing requires deep breathing like some forms of strenuous exercise, singers take in more oxygen, improve functioning of their heart and lungs, and release muscle tension.[5] All other things being equal, people who sing are healthier than people who do not. Further, singing together in groups is risk-free, economical, easily arranged and managed, and a powerful pathway to physiological and psychological well-being.[6] Vocal health is best assured by regular singing, which also renders speech more resonant, expressive, and colorful.

Singing engages the same areas of the brain that are active for language, including Broca's area (associated with grammatical structure) and Wernicke's area (associated with language and vocabulary acquisition). Indeed, singing may be a precursor to language learning.[7] The brain map below highlights the areas of the brain active in speech and language acquisition.

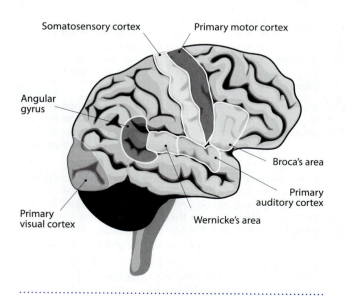

Singing and language (speaking) activate the same areas of the brain.

THE VOICE AS A PERSONAL INSTRUMENT

Speaking and singing voices share properties and functions, and are rooted in the anatomical structure of the voice. As babies babble their vowels and consonants, their earliest attempts at speech are very much like singing. All vocalizations emanate from the fundamental human need for expression, and from the same vocal cords and breathing apparatus whether one is speaking or singing. Some tonal languages, such as Mandarin, use singing-like inflections or tones to differentiate otherwise identical words. In English, similar inflections change statements into questions, or add emphasis or other subtle layers of meaning. In elementary school, children are taught to read with comprehension and expressiveness, so it follows that improving singing skills also improves reading skills (Chapter 10 describes many other ways music helps language arts). Children who sing frequently at home and at school typically develop skillful singing and a genuine musical interest that stays with them through their adult lives.

THE ADULT VOICE

While they may not find themselves Internet-famous or competing on *The Voice*, most adults are able to sing reasonably well, in tune and in rhythm. Most teachers do not actively study voice, but many do sing, automatically and without much effort, shifting from the clipped consonants of speech to the sustained vowels of song. Teaching is a voice-based profession, and some teachers practice singing well as part of their physical well-being, even seeking training through voice lessons and choir memberships. Adults who have sung often, whether in choirs, in the car, at work in the yard, or in the shower, will sing with greater ease than those who intentionally quieted their singing voices after childhood. Yet even self-proclaimed non-singers who say they can't carry a tune in a bucket may catch themselves singing along to their iPods and radios. It is natural, normal, and enjoyable for adults to sing.

Adults sing with stronger, more resonant voices than children.

Box 4.1 invites you to recall and reminisce on songs and singing experiences from your childhood and youth. It is designed to highlight the importance of singing and songs throughout childhood, and encourages you to consider how important songs and singing experiences are to all children, regardless age or place. Children, too, may find that the suggestions in Box 4.1 raise their attention to the presence of music in their lives.

The adult voice is the result of many years of vocalizing in multiple ways—talking at volumes that range from near-whispers to shouts, laughing and crying, humming, chanting, and singing. At maturity, the adult singing voice runs the

---

BOX 4.1 BECOMING ATTUNED TO SINGING

1. Think of children's songs that you know from your own childhood. Develop a list in several categories, including (a) those you remember well, (b) those you remember partially, (c) those whose melodies but not words you remember, and (d) those whose words but not melodies you remember. How many songs do you know? How did you learn them? Why can you remember some songs to this day?

2. Teach a remembered childhood song to someone else. (Talk with friends and family members to recall all of the song's words and melody.) What steps do you take to teach this song? How well does your student learn the song?

3. Record a remembered childhood song from your mother or father, grandmother or grandfather, aunt or uncle. Is it a song that you know? Did you learn it from them? What does the song-giver tell you about the song? Share the recording with your colleagues as well as information on the song-giver and the song's meaning.

4. Record a friend singing a remembered childhood song. Is it one you remember, too? Why or why not? Share the recording with your colleagues as well as information on the song-giver and the song's meaning.

gamut from nasal to throaty, from breathy to bell-like, and from open and relaxed to tense. These qualities are acculturated into the singing voice early on, although new vocal styles and techniques can be learned over time by mature singers, too. Every adult voice has a maximum pitch range (lowest to highest possible pitches) as well as a tessitura (a range of fewer, less extreme pitches that are more comfortable to sing). When they want to maximize expression, adults sing with modulating loud-soft dynamics, faster and slower tempi, and carefully shaped words and phrases.

Voice ranges of adult women often remain fairly close to the range of 12-year-old children's voices; however, some women contain their singing to the lower end of their mature speaking range. This is because even though their singing voices often retain the full and higher range of pitches, adult women's speaking voices tend to lower and thicken with age. Singing range does change for children, from the span of just a few pitches above middle C (C4) at about ages four to six, to as much as two octaves by the onset of adolescence.[8] Women's natural vocal ranges are near to that of children, and thus women make excellent singing models for children. After adolescence, men sing at least an octave lower than they once sang as children. This can complicate matters for some children, who attempt to sing in the lower octave, and the result is a rumbling and unnatural voice that not only sounds unmusical and out-of-tune, but also challenges their vocal health. If adult male singers hear children struggling to match their low pitches, they should switch to their high falsetto voices, and sing lightly to provide a model closer to the children's vocal range and timbre, or use a keyboard instrument or recording to play the melody in the children's range.

THE CHILD VOICE

The voice of a child is distinctive, in its light and soft indoor singing and in its outdoor timbre of calling and shouting. Generally, the younger the child, the softer the voice and more limited the range, but as children grow, so does their vocal potential. As their singing range increases, their voices become stronger and their pitch more accurate. Because singing is a physical activity that involves fine control and coordination of the laryngeal vocal folds, the oral cavity of the mouth, the many muscles of the lips and tongue, and the breathing muscles, it is no wonder that children's voices change significantly from preschool to school-age and into adolescence and adulthood.

Individual differences are to be expected in any facet of children's growth and across skill sets, but cultural differences appear as well, according to

African children singing

EXAMPLE 4.1

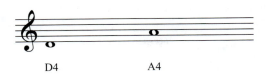

Comfortable singing range of kindergarten children

how particular societies value singing. The Maōri of New Zealand sing regularly, and children are surrounded by singing from their earliest memories. The Wagogo of eastern Africa enculturate their children through stories and songs, so that children sing easily and often in unison and in harmony at an early age. Children's singing potentials develop when nurtured, and thus their voices grow at different rates. That said, most very young children can hardly differentiate between their speaking and singing voices, and they slip from one to the other in their carefree and playful ways. As early as 18–24 months, they can imitate nursery rhymes, lullabies, and childhood chants like "Rain, Rain, Go Away," and they may invent their own songs about friends, family, pets, toys, or activities they enjoy. At this age, children delight in being playful with their voices and applying them in exploratory, imaginative, and dramatic ways. By kindergarten, they often sing in tune in a range of about five pitches (D4–A4; see Example 4.1) and are quick to learn the words, rhythms, and individual pitches of songs.

By the primary grades, most children have learned to sing expressively in tune and in time, and often do so with considerable enthusiasm and accuracy. They can switch between their lighter head voice and their heavier chest voice, and they alternately warble like songbirds or belt like a Broadway star. They learn by ear and imitate recordings and live models, just as they do for language acquisition. They typically sing in a range of about one octave, from C4 (middle C) or D4 to C5 or D5 (see Example 4.2), and although their vocal range continues to increase, they sing most comfortably and accurately in this one-octave range. When children receive sequential instruction in reading music (such as prescribed by the Kodály approach in Appendix 2), they are able to read melodies and rhythms as easily as they read words.

EXAMPLE 4.2

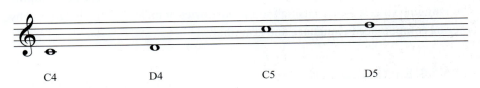

Comfortable singing range of first, second, and third graders

EXAMPLE 4.3

G3   B3   C5   G5

Comfortable singing range of fourth, fifth, and sixth graders

By the time children reach middle childhood (ages 8–10 or grades 3–4) and preadolescence (ages 10–12 or grades 5–6) and if they have been singing all along, their voices are strong, capable of a considerable range, and able to blend together harmonically in rounds and multipart songs. Boys' and girls' voices typically become more resonant (at age 8 or 9), and boys' voices may begin to drop in pitch as early as fourth grade or as late as seventh or eighth grade. Boys' voices typically become very unstable and unpredictable during puberty, and are accurate in a much smaller range (G3 to C4) until the adult male voice is firmly established. Some children become self-conscious about singing, especially solos, in later elementary school, so while most are physiologically well suited to sing two octaves, they prefer a more moderate, contained range (see Example 4.3). Children in fourth, fifth, and sixth grades are often motivated to sing by songs with rhythmic energy, accents, and syncopations. If songs are slower, unaccompanied, or in a foreign language, children may require extra preparation to appreciate their beauty and meaning. As always, the enthusiasm of their teacher and classmates inspires children to sing outside their comfort zones.

SONGS CHILDREN SING

Children sing what comes to them by way of their experience and training. If at home they hear lullabies and Disney themes, they internalize these songs and styles for singing in school and at play. If they hear Beyoncé, Taylor Swift, Justin Bieber, Kanye West, and other popular singers, this is the music that they are likely to sing. If their teachers play Mozart during math time, or Bach during creative writing exercises, these melodies and rhythms will settle themselves in their minds and children will hum them. If teachers offer children opportunities to sing songs, or to set rhyming words and poems to familiar melodies (or even two or three alternating pitches), children will benefit in triplicate: by developing their singing voices, by increasing their repositories of melodic knowledge, and by gaining competence in language and grammar.

SONGS BY CHILDREN

By the age of three, children invent songs. They explore the potential of their voices as they sing about what they're doing, from hopping and jumping to sliding and swinging. As they create stories that feature their friends, family members, and toys, they spontaneously sing what they know, imagine, and feel. Children's musical inventiveness may appear to peak in preschool, when there are fewer conventions to fence them in. But musical creativity can simmer for a few years, and when later occasions present themselves (such as opportunities for composing on the computer) children's natural inclinations to express themselves can come roaring back. Before their lives are filled with the seriousness of regulated routines, children can be wonderfully playful and artistic in making music.

Children sing and chant as they hop, jump, slide, and swing.

When children enter kindergarten, they come into the culture of playground songs, chants, games, dances, cheers, and jeers.[9] They chant and sing as they jump rope and play hand-clapping games. "Bounce High, Bounce Low" and "Charlie over the Ocean" are their songs, discovered by them or brought to them by other children. Other songs, from "The Farmer in the Dell" to "Cheki morena" and "A la rueda de San Miguel," are often generations old, and may come to them from parents and teachers, but they are nonetheless the songs of children through the ages and across different cultures. Through their own inventions, improvisations, and variations, children build a repertoire that they can claim as their very own.

SONGS FOR CHILDREN

Adults have always composed or selected songs to teach children valued principles, cultural knowledge, and artistic beauty. Some of the songs paint pictures, such as "Mountain Climbing," "Autumn's Here," and "De colores." Other songs tell stories, such as "The Ship's Carpenteer," "Barb'ry Allen," and "Froggie Went A-Courtin'." Still others offer portraits of people ("Ala De'lona," "Here Comes Uncle Jesse," "Leila," "Little Johnny Brown") or lessons for all time ("Music Alone Shall Live"). And of course there are silly songs, both traditional and composed, that are meant for children's amusement, from "B-I-N-G-O" to "Shortnin' Bread" and "All around the Kitchen."

A movement is well in motion by adult singer-songwriters to create and deliver songs to children that are both entertaining and educational. A wide array of online resources provides songs suited to children's interests, as well as to the interests of parents, teachers, and childcare workers who want children to enjoy music and learn about their world through songs. The trademark songs of long-established artists, such as Ella Jenkins, Sweet Honey in the Rock, John McCutcheon, Suni Paz, Woody Guthrie, Lead Belly, and Pete Seeger—and emerging artists, such as Elizabeth Mitchell and Sarah Lee Guthrie—are available from Smithsonian Folkways Recordings. These artists have rediscovered, composed, and performed folk and traditional

Ella Jenkins, Smithsonian Folkways artist, called "the first lady of children's music."

songs that engage children through call-and-response, recurring refrains, and cumulative verses that beckon young singers to stretch their memories.

OTHER SONGS: PATRIOTIC, POPULAR, AND ALL THE REST

School is where a child's song repertoire is formally fashioned, and where selected songs are validated for their social and educational benefits. Music was established as a curricular subject in the Boston schools in 1838, and other cities soon followed. Musician and educator Lowell Mason spearheaded the effort to make music a foundational experience for all children, and he persuaded educators and the public at large of the benefits of sequential lessons in singing and note reading for children's intellectual, moral, and physical development. For about 180 years, American teachers of all subjects have praised vocal music for its cultivation of the speaking voice, its potential to exercise the breathing apparatus and articulatory muscles, its provision of concentration at the beginning and end of a day (or subject, or class), and its contribution to the classroom's moral and social culture.

In school, children learn the music of their national culture, including patriotic songs like "America (My Country, 'Tis of Thee)," "America the Beautiful," and "The Star-Spangled Banner." They learn traditional songs many generations old that reflect the diversity of the American experience, including "Lift Every Voice and Sing," "Kwanu'te'," and "La raspa." The larger world comes to them, too, through international songs that have become standard in American schools: "Hava nagila," "Sakura," "Skye Boat Song," and "Arirang." School songs bring melodies and words that clarify and expand learning in other subjects, leading to a comprehensive education.

LEADING THE MUSICAL CLASSROOM

Music class is essential, but songs and singing activities in the general classroom at various times of day, throughout the school day, benefit children far afield from music class. Songs can be taught and learned by note or by rote, or by combining notes, words, listening, and iconic symbols (such as lines without notes that ascend and descend like pitches of a melody). Most of the world's folk, traditional, and popular songs are learned by listening to a lead singer. While music notation has been important for preserving songs for posterity and for learning complex music, notation is not necessary to learn most songs, and children learn quite readily through listening. Most classroom teachers teach songs orally and without notation, with or without recordings or instrumental accompaniment.

TIPS FOR SONG LEADING

Classroom teachers make excellent song leaders because they know their children, their speaking voices are familiar to their children, and children hear their singing voices as a natural variation of their speaking voices. Children like and trust their teachers, so are typically ready to follow their lead, be it in spoken word, chant, or song.

BOX 4.2 TIPS FOR EFFECTIVE SONG LEADING

1. Before teaching a song, practice singing it many times so that it becomes completely familiar. Sing it at home, in the car, on a walk, and alone in the classroom. Record it and listen back, if that increases your confidence.

2. Prior to singing, pitch the song to the children's singing range. Play the starting pitch on a recorder, bells, xylophone, or keyboard, and match the pitch by singing with the instrument. (See Examples 4.1, 4.2, and 4.3 for comfortable singing ranges of children of various ages.)

3. Establish a strong beat in the starting tempo by singing on the starting pitch: "one, two, ready, sing" for songs in duple meter. Nod or cue the singers to start with a hand gesture. Begin triple meter songs in the same manner: "one, two, three, ready now sing." Begin songs in quadruple meter with: "one, two, three, four, ready here we start to sing."

4. Teach the song by immersion—that is, sing it several times in full rather than in small phrases and segments, and invite children to join in singing when they feel ready.

5. Maintain eye contact with singers as they sing. Show delight in their singing with a relaxed smile. Don't concentrate so hard that it causes tension or frowning; children are perceptive to nonverbal cues and respond favorably to a relaxed and pleasant manner.

6. Consider conducting a steady beat in the air, or tap softly on a desk, table, or chair, to keep the singers together as they sing. You could also ask children to tap a steady beat on their laps.

7. So that singers end the song together, provide a cut off cue, such as putting your hands together high in the air, or drawing a big "C" (for "cut") in the air. Remind the singers to watch the conductor—either the teacher or a fellow student who is appointed to lead.

Still, there are teachers who may not feel completely comfortable singing and song leading. Sometimes they are shy about singing in public, often because they have little singing experience themselves. But the main function of song leading is not to perform, but rather to facilitate children's own singing by giving them an opportunity to listen to the song often to catch the melody, rhythm, and words. Some teachers may wish to use recordings to teach a song, or pick out a melody on a keyboard while singing. Notation and recordings of all songs referenced in this book are found on the companion website. Teachers may also wish to delegate some of the song leading to individual students, adding the role of the song-leader to the weekly list of teacher's helpers.

Box 4.2 offers some effective tips for song leading for both teacher and student song leaders. If you prefer to sing with a recording, select those that feature children's voices in their natural singing range rather than adult singers, whose voices are pitched far lower than children's. (The recordings on the companion website feature children's voices and adults singing in the range of children's voices.)

SINGING WITH YOUNG CHILDREN

From their earliest explorations, young children learn to imitate sounds and generate new sounds with their voices. They sing and chant nursery rhymes with parents and caregivers, and with preschool teachers, they continue their vocal play from babbling consonants to rhyming words in rhythm and pitch, absorbing the simple songs and chants of childhood. From preschool on into the primary grades, they grow their repertoire of songs, and their voices strengthen in intensity and widen in range. Teachers of young children can encourage full-body movement and invite them to invent expressive movements and new words. Box 4.3 offers strategies for singing with young children, and Box 4.4 provides a list of songs in this book that are suited to the voices and interests of children from preschool through second grade.

BOX 4.3 TIPS FOR SINGING WITH YOUNG CHILDREN (PRESCHOOL THROUGH SECOND GRADE)

1. Involve children kinesthetically

   - Keep a beat by patting the lap, or alternating pats and claps

   - Follow the rise and fall of the melody with raised and lowered arms

   - Nod, sway, and swing in place

2. Compile a list of familiar songs that relate to children's lives and to what they are learning in other school subjects. Talk with family and community members to find songs about people (mothers and fathers, sisters and brothers, teachers, bus drivers, mail carriers), animals, weather, and modes of transportation.

3. Invite children to create new words and phrases to familiar songs, or to add a new verse to songs like "Charlie over the Ocean" or "Draw Me a Bucket of Water."

4. Encourage free and creative movement, and share ways to make a song move.

BOX 4.4 SONGS SUITABLE FOR YOUNG CHILDREN

Preschool–Kindergarten

Bounce High, Bounce Low

Hey, Betty Martin

Hop, Old Squirrel

Let Us Chase the Squirrel

Little Cabin in the Wood

London Bridge Is Falling Down

Lucy Locket

Mighty Pretty Motion

Mos', mos'!

Mouse, Mousie

Rain, Rain, Go Away

Skip to My Lou

Suo gân

Teddy Bear, Teddy Bear

Yuyake koyake

Alle meine Entchen

Blue Bird, Blue Bird

Bow Wow Wow

Charlie over the Ocean

Charlie's Neat, Charlie's Sweet

Frère Jacques

Johnny Works with One Hammer

Just from the Kitchen

Kye kye kule

Little Johnny Brown

Little Sally Walker

Long-Legged Sailor

Punchinella

Rig-a-Jig-Jig

San Sereni

Sorida

This Old Man

Tingalayo

First and Second Grades

A la rueda de San Miguel

Alabama Gal

SINGING WITH CHILDREN IN THE INTERMEDIATE GRADES

Children's voices develop strength, agility, range, and intensity with age and experience. By the time children reach the intermediate grades (as early as third grade and up through sixth, when children are 8–9 to twelve years of age), they are ready to learn a wide range songs about a variety of topics. American heritage songs, along with songs from other cultures, are well within their singing ability. Classroom teachers can choose from an array of patriotic songs, ballads, lyrical songs, and singing games, and should challenge children to learn them in the original languages. Songs like "When Johnny Comes Marching Home," "Barb'ry Allen," and "This Land Is Your Land" offer historic perspectives and are melodically suitable for these children's developmental stage. For a non–Western experience, consider "Singabahambayo" (the Zulu of South Africa), "Quien es ese pajarito?" (Argentina), "Zum gali gali" (Israeli), and "Savalivalah" (Samoa). Classroom teachers can turn children loose to discover new songs, which can be matched to curricular content and concepts. Including a song in a report on a country or culture, for example, would add interest and cultural awareness to a reading and writing project. Box 4.5 provides a list of songs in this book that are especially suited to the voices and interests of children in third through fifth grades.

ADAPTING INSTRUCTION FOR VARIOUS NEEDS

Blindness and Other Visual Impairments

Teach folk and traditional songs aurally. Enlarge graphic notation to suit their capacity to read it. Investigate the Royal National Institute of Blind People (RNIB) website for sources of music in modified staff notation, as well as talking scores and traditional Braille notation.

Deafness and Other Hearing Impairments

Face children when song leading, adequately project and enunciate words, and speak at a reasonable pace. Share notation and sheet music, and play melodies on pianos and xylophones that are placed on wood floors so that the beat can be felt through vibrations. Use gestures to indicate higher and lower pitches of the melody. For students with limited hearing, wear a transmitter that sends radio signals to the students' ear receivers or amplifiers.

Behavior Disorders with Externalizing Behaviors

Steer children to a consistent and systematic regimen of singing as a physical exercise. Remind them to produce a solid vocal sound by focusing their attention on deep breathing, posture, and articulatory muscles.

Behavior Disorders with Internalizing Behaviors

Allow children to sing "inside" (mentally sing the words with melodies to themselves), listening to a live or recorded model and mentally rehearsing a song. Encourage singing in small groups, and place a withdrawn child with those children he or she is comfortable with. Do not require solo singing in front of a large group.

Mobility Impairments

Adjust children's posture for singing while sitting in wheelchairs, so that they are straight yet comfortable for proper breathing and a fully functioning diaphragm. Practice deep breathing for purposes of phonation.

Autism Spectrum Disorders

In close, face-to-face sessions with a child, model proper postural alignment, breathing, and articulation. Focus on each of these techniques separately, and then blend them together.

BOX 4.5 SONGS SUITABLE FOR CHILDREN IN THE INTERMEDIATE GRADES

Third Grade	Fourth and Fifth Grades
Ah, Poor Bird	Arirang
All 'Round the Brickyard	Billy Boy
Bambu	De colores
Barb'ry Allen	Erie Canal
Dance Josey	Feng Yang
Did You Ever See a Lassie?	Follow the Drinking Gourd
Four White Horses	Go Tell It on the Mountain
Hill an' Gully Rider	Haere, Haere
I Got a Letter This Morning	Hava nashira
I Went to California	Here Comes Uncle Jesse
Jubilee	Las mañanitas
Kaeru no uta	The Noble Duke of York
Kookaburra	Oh Freedom
La Raspa	Rise Up, O Flame
Leila	Savalivalah
Little David (Play on Your Harp)	Singabahambayo
Lovely Evening	Sing Together
Michael Finnegan	Skye Boat Song
Music Alone Shall Live	Swing Low, Sweet Chariot
Old Joe Clark	This Land Is Your Land
Quien es ese pajarito?	This Train
Rocky Mountain	Viva la musica
Sansa kroma	When Johnny Comes Marching Home
Scotland's Burning	With Laughter and Singing
Shalom chaverim	
Shortnin' Bread	
Weevily Wheat	
Zum gali gali	

SONG-BASED LESSONS

Integration singing into the classroom can bring joy and amusement as it furthers learning. Teachers can mix songs into their lessons for any number of functions, and can measure the each song's effectiveness during and after each lesson. Lesson Plan 4.1 provides four examples of inserting music into lessons in other subjects. The lessons suggest songs for specific ages and grade levels, and explain how they can be used to introduce, underscore, exercise, or otherwise advance learning. The frameworks for these lessons can be applied to any song, and the thoughtful teacher will find there is a wide spectrum of songs (including those featured in this book and on the companion website) that will spark learning in non-music lessons.

CHAPTER 4 | Their Singing Voices

LESSON PLAN 4.1

Song-Based Lessons

Song
"Mighty Pretty Motion"

Grade Levels
Preschool–kindergarten

Objectives

- Move the body with the melody and lyrics
- Explore the movement of hands, wrists, arms, shoulders, feet, legs, head, and torso
- Learn the names of body parts in English (particularly for English as Second Language students).

Materials
Song recording and notation

Procedure

1. Opening:
   - In a circle, the teacher sings or plays the song, focusing children by asking, "What is so 'mighty pretty' in this song?" (Answer: motion)
   - Explore freely and in imitation of the teacher various movements of the body that are "mighty pretty."

2. Continuing:
   - Sing the song through, beginning with the teacher in the middle of the circle modeling a "mighty pretty motion" that the children imitate.
   - Choose individual children to invent a "mighty pretty motion" in the middle of the circle, while everyone imitates and sings.
   - Remind children of motion possibilities, including less obvious body parts such as the head and shoulders.

3. Closing:
   - Ask children to turn to the right and walk to the beat as they sing the song together several times, moving on the teacher's cue their hands, then shoulders, then heads.

Assessment
Can the children identify body parts by name? Can they sing the song with melody and words? (Move around the circle to listen to small groups of children.)

Song
"Kookaburra"

Grade Levels
Third–fourth

Objectives

- Learn a popular Australian children's song
- Become acquainted with the kookaburra, a large kingfisher bird of Australia

Materials
Song recording and notation

Procedure

1. Opening:
   - The teacher sings or plays the song, focusing children by asking, "Do you know what a kookaburra is? How does the song describe it?" (Answer: It sits in a tree; it is "king of the bush"; it laughs.)
   - Explain that the kookaburra is a large laughing kingfisher bird of Australia, show a picture or two, and play a recording of its laughing call (available for free from Wikipedia). Using a globe, show the children where the kookaburra lives in Australia.

2. Continuing:
   - Sing the song through, asking children to join in by alternating pats and claps in a steady beat.
   - Rhythmically chant the three phrases, asking children to echo each phrase.
   - Sing the song through, asking children to fill in the missing words: "Kookaburra sits in the old (gum tree), Merry, merry king of the (bush is he), Laugh, kookaburra, laugh, kookaburra, Gay your (life must be)."
   - Clapping and patting a steady beat, sing the song through three times.
   - Invite children to sing it as a round. Divide the class into three groups. Group 1 begins the first phrase alone, continuing while Group 2 starts with the first phrase. Group 3 enters as Group 2 continues into the second phrase (with Group 1 now on the third phrase). Repeat the round three times.

3. Closing:
   - Learn a parody of the song, such as this one, popular in Australian schoolyards: "Kookaburra sits on electric wire, jumping up and down with his pants on fire."
   - Ask children to create their own parodies of "Kookaburra."

Assessment
Can children sing the song accurately? What have they learned about this land bird of Australia?

Continued on next page

Song
"Singabahambayo"

Grade Levels
Fifth–sixth

Objectives

- Learn a freedom song of South Africa

- Understand the importance of song in the South African movement to abolish apartheid

Materials
Song recording and notation, drum

Procedures

1. Opening:

   - The teacher sings or plays the song, stepping to the beat in a marching movement and focusing children by asking, "What about this song might suggest that people sang it during their struggle for freedom?" (Answer: The marching step akin to processionals through the city streets; "Haleluya" as a joyous cry of faith and belief in the peaceful resolution of challenges)

2. Continuing:

   - Sing the song through, asking children to pat just two fingers in the palm of the hand to keep the beat quietly.

   - Sing the song again, inviting students to come in on the Haleluyas.

   - Rhythmically chant the phrases, asking children to imitate each phrase. Use short phrases: "Singabahambayo thina," "kulomhlaba," "kepha sinekhaya," "e Zulwini."

- Clarify the meanings of the phrases: people marching for freedom, then going home with peace and joy in their hearts.

- Sing the song in the same short phrases, asking the children to imitate each phrase.

- Invite children to sing the whole song together.

- Sitting down, start children into a quiet march step: "right, left, right, left," to the beat. Play a drum to keep the stepping steady and in time. Add singing to the quiet march step, still sitting. Stand and sing the song while marching in place to the beat of the drum.

- Ask children to research online the importance of songs in the recent history of South Africa's struggle with apartheid.

3. Closing:

- Sing the song with intensity and volume, marching to the beat, following a leader around the classroom (and, later, in different shapes and directions around the playground).

- Show children where South Africa is located on a globe.

Assessment
Can children sing the song accurately? Can they sing while marching in time? What have they learned about the importance of freedom in the South African struggle for liberation?

Summary

As a fundamental human expression, singing underpins education in and through music—and the holistic development of children as thinking, expressive, social-emotional beings. Everyone has a voice, and the distance is short from speaking to singing. Classroom teachers can channel children's natural inclination to sing, weaving song throughout the school day to benefit learning and social-emotional growth. Integrating singing experiences adds joy, relaxation, and celebration to a classroom, and children deserve daily opportunities to raise their voices in song.

Review

1. What are the comfortable singing ranges of children of various ages? How do their voices develop as they grow?

2. What steps would you take to lead children in singing a song?

3. Describe the guidelines for teaching songs to young children.

Critical Thinking

1. Review the music standards on the National Association for Music Education's website. Examine the components of the first standard (singing), and decide which of them could be accomplished by integrating song into classroom practice.

2. Review the listed song titles for children in preschool through sixth grade (Boxes 4.4 and 4.5). Which songs can you sing alone or with others? Which songs have you known for a long time? Which songs have you learned in class or via the companion website?

3. Describe how children's voices differ from adult voices.

Projects

1. Examine the research on singing as a healthy endeavor, as reported in this book and in any late-breaking studies that you may find. Describe and discuss this research, then examine your own sense of well-being, including physical and social-emotional feelings that emerge from your experiences with singing.

2. Engage with children you know, or who may be available in your local lab school, in a discussion of favorite songs. Ask them to list all the songs they like, and invite them to sing them for you (and with you). Write a paper describing your experience and what you learned, and share their list of favorites.

3. Complete the suggested activities in Box 4.1, alone or with a colleague. Report the outcome to the class.

4. Alone or with a colleague, teach a song-based lesson according to the steps suggested in Lesson Plan 4.1. Apply these steps to another song, and design and deliver a new song-based lesson.

Additional Resources for Teaching

Campbell, Patricia Shehan. (2008). *Tunes and Grooves in Music Education*. Upper Saddle River, NJ: Prentice Hall.

Langstaff, John. (1996). *Songs for Singing Children*. Boston: Revels Records. The American Folk Song Collection.

Choksy, Lois, and David Brummitt. (1987). *120 Singing Games and Dances for Elementary Schools*. Upper Saddle River, NJ: Pearson.

Bolkovac, Ed and Judith Johnson. (1982). *150 Rounds for Singing and Teaching*. New York, NY: Boosey & Hawkes.

Online Resources: Audio and Songbook

digital.wwnorton.com/classroom

5

THEIR EARS: LISTENING TO MUSIC

IN THIS CHAPTER

Children as Listeners to Music

In the Classroom

Developing Listening Skills

Occasions for Listening

Listening to Music in the Background

Listening to Music in the Foreground

Listening to Music in Live Performances

Listening Responses through Other Arts

Summary

Review

Critical Thinking

Projects

Additional Resources for Teaching

After silence, that which comes nearest to expressing the inexpressible is music.

—Aldous Huxley, *Music at Night*

Children love listening to music.

CHILDREN AS LISTENERS TO MUSIC

Listening to music is one of life's most sensuous experiences. Music's vibrations not only touch our ears, but resonate throughout our entire body. Music stimulates us to sing, to move, or to sit with rapt attention and allow the sounds to surround and fill us. Music is made of organized sounds that please the listener, and that stimulate mind, body, and spirit. A true testament to the depth of feeling that music elicits is this sentiment, shared by the daughter of one of the authors of this book: "Mom, I would never want to lose one of my senses, but if I did, I would rather be blind than deaf. I can't imagine my life without music." Children, adolescents, and adults often share this sentiment, that listening to music is one of life's greatest pleasures.

Young children respond as vitally to music as adults do. They smile, bounce, clap, and dance, as well as listen attentively to music that captivates them. As children develop, they form strong preferences for various kinds of music, based on what they've been exposed to. At about age eight or nine, children are drawn particularly to the influences of peers and popular music. In the late teenage years or adulthood, people usually open up again to a wide range of music. Educators must expose children to music of various styles and genres to keep open and expand their preferential listening palates. Children at every age can absorb even the most complex music.

Most people can identify aurally hundreds, if not thousands, of pieces of music they have been exposed to through a lifetime, explain details about the music and the context in which particular pieces are known, and attach personal meaning to each piece. Music, in many ways, is a thread linking the different periods of one's life, marking special moments and connecting one to others.

IN THE CLASSROOM

VIGNETTE ONE

Ms. Piper has a box filled with long, colored scarves. She places a scarf at the seat of each of her kindergarten students. They are delighted, as they know what is coming. She asks them which pieces of music they want to move to, and they select *The Swan*, a slow, meditative piece by Camille Saint-Saëns, and "Jump for Joy" by Joanie Bartels. These pieces have very different musical energies, giving children the chance to express a variety of responses through free movement. They especially enjoy the scarves, which extend the flow of their movements. Ms. Piper has introduced a range of musical styles throughout the year, and children have learned to name the various pieces and identify some of their favorites. The children have also learned about their personal space and to control their movements through general space, so they don't run into each other or into furniture and other objects. Ms. Piper makes note of each child's response to the music and their abilities to convey the flow, tempo, and spirit of the music through their movements. She is pleased by their sensitivity and maturation, gained over the course of the year's listening experiences in her classroom.

You Will Learn

- the value of recorded music in class to enhance learning and create a rich environment

- a range of musical styles, and key trends, forms, and artists in various styles

- how to engage children actively in listening to music

- how to prepare children to attend performances of live music

- strategies for combining art with music, and how to use music to stimulate writing

Ask Yourself

- What is a favorite recording you listened to as a child? What attracted you to that music? How did you respond to it?

- When do you listen to music now?

- Why do you listen to music?

- How does listening to music affect you?

- What might listening to recorded music do for children in your classroom?

- What different occasions or reasons might prompt you to use recorded music in your classroom?

- What kinds of music would you choose for those occasions?

- What are some differences between listening to recorded music and listening to a live performance?

VIGNETTE TWO

Mr. Sanchez has set up a music listening center with headphones in his third-grade classroom. In it he places several recordings from a composer, performer, or group he features in a given month. He varies the monthly selections widely in terms of types and styles of music. Included in the center are pictures of the composer or performers and biographies. Mr. Sanchez also includes worksheets for the children to complete as they listen to a given piece. He incorporates musical vocabulary (see Table 5.1 and Appendix 1) to encourage children to respond using concepts they have learned. Children may also make drawings in response to the music or write a poem about the music. Often Mr. Sanchez introduces particular pieces in class before placing them in the listening center. Over the year, his children build an impressive repertoire of music. They suggest people and pieces to include in the center. The children are motivated to complete their other work so they can return again and again to the music listening center.

VIGNETTE THREE

Ms. Chen is a fine violinist and enjoys playing for her fifth-grade students, and they love listening to her play. Over the school year, she has introduced them to several pieces of music and various composers. The students have learned to ask for their favorite pieces by name. Ms. Chen has tried to expand their understanding of the violin by bringing in music from parts of the world where violin is central to the musical culture. These examples include mariachi music, Norwegian Hardanger fiddling, Appalachian bluegrass fiddling, and Irish fiddling. She challenges her children to find other examples of violin or fiddle music from other regions of the world and encourages them to find pictures in online encyclopedic resources of instruments from around the world. The children cut out and place their pictures on a world map. They discover that fiddle music occurs everywhere in the world, although the musical styles sound remarkably different.

DEVELOPING LISTENING SKILLS

All classroom teachers need to be prepared to teach music. With recent curricular focus on literacy and numeracy, some school districts are eliminating the position of music specialist and expecting classroom teachers to teach music themselves. This section on developing listening skills is equally useful for classroom teachers and for children, whose overall listening skills, such as phonemic awareness, rhyming, syllabication, and fluency in language arts, will transfer to other subjects.

Children's mental and physical development determines what they are ready to process musically.[1] Children as young as 3 months can match sustained pitches vocally. Children as young as 6 or 7 months appear to have acquired a sense of musical phrase, and by 8 months, a sense of what fits melodically in their culture. By the time children are in preschool they are developing vocabulary to describe what they hear. Concepts of tone color, dynamics, tempo, and style emerge early. Concepts of pitch, rhythm, and form come later, around the age of four. In kindergarten and the primary grades children continue to grow in perceiving music's elemental features. School-age children can recognize and apply a wide range of concepts to music listening experiences, provided they have a strong foundation in music education.

Teachers need to provide active listening experiences, in which children:

- ► regularly listen to music that is more complex and challenging than much of the music they are exposed to in their daily environments
- ► listen to a piece of music enough times so that it becomes familiar and no longer seems exotic
- ► gain conceptual tools for discussing and analyzing music, and perceive and respond to musical events in increasingly refined fashion
- ► discuss their musical preferences and attitudes without being judged for their choices or feelings
- ► reflect and document what they have perceived and felt while listening

Box 5.1 offers some active listening strategies that can help children perceive and respond to music in meaningful ways from preschool through the elementary years.

Infants and young children can perceive some elements of music, and this ability grows as they do. They have not, however, developed a musical vocabulary to describe these elements. Teachers can help build vocabulary and reinforce concepts by providing a collection of musical terms for children to draw from in discussions and writing. Such a strategy is useful for learning any subject, including music and the arts. Even if children visit music specialists for regular music classes, it is useful to know how teaching strategies overlap among classes and teachers—and how

BOX 5.1 ACTIVE LISTENING STRATEGIES FOR ENGAGING YOUNG CHILDREN

- Invite children to move to the music with their entire bodies—in personal or general space, interpreting the flow and spirit of the music as they sense it.

- Encourage children to shape the melody of the music using their hands or arms.

- Have children clap the steady beat or a recurring rhythm pattern in the music.

- Have children play pulses, rhythms, tonic pitches, or a simple repeating melodic part on classroom instruments to different sections of the music, using contrasting sounds to highlight the changes in the sections.

- Have children change movements for different sections of the music.

- Ask children to describe something they noticed about the music in their own words.

- Ask children to describe how the music made them feel, by using a single descriptive word, sentence, or phrase (for young children), or by writing a poem (for older children).

- As children become aware of various tone colors of instruments and ensembles, invite them to name the individual or collective sounds that they hear.

- Invite children to draw a map of the musical events as they unfold (they will need to listen to the music several times). Have children exchange their maps with other students and try to follow them as they are listening. Allow children to discuss what they discovered in that process. Are there things they would like to change in their maps?

- As children develop a music vocabulary, encourage them to apply that vocabulary in describing the music. Make a chart of music vocabulary available in the room (see Table 5.1).

TABLE 5.1 MUSIC WORD BANK

TERM	EXAMPLE	ALSO USEFUL FOR
Pitch	high/low; upward/downward/staying the same	fluency, expressive reading
Melody	phrases; contour (conjunct/disjunct)	expressive reading
Texture	thin/thick; monophonic (one line); polyphonic (interweaving lines); homophonic (chords)	linear thinking, detecting complexity
Harmony	consonant/dissonant; basic chord structures	awareness of the quality of sounds, awareness of sequences of sounds
Rhythm	steady beat; long sounds/short sounds; patterns of longs and shorts	math patterns, number sense
Tempo	fast/slow; getting faster/getting slower	expressive reading
Dynamics	loud/soft; getting louder/getting softer	expressive reading
Tone Color/Timbre	the individual sounds (of instruments or voices); the kind of group (band, orchestra, choir, African drum ensemble, Gamelan, etc.)	development of aural acuity for individual sounds and combination of sounds
Form or Structure	repeated pattern/contrasting pattern; repeated sections (AA); contrasting sections (AB, ABA, ABACA)	poetry
Style	jazz, reggae, pop, classical, blues, world beat, hip hop, electronica, etc.	visual sensitivity, enriching vocabulary

instruction in music class ties into instruction in the general classroom. Table 5.1 contains important terminology for learning about music, as well as how each concept pertains to other subjects.

OCCASIONS FOR LISTENING

When approaching listening activities with children, keep in mind:[2]

► Music listening is a skill that can and should be developed.

► Listening to music requires active and creative engagement.

► Children should engage with music from a variety of styles, genres, and cultures.

► Let the music guide your teaching; it will evoke the relevant concepts and the activities most appropriate for teaching those concepts. (Some music is quite complex and can illustrate many things at once. Choose to teach what is clear in a piece of music, such as the beat or the meter.)

► Music is suitable for children of all ages; instructional activities should be selected based on children's ages.

► Students should hear the same music several times, in brief segments, over time. The activities should become more involved with each listening opportunity.

► Listening activities should be multisensory, involving touch and movement of large muscles, sight, and hearing.

- ▶ Movement, like other concrete experiences, develops aural memory. For young or preliterate children, movement is often the only accurate musical response.
- ▶ Present tasks or questions before playing the music to focus children's attention on the salient features of the music.
- ▶ Design future instruction by taking cues from student responses during listening experiences.

LISTENING TO MUSIC IN THE BACKGROUND

It seems that everywhere we go, music is part of our environment. Indeed, music is a powerful force even when we do not pay active attention to it. Classroom teachers can harness the effects of music in a variety of ways to promote learning, attention, and relaxation in children.

There is extensive scientific research on how background music can influence people's behavior.[3] Music in grocery stores is carefully sequenced across a twenty-minute cycle to move from minimally intrusive and gentle to more upbeat and energetic, then cutting to silence for two minutes. In those two minutes, shoppers are more likely to buy a non-essential item. Restaurants play upbeat music at lunch to encourage people to eat more quickly and move out of the restaurant faster. In the evening, they usually play slow, dreamy music to encourage people to stay longer and consume more. In the non-consumer sphere, people in hospitals and dentist offices who are allowed to listen to their favorite music are often distracted from pain and will often heal more quickly. Fitness centers find that people exercise more if they can choose the music they listen to. Music has tremendous power to influence us emotionally and physically.

Listening to music releases dopamine and oxytocin in the brain, which make people happier. Also, it can help people solve problems more creatively. Music historian Joshua Berrett recommends that people choose tunes to match their to-do lists, with slower beats for calming down, a slightly faster tempo to improve spirits, and a quick tempo to get energized.[4]

Classroom teachers can put this research to good use in a number of ways. Different types of instrumental music could set the mood for different times of day. Calm, quiet music is good for times when children need to slow down and relax: as they come into the room in the morning or return after recess, or when they need to rest. More upbeat music could be used when children need to move and get the oxygen flowing to their brains again. Moderate tempo, minimally intrusive music could be used during group or individual project times. Instrumental music can help children focus, but vocals are often distracting. Sometimes, if children are really excited, their energy needs to be met with upbeat music, after which the music can be changed gradually to slow them down.

Background music can also reward children's academic achievement. Teachers have found that promising students a favorite recording often motivates them to complete their work in a timely fashion.[5] Unlike recess, free time, or tokens to be accumulated for trinkets, music is one of the few curricular subjects that can function as a reward.

> ## ADAPTING INSTRUCTION FOR VARIOUS NEEDS
>
> ### Hearing Impaired and Deaf
> Have children lean their heads against a vibrating surface, hold an inflated balloon next to their head, or feel the vibration through their feet with speakers placed on the floor.
>
> ### Specific Learning Disabilities and ADHD
> Engaging children in multiple ways while listening including tracking the score, moving to the music, playing instruments with the music, and following a listening map. This helps both focus and attention.

Not every child will like every kind of music. Personal taste affects how anyone receives music. What is valued by one person may be extremely annoying to another, so teachers should use caution with music that might provoke strong negative responses. Also, some children are extremely sensitive to background sounds or noise, and find it difficult to concentrate because sounds distract them.[6] Know that some children may struggle with having any music in the environment at all, especially when they are trying to learn something new.

Research by psychologist Frances Rauscher and neurobiologist Gordon Shaw on how listening to Mozart affects spatial intelligence led to the popular "Mozart effect" theory. For a while, their work and the myth that emerged from it inspired parents and teachers to feature Mozart and other classical music at bedtime, in the classroom, in the car, and even prenatally. Indeed, a number of researchers are discovering that learning to play and sing music does help language development, coordination, and other important brain functions crucial to learning,[7] but despite all the excitement about Mozart helping listeners learning math, the effects have been found to be transitory. Mozart's music is brilliant, to be sure, but listening to Mozart does not raise IQ scores or turn children into mathematical geniuses.

LISTENING TO MUSIC IN THE FOREGROUND

When music is in the foreground, children are invited to listen to the music and learn something about it. As children learn to listen actively to many different styles, they develop their listening skills and music moves to the front of their perceptions. The more they learn about various styles and come to know representative pieces, the larger their internal repertoire of wonderful music, and the deeper their musical literacy.

Classroom teachers are in a unique position to help children become musically literate. Just as teachers read important children's literature aloud to build literacy, they can play key works of music throughout the year to build musical literacy. Children who are exposed to the best works of literature, art, and music feel their worlds expand and discover possibilities for deep appreciation and knowing.

Classroom teachers might place music in the foreground by choosing a composer, composition, or style to feature every two weeks, or every month. A station in the room could display photographs, scores, picture books, and biographies, as well as recordings for students to listen to. Once the music or artist of the month is introduced and children learn background material, they can go to the music center to explore the topic in more depth and complete research and writing assignments about that music, composer, artist, or style. Children can give reports that include images and music. Play the selected music often so that they might deposit it, along with information related to it, in their long-term memory. Multiple listenings are required for children to know the music (and to value it). With any foreground music activity, place the title, composer, and performer(s) of the musical work on the board, so children know what and who they are listening to.

CLASSICAL MUSIC

Many nations have a classical or art music tradition. European classical music is divided into historical periods from the Middle Ages to the present, including Medieval, Renaissance, Baroque, Classical, Romantic (or nineteenth century), and Contemporary (twentieth and twenty-first centuries). Musicians from throughout the world are drawn to European classical works by renowned composers, and any musical work of high quality, regardless of historical period, style, or genre, can be selected for listening.

ORCHESTRAL MUSIC

Much classical music is written for the symphony orchestra. At the heart of the orchestra are the strings (violins, violas, cellos, basses). The wind section includes the brass (trumpets, trombones, French horns, tubas) and the woodwinds (piccolos, flutes, clarinets, oboes, English horns, bassoons). The percussion section features timpani, snare drums, bass drum, and other instruments played by hitting or striking such as triangles, bells, güiros, and claves. In addition, orchestras occasionally include harp, piano, organ, celesta, and guitar for some compositions.

The orchestra has grown in size over the centuries from a small, mostly string group in the Baroque period to a huge full orchestra in the nineteenth century (the Romantic period) that continues to the present day. Typically composers write music for a certain combination of instruments that produces the sound they are imagining. For example, Camille Saint-Saëns, a French composer of the late Romantic period, assigned different instrument sounds to fourteen different animals, one for each movement, in his composition *Carnival of the Animals*. (This type of music is called *program music*, in which composers want listeners to associate certain stories or images with the music.) Many of the movements, including *The Swan* and *Aquarium*, stand alone and have entertained people for many years in concert and film.

Over time, children may listen to all the movements of *Carnival of the*

The modern symphony orchestra consists of four families of instruments: strings, woodwinds, brass, and percussion.

Animals. Teachers can use the music to promote literacy by reading the story in one of several books by the same name (the bibliography at the end of this chapter gives many relevant books). Children can imagine what sounds from the orchestra they might use to exemplify a kangaroo, a donkey, or fish in an aquarium. Once they've made their predictions, they can listen to Saint-Saëns's music to see if their ideas match the composer's. Eventually, children will be able to appreciate the entire work, and may make masks or puppets and dramatize or move to the music as it unfolds. (See Chapter 14 for a series of lessons based on *The Aquarium* that integrate other arts.)

BALLET

Ballet music accompanies a highly specialized dance form originating in Europe, wherein dancers wear costumes to help tell a story, and female dancers wear pointe shoes requiring great strength and balance. Composers and choreographers collaborate in choosing a theme or story before the music is composed and dance movements choreographed. Three famous composers of ballet music are the Russians Pyotr Il'yich Tchaikovsky and Igor Stravinsky, and the American Aaron Copland. (Music by each of these composers is suggested in Appendix 3.)

Perhaps the most familiar and fascinating children's ballet is *The Nutcracker*, by Tchaikovsky. It tells the story of young Clara's family Christmas gathering, after which a nutcracker and other toys come alive and fight a battle. With Clara's help, the Nutcracker defeats the evil Mouse King, then turns into a Prince and takes Clara to the Land of Sweets. Teachers can achieve music and literacy goals by reading aloud from books such as *The Nutcracker Ballet* by Vladimir Vagin while the music plays softly in the background.

OPERA

Opera is often called the most complete art form within the realm of European art music, because it combines orchestra, singers, elaborate costumes, stage sets and props, dancing, and acting (and sometimes fencing, juggling, gymnastics, and other vigorous physical activities). Children are more familiar with the musical, whose music sounds decidedly more popular, and most operas are written for adult audiences and have adult themes, such as love, loyalty, and betrayal, and complex stories about mythic characters, but some, such as *The Magic Flute* by Mozart, are more playful and comical. Two operas, *Hansel and Gretel* by Engelbert Humperdinck, and *Amahl and the Night Visitors* by Gian-Carlo Menotti, are particularly child-oriented and easily understood and enjoyed by children.

A child's drawing of a scene from *The Nutcracker*.

Many children can also relate to more adult themes and styles, as testified by adults who fell in love with opera when they were children by listening to Metropolitan Opera broadcasts on Saturday afternoons. The beauty of the music and the voices enthralled them. Such stories suggest that instead of limiting children's experience of opera, we should expand it. Classroom teachers can acquaint

CHAPTER 5 | Their Ears: Listening to Music **83**

LESSON PLAN 5.1

Famous Composers from Europe

Europe during the Baroque and Classical periods produced many amazing and highly gifted composers whose music has lasted through the centuries. The following activities engage children with music from three notable composers: Bach, Mozart, and Beethoven. (Further recommended listening selections are found in Appendix 3.)

Johann Sebastian Bach, 1685–1750, Germany, Baroque style

- *Jesu, Joy of Man's Desiring* (piano)
- Toccata and Fugue in D Minor (organ)
- Cello Suite No. 3 in C Major, II (cello)
- Prelude and Fugue in C Minor (piano)

Suggested activities:

- With *Jesu, Joy of Man's Desiring* or Cello Suite No. 3, have children trace the melody in the air with their hands or on paper with pencil or marker. Encourage them to move their bodies through general space to the flow of the music.
- Listen to "Mr. Bach Comes to Call" by Classical Kids Productions or read *Bach,* by Ann Rachlin (from the Famous Children series). Have children research the life of J. S. Bach and write a story about some aspect of his life.

Wolfgang Amadeus Mozart, 1756–1791, Austria, Classical style

- 12 Variations on "Ah, vous dirai-je, Maman" ("Twinkle, Twinkle Little Star") (piano)
- Concerto for Flute, Harp, and Orchestra in C Major (flute and harp)
- Symphony No. 40 in G Minor (orchestra)
- Piano Sonata No. 11 (Turkish March) (piano)

Suggested activities:

- Sing "Twinkle, Twinkle Little Star" with children, then listen to the many ways Mozart changed the melody. Listen repeatedly, and encourage children to use music vocabulary such as "melody," "rhythm," "meter," "harmony," "bass," and "treble" to describe the changes.
- Find pictures of the flute and the harp. Discuss how they are played. Imagine the sounds. Listen to the Mozart Concerto, and notice when each of these instruments is playing and how they relate to each other. Divide the class into two sections and invite children to pretend to play either the flute or the harp when they hear these instruments.
- Read biographies of Mozart for children, such as *Amadeus Mozart* by Ibi Lepscky or *Mozart* by Catherine Brighton. Invite children to draw a scene from Mozart's life and write a short description of the action depicted in the illustration.

Ludwig van Beethoven, 1770–1827, Germany, Classical style

- Rondo in C Major (piano)
- Symphony No. 5 in C Minor, I (orchestra)
- Piano Sonata No. 14 in C Minor (*Moonlight*), I (piano)
- Symphony No. 6, IV (*Storm*) (orchestra)

Suggested activities:

- Read *Rondo in C,* by Paul Fleischman. Listen to the music and find sections that repeat. Ask children to consider how repeating sections relate to the images in the book.
- Notice the repeated opening melodic pattern in Symphony No. 5. Turn to a discussion of visual repetitions in nature, in our homes and school surroundings, and in art.
- Contrast the *Moonlight* Sonata with the storm movement from Symphony No. 6. How does Beethoven create these moods musically?
- Read *Beethoven Lives Upstairs,* by Barbara Nichol, or watch the video or listen to the story by Classical Kids Productions, then discuss Beethoven's life. What were some of his struggles? How did he overcome them?

them with the genre through stories and selected pieces from various operas. In *Sing Me a Story*, by Jane Rosenberg, children can read the stories of operas and view pictures, then make puppets of leading characters and dramatize the stories. A culmination of the unit is listening to the music (or even viewing scenes) from some of the operas they study. Lesson Plan 5.3 is designed to develop children's understanding of the treasured German opera *Hansel and Gretel*. (See Chapter 8 for how to obtain support from existing opera companies to help students stage their own operas.)

84 PART II | The Musical Makeup of Children

LESSON PLAN 5.2

Music from *The Nutcracker*

Grades
Second–sixth

Objectives

- Internalize key elements of *Trepak* and the March from *The Nutcracker* by moving to the music.

- Coordinate movements with the music, changing movements to reflect changes in the music.

- Discover and respond to the overall structure of two different pieces from *The Nutcracker*

- Build a repertoire of classical music.

Materials

- Hands and bodies

- Open space to create large movements

- Audio recording of the *Trepak* and March from *The Nutcracker*

- Video recording of the *Trepak* from YouTube

- Four large cards with one letter printed on each: A, A, B, A

Sequence A: Trepak (Russian Dance)

Introduction: Review the story of *The Nutcracker*. Tell the children how the Russian composer, Pyotr Il'yich Tchaikovsky, composed music that turned this story into a ballet—a story told through dance. Ask the children whether any have seen a ballet or are taking ballet lessons. Many musical selections from *The Nutcracker* are played as symphonic or orchestral works in a suite, apart from the actual ballet. One of those pieces is the *Trepak*, or Russian dance.

1. Before listening, invite students to consider how a dance featuring men in the costumes of Russian soldiers might look. Collect their ideas and put them on the board.

2. Ask them: if they were going to compose music for such a dance, what beat and speed would they choose (steady/unsteady; fast/slow/changing)? Would the dynamics be loud or soft or changing? What instruments would they feature from the orchestra and why? Write their ideas on the board.

3. Listen to the music to see what Tchaikovsky actually did. He created a short and lively piece with a strong, steady beat and lots of accents or stresses. Compare children's ideas with those Tchaikovsky used.

4. Listen again, inviting children to tap one hand to the beat with their other hand. Monitor to see who is keeping the beat accurately, and model the beat for children who might be struggling.

5. During the next listening, invite children to notice when the strong beat seems to lift the music into the air. Write the following pattern on the board and tap below each x, guiding the children's tapping as the music unfolds.

A section: **X**xxx **X**xxx xxxx xxxx **X**xxx **X**xxx xxxx xxxx   [tap on hand]
B section: xxxx xxxx xxxx xxxx xxxx xxxx xxxx xxxx   [tap on head]
A section: **X**xxx **X**xxx xxxx xxxx **X**xxx **X**xxx xxxx xxxx   [tap on hand]

Ask children to create a lift with their tap on each large **X**, making that beat bounce higher off of their hands than the others.

6. After students have performed these patterns successfully with their hands, challenge them to make up movements to these patterns in general space, taking care to avoid running into each other or furniture. How would they show the strong beat with their bodies? How do they move differently to the beat in the B section vs. the A section? Discuss their choices with them. Invite them to reflect on what they did to make the music come alive.

7. Once they have interpreted this piece through their movements, search the Internet for a video of *Trepak*, and watch professional ballet dancers perform this dance. Ask the children to reflect on how the dancers' movements are similar to theirs and how they were different.

Sequence B: March

Introduction: Tell students that Tchaikovsky also composed a march in *The Nutcracker*. Invite them to imagine a stage full of wooden nutcrackers dressed as soldiers.

1. How might wooden nutcracker soldiers move if they were going to march? Invite one or two students to demonstrate their ideas.

2. Have students listen to the March to identify elements that suggest nutcracker soldiers moving stiffly. Ask if there is a part that contrasted, when the movements seemed less stiff. Listen again and have them raise their hands when they hear that part. Ask them to describe that music.

3. Set the music to a hand dance using stomps, pats, claps, and snaps (see Table 5.2).

4. Over time, do these movements until most children appear comfortable coordinating them with the music.

5. Divide the class into two sections (A and B). Students in the A group will do the hand dance to the music that represent the soldiers marching. Students in the B group will do the hand dance to the less stiff, freer part. Ask each group how many times they did their patterns from the beginning of the piece. Write the letters on the board to represent the overall structure of the music: AABA. Tell students that those letters represent the form of the music.

6. Create four large cards, three with A and one with B. Give one card to each of four children in the order AABA. As the other children perform the hand dance to the music, have the children in front hold up their cards when their section is playing.

7. Have children work in groups of four or five to create a pattern using A and B, such as ABA or AABB and, using found sounds from around the room, compose a short piece showing repetition and contrast of ideas following the pattern they've chosen. Each idea should be at least four beats long. Have children share their form with the class before they play their piece. Invite all students to notice whether each group followed their form and reflect on the ways they showed repetition and contrast.

TABLE 5.2 HAND DANCE FOR MARCH FROM *THE NUTCRACKER*

	BEAT 1	BEAT 2	BEAT 3	BEAT 4	BEAT 1	BEAT 2	BEAT 3	BEAT 4
Phrase A1	stomp	pat pat pat	pat	pat	clap	clap	snap	rest
Phrase A1 (repeat)	stomp	pat pat pat	pat	pat	clap	clap	snap	rest
Phrase A2	Hold up two fingers of one hand to make bunny ears that hop up arm in eight beats. Bunny ears hop down arm in eight beats.							
Phrase A1	stomp	pat pat pat	pat	pat	clap	clap	snap	rest
Phrase A1 (repeat)	stomp	pat pat pat	pat	pat	clap	clap	snap	rest
Phrase A2	Hold up two fingers of one hand to make bunny ears that hop up arm in eight beats. Bunny ears hop down arm in eight beats.							
Phrase B	Start with arms high over head and slowly drop down in eight beats. Lift arms to chest height in four beats. Drop arms to sides in four beats.							
Phrase B	Repeat above.							
Phrases A1 and A2	Same as above with repeat.							
Phrases A1 and A2	Same as above with repeat.							
Phrase C	Pretend to play the flute, moving fingers rapidly for eight beats. Pretend to play the violin, moving fingers rapidly for eight beats.							
Phrase C	Repeat above.							
Phrases A1 and A2	Same as above with repeat.							
Phrases A1 and A2	Same as above with repeat.							
Phrase B	Repeat above.							
Phrase B	Repeat above.							
Phrases A1 and A2	Same as above with repeat.							
Phrases A1 and A2	Same as above with repeat. On final beat: clap!							

LESSON PLAN 5.3

Music from *Hansel and Gretel*

Grades
Second–sixth

Objectives

1. Familiarize students with some of the essential aspects of opera—a story told in song with costumes, dancing, acting, and complete staging, accompanied by an orchestra.
2. Perform "Evening Prayer" from *Hansel and Gretel* with expression, using the voice to convey the emotion of the song.
3. Learn the role that an overture plays in an opera, and discover how the melody of "Evening Prayer" is used in the overture to *Hansel and Gretel*.
4. Perform "Brother, Come and Dance with Me" as a dance and a song, expressing Hansel and Gretel's playful spirits as they sing the song.

Materials

- Illustrated children's book of *Hansel and Gretel*
- Large, empty space for dancing
- Recording of "Brother, Come and Dance with Me" and "Evening Prayer"
- Video of "Evening Prayer" and the Overture (available on YouTube)
- Art materials for drawing a picture or building a diorama

Sequence A: "Brother, Come and Dance with Me"

Introduction: Present the idea that stories can be told by singing them. Invite children to share stories they know that are presented in that form. (Many will cite Disney or Broadway musicals.) Before musicals and before film, composers often turned stories into operas. Discuss the operatic qualities stated above. We are going to learn about an opera written by a German composer, Engelbert Humperdinck. (Print his name on the board and have children repeat it.) It is based on the German fairy tale *Hansel and Gretel*.

1. Read the story of Hansel and Gretel from a children's picture books. Discuss how the children must have felt at different points in the story.
2. Invite students to share or write their own stories of when they've felt happy or frightened or alone.

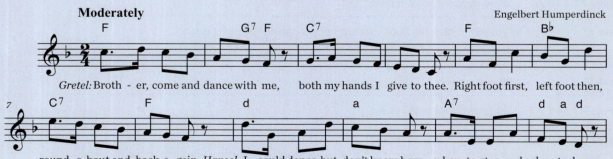

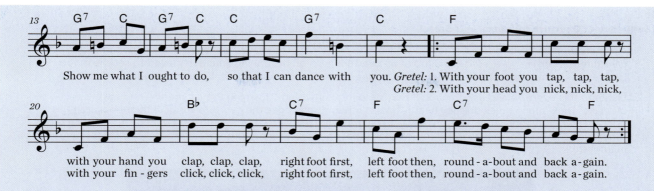

3. Learn to sing the song "Brother, Come and Dance with Me." Discuss the happy spirit of the song, which is sung early in the opera (when the children still live at home with their parents).

4. Once children can sing the song with ease, have them choose a partner (it is not necessary for boys to pair up with girls), face each other, and sing the words, one phrase at a time, while acting out the movements suggested.

5. Continue through the entire song. Practice singing and moving until everything flows smoothly. Gently encourage students who are struggling or need more practice.

6. Decide which of the pair will sing Gretel's part and which Hansel's, sing the song in those roles, and then switch roles and repeat the song.

Sequence B: "Evening Prayer"
Introduction: The mood of "Brother, Come and Dance with Me" is happy and upbeat, but in almost every good story there is also tension that brings a change in mood.

1. Review the point in the story when the children are in the woods at night, trying to fall asleep. Discuss the feelings they might have had. Share ideas about the kind of music Humperdinck might have written to comfort the children.

2. Listen to "Evening Prayer," from the opera. Discuss whether the students' ideas were similar to Humperdinck's.

3. Learn to sing "Evening Prayer." Children can move their arms in an arcing rainbow shape for each phrase of the song. Learn to sing each phrase in one breath, connecting the words with the flow of the breath. Over time, sing it in a way that expresses how Hansel and Gretel were feeling. Tell children that in performances of the opera, fourteen actors dressed as angels surround the children as they fall asleep.

4. Invite children to draw a picture or build a diorama staging this scene.

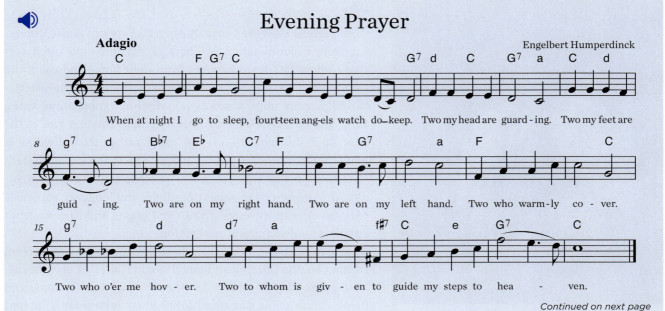

Continued on next page

Sequence C: Overture to *Hansel and Gretel*

1. Once children know "Brother, Come and Dance with Me" and "Evening Prayer," have them listen to the Overture to *Hansel and Gretel*. Explain that an overture is an orchestral introduction played to set the mood before the opera begins. The overture often includes portions of music that will occur throughout the opera.

2. Listen to this overture and ask children if they recognize anything ("Evening Prayer" begins and ends the overture). How many times do they hear it? What other moods does the overture suggest might occur in this opera? Over time, replay the overture so that children will internalize this beautiful music and cue their ears to other melodies and themes that will return later. If possible, watch a performance of *Hansel and Gretel* sung in English.

Hansel and Gretel in the woods at night

JAZZ

Louis Armstrong

Jazz is often called the one truly American style of music, emerging from a combination of complex rhythms and pitch sets that enslaved Africans brought from their homelands with the harmonies of European traditions. The five main characteristics of jazz are improvisation, polyrhythm, syncopation, swing time, and blue notes. Swing time lengthens the first half of the beat (and shortens the second half), rather than dividing it equally. Blue notes are pitches played a half-step lower (flatted) within the major scale. Jazz was preceded by the blues (usually African-American songs of sadness and longing), spirituals (African-American songs of faith and hope), and African drum rhythms for dancing and celebration.

Jazz began in New Orleans, where Afro-Caribbean drummers from Cuba, the Dominican Republic, and Haiti met up with ragtime piano players and blues singers. Musicians in Dixieland bands, often using discarded army brass instruments, played early forms of jazz that are still popular today, especially in the French Quarter of New Orleans. Louis Armstrong, one of the most famous of those Dixieland players, was greatly renowned for his gravelly voice and his trumpet playing. One of his most inspiring songs is "What a Wonderful World," an excellent choice for children, which can also be signed using American Sign Language. Listen to Armstrong sing "Bye Bye Blackbird" and "I Got Rhythm" to hear how he brings the swing feeling of jazz to those songs.

Jazz musicians traveled up the Mississippi River in the early twentieth century to Memphis, St. Louis, and Chicago. Along the way, new forms of jazz emerged, including the swing music of Count Basie and Duke Ellington, the scat singing of Ella Fitzgerald and Sarah Vaughan, the bebop of Charlie Parker, and the cool jazz of Miles Davis and John Coltrane. Jazz continues to flourish in America, and has been fused with classical, rock, and popular music by Randy and Michael Brecker, Chick Corea, Pat Metheny, Trey Anastasio and Phish, and Nguyên Lê. Many young people perform jazz in middle and high school ensembles.

Ella Fitzgerald

Select one or two jazz recordings, such as "Take the 'A' Train" or "Linus and Lucy," to play for children in class (consult Appendix 3 for additional options). Invite younger children to move to the music, as most naturally will; it is challenging to sit still in response to jazz. Encourage older children to research and report on the history of jazz or on the life of a famous jazz performer. Box 5.2 suggests illustrated books for elementary children to use in exploring jazz.

BOX 5.2 PRINT RESOURCES ON JAZZ FOR ELEMENTARY CHILDREN

History, Essence, and Artists of Jazz

I See the Rhythm by Toyomi Igus and Michele Wood (Illus.)

Jazz: My Music, My People by Morgan Monceaux

Jazz on a Saturday Night by Leo and Diane Dillon

Music Over Manhattan by Mark Karlins and Jack E. Davis (Illus.)

This Jazz Man by Karen Ehrhardt and R. G. Roth (Illus.)

Who Bop? by Jonathan London and Henry Cole (Illus.)

Stories of Specific Jazz Artists

Before John Was a Jazz Giant: A Song of John Coltrane by Carol Boston Weatherford and Sean Qualls (Illus.)

Charlie Parker Played Be Bop by Chris Raschka

Dizzy by Jonah Winter and Sean Qualls (Illus.)

Duke Ellington by Andrea Davis Pinkney and Brian Pinkney (Illus.)

Ella Fitzgerald: The Tale of a Vocal Virtuosa by Andrea Davis Pinkney and Brian Pinkney (Illus.)

Satchmo's Blues by Alan Schroeder and Floyd Cooper (Illus.)

Skit-Scat Raggedy Cat: Ella Fitzgerald by Roxane Orgill and Sean Qualls (Illus.)

When Louis Armstrong Taught Me Scat by Muriel Harris Weinstein and Gregory Christie (Illus.)

Invite them to discuss what they learn from these books about jazz style and American history. Ask them whether they know someone who plays jazz, such as an older sibling or neighbor. Invite a local jazz musician to come perform for students. Jazz music can enhance social studies projects, provide interesting stories for children to read, and affect the mood of the classroom by increasing the energy level (with fast jazz) or lowering it (with mellow jazz). Jazz at Lincoln Center in New York City has a wonderful array of videos and educational materials available online for children, teachers, and parents.

POPULAR MUSIC

Popular music is a culture's commercial music, recorded by artists who are promoted as pop stars. It pervades every culture to which mass media travels—by radio, TV, cell phones, the Internet, video games, and film. Popular music changes quickly, and the music of one generation of young adults will be completely different for those even four or five years younger. Children respond to popular music, with its catchy repeated rhythms and melodies.

Children come to class already immersed in popular music. They don't need teachers to educate them here; however, teachers could integrate popular music when it is topically relevant to a curricular point or a current issue. Older children may want to share in class some of the music they are listening to, and can learn to articulate orally and in writing what makes this music meaningful to them, and how it its lyrics, melody, rhythm, and harmonies are constructed. Popular music may motivate them to read, analyze, and organize their ideas about their favorite groups or artists (teachers should set boundaries for acceptable lyrics).

FOLK AND AMERICAN ROOTS MUSIC

Folk music is the expressive songs and instrumental tunes of a particular people or region that evolved over many years, usually transmitted orally and with no known composers. American cowboy songs, Mexican American corridos, African-American spirituals, and Anglo-American songs of the Appalachian and Ozark Mountains are all examples of folk music. Folk music is recognizable by the quality of the singing, the focus of the lyrics, and the type of instruments played. Folk music exists throughout the world, and some of the American folk genres are referred to as roots music, in reference to their foundational influence on popular genres such as country, rock, and singer-songwriter styles.

In the late 1950s and early 1960s, a folk music revival grew in America, featuring singers such as The Weavers (including Pete Seeger), Woody Guthrie, Lead Belly, and Odetta. They were followed by folk rock musicians such as Peter, Paul, and Mary; the Kingston Trio; Joan Baez; Bob Dylan; the Mamas and the Papas; Paul Simon and Art Garfunkel; and James Taylor. Often accompanied by guitars, they sang soulful and engaging songs about such as war, peace, oppression, and hope that spoke to the public imagination. Folk singer-songwriters of today, including Ani DiFranco, Ben Harper, and Gillian Welch, carry on the spirit and sound of the folk revivalists.

The Smithsonian Folkways Recordings provide an extensive online collection of folk music from many cultures and regions, as well as lessons for teaching (many are referenced in Appendix 3). The broad spectrum of musical genres and styles in this archive may seem overwhelming at first (genres include blues, bluegrass, Cajun, Celtic, children's, historical song, jazz, Judaica, Latin, old-time, struggle and protest, and world music). But this resource offers audio and video recordings (including videos of musicians and dancers) as well as written descriptions of the music—much of the material coming firsthand from musicians of all genres.

Folk songs' historical relevance suit them ideally for incorporation into classroom projects with children, and the songs in this book epitomize the American folk tradition, including children's songs and heritage songs of various times and places. Children in the intermediate grades would do well to research artists, be their songs ballads (which tell stories and portray particular characters), songs of romance, or protest songs. They can write reports about the artists, their songs, and their messages. Children of all ages learn more about history by singing and studying the folk music of historical and contemporary cultures, and integrating folk music into history and geography lessons enlivens the curriculum.

Lesson Plan 5.4 moves children from singing an American folk song, "Hush, Little Baby," to singing the song along with three different literary versions, to listening to instrumental versions of the song and drawing connections between the print versions and the recorded versions.

WORLD MUSIC

World music is a term widely used to refer to folk, traditional, popular, and art music from every region of the world, especially outside the realm of Western Europe. The Internet and globalization have exposed more listeners to many world music practices. Smithsonian Folkways Recordings is a rich resource for world music and strategies for teaching the world's musical cultures, with its extensive archive of recordings, videos, and lessons. From women singers in Central Asia to gong players in the Philippines, accordionists in Columbia, string players in Ethiopia, court orchestras in Cambodia and Thailand, sitarists in North India, pan pipers in Bolivia, and bagpipers in Bulgaria, France, Ireland and Scotland—and so much more—the collection is immediately available for lessons on listening, singing, playing, and cultural understanding. World music becomes particularly relevant when studying the people and culture of a world region in a social studies class (see Appendix 3 for a sampling of world music recordings).

Professional western musicians enjoy the new sonic possibilities of world music, and many have been influenced by new sounds and structures. They often incorporate these elements into their own compositions and improvisations, and their efforts are available on recordings and in films. A half-century ago, George Harrison of the Beatles went to India to study with the great Indian sitarist Ravi Shankar (father of jazz singer Norah Jones and contemporary sitarist Anoushka Shankar). In 1985, Paul Simon traveled to Johannesburg to record his album *Graceland* with South African musicians. More recently, the Kronos Quartet (two violins, viola, and cello) collaborated with a Chinese pipa (plucked lute) virtuoso in Tan Dun's *Ghost Opera* and with the Zimbabwean Dumisani Maraire in *Pieces of Africa*. Cellist Yo-Yo Ma collaborated with musicians from many cultures in Central Asia, China, India, and Turkey along the Silk Road, and he joined them on tour to share the variety of musical impulses that early travelers along that route

LESSON PLAN 5.4

Music from "Hush, Little Baby"

Using "Hush, Little Baby" by Heidi Grant Murphy and Auréole, and "Hush Little Baby" by Yo-Yo Ma and Bobby McFerrin

Grades	Pre-K–second
Repertoire Goals	Internalize a sense of style that comes from contrasting versions of a familiar song. Understand that one piece can occur in many different arrangements.
Concept Goals	Review the meaning and traditional style of a lullaby. Understand that improvising is a way to be musically playful.
Skills Goals	Physically and vocally respond to the flow and mood of the music. Aurally perceive ways that a familiar work has been altered. Experiment with musically altering other familiar works.
Literature Goals	Become familiar with contrasting styles of illustrating a familiar song and to connect that with similar styles in music. Write and illustrate an arrangement of that song.
Day 1	Read the picture book *Hush, Little Baby* as illustrated by Aliki (1968).
	Discuss the sequence and the predictability of the rhymes. Learn to sing the folk song "Hush, Little Baby." Sing it as you follow the pictures in the book.
Day 2	Bring in a doll or stuffed animal. Pretend to put it to sleep by rocking it. When it resists falling asleep, suggest that a lullaby might help. Have the children listen carefully to see if they can help rock pretend babies and also sing the lullaby. Begin to sing "Hush, Little Baby" on the neutral syllable "loo." Watch to see when children recognize the song and enter in. Have them name the song and then sing it while they pretend to rock their babies and put them to sleep. Gently place the sleeping babies away as you play the recording of "Hush, Little Baby" by Heidi Grant Murphy and Auréole. Invite children to stand, find a place in space, and gently move to the flow of the music. Extend their movements by having them used colored scarves or streamers to show the flow. Invite children to share what they noticed about the music and how it made them feel.
Day 3	On the board, put the words *word* and *bird*, *sing* and *ring*, *down* and *town*, and so on. Invite children to help read them. Ask them what song the words are from. Sing the song using soft, soothing voices. Discuss the flow (gentle) and dynamic quality (soft) of the lullaby. Tell them you are going to play a recording of two men performing "Hush, Little Baby." Ask them to listen to decide whether they think it will put the baby to sleep or not. Listen and discuss their responses as to why it would not put the baby to sleep. (It is loud and fast.) Have the children stand, face a partner, and hold hands. Play the recording again while the children rock back and forth to the flow of the music, creating an imaginary cradle.
Day 4	Introduce children to the names of the two musicians who performed the second recording of "Hush, Little Baby." Show them their pictures. Discuss the fact that they are both famous musicians who love to experiment or play with sounds. (Children may have seen them on *Sesame Street* or in TV ads.) Listen to their arrangement of "Hush, Little Baby" to discover what they did to make it different from the original. Discuss those ideas (faster, louder, different words, higher pitches, sliding, mouth sounds, clapping). Have children join in vocally with the recording, trying some of the techniques. Discuss the delightful character of this style of singing. Read the book *Hush, Little Baby* illustrated by Margot Zemach (1976). Does its quality capture more of the original version of the song or the Yo-Yo Ma–McFerrin version? Why?

Kindergarteners listen to three different versions of "Hush, Little Baby."

Extensions
1. Have the children develop their own vocal improvisations (playing with sounds) using familiar nursery rhymes.
2. Take another lullaby and turn it from a gentle piece to an upbeat piece by improvising.
3. Share the book *Hush, Little Baby* by Sylvia Long (1997). Have the children discuss what is different about this book. Encourage them to create their own version of "Hush, Little Baby," illustrate it, and then bind it into their own book.
4. Listen to other selections from the album *Hush*, such as "Flight of the Bumblebee" by Rimsky-Korsakov. Discuss how the various effects were created.
5. Find out more about Bobby McFerrin and Yo-Yo Ma (videotapes from PBS, other recordings). Build their names into the children's vocabulary. Compare Yo-Yo Ma's cello style on "Hush, Little Baby" with a more traditional style. Discuss the differences.

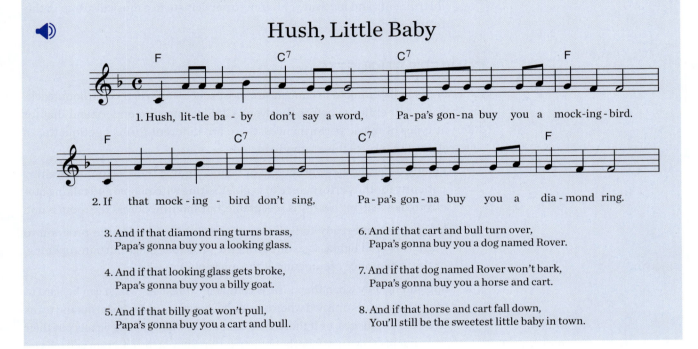

would have encountered. Like professional artists, so too can children be encouraged to discover sound sources from the world's cultures and to mix new melodies, rhythms, and forms into the music they know best as they create music vocally and on percussion instruments, keyboards, guitars, and other instruments.

LISTENING TO MUSIC IN LIVE PERFORMANCES

Perhaps the ultimate experience of music is a live performance, which offers children a chance to see and hear music and musicians in action and thus to engage with and understand music more fully. Teachers can offer live performances to children by tapping any number of resources:

- outreach groups from local symphony, chamber music, opera, or musical clubs (often low-cost or free)

- ► school trips to musical performance venues
- ► artists who visit for long-term residencies in classrooms or the school as a whole
- ► individuals or groups engaged for assemblies and classroom visits through PTA funds
- ► local cultural groups who sponsor performers
- ► parents, grandparents, and other relatives, or friends of teachers, students, or families who are willing to perform for classes or the school
- ► the students themselves
- ► students in the district's middle and high schools who can demonstrate on instruments and motivate children to participate in a musical group in the future

CONCERT ETIQUETTE

Experiences in listening to live music are most successful when classroom teachers prepare their children before the event. Children need to understand that for different types of music performances, there are different forms of etiquette. In classical music concerts this etiquette includes:

1. quietly entering the concert hall or venue, finding their seats, and waiting patiently for the performance to begin. Visiting with people and talking quietly to those sitting nearby is acceptable, but shouting across the room is not.

2. being quiet and ready to listen once a signal is given for the program to begin (lowered lights, a gesture from the principal, stage curtains opening, or the appearance of someone at the microphone).

3. applauding only when the music is completely finished (which can be hard to tell). The music is finished when the conductor drops his or her arms and turns to face the audience, or if there is no conductor, when the musicians put their instruments down and face the audience. (A review of the program will tell you how many musical works are planned and whether these works are organized into sections. For a musical piece with several sections or movements, it is customary to wait until the entire piece has been performed before applauding.)

Folk music, popular music, and world music concerts sometimes have more relaxed expectations of audience behavior. Often there are no printed programs, there may be more socializing prior to or between pieces, and sometimes people spontaneously join in the musical performance by singing, clapping, or dancing. Teachers need to be explicit when teaching the appropriate behaviors, and model them with their own behavior.

PREPARING CHILDREN TO UNDERSTAND THE MUSIC

Teachers may prepare for performances by attending to the music itself. Many organizations and artists send teachers materials to help prepare their children for the listening experiences, including child-oriented activities that teachers can easily adapt for their own classrooms. It is always rewarding to children to have heard at least some of the music ahead of the live performance, or to have learned about the music, musicians, instruments, or cultural or historical era of the featured music.

Many in-school performers invite children to ask questions about the music or the instruments. Ask children to think of questions they would like to have answered. It is also valuable to offer follow-up activities that may encourage children to listen to the music again. This kind of thoughtful engagement increases children's cultural competence.

LISTENING RESPONSES THROUGH OTHER ARTS

Artists in one form have always inspired creativity in other forms. Children enjoy responding to music through other art forms, and program music, a genre of Western art music written with a particular story or image in mind, has strong appeal. Children can readily translate program music into visual images, poetry, or movement, particularly if they know the intent of the composer. *Pictures at an Exhibition,* by Modest Musorgsky, in which each movement suggests a painting in an art gallery, and *Peter and the Wolf,* by Sergei Prokofiev, which tells the story of young Peter encountering and capturing a wolf, are two seminal examples of program music. Most Western art instrumental music is absolute music, or music that is not intended to convey images or stories, yet it, too, can evoke powerful responses in other art forms. After repeated listening to nearly any piece, children will often respond emotionally and cognitively by creating images, poetry, or movements that are quite true to the composer's intentions.

DRAWING OR PAINTING IN RESPONSE TO LISTENING

To stimulate children's artistic responses to music, give them art materials, instruct them to draw images in response to the music, and play a recording thoughtfully selected for this purpose. Invite them to focus on the music's tone colors, rhythms, melodies, form, harmonies, and overall mood as they create their images. Finally, provide time for children to process the connections they have made between the music and their art work, either verbally or in writing.

One particularly interartistic set of experiences was conceived by concert pianist Dr. Amy Grinsteiner, who collaborated with a second-grade classroom teacher. First, the teacher introduced the children to various elements of drawing, such as shading, design, line, color, contrast, shape, and value. Grinsteiner entered the project to play samples of J. S. Bach's *Goldberg Variations,* a piece of absolute music, and introduce key music vocabulary such as texture (thick/thin), volume (loud/soft), tempo (fast/slow), and pitch (high/low). She encouraged children to describe how the music made them feel and how they might represent their feelings artistically. Each child was assigned a variation to listen to through headphones while responding by drawing. Their artistic expressions were abstractions of the music that came

Peyton Dirkes, Variation 20

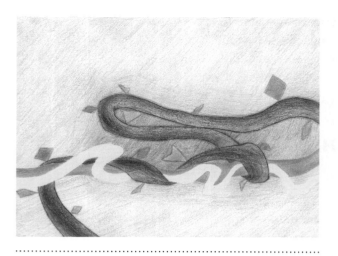

Aubree Eiynck, Variation 25

alive with motion, color, and a sense of the structure and elements of the music, and children were encouraged to reflect upon the music and their drawings. Afterward, children and their parents and families attended Grinsteiner's performance of the entire *Goldberg Variations*, during which the children's artworks were projected. As a result, children truly owned the music because they had listened to it several times and expressed themselves artistically in response to the music. The accompanying figures represent two of their drawings.

Another fun listening strategy is to play a piece of program music without telling children the composer's intent. Encourage them to draw what they imagine as they listen. These images, and the composer's title and intent for the music, can then be discussed and dissected. This sequence can also be reversed: children select a painting or photograph, which then inspires a group or individual musical composition in response to the image.

WRITING IN RESPONSE TO LISTENING

Music's evocative qualities stimulate children's imaginations. Children are accustomed to music with images and words in film, but they are probably less experienced with connecting music to writing poetry. Children can write poetry in response to music at any age, with younger children dictating words and older children writing at whatever level they are capable. They can write poetry about images or feelings the music evokes (see Lesson Plan 5.5), or based on the rhythms, instrumental and vocal colors, or timbres of the music itself, as in the *Goldberg Variations* project. Both hold music at the core of the activity but allow development along other expressive avenues.

The poems below were written by children in response to hearing a recording of the cellist Yo-Yo Ma play Tan Dun's theme music from the film *Crouching Tiger, Hidden Dragon*. None of the children recognized the music initially, nor did they know that the music was scored for film. Their poetry, however, remarkably reflects the film's spirit and essence. At the close of the lesson, children were excited to learn the performer's identity, and those who had seen the film were especially amazed to recognize how closely their poetry related to the film's characters and story.

Poem by Maddie
I have given up
It is time to go back
I have failed in my travel
I look over the great city and it looms

I run
The world is upon me
The excitement fills inside

CHAPTER 5 | Their Ears: Listening to Music 97

LESSON PLAN 5.5

Writing Poetry in Response to Music

Grade Level
Fifth–sixth

Objectives

- Use music to stimulate creative poetic writing
- Reflect on aspects of the music that stimulated the poetic responses
- Share and contrast responses from other students, discussing similarities and differences

Materials

- Examples of descriptive poetry
- Musically expressive recordings without words, such as Tan Dun's theme from the film *Crouching Tiger, Hidden Dragon*; *Grand Canyon Suite* by Ferde Grofé; or *Pictures at an Exhibition* by Modest Musorgsky
- Paper and pencil for each child

Procedures

1. Introduce children to different styles of poetry, including poems that are rhymed and metered and poems that are in free verse. Discuss the differences. Ask them which they think might be more challenging to write and why.

2. Play recorded music without telling children its name or any other information. Invite them to listen to the music with their eyes closed and notice what images or feelings the music evokes. Create a word bank of those images and feelings.

3. Play the music again and invite the children to write a poem in response to the music using whatever style of poetry writing seems to fit what they want to express.

4. Play the music again, inviting them to review their poems and make any changes they wish to make.

5. Children form pairs and share their poems.

6. Ask if anyone wants to share his or her poem with the entire class.

7. Listen for any commonalities in the poems. Discuss both the commonalities and differences. Discuss how the poems match elements in the music.

8. Play the music again and share the name of the music as well as the performer(s) and composer. Discuss the music. If the music has a programmatic intent, check that intent against what the children wrote. Notice any relationship between the two. Discuss how music can communicate ideas without using words.

Do I have time?
Is it there?
Am I ready to trust myself?

The grass droops
The wind stops
The waves fall back
The world is waiting

Poem by Alex

The traveler sets off, through land of green
He is skilled as a warrior though he's just a teen
His way on the road is going to be tough
To accomplish this task, he must be strong and lean.

Through his journey he will meet foe and friend
He knows there will be death in the end.
He goes anyway, by will of love.
He sets on the journey, the town to defend.

LISTENING TO MEET MUSIC STANDARDS

1. Singing. Invite children to sing the themes of music they are listening to. Encourage children to listen carefully to various vocal styles, describe those styles, and then try to sing in those styles.

2. Playing. Have children play along with recorded music, entering on certain rhythmic patterns in the music or playing with various sections to show the form of the music.

3. Improvising. Listen to jazz musicians improvising with their voices and instruments. Learn to identify when that is happening in a piece. Try improvising using vocal syllables.

4. Composing and arranging. Listen to some music by Philip Glass, who uses limited resources and repeated patterns in his compositions. Compose a piece for only one instrument using patterns that repeat over and over and change very gradually.

5. Reading and notating. Provide scores or notation for some of the music you are listening to. Follow along as you listen to the music. Have someone stop at an unexpected point in the music. Indicate on the score where that is.

6. Listening. Expand children's listening experiences by having them research particular composers or artists, recommend a piece they think everyone should listen to, and justify their choice. Share that piece with the class.

7. Evaluating. Listen to two or more interpretations of the same piece of music by different performers. Critique the performances, deciding which is the most interesting or effective and why. Build a case for your decision.

8. Connecting to other arts and curricular areas. Listen to program music written to create images of nature or other aspects of the curriculum you are studying. Discuss how the composer paints a picture in sound.

9. Connecting to culture and history: Listen to music from various periods or cultures you are studying. Discuss how it reflects that period or culture. Compare and contrast the music to contemporary music. How does contemporary music reflect our time and culture?

Summary

Listening intelligently to music increases not only children's pleasure, but also their learning in other school subjects. Classroom teachers can tap into the power of music listening to motivate students in other arts, language arts, math, and social studies. Far from stealing time from instruction in other subjects, music adds exciting new dimensions to that learning.

Review

1. What are the differences between listening to music in the background and music in the foreground?

2. What does it mean to build musical literacy?

3. Name five ways to actively engage children in listening to music.

4. What various styles of music should be included in the classroom?

5. What is the difference between program music and absolute music?

Critical Thinking

1. How might children benefit from music in the background in a classroom? When might background music be problematic? With that knowledge, how, when, and why would you plan to use music in the background?

2. What are the advantages of actively engaging children in responding to music, rather than letting it wash over them like a tonal bath?

3. What do you think it means to be an educated person? How might being musically literate enhance one's education?

4. Why might children's experiencing performances of live music be more valuable than only listening to recorded music?

5. With which styles of music are you most familiar? How might you use those with children? How could you expand your repertoire?

Projects

1. Download several pieces of instrumental music you might use in the background in your classroom to calm children down, lift their spirits, or energize them. Rationalize your musical choices.

2. Select a piece of music you believe should become part of children's internal repertoire and explain your choice. At which grade level would you introduce this music? Develop a series of activities for children of that age to internalize the music.

3. Review some of the books listed in this chapter to introduce children visually to music or musicians. Listen to the music that pertains to the book. Develop several ways to use the music and book to enhance children's understanding.

4. Develop a response sheet for use in a third-grade (or older) classroom music center. Include questions that encourage appropriate music vocabulary to describe the music, and also questions that target children's emotional responses to the music. Children may make judgments about liking or not liking a piece of music, but they should justify they decision based on the music itself.

5. Select several pieces of music by one composer or artist for use in a music center for children. Include children's books and biographical information to enhance their understanding. Develop questions about the music and the composer or artist for children to answer as they work in the music center.

6. Identify key works of music in each genre discussed in this chapter (orchestral music, ballet, opera, jazz, popular, folk, and world). Familiarize yourself with them, and list ways you would use them in your classroom based on ideas from this chapter and your own creative thinking.

Additional Resources for Teaching

American Folk Music

Chase, Richard. (1971). *American Folk Tales and Songs* (Dover Books on Music). New York, NY: Dover Publications.

Gourley, Robbin. (2015). *Talkin' Guitar: A Story of Young Doc Watson*. New York, NY: Clarion Books.

Guthrie, Woody and Kathy Jakobsen. (1998). *This Land Is Your Land*. New York, NY: Little, Brown.

Hopkinson, Deborah and S. D. Schindler. (2009). *Home on the Range: John A. Lomax and His Cowboy Songs*. New York, NY: Putnam.

Kidd, Ronald and Linda Anderson (Illus.). (1992). *On Top of Old Smoky: A Collection of Songs and Stories from Appalachia*. Nashville, TN: Ideals Publications.

Robertson, Robbie, Jim Guerinot, Sebastian Robertson, and Jared Levine. (2013). *Legends, Icons & Rebels: Music That Changed the World*. Toronto, ON: Tundra Books.

Silvey, Anita. (2016). *Let Your Voice Be Heard: The Life and Times of Pete Seeger*. New York, NY: Clarion Books.

Ballet

Angus, David and Jenny Agutter (Narr.). (2001). *Ballet Stories: Swan Lake, Coppélia, Sleeping Beauty, Nutcracker, Giselle* [CD]. Surrey, England: Naxos Audiobooks.

Chappell, Warren (Illus.). (1961). *The Sleeping Beauty: From the Tales of Charles Perrault*. New York, NY: Knopf. [Music by Peter Tchaikovsky.]

Demi. (1994). *The Firebird*. New York, NY: Henry Holt & Co. [Music by Igor Stravinsky.]

Hautzig, Deborah and Diane Goode (Illus.). (1986). *The Story of the Nutcracker Ballet*. New York, NY: Random House Books for Young Readers.

Helprin, Mark and Chris van Allsburg (Illus.). (1989). *Swan Lake*. Boston: Houghton Mifflin Co. [Music by Peter Tchaikovsky.]

Jeffers, Susan. (2007). *The Nutcracker*. New York, NY: HarperCollins.

Vagin, Vladimir. (1995). *The Nutcracker Ballet*. New York, NY: Scholastic, Inc. [Music by Peter Tchaikovsky.]

Biographies of Composers

Krull, Kathleen and Kathryn Hewitt (Illus.). (2013). *Lives of the Musicians: Good Times, Bad Times (and What the Neighbors Thought)*. Boston, MA: HMH Books for Young Readers.

Rachlin, Ann. (dates below). *Famous Children*. Hauppauge, NY: Barron's Educational Series.

(1992) *Mozart*

(1993) *Tchaikovsky*

(1993) *Brahms*

Venezia, Mike. (dates below). *Getting to Know the World's Greatest Composers*. New York, NY: Children's Press.

(1995) *Peter Tchaikovsky*

(1995) *George Gershwin*

(1995) *George Handel*

(1995) *Aaron Copland*

(1996) *Ludwig van Beethoven*

(1996) *Wolfgang Amadeus Mozart*

(1996) *Duke Ellington*

(1997) *The Beatles*

(1997) *Igor Stravinsky*

(1998) *Johann Sebastian Bach*

(1998) *Leonard Bernstein*

(1999) *Johannes Brahms*

(1999) *John Philip Sousa*

(2000) *Frederic Chopin*

General Resources

Ardley, Neil and Poul Ruders. (2004). *A Young Person's Guide to Music.* London, UK: DK Children.

Hurd, Michael. (1980). *The Oxford Junior Companion to Music.* London, UK: Oxford University Press.

Spence, Keith. (1995). *The Young People's Book of Music.* Brookfield, CT: Lerner Publishing Group.

Jazz

Gollub, Matthew and Karen Hanke (Illus.). (2000). *The Jazz Fly.* Santa Rosa, CA: Tortuga Press.

Gray, Libba Moore and Lisa Cohen (Illus.). (1996). *Little Lil and the Swing-Singing Sax.* New York, NY: Simon & Schuster.

Isadora, Rachel. (1979). *Ben's Trumpet.* New York, NY: Mulberry Books.

Schroeder, Alan and Bernie Fuchs (Illus.). (1995). *Carolina Shout!.* New York, NY: Dial Books.

Shange, Ntozake and Romare Bearden (Illus.). (1994). *i live in music.* New York, NY: Welcome Books.

Opera

Lesser, Rika and Paul O. Zelinsky (Illus.). (1999). *Hansel and Gretel.* New York, NY: Penguin Group. [Music by Engelbert Humperdink.]

Menotti, Gian Carlo and Michele Lemieux (Illus.). (1986). *Amahl and the Night Visitors.* New York, NY: HarperCollins. [Music by Gian Carlo Menotti. Also available on DVD.]

Rosenberg, Jane. (1989). *Sing Me A Story: The Metropolitan Opera's Book of Opera Stories for Children.* New York, NY: Thames & Hudson.

Symphonic Music

Prelutsky, Jack and Mary GrandPré (Illus.). (2010). *The Carnival of the Animals.* New York, NY: Knopf Books for Young Readers. [Book and CD; music by Camille Saint-Saëns.]

Raschka, Chris. (2008). *Peter and the Wolf.* New York, NY: Atheneum/Richard Jackson

Turner, Barrie and Sue Williams (Illus.). (1999). *The Carnival of the Animals: Classical Music for Kids.* New York, NY: Henry Holt.

Voigt, Erna. (1980). *Peter and the Wolf.* Boston: David R. Godine. [Music by Sergei Prokofiev.]

World Music

Ajmera, Maya, Elise Hofer Derstine, and Cynthia Pon. (2014). *Music Everywhere!* (Global Fund for Children Book). Watertown, MA: Charlesbridge.

Barber, Nicola and Mary Mure. (1995). *The World of Music*. Parsippany, NJ: Silver Burdett Press.

Ober, Carol and Hal Ober. (1994). *How Music Came to the World: An Ancient Mexican Myth*. New York, NY: Houghton Mifflin Harcourt.

Titon, Jeff Todd (Ed.). (2008). *Worlds of Music: An Introduction to the Music of the World's Peoples*. New York, NY: Cengage.

Recorded Music Sources

The commercially recorded listening examples in this book can be purchased from iTunes and other online music stores. Sources are suggested in Appendix 3. Talk with your music specialist about borrowing recordings from the music room, including recordings that accompany music books and textbooks. Most public libraries also loan recordings.

Online Resources: Audio and Songbook

digital.wwnorton.com/classroom

6

THEIR MOVING BODIES

Activity and participation get more blood to more brains. Activity and participation make children happier. Activity and participation in a music-dance tradition prepares children for a life well lived at a great many deep and mostly unconscious levels: how to be in time, in tune, in graceful synchrony with other people, how to be an energetic presence, a shining individual with tight relationship with many others simultaneously.

—Charles Keil, *Dance Daily. Dance Early. Dance Now.*[1]

IN THIS CHAPTER

In the Classroom

Children, Rhythm, and Movement

Rhythmic Movement in Development

Exploring Movement

Safe Movement Activities

Components of Rhythm in Movement

Moving Rhythmically in Early and Middle Childhood

Rhythmic Movement in Speech and Song

Movement in Manageable Dance Experiences

Singing Songs, Signing Songs

Summary

Review

Critical Thinking

Projects

Additional Resources for Teaching

Additional Songs for Singing

Activity and participation make children happier and more ready to learn.

103

You Will Learn

- why it is important for children's bodies to move regularly and musically

- how children develop movement capabilities as they grow

- many practical techniques for incorporating movement and music activities into all curricular areas

- ideas for signing songs with American Sign Language to combine language arts and music through movement

- stylized dance steps that children can easily learn in classrooms

Ask Yourself

- When you least expect it, do you ever find yourself moving and grooving to the music on your mobile device, in the car, or at home?

- Do you dance with others? By yourself? What music do you dance to?

- As a child, did you dance, formally or informally? What sort of dancing did you do, and to what kinds of music?

- How did you feel when you danced? Did those feeling inspire your dancing, or vice versa?

- What do you observe when you see children dancing?

- Have you noticed the rhythm in rhymes, poetry, and in spoken conversations, where some syllables are accented, some words are elongated, and some phrases are more rushed (or leisurely) than others?

- Speak aloud a favorite poem. Do you notice the rhythmic movement of the syllables, words, and phrases?

Watch children on the playground, at the bus stop, in the cafeteria, in their individual and group classroom activities, or as they line up for recess. They are unlikely to be standing up perfectly straight, silent, and still. Instead, children move, and they frequently move in a musical manner. They may sway, hop, rock, nod, and gesture animatedly while talking to their friends. Their movement is alternately regular and sporadic, slower and faster, and choppy and smooth. They cannot help but move independently or in synchrony with others, and when the music starts they are drawn to its rhythms, timbres, textures, and articulations. Teachers recognize children's penchant for moving to music, and they find that their classrooms can be made more joyous and more energetic (in controlled ways) and that children learn more through movement and the dance.

IN THE CLASSROOM

VIGNETTE ONE

Ms. Smith's kindergarteners merrily motor through their half-day class. Ms. Smith greets the children at the door and watches how they skip, gallop, and hop to their cubbies to hang their jackets and coats, and on to their assigned seats at the six-person work tables. Before they begin their coloring, cutting, and pasting projects, she often captures their attention and organizes them by playing a drum pattern, inviting them to clap, pat on the table, or chant on a steady "pah" syllable (most need no invitation at all, and begin moving rhythmically when the drum starts). While they work on their art projects, she may play recorded selections from Mozart's *Eine kleine Nachtmusik* or Stravinsky's *Rite of Spring*, piano music by J. S. Bach or Claude Debussy, or the latest Kronos Quartet recording. She delights in watching them connect with the musical pulse they hear, hand-patting or head-nodding as the music plays. Ms. Smith has the children stretch high and bend low as they finish their table work, reaching to the sky when she plays a high-pitched tone bell and then dropping to the floor when they hear her wood blocks click. Back and forth, rising and falling they go, responding to the cues they hear. She leads them through their group, counting to twenty, playing a steady pulse on the wood block, first slow and then faster over several trials, and watches how the children count and tap with her. In their sharing circle, she tells the classic story of Goldilocks and the Three Bears while Beethoven's Sixth Symphony plays softly in the background, and encourages their animated enactments of gulping down the porridge from imaginary bowls, scoffing at imaginary chairs, and reclining onto imaginary beds. She gives them time to dramatize the story, and notices how the musical sounds they create with their voices influences their dramatic play. Before lunch, the children have danced their way through the singing games they know, "London Bridge Is Falling Down," "Bambu," and "Sorida." As children prepare for departure, Ms. Smith settles them down for a few minutes of quiet listening to a Javanese gamelan piece (from *Yogyakarta: Gamelan of the Kraton*, Celestial Harmonies recordings), and notices that nearly half the children are tapping rhythms they hear on the floor. In a single morning, Ms. Smith and her children have experienced music and movement in an array of ways. Ms. Smith has harnessed the natural inclination of her young students to focus and engage kinesthetically.

VIGNETTE TWO

Over seven years of teaching, Mrs. Lehman has learned that she can use a variety of music to gather her children together and create communal experiences that break from their individualized assignments. Her mobile device is full of music she uses in her own workouts—from salsa numbers by Eddie Palmieri to Israeli hora dances, tunes by Ofra Haza, and Pat Metheny's progressive jazz pieces–and when she cranks up the music in class, her children respond immediately. Several times each week, her class moves to music, often for just five or ten minutes, when she leads the children in a simple four-step pattern or an arm exercise of up, down, right, left maneuvering. She allows the children to lead their classmates in invented four-beat movements as well. Following their brief musical workouts, the children return to their work energized and focused. Mrs. Lehman has channeled her own interest in the physicality of music to stimulate her children to loosen up, get physical, and then attune themselves to the classwork ahead.

VIGNETTE THREE

On recess duty one October afternoon, Ms. Soto saw her fourth grade students in a brand new light. There they were, most of her crew, dancing their hearts out. One girl had set up an iPod and speakers, and her classmates were arranged in several lines on the blacktop, stepping forward and back, twitching their shoulders and wiggling their hips, swaying side to side. Their routine was impeccable, and all the girls (and more than a few boys) were precisely in step and in time with each other. Ms. Soto has since set aside a half hour on Friday afternoons for children to practice and develop their dance routines. A few of the boys still prefer not to dance, but she has supplied them with percussion instruments to play along with the dance music. The children are planning to sign up the whole class for the school's annual talent show. In thirty minutes per week, Ms. Soto's fourth graders are collectively creating a movement piece, dancing in attention to time, patterns, and form, and enjoying a healthy social-emotional outlet with their peers.

VIGNETTE FOUR

In a language arts unit on Emily Dickinson's poetry, Mr. Andrews wants his sixth-grade students to memorize *A Bird Came Down,* so he teaches them to recite the poem together as choral speech (this technique and others from Orff Schulwerk for mixing movement into speech and song may be found in Appendix 2). When some students have trouble memorizing, he adds movement and gesture to the learning process. When the children say, "A bird came down the walk— / He did not know I saw—," they move together in small, soft, gentle steps. After they recite the line, "And then hopped sidewise to the Wall / To let a Beetle pass—," they maneuver left or right in delicate hopping steps. As the children emphasize important words and phrases, they internalize the words' meanings through these movements. Through rhythmic speech and associated gestures, the children perform the poems, and Mr. Andrews records a video that he posts on a private YouTube channel for parents as a report of their progress in language arts. Even though his sixth graders are moving into the awkward age of low movement activity, when they are highly conscious of and sometimes embarrassed by their physical selves, Mr. Andrews wisely recognizes that uniform group movement can not only teach but also cement information, all while offering an outlet for creative expression.

CHILDREN, RHYTHM, AND MOVEMENT

For children, music and movement are inseparable: one begets the other. Music naturally triggers their bodies to respond kinesthetically, and they move their heads, shoulders, arms, hands, fingers, legs, feet, toes, and torsos to musical rhythms. Children may tap out internal music (a tune or groove they hear inside themselves), and may spontaneously begin singing or chanting. They move to music at an early age, joyfully, wistfully, in ways both gentle and hearty, dreamily and with astonishing vigor. One child may happily pat a pulse into his lap, while another child responds to the very same music by whirling and twirling, or hopping and jumping to the rhythm they hear. As children relate and respond to music spontaneously through movement, they come to understand music's rhythm, form, and meaning by performing the patterns of an associated dance: a jig, a hora, a cumbia, a square dance, or the latest hip-hop or techno groove. The ear–body–brain connection is a critical one, and children's movement connects what they hear to what they can process and understand.

Children dance, move, and groove to the music they experience. Most successful teachers recognize that the Cartesian dualism of mind and body is unnatural, because minds and bodies are intimately related. Children's minds receive signals from their bodily movements just as surely as their bodies respond to the ideas of their minds, and thus their brains learn better when their bodies are engaged. These teachers know that their children enjoy physical play, outdoor sports, and a wide spectrum of activity that requires their bodies to move, and thus they incorporate children's physical activities and kinesthetic means of learning by doing into the school day. They insert creative movement and clapping, patting, snapping, and stamping into the lessons they teach across a variety of subjects. They insert music and movement into the school day to alleviate routine and stress, stimulate thought, and encourage their students' social bonding and community building.

In addition to the more standard visual and aural means of learning, rhythmic movement involves children in holistic experiences and balances their sensory and intellectual selves. Teachers need not be expert dancers to model kinesthetic ways of learning. Just as teachers nod their heads in time to

Children move instinctively to any music they hear.

tunes on the car radio, exercise to music, or dance informally at home, at clubs, or at parties, they can lead kinesthetic activities in their classrooms. The movement and dance that they offer to children is not just energizing or amusing; they ensure that deep learning happens through the integration of body and mind.

RHYTHMIC MOVEMENT IN DEVELOPMENT

From an early age, children sense and show rhythm in their movements. Infants wiggle, rock, thrust, bounce, and kick, and toddlers from two years old expand this kinesthetic activity by imitating dancers, conductors, athletes, and family members at work or play. Most children enter kindergarten impressively coordinated to run, hop, jump, and gallop, and by the close of that first year, they can even skip and jump rope. From then on, children develop the fine motor skills to write, draw, paint, color, and engage in all sorts of complex intricate activities.

Children enjoy physical activity throughout their elementary school years and participate enthusiastically in singing games, action songs, and simple folk dances. Many children as young as five are motivated to move by the pulse of a drum, woodblock, guitar, or piano. Most first graders demonstrate beat competence, or the ability to match an external beat with some motion of the body. By six or seven years of age, most children respond physically to music's shorter and longer rhythms, faster and slower tempos, and different aesthetic qualities. They can conduct the 1-2-3-4 metric pulse of marchlike music or the 1-2-3 meter of a waltz or minuet. They can imitate short rhythms on drums, rhythm sticks, cowbells, tone bells, and xylophones. Most third graders have achieved the small-muscle coordination required for recorder playing, and by fourth grade, children develop the motor control and coordination essential for playing instruments of the band and orchestra. As students move through elementary school, their kinesthetic sense lights their way to finely-tuned musical performances as singers, players, and dancers. Classroom teachers can further illuminate this path with live or recorded music.

EXPLORING MOVEMENT

Moving to music in ways that reflect sonic qualities (rhythm, pitch, and dynamics) and their arrangements in repeating or contrasting sections is a panhuman ability as widespread as talking and walking.[2] Dancing is thought and feeling converted into organized, meaningfully expressive physical movement. Many teachers have discovered movement's power to enhance children's learning through workshops in dance, Dancercise, Zumba, step, and a variety of other dance exercises, and in the pedagogical practices of Orff Schulwerk and Dalcroze Eurhythmics. For others, simply turning the music on is

Deep learning happens when bodies move as minds focus.

a trigger to head-bobbing, toe-tapping, finger-snapping, and a few shuffle steps across the floor.

Box 6.1 asks teachers to recall some of their childhood movements to music. By trying the movements and analyzing when and how each part of the body moves, teachers can better understand how important and meaningful movement is for their students. Teaching requires physical stamina and energy, and when teachers reflect on their own capacity to move and to dance, they learn how to incorporate movement into daily classroom activity.

BOX 6.1 MOVEMENT, THEN AND NOW

1. Recall the singing games and action songs of your childhood. List them, and compare them to the action songs on this book's companion website, such as "Bounce High, Bounce Low," "La raspa" and "I Went to California." What sorts of movements are expected in these playful musical expressions? Try them out with friends and colleagues, children, and family members, and reflect on the difficulty or ease with which the movements fit the music.

2. Think of the dancing you did as a child, whether at dance lessons or at family gatherings, parties, weddings, and school settings. Do you remember the steps, hand and arm gestures, and body positions? What sorts of steps and gestures can you still do? Choose a remembered movement to share with a small group of colleagues, and join together everyone's movements into a connected set of gestures (with or without music).

3. Play a favorite recording of music from your childhood. Listen for a slow pulse, and clap it, tap it, and walk to it, then double the speed of that initial pulse, and clap, tap, and walk it. Return to the slower pulse. Change directions while walking, move your arms up and down, forward and back. Lower your body, bending your knees as you walk, then rise up very high, stretching your arms to the ceiling. These movements to music will loosen up your body and generate further ideas for movement.

4. Video the movements of children at play, in sport, or while playing schoolyard games. Reflect on the movements exhibited, and note the regular rhythms of certain swings of the arms, turns of the head, and steps of the feet. Try out the movements, and consider how they match the movement repertoire that you already have. Could these movements be brought into a classroom activity in some way? How?

MOVING TO MEET MUSIC STANDARDS

1. Singing. Children gesture and move to action songs, singing games, and folk dances, which helps focus attention on the words and create enthusiasm for joyful, strong singing.

2. Playing. Partial- and full-body movements are required to play instruments. Dalcroze Eurhythmics recommends preparing students with movement that approximates playing instruments.

3. Improvising. Children can improvise movements, fitting their actions to the music's characteristics.

4. Composing and arranging. Making up movement routines to music creates meaningful musical expression, whether through ballet or on *Dancing with the Stars*.

5. Reading and notating. Dance masters have developed viable notational systems for dance movement, and children can use dance notation to learn new dances and write down their own dance steps and routines.

6. Listening. Movement strengthens listening skills, as children must listen carefully to music's many

qualities of rhythm, melody, form, dynamics, articulation, and tempo, and match each with appropriate movement.

7. Evaluating. Children can easily see their own movements (especially on video) and others' movements, and can develop and apply criteria to evaluate movement performance, both for precision of execution and for musical affect.

8. Connecting to other arts and curricular areas. Movement can dramatize stories and poems, reinforce math concepts in numerous ways, and goes hand in hand with physical education, particularly gymnastics and aerobics.

9. Connecting to culture and history. Movement and dance exist throughout history and across cultures. Discover as a class or through individual research the qualities and styles of dance in various historic periods, such as the Middle Ages or the American Revolution, and in cultures such those of as China, France, Mexico, the Ewe (Ghana), and the Zulu (South Africa).

SAFE MOVEMENT ACTIVITIES

Most music movement activities, such as tapping, clapping, conducting, stretching and bending movements, and actions for songs, do not require large spaces and can be done sitting or standing at a desk. For movements that require more space, some preparations are necessary for safety. At a minimum, move classroom furniture to the sides of the room to create enough space for the children to move without bumping into anything. Better yet, use another location in the school: the gym, cafeteria, or stage. Teachers may need to establish boundaries in a large space where children could spread out too much and lose focus on the music (resulting in minimal learning, if not chaos!). Folk dance and creative movements can also take place outdoors, on a playground or field. Outdoor music equipment must be stronger than indoor, as there will be no reverberation from walls and ceiling; the teacher may need to use a drum if recordings cannot be heard at an adequate volume.

Obstacles are out of the way in a movement-safe classroom.

Teachers should set expectations for children's attention and compliance before starting the movement. Children can become so enamored with skipping, galloping, jogging, and jumping that they forget to focus on the music. Movement may feel social to them and motivate them to chat, laugh, and play. Teachers lay the basic groundwork for respecting others ("move without touching anyone") and remind children to connect the music to their movements ("listen to specific parts of the music to guide your movements").

COMPONENTS OF RHYTHM IN MOVEMENT

Like movement, rhythm is a constant presence in human life, and children's activities are replete with rhythm's regular recurring pulses. Their *rhythmicking* qualities (engagement in some manner of rhythmic behavior in movement or vocalization) are part of their very identities as children.[3] They develop rhythmic facility because rhythm is embedded in movement in language, and they learn through chanting, singing, listening, and playing music to discern pulse (beat), meter (cycles of accented and unaccented beats), tempo (faster or slower speeds in music), and rhythm (durational patterns of longer and shorter sounds).

In music classes throughout elementary school, children learn about timing, mostly through movement. They identify and perform rhythms and meters in different tempos, from simple beats to sophisticated syncopations and layered rhythms (called *polyrhythms*), which they then apply to other subjects. Teachers can draw on children's rhythmic skills by having them clap, tap, or step in place to reinforce timing, flow, and emphasis of spelling words, a sentence, a couplet, or a poem.

MOVING RHYTHMICALLY IN EARLY AND MIDDLE CHILDHOOD

Children in early childhood settings, kindergarten, and first grade move regularly, spontaneously and joyfully to music. Box 6.2 offers suggestions for movement in the early years, some of which emerges naturally but also arises from carefully crafted lessons.

Children in middle childhood continue to enjoy simple rhythmic activities such as keeping the beat and moving appropriately to the qualities of the music they hear, but they can also perform more complicated and subtle rhythmic movements. As coordination improves leading up to adolescence, children are able to move in increasingly complex patterns, combining a variety of large- and small-muscle movements into a pattern and changing patterns at the beginnings of music phrases. Not only can these children match the beat, they are also sensitive to meter groupings and aware of how many beats group into a phrase. They can continue one pattern in their muscles while their brains think ahead to select movements for the next pattern. This is a fun way for the brain to strengthen the same processes used for number sense, grouping, sequencing, and predicting. Movement prepares the brain to connect abstract math concepts with concrete muscle memory (see Chapter 12). Children in third through sixth grade enjoy the challenges of moving rhythmically through experiences such as those suggested in Box 6.3.

BOX 6.2 EARLY CHILDHOOD MOVEMENT

In silence or while listening to music, children imitate the teacher moving various body parts, in a variety of directions and levels. In miming, they learn by observing possibilities for movements forward, backward, sideways, up, and down, and towards particular parts of the room (such as the door or windows).

- Invite children to walk to a pulse played on a drum, rhythm sticks, piano, xylophone, or other instrument. Make variations:
  - Change the steady beat to a lopsided rhythm of long-short and expect their walking steps to turn into galloping or skipping.
  - Change speed faster and slower and expect them to match the tempo with their movement.
  - Change the dynamic levels and expect them to tiptoe on soft sounds and to stamp with loud sounds.
  - Stop playing occasionally and expect them to freeze.
- Invite children to help their favorite stuffed animal, action figure, or doll dance to the music selections they hear. Remind them that they will need to listen to the music very carefully to help their toys dance in ways that match the musical qualities.
- Distribute colorful scarves, flags, or strips of cloth for children to move in the character of the music.
- Ask children to pat, clap, or tap every other pulse to emphasize odd numbers (on one, and three) or even numbers (on two and four).
- Build movement into a story. As you tell or read the story aloud to the class, stop to dance or perform a rhythmic movement, or to enact a situation in ways that incorporate movement.

RHYTHMIC MOVEMENT IN SPEECH AND SONG

Children respond enthusiastically when their spoken words are accompanied by body percussion or instruments, and when they sing songs that include rhythmic movement. Excellent teachers know that rhythm and rhythmic movement are very effective techniques for reviewing, reinforcing, practicing, and retaining skills and concepts in language arts, math, science, and the social sciences.

RHYTHM IN SPEECH

In every language, words and phrases are spoken in conventional patterns of longer and shorter sounds, with particular phonemes and syllables stressed to create rhythm and meter. Phonemic awareness and syllabification are key concepts in language arts, and teachers can use rhythm and instruments to make children aware of these speech components. Music teachers often employ Orff Schulwerk techniques (see Appendix 2), in which speech rhythm informs

---

BOX 6.3 MIDDLE CHILDHOOD MOVEMENT

- While listening to a variety of music, use hand movements or stepping to show:

  - Tempo: fast, faster, slow, slower, speeding up, slowing down;

  - Space: forward, backward, sideways, diagonal, high, low, medium;

  - Energy: heavy, light, strong, limp, flowing, erratic, etc.

These movements can be done by each child independently, or as a group following a leader.

- Lead children in hand gestures to a variety of recorded music (start with double movements, such as pat-pat, clap-clap, snap right-snap right, snap left-snap left). As they become accustomed to the hand gestures, add different movements in a longer sequence (pat different body parts, jerk thumbs over shoulders, shrug shoulders, step right, step left, etc.). Later, divide the class into groups of 4 or 5 students, play recorded music, and let each group invent their own hand jive and then take turns leading the class.

- Ask children to each invent and show a duple (two-beat) movement pattern, such as 1) touch head, 2) touch shoulders. Select two student leaders to stand in front and lead the class in their movement patterns. Play march music in duple meter. One student leads the class during the first phrase, the other leads during the next phrase. They alternate leadership for several phrases, and then choose classmates to take their places. Repeat the activity above, but in triple (three-beat) meter with three movements (such as pat-clap-snap) while listening to European waltzes and minuets, Mexican sones or corridos, and selected triple-meter folk songs of Korea, Sweden,

and Latin American cultures in Argentina, Chile, and Bolivia. Repeat with four movements and move to quadruple (four-beat) meter dance music (such as samba, hip-hop, reggae, rock, pop, and country music).

- Children enjoy clapping patterns with a partner. Start with simple patterns, such as 1) pat lap, 2) clap own hands, 3) clap right hands, 4) clap own hands, 5) pat lap, 6) clap own hands, 7) clap left hands, 8) clap own hands. Children can do these patterns while singing a song or moving to recorded music in quadruple meter.

- Designate a different movement for each of several instrumental sounds, such as stepping to a drum sound, clapping to a xylophone sound, and hopping on one foot to a woodblock sound. Play repeated beats on one instrument, then change the instrument at any point. When children can change movements quickly and to match the different sounds, play recorded music while also tapping the beat on different instruments. This experience builds listening and direction-following skills.

- Encourage students to research dances of historic periods and cultures, such as European Renaissance dances, nineteenth-century Russian ballet, Cambodian court dance, Māori haka, Indian Bharata Natyam, Mexican folkloric dance, Japanese Bon Odori dance, Greek folk dances like the Tsamikos and Syrtos, and American popular dances such as tap, the Lindy hop, the twist, and hip-hop. Ask them to find performances of these dances online, and then to describe the dance with words, demonstrate the movements, and report on who dances the selected dance form, where and under what circumstances it is danced, and how the dance movement reflects the values of people in a particular time and place.

children's musical education and development (along with song, movement, and performance on pitched and unpitched instruments such as xylophones, drums, wood blocks, and shakers). Teachers across all grade levels and subjects are employing the Orff approach when they rhythmically chant words, phrases, sentences, paragraphs, and poems with their children, and when they lead them in a repertoire of body percussion such as clapping, patting their laps, tapping, snapping, and stamping (Box 6.4 offers exemplar strategies for combining speech and rhythmic movement).

SONGS THAT MOVE

When children sing, they feel the music and they move, often without any suggestion by parents, teachers, or other children. Many songs invite them to make particular actions, play movement games, or dance along to the rhythm and phrasing

---

BOX 6.4 INTEGRATING RHYTHMIC MOVEMENT INTO SPEECH

1. Name chants

   - Have children stand in a circle.
   - All children chant each child's name four times.
   - Start the children patting a steady beat and go around the circle again, chanting each child's name four times to the steady beat (all names are spoken in one beat, so those with more syllables need to be spoken faster).
   - In the third round, have children pat their laps on the strong syllable(s) of each name and clap on weaker syllables (this may take time and practice, especially on names with several syllables).

   Examples of children's names broken into syllables:

Kate				**Kate**				**Kate**				**Kate**			
Jack-	son			**Jack-**	son			**Jack-**	son			**Jack-**	son		
An-	tho-	ny		**An-**	tho-	ny		**An-**	tho-	ny		**An-**	tho-	ny	
An-	a-	**sta-**	sia	**An-**	a-	**sta-**	sia	**An-**	a-	**sta-**	sia	**An-**	a-	**sta-**	sia

   - Emphasize syllabification (and check for understanding) by asking children to group by the number of syllables in their names.
   - Play a steady beat on a drum and have all the children with one-syllable names chant their names and show the accent pattern with pats.
   - Do the same for other groups, showing the accent patterns with pats and claps.
   - Finally, combine all chanting, patting, and clapping at once.
   - Apply the same learning sequence to colors, animals, food, proverbs, rhymes, poems, or geographical names.

2. Rhyme chants

   - Chant this rhyme, speaking louder on the boldfaced words to accent them; think rather than chant "(rest)."

   One two **three** four **five** (rest) (rest) I **caught** a **fish** a- live (rest) (rest) (rest)

   Six seven **eight** nine **ten** (rest) (rest) I **let** it **go** a- gain. (rest) (rest) (rest)

of the song. Action songs (Box 6.5) have rhythmic gestures that reinforce the meaning of the text. Singing games (also Box 6.5) include counting songs, hand-clapping songs, and circle games in the round in which children may pass an object around the circle, interact with a leading child in the center of the circle, or chase a teasing child outside the circle.

MOVEMENT IN MANAGEABLE DANCE EXPERIENCES

Folk and popular dance is physically, socially, and musically rewarding to children. Dance is an excellent outlet for lively children who are drawn to movement for both learning and venting their emotions and pent-up energy. It provides children with kinesthetic activity, and it invigorates their thinking processes with more oxygen for the brain and better circulation of blood through the muscles. Folk and popular dance teach children basic concepts of rhythm and form, auditory discrimination, repetition, sequencing, patterning, and counting. Performed in lines or circles, with or without partners, dancing teaches awareness of personal space and others' space; when bodies are shoulder to shoulder or hand in hand, dancers need to be highly aware of their own personal space and that of

Circle songs allow children to invent movements and take turns being the leader.

BOX 6.5   ACTION SONGS AND SINGING GAMES

Action Songs

"Teddy Bear, Teddy Bear" (preschool–kindergarten): Act out the words of the song text.

"Little Cabin in the Wood" (preschool–second grade): Act out the words of the song text.

"Johnny Works with One Hammer" (preschool–second grade): Verse 1, pound one fist on knee. Verse 2, pound two fists on knees. Verse 3, pound two fists and one foot. Verse 4, pound two fist and two feet. Verse 5, pound two fists, two feet, and nod head. On "then he goes to sleep," rest head on hands.

Singing Games

"Punchinella" (first–fourth grades): Children form a circle, facing in, joining hands, with one child in the center. Children circle right for verse 1, stop and imitate the center child's action for verse 2, then circle right again as the center child spins and chooses a new child as a replacement.

"Sansa kroma" (first–fourth grades): Children form a circle, each holding a block (or pebble or stick) in their right hands. They say in rhythm, "Tap, tap, pass, take," and then practice the four-beat movement with gestures:

1	2	3	4
Tap floor.	Tap chest.	Pass object to right.	Take object from left.

For practice, instead of releasing the block, simply pretend to pass and take without moving it from hand to hand. Once the movement is perfected, release the object to the person on the right on count three, and take the object from the person on the left on count four.

Many dances employ the circle formation.

other dancers next to them or across from them. Children learn a great deal from well-managed dance experiences: their brains must coordinate auditory input and muscular direction within a stylized social context.

Songs that dance (Box 6.6) refer to regular and purposeful movements that reflect the rhythm and form of a song. Not just young children, but also children in the upper elementary grades are energized and engaged by carefully selected songs that move. Classroom teachers can use these songs to build community among their students and reinforcing concepts taught in many subject areas. Music specialist teachers in elementary schools will have suggestions for recordings and for integrating these songs with movement.

BOX 6.6 SONGS THAT DANCE

With each of these songs, follow the learning sequence, beginning with just listening to the song without doing any movements, then adding movement words, then repeating the words while doing the movements, and finally thinking the words while doing the movements.

"Skip to My Lou" (kindergarten–third grade). Children form a circle, joining hands in a relaxed manner. The movement proceeds in four phrases:

Phrase 1: *Circle right, step, step* (4 beats)

Phrase 2: *Circle left, step, step* (4 beats)

Phrase 3: *"Where is my partner?"* (4 beats)

Break formation, search for lost partner

Phrase 4: *"There is my partner"* (4 beats)

Find a new partner and lock right elbows

Chorus: *Partners skip clockwise with right elbows hooked* (16 beats)

"Hava nashira" (fourth–sixth grades). Children form a circle, joining hands with arms relaxed and swinging gently at the side. Beginning with weight on the left foot, they move in a grapevine step to the right, in this sequence:

1. *Right foot **side** step to the right*
2. *Left foot **cross** over front of right foot*
3. *Right foot **side** step to the right*
4. *Left foot cross **behind** right foot*
5. *Right foot **side** step to the right*
6. *Left foot cross over right foot and **touch** toe*
7. *Left foot **side** step to the left*
8. *Right foot cross over left foot and **touch** toe*

(When teaching, say all the words; when dancing, say only the boldface words.)

"Gonna Sing When the Spirit Says Sing" (fifth–sixth grades). Children stand in two or three lines, facing front and spaced apart for foot movement. Starting with weight on the left foot, they step-touch right and left, clapping on beats two and four:

1. *Right foot side step to right*
2. *Left foot touch left toe near right foot, clap hands*
3. *Left foot side step to the left*
4. *Right foot touch right toe near left foot, clap hands*

"Ala De'lona" (fourth–sixth grades). Children form a circle and lightly link pinky fingers, with hands at chest level and elbows down in a "W" hold. The teacher stands inside the circle to demonstrate the foot movements without the arm movements. Starting with the weight on the left foot, chant the words rhythmically, moving in a grapevine step to the right. On beats 6 and 8, lift the foot in the air:

1. *Right foot **side** step to the right*
2. *Left foot **cross** over front of right foot*
3. *Right foot **side** step to the right*
4. *Left foot cross **behind** right foot*
5. *Right foot **side** step to the right*
6. *Left foot cross over right foot and **lift** left foot*
7. *Left foot **side** step to the left*
8. *Right foot cross over left foot and **lift** right foot*

(When teaching, say all the words; when dancing, say only the boldface words.)

BOX 6.6 SONGS THAT DANCE (*continued*)

Following this teacher demonstration, repeat the process with children chanting the movement words, then performing the movements in rhythm while saying only the boldface words, and finally thinking the words in rhythm while doing the movements. Once everyone can perform the work automatically, the teacher can demonstrates the arm movements without (and then with) the foot movements, following the same process as above. (Note that this dance can also be performed with hands held, arms down, without the more sophisticated arm movements.)

1. *Sway arms to the **right***

2. *Sway arms to the **left***

3. *Swing arms **down** below belt and bow*

4. *Swing arms **up** to chest level*

5. *Sway arms to the **right***

6. *Sway arms to the **left***

7. *Swing arms **down** below belt and bow*

8. *Swing arms **up** to chest level*

When the children are comfortable doing the arm movements, combine foot and arm movements as follows:

1. *Right foot **side** step to the right; sway arms to the **right***

2. *Left foot cross over front of right foot; sway arms to the **left***

3. *Right foot side step to the right; swing arms **down** below belt and bow*

4. *Left foot cross **behind** right foot; swing arms **up** to chest level*

5. *Right foot **side** step to the right; sway arms to the **right***

6. *Left foot cross over right foot and **lift** right foot; sway arms to the **left***

7. *Left foot **side** step to the left; swing arms **down** below belt and bow*

8. *Right foot cross over left foot and **lift** left foot; swing arms **up** to chest level*

FOLK AND OTHER PATTERN DANCES

Dances are best taught and learned beginning with listening and then moving through a sequential process:

1. **Listen** to the music to get the feeling of the pulse, rhythms, character, and style, and to learn the music's sequence of phrases;

2. **Say** each movement of the dance in simple language, chanting rhythmically such dance language as step-slide, step-point, back-slide, front-point;

3. **Repeat saying** the dance movements **while doing** the movements;

4. **Think** the words **while doing** the movements, without and then with the music.

This sequence helps children process the directions, focusing on language first and then tying language to movement. This forms important synapses among different parts of the brain, and thus strengthens memory. Three folk dances are particularly well-suited to this sequential learning process: the hora, the square dance, and the jig.

The hora is a circle dance from the Balkan countries of southeastern Europe, including Romania, Bulgaria, and Macedonia, and is popular as well in Israeli and Jewish communities; while its name may vary across languages, the dance steps are the same. Its movements comprise a grapevine step, in which the feet weave in front of and behind one another, and then step-lift, step-lift, once for each foot.

The jig is associated with Ireland, but it originated in France (gigue) and Italy (giga). With the sound of a 6/8 melody comes the stepping of the jig, in which the weight of one hopping foot is counterbalanced by the alternate foot's thrust or point. While the rapid count of six beats races by, the emphasis is felt on 1 and 4 in a kind of duple meter, each beat divided into three parts.

The square dance is a folk dance for four couples that dates to early Anglo-American communities and is related to the country dances of England and France. The four couples are arranged in a square, with one couple on each of the four sides. They dance forward to the middle of the square and back again, sometimes together, sometimes just boys or just girls. They may move around the couple on the opposite side, or join hands in the middle and rotate around the square, or bow, shake hands, or move around the person in the corner next to them. Many examples of the hora, jigs, and square dances can be found on the Internet, including music and illustrations of the various maneuvers.

POPULAR DANCES

Children enjoy moving to a variety of popular pattern dances, including salsa, cha-cha, and country line dance. The music for these dances is often irresistible, and while children may have their own ideas for how to move, they can learn the standard footwork and body positions for these standard dances.

Salsa is a popular Latin-American dance form, originating in Cuba at the confluence of Spanish and African cultures, that has been embraced throughout the world for its rhythmic energy. The groove for this dance comes from the layered rhythms of several instruments including claves, congas, timbales, piano, bass, maracas, guiro, and cowbell. The basic salsa step involves six steps in eight beats: moving forward on two steps and rocking, followed by moving backward two steps and rocking. Much of the body remains still during the stepping, but the hips and arms are always in motion. Salsa can be done with a partner, in lines, or alone.

Another Cuban-origin dance is the cha-cha, which has the following foot pattern: slow step, slow step, fast stamp, fast stamp, fast stamp. Typically danced by partners, it can also be danced in lines. The torso is fairly still except for the hips, which move in every beat.

Country line dancing takes place in a line, with all dancers facing the same direction and engaged in a sequence of choreographed steps. This phenomenon of slides, steps, stamps, and boot-scoots was brought to international attention in the early 1990s and since then the dance has been performed to a great variety of country music tunes. Many examples of this style of line dancing (and of salsa and the cha-cha) are available online.

SINGING SONGS, SIGNING SONGS

Music, language, and movement connect when children use American Sign Language (ASL) while singing the words of a song. ASL bonds students together in mutual activity and demonstrates solidarity in performance for an audience. Every child's attention is riveted, even those with learning disabilities, mild autism, and hearing problems. Signing and signing is more personal and intense than choral singing alone. All children know their actions are individually accountable and clearly on public display—there is no place to hide—and all want to demonstrate their competence in mastering the movements. In our digital age, ASL is easier to learn than ever (consult Signing Savvy, Masters Tech Home, and others). Websites

ADAPTING INSTRUCTION FOR VARIOUS NEEDS

Blind or Visual Impairments

In moving to the music, gently shape the body to the expected movement—the arms, wrists, hands, head, torso, and legs. Give every movement shape a name, so that the muscles will remember how to find their way to Move A, Move B, Window, O-shape, Elbow swing, etc.

Deaf or Hearing Impairments

Residual hearing can be enhanced when movement and dance is in response to live piano on wood floors, music especially rich in bass tones, or amplified music. Musically expressive movement among the hearing-impaired is also aided by counting steps or beats visually with the fingers and by communicating through signs. Vibrations can be felt through some floor surfaces, especially when children take off their shoes.

Behavioral Disorders with Externalizing Behaviors

Help children gain better control of their bodies by having them restate the safety rules for movement and giving them extra practice stopping, starting, and staying with the music. Sometimes assigning a buddy for them to stay close to and follow helps.

Behavioral Disorders with Internalizing Behaviors

For the withdrawn child, partnering and grouping with trusted friends, along with regular encouragement at various stages of progress, will assist full movement engagement.

Mobility Impairments

Modified movement is possible for children in wheelchairs and on crutches. Aides, teachers, parents, and other children can be helpful in engaging children and working through physically integrated movement exercises to strengthen their bodies and develop their coordination. Movement practice sessions can be scheduled outside class time.

Autism Spectrum Disorders

In one-on-one sessions, or with face-frontal direct attention to the children, explore small and large movement that links directly to the tempi, pulse, rhythms, dynamics, articulations, and phrasing of music played on drum, piano, or recordings.

show videos of the sign actions and explain the rationale for the movements, adding insight into the meanings of many words.

Songs best for signing have repetitive patterns of simple words and a moderately slow tempo. It is not necessary to sign every word of the lyrics, nor does the choir need to sign the entire song—sometimes a neutral step-clap pattern is fine on the verse, while signing is more natural for the refrain. "We Shall Overcome," "Taps," and "Keep Your Hand on That Plow" (also known as "Hold On" and "Keep Your Eyes on the Prize") all lend themselves to signing.

Summary

To dance is human,[4] and movement proves that music is alive and well in children's experience. Their growing bodies need to move, and they enjoy moving in all kinds of ways, stretching and exercising their muscles and moving in time together with others. Children cannot always keep still; the body supports the brain, and if the body is not happy, children cannot function at full intellectual and emotional capacity. The more teachers can do to incorporate movement into all their lessons, the better for children's learning, growth, and social-emotional well-being. Movement in rhythmic ways advances all children's knowledge, skills, and sensitivities, and it is crucial for children whose preferred learning mode is kinesthetic. For all learners, teachers included, movement to music brings smiles and happiness.

Review

1. Discuss the benefits of rhythmic movement and physical play for children in school.

2. Enumerate a set of safety rules for movement in the classroom.

3. How are action songs different from singing games and songs that dance?

Critical Thinking

1. Read aloud a poem or excerpt from a book. Listen carefully as you read, and try to feel and tap the beat, both the louder (accented) and softer (unaccented) beats. How easy or hard is it to feel the rhythm of the speech?

2. Explain how movement experiences differ for younger and older children.

3. Consider the different styles of movement found in various folk and popular dances. Where is the core area of movement in dances such as the hora, the jig, salsa, and the cha-cha? How might culture determine movement style?

Projects

1. Alone or with a colleague, engage in several of the movement-related activities suggested in this chapter. Keep a journal of your thoughts and feelings about these experiences, and draw from it for discussion with colleagues.

2. Enroll in a local workshop in dance, be it folk dance, country line dance, creative or modern dance, salsa, or another genre. Learn basic steps and positions, and practice them at home with recorded music. Then, teach the routine or techniques to a friend and write a short reflection on how this dance might fit into the classroom and how similarly (or differently) you would teach it to children.

3. Explore the possibilities of movement in Orff Schulwerk and Dalcroze Eurhythmics. Talk to experts in these methods, enroll in a class, search the Internet for video examples, and read about these methods in their professional periodicals (American Orff Schulwerk Association and Dalcroze Society of America). From experience and searching, describe to the class those teaching ideas that you will implement in your classroom.

Additional Resources for Teaching

Abramson, Robert M. (1998). *Feel It! Rhythm Games for All*. Miami, FL: Warner Bros. Publications.

Frazee, Jane, and Kent Kreuter. (1997). *Discovering Orff: A Curriculum for Music Teachers*. London, UK: Schott.

Goodkin, Doug. (2002). *Play, Sing & Dance: An Introduction to Orff Schulwerk*. London, UK: Schott.

Longden, Sanna, and Phyllis Weikart. (1998). *Cultures and Styling in Folk Dance*. Ypsilanti, MI: High Scope Press.

Mead, Virginia Hoge. (1996). *Dalcroze Eurthymics in Today's Music Classroom*. London, UK: Schott.

Schnebly-Black, Julia, and Stephen F. Moore. (2003). *The Rhythm Inside*. Van Nuys, CA: Alfred Publishing.

Additional Songs for Singing

Come, Let's Dance	Jubilee	Ring around the Rosie
Dance Josey	This Old Man	Schottische
Dance the Kolo	London Bridge Is Falling Down	Weevily Wheat
Draw Me a Bucket of Water	The Noble Duke of York	
Guru ndiani	Rig-a-Jig-Jig	

Online Resources: Audio and Songbook

digital.wwnorton.com/classroom

7

THE INSTRUMENTS THEY PLAY

The music you make is shaped by what you play it on.

—Mark Knopfler, Dire Straits

The power of musical instruments is apparent in their appeal to children.

IN THIS CHAPTER

Children and Instruments

In the Classroom

Sound Exploration and Discovery

Sources of Sound and Kinds of Instruments

Occasions for Play

Instruments and the Teacher

Summary

Review

Critical Thinking

Projects

Additional Resources for Teaching

You Will Learn

- a range of sound sources that can serve as instruments for children

- techniques for playing a variety of instruments typically used in the elementary classroom

- the origins of many traditional classroom instruments

- a range of ideas for using and integrating instruments in all elementary subjects

Ask Yourself

- What instruments, if any, did you have in your household growing up, who played them, and how well did they play?

- What instruments did you play as a child at home or in school?

- As a young child, did you ever invent instruments out of non-music objects? If so, what were they and how did you use them?

- Why do you think children are attracted to playing instruments?

- What instruments did you play as a teenager or beyond?

- If you were to learn to play an instrument now, what would it be and why would you like to learn to play it?

- How might you use instruments that you play in your classroom?

CHILDREN AND INSTRUMENTS

There is something magical about children acting upon their world and getting results that excite and please them, as happens with musical instruments. Watch a young child exploring a piano keyboard for the first time, and observe the range of actions, from vigorous pounding to delicately touching one note at a time. See their surprise, curiosity, and satisfaction. Watch children explore their environment for objects to strike, bow, pluck, strum, or blow to make a satisfying sound. Note their concentration and pleasure.

When children play instruments, they physically extend their bodies and create actions that make sounds, and they are fascinated by the sounds themselves. There is a feedback loop from action to sound, back to action, back to sound. In the midst of this doing and listening, children respond physically, emotionally, and cognitively. Playing instruments engages the whole child.

IN THE CLASSROOM

VIGNETTE ONE

Ms. Bernstein's kindergarten has an instrument center with rhythm instruments and small xylophones with mallets. It is one of many centers in her room where children can go to explore and play on their own. Throughout the year, she adds new and more complex instruments to challenge her children's thinking and extend their play. They can listen to recorded music in the center and play along on their instruments. Toward the end of the year, Ms. Bernstein encourages children to create patterns of sounds. She adds colorful blocks to the music center, inviting children to symbolize their patterns with different colored blocks.

VIGNETTE TWO

Mr. Mitsuyu knows that his third-grade students need energy breaks at various points in the day. He began the school year by punctuating the day with opportunities to move, having them echo simple four-beat patterns with clapping, stamping, snapping, and patting, but over time the students have explored other sounds they can make using their bodies as percussion instruments, and Mr. Mitsuyu has extended the echos to eight-beat patterns to challenge their memories. Sometimes they establish an interesting eight-beat pattern that they repeat as an ostinato, over which Mr. Mitsuyu invites different students to improvise with contrasting rhythms and sounds.

VIGNETTE THREE

Mr. Bridges and his fifth graders have been exploring West Africa in social studies. Because West Africa is renowned from its drumming, they decided to work together with some parents to build drums out of large PVC pipes and animal skin. Once the drums were built, Mr. Bridges showed the children pictures of kente cloth from the region and had them design their own similar patterns on large pieces of paper they then used to decorate the drums. After that, Mr. Bridges gave each child a grid of eight spaces across and six spaces down, inviting them to invent patterns of one, two, or three sounds in a row followed by a rest or silence (with only one sound per box). Mr. Bridges modeled this by showing a pattern of one sound and one silence repeated across the eight boxes.

Once the children completed the patterns, they put different patterns on the board and tried performing them using body percussion. Then they divided into groups, and different groups kept different patterns going over and over in layers, like the multiple rhythm patterns in West African drumming. Finally, they performed these patterns on their drums, playing with hands and sticks.

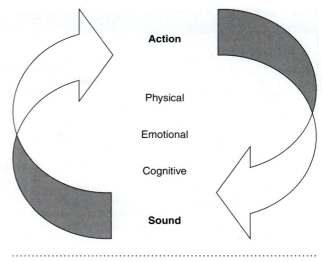

Actions make sound makes actions.

SOUND EXPLORATION AND DISCOVERY

Guided sound play or exploration familiarizes children with instruments and their sound possibilities. This kind of play and discovery is a solid learning strategy for children of all ages. When children become aware of the timbre, or tone color, of various instruments, they begin to build an internal sound vocabulary. This vocabulary will inform their choices of instruments for composition or to accompany a song.

Physically, children temper their hand gestures to create certain sounds and patterns of sound, and change the quality of their gestures to shape the sound. This is the beginning of technical competence, even with the simplest instruments. A teacher might ask:

- Can you play that sound louder? Softer?
- Can you make a short sound? A long sound? A sustained sound?
- Can you play an even pattern? An uneven pattern?
- Can you play a rough sound? A smooth sound?
- Can you play a high sound? A low sound?
- Can you play a short pattern over and over? Backward?

The first thing children will discover during these guided explorations is that they can control the sounds that they make. The second is that what they can or cannot do depends on the instrument that they are using. For example, not all instruments have pitch (high or low sounds), although they may have timbral differences (such that where or how the player makes contact with the instrument affects the sound quality).

Once children have become familiar with individual instruments, they can start to collaborate on a range of instruments based on the qualities of their sounds. These activities can begin in late kindergarten and extend through the elementary school years. Children may group the sounds accordingly:

- Find all of the ringing (metal) sounds.
- Find all of the skin (drum) sounds.

PLAYING INSTRUMENTS TO MEET MUSIC STANDARDS

1. Singing: Encourage children to experiment with various instrumental tone colors as they decide which instruments to use to accompany a particular song or chant. Over time, try different possibilities until they find one that is musically satisfying.

2. Playing: Over time, have children play a variety of pitched and unpitched percussion instruments, learning correct technique for each of them and building a sense of competence in playing. Play by ear and from scores.

3. Improvising: Encourage children to improvise on instruments using question and answer form. Have the drums agree upon a four- or eight-beat pattern they will play as a question, and have the woods improvise an answer with a different rhythm that fits within the four or eight beats.

4. Composing and Arranging: Invite children to compose works on classroom instruments to accompany children's literature, videos, songs, raps, or chants that they have created or learned.

5. Reading and Notating: Have children read their instrument parts from standard notation prior to playing. Help them by using word chants or rhythm syllables to read the notes.

6. Listening: Expand children's aural awareness of various instruments and instrumental groups by playing recorded music of symphonic orchestras, jazz bands, wind ensembles, recorder ensembles, guitars, rock ensembles, etc. Help children identify the various instruments alone and in ensemble.

7. Evaluating: When children are creating instrumental accompaniments, encourage them to critique the accompaniments and to modify them until they are satisfied with the results.

8. Connecting to other arts and curriculum areas: Have children design an instrument, labeling its parts and describing how they think it will sound. Encourage them to give it a creative name. If possible, have them construct the instrument.

9. Connecting to culture and history: When studying another culture, subculture, or particular time or place in history, encourage children to discover instruments of that time and place. Have them determine the instruments' sources and how they relate to travel through those regions, patterns of migration, or materials available in that region.

> ▶ Find all of the wooden sounds.
> ▶ Find all of the rattling sounds.
> ▶ Find all of the scraping sounds.

Note that some instruments may belong in more than one group.

Once the basic sound qualities have been established, invite children to rearrange themselves:

> ▶ Find all of the instruments that play a pitch you can sing.
> ▶ Arrange these instruments from lowest to highest.
> ▶ Arrange the instruments based on how long the sound sustains after the instrument is struck or shaken once.

Once grouped, a child or series of children can act as the conductor, directing which group should play its sounds and for how long. The conductor may indicate that more than one kind of sound will play at a time.

SOURCES OF SOUND AND KINDS OF INSTRUMENTS

Sound sources are not limited to traditional musical instruments: almost any object can produce some kind of vibration and sound. Children enjoy experimenting with the or sound qualities of different objects, from wooden spoons and metal pots to blades of grass and cans full of rocks. Classroom teachers can build on this natural curiosity, starting with the ideas that follow.

FOUND SOUNDS

Found sounds come from objects in the environment that can be manipulated to create sounds and used to make music. One experiment is to give children ten seconds to discover how many different sounds as they can make with a piece of paper. At the end of ten seconds, they can be invited to share their techniques and have their classmates try to recreate the various sounds. Children may describe the sound using onomatopoetic words such as *rip* or *swish*, and may also describe the sound-making technique using verbs (*tearing* or *blowing*). Children can search the classroom for good sources of sound, such as rulers, pencils, tabletops, or grates over heating ducts, and may explore and describe those sounds. Children of all ages enjoy bringing interesting objects from home, such as wood spoons, metal tongs, plastic containers, and other implements from the kitchen or garage that make unusual sounds. Once explored, shared, and discussed, the objects may be used in various improvisations and compositions. Chapter 8 is full of ideas for organizing sounds creatively.

BODY SOUNDS

The body is an astonishing source of sounds. Body percussion is made by clapping, snapping (beginning in second grade), stamping, patting (knees or laps), and rubbing. Give children the opportunity to explore a full range of body sounds, and listen carefully to the variety of timbres they produce. Put body percussion into a sound composition, such as a rainstorm, in which different sections perform finger snapping (*sn*, for raindrops), clapping (*cl*, two sharp claps for lightning), and stamping (*st*, for thunder).

Integrate and enhance language arts skills with music. Read *Listen to the Rain* by Bill Martin and John Archambault to see how the flow of the book matches the flow of this body percussion piece. Read the book expressively, changing dynamic levels. Have children read the book's poetry, changing the dynamic levels. Tell the story page by page, using only body percussion.

Mouth sounds[1] are also body sounds; children enjoy vocalizing colorfully with their mouths. Ask children to think of at least two different sounds they can make with their mouth, and suggest that they use their hand to help make those sounds if they wish.

Ask children to choose their favorite mouth sounds and experiment, share, replicate, and discuss the sounds. Select a conductor, to move his or her arms like the second hand on a clock. During a period of one minute, children will each make a single chosen mouth sound only two times, at whatever time they desire within that minute. Record this improvisation of mouth sounds, listen to it,

(start softly . . . . get louder . . . . and louder . . . . . really loud . . . get softer . . . die away)

sn . . . .

cl _____ **XX** _____ xx _____

st _____ **XXXX** _____ xxxx _____

To perform this rain composition with body sounds, children begin by rubbing their hands together softly (for the wind that precedes a storm), then patting index fingertips together (for a soft rain), then snapping (larger raindrops), then patting their laps (heavy rain), then clapping and stamping for thunder and lightning. As the storm begins to abate, children go back through the motions in reverse order, and the rain dies away.

The body as a percussion instrument

and then discuss the results. What did the children find interesting? What would they change to make it more interesting, if they were to do it again? Try this improvisation another time and note changes in the creative product. Children may want to change the parameters, mixing mouth sounds with body percussion, offering three different sounds, finding their own individual rhythm for one mouth sound, or adding gestures to the sounds.

A variation on this technique can enhance spelling skills: divide the week's spelling words among the children and ask them to say a word and spell it twice in one minute, at whatever speed, rhythm, and volume they choose. Record their spelling improvisation, listen to it, and discuss the results. Once children have had the opportunity to use vocabulary words in a creative way, they will own them and become much less likely to forget them. This exercise can also be used with multiplication tables to build math skills (see additional ideas in Chapter 8).

INVENTED AND CONSTRUCTED INSTRUMENTS

Most schools have enough money for physical education equipment. Fewer have the resources to place instruments in classrooms throughout the school. More often, there are no instruments available in classrooms, so that enterprising teachers must acquire a collection of instruments themselves. Students can help with this effort:

- ▶ Have children invent instruments out of wood, tin cans, pieces of metal, plastic containers or boxes, PVC pipe, bottles, nylon string, and so forth. Children of all ages will find interesting ways to create instruments by combining materials.
- ▶ Often, fifth and sixth graders go to environmental camps for several days to study science and nature. This presents an excellent opportunity for a summer project: to create instruments out of objects they find in nature such as wood, seed pods for rattles, grasses for whistles, tubes for horns, hollow logs for drums, and so on. Experiment with various sounds. Lead them in discussions of some of the earliest instruments and what they were made of.
- ▶ Children of all ages enjoy building instruments, following directions from books or websites. Parents can help create more complex instruments. Use these in your classroom for projects involving accompaniment, improvisation, or composition (see Chapter 8 for ideas on how to construct instruments). Instruments can also be used for studying the science of sound and the mathematics of measurement and tuning (see Chapter 13).

- When studying a culture or subculture, children can explore instruments traditional to that region and construct some of the simpler ones themselves. They can study how the instruments relate to the geography and climate as well as the history of that region, and how people construct instruments out of the materials available to them.

STANDARD CLASSROOM INSTRUMENTS

Most of the instruments described below are available in elementary school music rooms. Teachers can often borrow them from the music specialist for limited use, or they might be purchased through a grant from the PTA or special fundraising projects. Some teachers enjoy collecting instruments as they travel and adding them to their classroom collection.

Cabasa, shekere, maracas, and rattles

Unpitched percussion instruments

Hand percussion instruments are the most familiar and accessible instruments for young children and come in various sizes, shapes, and weights to accommodate the growing child. Smaller versions are best for younger children in preschool, kindergarten, and first grade. From second grade onward, children can generally manage regular-sized instruments. Even though these unpitched percussion instruments are often thought of as children's instruments, they all feature in orchestral and wind ensemble music as well as ensembles around the world. Many are of ancient origin, and all add unique sound colors to music.

Gourds
- Maracas (shakers) were originally made of natural gourds with dried seeds inside. Now many are made of plastic with handles, or simply a small egg shape without a handle that can be held easily by small hands. Mexico and Latin America are home to the maracas.
- Rattles of various constructions appear throughout the world and may have derived from large seed pods such as those from the jacaranda tree.
  - In Nigeria, the shekere is made from a gourd with external netting strung with small cowrie shells or beads; the instrument goes by other names in other parts of West Africa.
  - Among the Shona people of Zimbabwe, the hosho is a woven basket rattle with beads or small stones inside.
  - Rattles made by certain groups in the Andes mountains of South America (especially Bolivia, Ecuador, and Peru) are made of goat hooves.
  - Young children may construct rattles using materials as simple as boxes, envelopes, or small plastic containers to hold beads or seeds. Children learn math concepts, such as volume, by determining the amount of beads that makes the best sound.

Woods
- Rhythm sticks come in pairs; one is smooth and the other is grooved. Sticks can be played by children at any age but are often used by younger

Rhythm sticks, claves, güiro, and sand blocks

children. They can be struck or rubbed, and are well suited to keeping the beat or creating special effects. They can be amplified by placing the end of a grooved stick on a desk and rubbing it with the other stick (the effect is a wonderful sound for a growling bear).

- Claves are thick rosewood sticks about one inch in diameter. The dense wood gives claves a sharp, bright sound that readily cuts through other sounds. Holding the claves properly poses a bit of a physical challenge: cup the fingers of one hand, lightly curling them over to create a kind of tunnel. Balance one clave on top of the fingernails. Hold one end of the other clave lightly with the other hand, and strike it against the suspended clave, allowing it to bounce. The hollow part of the cradling hand is a resonating chamber for the sound. The most familiar Latin American rhythm for the claves is depicted below, where X = *strike*, and blank = *silence*.

1	2	3	4	5	6	7	8
X		X	X		X	X	

- Sand blocks are made of two pieces of wood, about 3" x 5", faced on one side with sand paper. A small handle is attached to the back. Various grades of sandpaper can be used for coarser or gentler sounds. Rubbing sand blocks together makes the sound of a train or other swishing sounds. They help children feel music's pulse and meter.
- Wood blocks (for larger hands) are hollow rectangular pieces of wood that are held lightly in one hand struck with either a wooden or a hard rubber mallet. A tone block works well for smaller hands; it has a handle that can be held more easily by younger children.

Woodblock, bass xylophone, and suspended cymbal

- Temple blocks are large hollow blocks of graduated sizes mounted on a stand. They suggest several different indefinite pitches; the larger the block, the lower the pitch. Like woodblocks, they are struck with a wooden or hard rubber mallet. They originated in East Asia and can be used authentically with songs from China, Taiwan, Japan, Korea, and Vietnam, or to add a beautiful variety of color to various compositions or arrangements from anywhere in the world.
- Slit drums come in various sizes and are hollow boxes of fairly dense wood. Slits on the top create tongues of various sizes, which produce different approximate pitches according to their size. They are usually played with a hard rubber mallet and are modeled on the sub-Saharan slit log drums, but are much smaller and more easily

managed by children. They are useful for repetitive patterns to accompany songs or they can be used for improvisation and composition.

- Güiros, sometimes called "fish" and pronounced "wee-row," are long hollow enclosed tube shapes with a ridged surface. They are played by scraping a small wooden or metal stick over the ridges. Some güiros from Latin America are made of metal, but the typical güiros used in schools are wood. Grasp the instrument with the thumb and middle finger of one hand through the two holes on the bottom, and scrape the ridges with the accompanying stick. This instrument is easier for older children.

Hand or frame drums, and rattle drums

Skins (Drums)

- Hand drums have a round wooden frame and a skin head. One hand holds the frame, and the drum head is struck by either a mallet or by two fingers of the other hand. Younger children hold the drums in their laps to play them, but older children need to hold them vertically by the frame for better tone. Some hand drums have metal tuning pegs that tighten or loosen the surface of the skin, raising or lowering the pitch. Frame drums are often used among the indigenous people of the Americas from the Northwest to northern Canada and Alaska (in humid climates, drum heads can lose their surface tension, requiring the heads to be dried out with a hair dryer or tightened mechanically).
- Bongo drums come in pairs of unequal size, and are held together by a crosspiece. They are from the Caribbean and are played with the fingertips, palms, and thumbs, adding rhythmic elements to the music. They are usually held between the legs and tipped slightly away from the body, so the angle of the head matches the angle of the arms.
- Conga drums are long, upright, wooden barrels with skin heads stretched tightly across the tops. The conga drum produces a wide variety of timbres as the player strikes the center or edge of the head with the palm or heel of the hand (either flat or cupped), the fingertips, or with a stick on the wooden side of the drum. The conga's sounds and playing techniques have been honed in Cuba and other parts of Latin America. Congas come in different sizes and are sometimes played in pairs. Older children can experiment with tapping and slapping the drum heads. Guide them to discover how the sound changes from the center of the

Children with bongos in music class

Chinese gong, Chinese opera gong, suspended cymbal, clash cymbals, and finger cymbals

drum to the edge and according to what part of the hand they use to play the rhythms.

- Djembe drums are found throughout West Africa, including Ghana, Guinea, Mali, and Senegal, and are enjoying a rise in schools as teachers engage children in West African drumming. Djembes come in various sizes, wide at the head and narrow at the bottom. They are played at the center with the hand (either flat or cupped) and at the edge with the fingertips. Commercial models are very colorful and fun for children.
- Rototoms are drums with rotating heads that can be tuned like tympani.

Metals

- Cymbals have a long history in the Middle East, China, and Southeast Asia, and are made of brass or steel. They come in small sizes with handles (easier for small children), and are typically played by striking the cymbals together. They can also be rubbed together or struck with a metal stick.
- Larger cymbals, used in marching bands and sometimes called crash cymbals, can make a variety of sounds, from a subtle "zing" with a brush to quite an intense clash. Too heavy for some children to hold, they can be mounted on stands.
- Finger cymbals are quite small and, depending on their construction, can sound very delicate or quite piercing. They are commonly found in Middle Eastern music, and are often played by dancers. Finger cymbals are paired, and sometimes held together with a string. Elastic loops are usually attached to finger cymbals used in schools. They can be played by gently striking the edge of one with the edge of the other, creating a sustained ringing sound, or they can be clapped together to make a more muffled sound. The loop on one cymbal can go around the middle finger and the loop of the other around the thumb of the same hand. Players bring the cymbals together in short, sharp strikes. This method of playing is difficult for younger children but might be tried by older children.

A child playing a triangle

- Triangles are solid steel bars bent into a triangular shape with one corner left unconnected. They hang suspended on string from one of the connected corners (if a string is not available, use a rubber band or paper clip to suspend the triangle, so it can vibrate freely). Triangles are struck by a metal bar on the side opposite the open corner. They come in various sizes; the larger the size, the lower the pitch. The triangle has a bright sound that sustains for some time, unless touched by a finger. A player can roll the striker in one of the closed corners to create a "come to dinner" effect.

- Tambourines are single-headed frame drums from the Middle East with pairs of metal discs mounted in the frame that produce a jingling sound. The player holds the tambourine in one hand, by the part of the frame without discs, with the thumb on the outside of the frame and the other fingers on the inside. Playing techniques include shaking for a rolling jingle and tapping the head with the other hand to produce a rhythm.
- Jingle bells are small bells affixed to a stick or a wrist or ankle band. They are played by shaking and are usually associated with the winter season (hay rides and reindeer), but they are also used in some Native American pieces, or for a festive effect in other compositions.
- Gongs originated in East Asia and are metal discs with curved edges. The Chinese use flat gongs of various tunings and even have gongs that change pitch when struck, much like the tonal nature of their languages. Knobbed gongs feature in the gamelan orchestra music of Indonesia. Gongs may be struck with soft felt- or cloth-covered mallets, which must bounce off the gong to allow it to ring with a sustained sound, or with a hard wooden mallet (especially in Chinese festival music). In large gongs, the best tone is achieved by getting the gong vibrating (warming it up) with a series of soft, quick strikes before the main strong strike.
- Cowbells, originally worn around the necks of Swiss cows to help their farmers locate them, became popular in the Caribbean music of Cuba, Puerto Rico, and the Dominican Republic, and in many Latin-American styles. They are held by the handle and can be struck either at the mouth of the bell for a lower sound, or high up on the bell for a higher sound. Holding the bell body in the hand damps the sound, producing a tight, short, metallic sound. Care must be taken not to play the cowbell too loudly. A shorter, lighter mallet can help it from becoming too overwhelming.
- The double iron agogô bells is a pair (or sometimes a trio) of bells, one smaller and one larger, popular in West African cultures. They are played with an iron striker or hard wooden mallet, and are timbral and polyrhythmic components of drumming ensembles from Ghana, Nigeria, the Republic of Benin, and the Ivory Coast. Children as young as second grade can begin to experiment with these combinations, and older elementary children will be able to tackle complex rhythms.

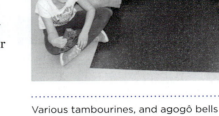

Various tambourines, and agogô bells

Taiko drum

Other unpitched percussion instruments Music specialists or district music supervisors might have other, less common, instruments available for short-term loan to classroom teachers, such as the bass drum, taiko drum, vibraslap, rasp, whip (or slapstick), and cuíca. See what is available to learn and share with children.

Bass xylophone, alto xylophone, and soprano xylophone

Pitched percussion instruments

Carl Orff, the German composer, music educator, and creator of Orff Schulwerk, advocated child-centered musical learning on a variety of simple pitched and unpitched percussion instruments. These Orff instruments, many of which are described above, include the barred percussion instruments xylophone, metallophone, and glockenspiel. These are most likely to be used in the music room with a specialist, but they also provide an amazing variety of beautiful sounds for children and teachers to experience in the general classroom. They come in many different sizes and tone colors, and can be played in ensembles or used for composition and improvisation. The bars can be removed and rearranged to set up different scales or intervals. Sharp bars can be substituted for F bars to play in the key of G, and flat bars can be substituted for B bars to play in the key of F. There are even special Orff sets with bars for the complete chromatic scale over several octaves, but these are likely too complicated for most classroom teachers, especially those without piano experience.

- ▸ Glockenspiels are metal-barred instruments with narrow pitch ranges. They come in soprano and alto registers and can be played with one or two rubber mallets, adding a bright and high-pitched sound to the music. They were inspired by the German glockenspiels often played in marching bands.
- ▸ Metallophones are also metal-barred instruments, as their name suggests. They come in soprano, alto, and bass registers and are played with one or two felt mallets. They were inspired by the metal-barred instruments of the Southeast Asian gamelan. They produce ringing sounds that can sustain or be damped by touching a finger to the vibrating bars.
- ▸ Xylophones are wooden-barred instruments of several different sizes, including soprano, alto, bass, and contrabass. They are usually played with a hard rubber or string-wrapped mallet using a sharp, short, striking motion. Classroom xylophones can be as short as one diatonic octave from C4 to C5, or they can be chromatic, including both white and black keys of a piano keyboard. Inspired by the xylophones of Africa, they provide a bright sound well suited to melodies or tuning pitches for singing.
- ▸ Timpani are headed drums with a spinning tensioning system that tunes the drums to any pitch in the timpani range. They are played with felt or wrapped mallets and provide a deep reverberating sound.
- ▸ Pianos, electronic keyboards, and melodicas are played with the fingers and require some dexterity. They

Bass metallophone, alto metallophone, soprano metallophone, and glockenspiel are excellent for playing melodies and harmonies as well as improvising. Electronic keyboards can often be programmed to play a range of interesting sounds, which children love to use for special effects in compositions. With a keyboard in the room, children who are studying piano may share some of their pieces with the class. The melodica (also called pianica or blow-organ) has the reedy sound of the harmonica, but pitches are played on a small keyboard.

Rototoms

Table 7.1 outlines when children are able to play various instruments with some ease and accuracy. The complex motor coordination of eye, ear, mind, and body usually comes together about age eight or nine, but there are always individual differences between children, depending on their natural aptitude and previous musical experiences. Some children who struggle with complex motor coordination may never find playing some instruments easy; teachers may simplify their parts or provide more time and practice, with or without a student learning partner. All children, regardless of ability, should have the opportunity to explore and play the kinds of instruments outlined above.

Family-owned instruments A favorite elementary language arts and social studies assignment asks children to explore their family tree and write a short history of their family. Documentation for this work typically includes pictures, interviews, and cultural artifacts, and children may develop a display or give an oral report on their family history. Music is important in many families, and some may own instruments that have been handed down over several generations. As a part of presenting their historical research, children could bring instruments to show to the class, if parents grant permission (ensure that these instruments are transported and stored safely; check with your school principal before children bring valuable instruments to school).

Children may place instruments from their families' cultures on maps for a geographical study, and research similar instrument types in other cultures, sharing their findings in oral and written presentations. Teachers could even invite adults from families who have maintained musical traditions to perform for the children, or have a family music-making night sponsored by the school.

ADAPTING INSTRUCTION FOR VARIOUS NEEDS

Intellectual Disabilities
For children who struggle to maintain an instrument part in a piece, select a part that is simple and repetitive, such as the steady beat. Place this student near someone who is confident on that part and have them match each other.

ADHD
Children who struggle to pay attention in other areas of learning may succeed in playing rhythm instruments with repeated patterns as they are receiving feedback through eyes, ears, touch, and large muscles; however, they may have trouble reading patterns, so trace patterns using verbal syllables as you present them, or teach them by rote imitation.

Emotional or Behavioral Disorders
Before distributing or playing instruments, review correct techniques for playing and how to respect instruments. For example, it is particularly important that children not play drums with sharp objects or play xylophones or metallophones with any object other than the correct mallet. Make sure children are aware of consequences if instruments are not respected.

TABLE 7.1 DEVELOPMENTAL SEQUENCE FOR PLAYING INSTRUMENTS

AGE	MUSICAL-MOTORIC DEVELOPMENT	INSTRUMENTS AND TECHNIQUES
Less than two years	Rocking, nodding, swaying Capacity to grip and grasp	Rattles (shaking) Jingle bells (shaking)
Two to three	Short periods of rhythmic regularity	Hand drum (hand tapping) Sticks (striking)
Three to four	Longer periods of rhythmic regularity Sensitivity to pulse Swaying of arms	Claves (striking) Sticks (rubbing) Woodblock (mallet striking, rubbing) Sandblocks (rubbing) Tambourine (shaking, striking) Güiro (rubbing) Maracas (shaking) Gong (mallet striking) Cowbell (mallet striking)
Five to six (kindergarten to first grade)	Maintenance of pulse Alternation of hands Basic eye–hand coordination	Finger cymbals (striking rim to rim) Bongo drums (hand striking) Timpani (mallet striking) Cymbals (striking) Triangle (mallet striking) Keyboard (one hand)
Seven to nine (first and second grades)	Eye–hand coordination	Finger cymbals (striking; attached) Slit log drum (mallet striking) Temple blocks (mallet striking) Conga drum (hand striking) Goblet drum (hand striking) Double iron agogo bells (mallet striking) Tone bells (mallet striking) Xylophone (simple drone, bourdon, ostinato; two mallets striking) Keyboard (both hands, melody with chords) Recorder G4–D5 (holding, blowing, fingering) Autoharp (chording)
Ten to twelve (fourth through sixth grades)	Increased eye–hand coordination Finger flexibility Control of breathing	Xylophone (moving drone, ostinato, melody; two mallets striking) Keyboard (both hands, two moving parts) Recorder C4–G5 (tonguing, fingering) Guitar (chording, strumming)

OCCASIONS FOR PLAY

In a musically vibrant classroom, various instruments should be made available for children to use throughout the school year. These instruments could be kept in a music center, readily available for many projects and activities. The following ideas suggest some of the ways that instruments could be used.

PERFORMING RHYTHM PATTERNS

Children develop rhythmic performance when they begin walking, running, and speaking. Walking maintains a steady beat; running subdivides the beat; and speaking introduces rhythms or patterns of longs and shorts. In some sense, all of life is lived in rhythmic patterns as we move through the activities of each day and as we perceive and predict the motion of objects. Children on the playground express complex rhythms as they chant or sing while jumping rope or bouncing balls.

Teachers can lead children of any age in clapping or playing simple rhythm patterns. One group may maintain a steady beat while others play one or more patterns synchronized with the beat. As children mature, they can perform increasingly difficult patterns. Begin performing patterns with the body, using different sounds for different patterns to create contrast, then transfer the patterns to instruments (you can find ideas for pattern music in Chapter 12). The teacher or student leader can establish the beat and the tempo first by tapping four beats on a drum or chanting "one-two-ready-go" for a pattern in duple meter, or by tapping three beats on a drum or chanting "one-ready-go" for a pattern in triple meter.

ACCOMPANYING CHANTS

Throughout the world, children chant or sing songs accompanied by hand-clapping patterns that are so rewarding to perform, they will try them over and over until they are successful. Children love to chant simple rhymes in a steady rhythm. As they grow older, they love to rap to a beat—another form of chanting, but more contemporary and complex. Chants can be accompanied by hand clapping, other body percussion, or simple instruments.

Chants can be built from spelling or vocabulary words, or from other subjects, including social studies (names of cities, states, and countries), math (multiplication tables), and science (names of plants, trees, animals, or the human skeletal structure), to name just a few. One of the most delightful kinds of chant is made of children's names (especially useful early in the year, when children are becoming acquainted). Other chants are great for counting out children to lead a game or classroom activity. Chants can be constructed of nonsense words, too. The key is to create a chant that rhymes, and to chant it over a steady beat. Once the chant is established, some children can maintain the steady beat while others clap or play the rhythm of the chant. Over time, more complex accompaniments can be added, like ostinatos clapped or played on instruments.

ACCOMPANYING STORY READINGS

Students as young as kindergarten age can enhance story reading by introducing instrument sounds to highlight certain words and convey setting and plot, as if they were producing a radio drama with sound effects. Children will not only have fun deciding how sounds enhance words, but will also read with more comprehension and expression, important goals of language arts (see Chapter 10 for more ideas).

ACCOMPANYING SONGS

Most songs invite accompaniment, often with simple rhythmic percussion instruments but sometimes with melodic or harmonic instruments. The key is to choose instruments that fit the nature of the song and create accompaniments that can children can manage. And, of course, make the choices musical. There are so many sound possibilities that too many instrumental sounds will obscure the song's melody and words. Not everyone needs to play an instrument at once; over time, repeat the song and invite new children to play the accompaniment. Younger children will need to focus on playing the beat or the rhythm, while older children can play every other beat or the offbeat, or add contrasting rhythms such as ostinatos. Children or teachers with keyboard, guitar, or autoharp experience could accompany songs harmonically.

When helping children create accompaniments to a song, the teacher may ask them:

- ▶ What is the mood of the song? What instruments might help create that mood?
- ▶ What is the dynamic quality of the song? What instruments lend themselves to that dynamic? How would you play them to create that quality?
- ▶ Would a rhythmic accompaniment be best, or should we choose some sounds to create an impression of the mood or create a scene for the song?
- ▶ Shall we create a harmonic accompaniment with autoharps, keyboards, or guitars?
- ▶ Where is the song from? What kinds of instruments would traditionally be used to accompany songs from that culture or region?

These decisions require both musical sensitivity and some musical knowledge. With younger children may need to be told what and when to play. They are certainly capable of responding to the first two questions and perhaps to the third in limited ways. The key is to trust their musical decision making. Even young children can be remarkably sensitive to musical nuance.

"Tingalayo" is delightful for children's singing and rhythmic performance. A simple accompaniment involves half the class playing the steady beat on woodblocks or coconut shells (like the hoofbeats of the donkey) while the other half plays the rhythm pattern ("come little donkey, come" or "ven, me burrito, ven") on maracas or shakers each time it occurs in the song.

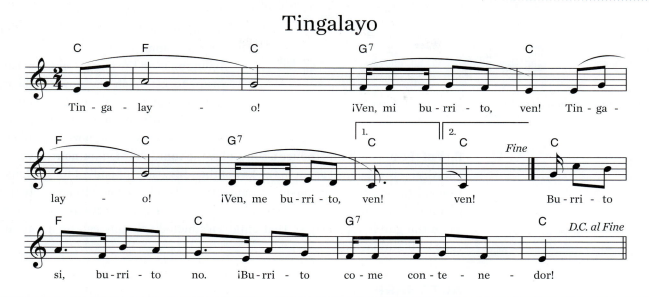

INSTRUMENTS AND THE TEACHER

Many teachers have had rich musical experiences growing up and already know how to play at least one instrument; others have had minimal experience. Regardless of your musical background, there are many instruments available for accompanying children's musical activities in the classroom. The following instruments could be learned in a college music methods class, private or group lessons, or courses available online or on DVD.

KEYBOARD

Teachers can use the piano or electronic keyboard to introduce the melody of a new song and later play both the melody and harmonies in a full accompaniment. The final phrase of the song, played in rhythm and tempo, will prepare children to sing the song in the correct key with the correct intonation and style. If the teacher is not an accomplished piano player, an electronic keyboard loaded with software and sound files can do the job.

GUITAR

Guitars are frequently used in elementary classrooms to accompany folk, traditional, heritage, and children's songs, most of which require just two or three chords. Teachers learn to play chords from keys most common to children's songs (such as D, G, and e; see tablatures above), usually in the guitar's

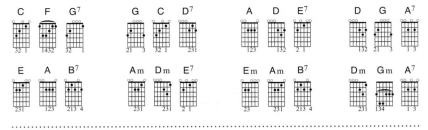

Tablatures of common guitar chords to accompany children's songs

first position close to the tuning pegs (rather than far up on the fretboard). Either acoustic (steel strings) or classical guitars (nylon strings) can be used for classroom purposes. In accompanying songs on the guitar, teachers can strum to establish the key, the beat, and the meter of the song, and must move fluently from chord to chord in several keys to support the steady flow of the music. To introduce a song, play the tonic chord, dominant-seventh chord, and tonic chord again in the key of the song (see Appendix 1 for explanations of these and other music fundamentals). Teachers who already play the guitar well may be able to play melodies in familiar keys to accompany singing. Tune the guitar regularly so that children's melody-singing can be harmonically well-supported.

AUTOHARP

The autoharp is a folk instrument that is played on the lap or a table, or held in a vertical position. It is "automatic" because it has a series of bars over the strings that block out some of the strings when the player presses a key, leaving other strings that fit within a major or minor chord free to vibrate. The keyboard of the autoharp is arranged according to common chord groupings used in most folk music. The purpose is to provide harmonic support to a song. The left hand presses the buttons on the autoharp. The index finger is placed on the tonic (I) chord of the song, the middle finger on the dominant (V) chord, and the ring finger on the subdominant (IV) chord. The right hand strums with a pick, either to the right of the bars or above the bars and on the left close to the bars. Strumming begins with the lower (thicker) strings and sweeps upward, and the rhythm pattern can be as simple as strumming once per beat. Establish the meter by strumming the downbeat a little stronger than the other beats. Establish the key and flow of the song by playing the tonic, dominant, tonic chords in meter and tempo before the children enter singing.

Autoharp

RECORDER

The recorder is a wind instrument from medieval Europe. Traditional recorders were made from wood, but they are now available in plastic. Recorders come in various sizes, playing at registers from high to low: sopranino, soprano, alto, tenor, and bass (most schools use the soprano recorder). Typically, recorders are taught in the third or fourth grade, when most children's fingers have grown big enough to cover the holes completely. Classroom teachers who have learned to play the recorder can use it to give children the starting pitch of a song or to play an entire melody for them.

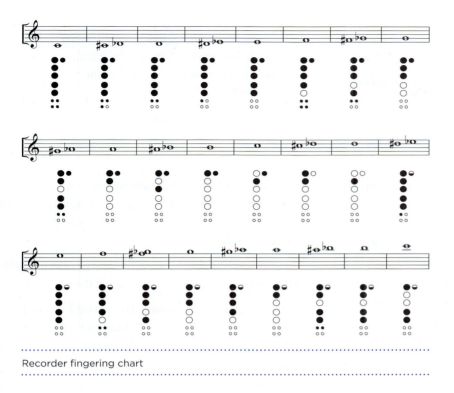

Recorder fingering chart

PERCUSSION AND OTHER INSTRUMENTS

Percussion instruments are played by striking, and most of the instruments listed in this chapter are percussion instruments. Teachers who play percussion can use their own instruments to accompany singing as appropriate.

Classroom teachers who played keyboard, band, or orchestral instruments through high school or college may bring their own instruments to school and share what they sound like, what they are made of, and how to play them. If appropriate, use them to accompany children's singing.

Summary

Children thrive when making music, whether they are singing, chanting, playing instruments, composing, improvising, arranging, or dancing and moving to music. As they learn to play instruments, they become even more musical, adding richness, color, and creativity to every subject taught in the general classroom.

Review

1. Name some ways the body can be used as an instrument.

2. Name two instruments from each of the following categories:

   Woods   Metals

   Skins (drums) Pitched percussion

   Gourds

3. Name three different ways children could use instruments in your classroom.

Critical Thinking

1. Why is instrument-playing so attractive to children?

2. How might you build a collection of instruments for your classroom?

3. What coordination skills might children gain from learning to play even simple instruments?

4. Name some physical, emotional, and cognitive benefits of playing instruments.

Projects

1. Build a collection of found sounds from interesting objects in your world. List the variety of sounds you can create, using descriptive names for the sounds such as *hollow*, *scratchy*, and so on. Categorize the sounds based on their qualities.

2. Find books or online resources for making simple instruments. Construct and decorate two or three simple instruments or one complex instrument to begin an instrument collection for your classroom. Determine the efficacy of your instrument by the quality of sound it makes.

3. Select three songs to add instruments to. Develop a plan for which instruments you would add. Assemble a group of players and experiment with how those instruments sound with the songs. Once you are satisfied, teach the songs and the instrument parts to a group of children.

4. Learn two songs or chants with hand jives and practice them until you can coordinate all of the elements.

5. Create a chant using words from a unit of study you would implement in school. Decide what instruments or body percussion you would use to accompany the chant.

Additional Resources for Teaching

Hopkin, Bart. (1996). *Making Simple Musical Instruments: A Melodious Collection of Strings, Winds, Drums & More*. Asheville, NC: Lark Books.

Martin, Bill Jr., John Archambault, and James Endicott (Illus.). (1988). *Listen to the Rain*. New York, NY: Henry Holt and Co.

Newman, Fred. (2004). *Mouth Sounds: How to Whistle, Pop, Boing, and Honk for All Occasions and Then Some*. New York, NY: Workman Publishing.

Scoville, John and Reinhold Banek. (1995). *Sound Designs: A Handbook of Musical Instrument Building*. New York, NY: Ten Speed Press.

Shepard, Mark. (2001). *Simple Flutes: A Guide to Flute Making and Playing*. Arcata, CA: Simple Productions.

Waring, Dennis. (1991). *Making Wood Folk Instruments*. New York, NY: Music Sales Corp.

Online Resources: Audio and Songbook

digital.wwnorton.com/classroom

8
THEIR CREATIVE IMAGINATIONS

Creativity involves breaking out of established patterns in order to look at things in a different way.

—Edward de Bono

Creativity is a natural extension of our enthusiasm.

—Earl Nightingale

IN THIS CHAPTER

Children as Creators of Music

In the Classroom

Composing Music in the Classroom

Developing the Musical Imagination

Using the Body and the Voice

Creating Musical Instruments

Improvising and Composing

Inventing Chants and Raps

Composing Songs

Other Arts and Composing

Summary

Review

Critical Thinking

Projects

Additional Resources for Teaching

Children are natural inventors when it comes to just about everything, including music.

You Will Learn

- how to help children create music to reinforce both musical and non-musical learning

- a broad repertoire of sound sources for creating music, from hambone body percussion and mouth sounds to constructing instruments

- a variety of ways to teach improvisation and composition to children

- more about your own musical imagination by creating tunes, songs, and raps

Ask Yourself

- Have you ever simply played with sounds by vocalizing with your mouth, singing or whistling a random tune, or exploring patterns on a keyboard or other instrument?

- Do you believe everyone has the capacity to invent with music? Why or why not?

- Do you believe it is possible to compose music without writing it down?

- Do you think it is possible to invent your own way of notating music?

- Are you confident leading children to invent songs?

- Have you ever made up a song or personally known someone who has?

- Why is it important to nurture and develop creativity in children?

CHILDREN AS CREATORS OF MUSIC

Children are naturally curious about sounds and love putting them together. Infants babble, squeal, squawk, coo, and gurgle. They repeat favorite sounds endlessly. Toddlers explore various musical toys, determining how their actions trigger the sounds. Preschoolers sing self-made songs as an extension of play or to comfort themselves. Kindergarten and primary-grade children enjoy personalizing singing games and hand-clapping and rope-jumping songs. In the intermediate grades, children use computer programs for songwriting and composing. with sound. They invent chants and raps, and movements to go with them. When children encounter new instruments, they want to know how they work and how the sounds are made. With this information, and their curiosity and natural playfulness, their musical creativity can grow.

IN THE CLASSROOM

VIGNETTE ONE

Mrs. King is a first-grade teacher who believes that all children can learn to sing. She realizes that, for some, this is a matter of building confidence, learning to support the sound, and thinking of themselves as singers. Once a week, she leads a song circle in which different children volunteer to improvise a song on a topic of interest to them, such as their pet, playing with a friend, or the story of a book they have read. Mrs. King knows that preschoolers create songs readily and spontaneously, but that first graders often hesitate and may need space and encouragement.

VIGNETTE TWO

Mr. Allen's fourth graders studied the planets and galaxies. The students constructed a model of our solar system, making the sun, planets, and some of the moons in relative size to each other by covering balloons with papier mâché. When the paper dried, they painted each body with colors to match pictures they had viewed and suspended them from the ceiling of the classroom in relative distance from each other. Mr. Allen then encouraged children to discuss the name of each planet and its corresponding character from Roman mythology. How does each planet's name reflect its qualities? What do scientists know about the climate and other features of each planet? Mr. Allen divided the students into groups of five and assigned each group a different planet. Once the group had discussed the characteristics of their particular planet, they chose sounds to use in a short instrumental piece about their planet. They shared their compositions with their fellow students and received suggestions for refining them. Once the compositions were completed, they searched the Internet for electronic music, stars, and galaxies, and listened to how other composers represented outer space in music. Finally, they explored the tone banks of a synthesizer, a Qchord, and various cell phone apps to add to their compositions and create an electronic suite, one composition for each planet. They used the suite to accompany a presentation about the planets to their parents.

VIGNETTE THREE

Mr. Sanchez's fifth-grade class filmed key historic sites in their community as part of their study of local history. Once the film was completed and edited, the children decided it would be more interesting if they added a sound track, including music. Rather than use preexisting music, Mr. Sanchez encouraged the students to compose their own music. They talked about the spirit and geography of their region, and brainstormed ideas for theme music that spoke to the essential character of the community. Over time, the children worked to refine their ideas and set them to music, using a variety of sound sources including instruments they created and instruments they play in band and orchestra. They also researched songs that were popular when local historic events took place, and made a recording of their theme music with portions of historic songs woven in. Finally, they edited their sound track to match the moving images in their film.

COMPOSING MUSIC IN THE CLASSROOM

Composing music in a classroom is not without its challenges, but children flourish when their creativity is encouraged. Some teachers may fear loss of control if they turn children loose with instruments, but a few guidelines should help teachers move beyond these fears and allow for the musically creative process to unfold on a regular basis. Children's musical growth and enthusiastic engagement in learning make this risk of student experimentation worthwhile.

1. Freedom to do everything bewilders children with too many choices, so teachers need to specify a limited assignment or idea for individual and group improvisations or compositions. As children begin to discover their potential as composers, they can make their own choices for some features while working within the safety of teacher-prescribed elements. Many such ideas are included in this chapter.

2. Musical creativity requires a period of sound exploration and discovery. This process can look and sound like chaos, so the teacher needs to develop a nonverbal signal system to get their attention, such as turning off the lights. When the room is dark, all sounds stop and children turn to face the teacher. Try that signal two times in a row. If they don't stop the first time, they will learn by the second time.

3. Depending on the assignment, children should be able to explore a variety of sound sources to use for their composition (see Chapters 7 and 13 and later in this chapter for ideas). A synthesizer in the classroom can be a wonderful sound source capable of much variety.

4. When grouping children for collaborative work, you may choose to count them out (e.g., all of the 1s, go to that corner, etc.) or match them according to desk placement, but use care: try to avoid putting all of the strong leaders or all of the introverts in any given group. There needs to be a mixture of personality types. As children mature, some may want to work on their own, but collaboration can bring many riches.

DEVELOPING THE MUSICAL IMAGINATION

Creative thinking diverges from standard, expected responses. Divergent thinking is "thinking outside the box" or "coloring outside the lines." It comes naturally to young children as they learn about their world and its myriad possibilities. Children in preschool and kindergarten create their own drawings, poetry, dances, and songs. They feel no need to copy the work of others, although they are certainly capable of learning various artistic expressions. The majority of four-year-olds measure highly creative on most tests of creative thinking; however, once they enter school children are increasingly required to produce right answers—a process known as convergent thinking. Emerging research suggests that constant testing and pressure to teach to the test inhibits children's creative development, especially if the emphasis is on getting the right answers.

In a recent examination of 300,000 tests of creative thinking administered since 1970, neuroscientist Kyung Hee Kim found that creativity has decreased among American children in recent years.[1] Kim determined that since 1990, children have become less able to produce unique and unusual ideas. They are also less humorous, less imaginative, and less able to elaborate on ideas. Children need time to play and imagine in order to develop their inherent creativity. Teachers can help by being open to unexpected responses. Rather than dismissing children's unique responses, they might ask, "how did you arrive at that answer?" And, teachers need to welcome diverse answers for the problems being posed. One task that encourages a variety of creative responses is composing and improvising music.

Even without an extensive musical background, small groups of children can compose quite complex and interesting pieces around various themes or musical ideas. The teacher's role is to establish a structure or assignment, give students materials and time, and let their creativity emerge. Children are endlessly enthusiastic and imaginative; they simply need some structure and guidelines within which to create.

USING THE BODY AND THE VOICE

Our bodies and voices are our primary instruments. They are an important first resource for sounds, and are absolutely free of charge. Invite children to see how many different sounds they can make with their hands: clapping, snapping, flat-hand clap, cupped-hand clap, hand-to-chest pat, hand-to-leg hambone rhythm, and so on. Once they've discovered several contrasting sounds, they can invent a short rhythmic piece for hands such as Example 8.1, which uses contrasting sounds to produce simple rhythms.

Children in the intermediate grades can create pieces with more complex rhythms, more sounds, and various patterns layered in different parts, such as Example 8.2. These pieces might feature categories of chanted words that fit the various rhythms, such as fruit (blueberry, kiwi, pear), cars (Cadillac, Jaguar, Ford), or sports teams (Mariners, White Sox, Cubs). Children especially enjoy figuring out the syllables for their first names and then adding them to a spoken rhythmic piece such as this one.

EXAMPLE 8.1

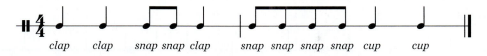

EXAMPLE 8.2

Hand jives have long been popular among children. Also known as hand clapping, hand jive movements progress from simple to complex patterns of clapping with partners or members of a small circle of players, and may include snapping, hand shaking, and patting the lap, chest, or head. Hand jives often accompany chants and songs. The hand jives in Example 8.3 move from simple to more

EXAMPLE 8.3

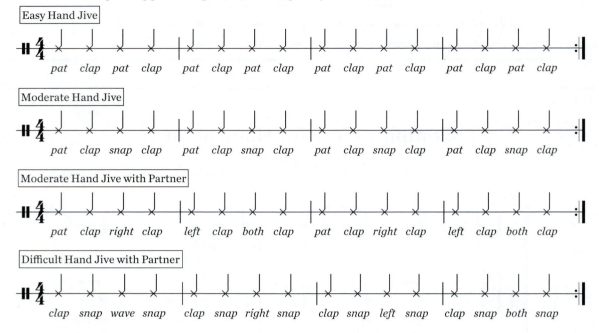

complex. On playgrounds around the world, children as young as four perform fairly complex hand jives, and the patterns become more complicated among children in the upper elementary grades. Girls more than boys engage in hand jives on the playground, but boys are known to accept the challenge in the classroom. These hand rhythm sequences are excellent for building complex perceptual motor coordination in children, and patterning is very important to brain development. Try applying these hand jives to jump rope rhymes or playground songs, such as "Miss Mary Mack" (Example 8.4).

When the body is used as a musical instrument, it becomes a corpophone (from Latin *corpus*, meaning body, and Greek *phon*, meaning sound). Corpophones have been used for centuries throughout the world to make music. African-American slaves were not allowed to use drums, so they created complex rhythms with various parts of their bodies, especially by slapping with their hands. This activity is referred to as "hambone." Hambone performance techniques include stamping the feet, slapping the thighs, hitting the chest, clapping, snapping, and making popping sounds with one's mouth. Hambone demonstrations online offer many ideas for using the body as a percussion instrument. Encourage students to try some simple patterns using their thighs, chest, and clapping in a similar way. Over time, challenge them to try more complex patterns. Once children learn how to use their bodies as percussion instruments, they will discover many ways to be inventive.

Mouth sounds can be voiced by using the vocal chords, as in speaking, or unvoiced by making various buzzing, clicking, and popping sounds with other parts of the mouth and throat. A single person can alternate or combine voice and

 **EXAMPLE 8.4**

mouth sounds. Whole stories can be told using mouth sounds alone, or mouth sounds can be combined with words to enhance the story. Mouth sounds have recently gained popularity with the resurgence of a cappella singing and subsequent rise of beatboxing, a process by which the performer imitates a drum machine with the voice. Bobby McFerrin has elevated mouth sounds to a form of high artistic expression in his amazing combinations of voice, body, and mouth sounds in performance. Search the Internet for examples of mouth sounds and beatboxing. As children become familiar with the possibilities, encourage them to include mouth and voiced sounds to tell their original stories or create musical pieces to share.

CREATING MUSICAL INSTRUMENTS

Chapter 7 offers ideas for inventing and constructing simple instruments. The more sounds from which children can choose when they compose, the more creative their compositions will be. The key is to have children create enough instruments so that they have a range of sound sources available when they want to compose.

The photograph at the top of page 146 depicts invented instruments with a variety of tone colors. The ideas for instruments below are presented from simple to complex (children may require help from parents and grandparents to construct some of the more complex instruments). Children can also imagine and invent their own instruments. Resources on instrument construction can be found online.

PERCUSSION INSTRUMENTS

- Rattles: Partially fill any small container, such as plastic eggs or boxes, with beads, pebbles, rice, or beans. Partially fill hollowed, dried gourds or dried leather pouches with rice or beans.
- Drums: Place any sized cylindrical container upside down and beat on it with dowel sticks. Cover a cylindrical container with rubber from a balloon

Invented instruments create a variety of tone colors.

and attach with a rubber band. Play with unsharpened pencils or fingers.
- For African-style drums, use large PVC pipe and untreated leather, which can be found in a leather shop or online. (Look for goat skin; it's thinner and easier to work with than cow skin.) Play with hands or sticks.
- Slit drums: These are a bit more complicated, but with woodworking tools and quality hardwood, you're ready to tackle any of the tutorials available on the Internet.
- Sticks or rasps: Use plain dowels of various thicknesses. File notches in one e dowel, and scrape it with the other. For different pitches, scrape notched flexible PVC pipes of various lengths.
- Xylophone: Cut different lengths of copper tubing, rest on notched foam, and strike with a metal striker. (This project would definitely need some help from parents or grandparents, but the result is a beautifully sounding instrument. Consult the Internet for instructions.)
- Tambourine: Punch holes regularly around the edge of an aluminium pie plate. Attach jingle bells or pull tabs from soda cans to make a ringing sound.
- Rainstick: Partially fill a mailing tube with rice or small beads. Push or hammer small nails into the side of the tube (to keep all the "rain" from falling at once). Cover the ends with rubber or a balloon and attach with colorful tape. Decorate by drawing or layering colored tissue paper.

WIND INSTRUMENTS

- Blow across the top of a glass bottle.
- Blow into a golf club divider tube using a buzzing sound, with lips pursed.
- Plastic straw oboe: Flatten a straw on one end and cut notches on either side. Buzz through the flattened end.
- Bottle scale: Collect eight tall glass bottles of the same size. Leave one empty, then fill the rest with incremental levels of water, blowing across the top to check tuning. Create a scale.
- Kazoo: Cover both sides of a small comb with wax paper, and hum into the comb. Or cover the end of a cardboard tube with wax paper fastened with a rubber band, and hum into the tube.

STRING INSTRUMENTS

- Stretch rubber bands of various sizes across a cigar box or other sturdy box.
- Monochord: Cut a 16" length of 2" x 4" wood. Put a large eye bolt at either end and string a guitar string or nylon string in between. Play by plucking

CHAPTER 8 | Their Creative Imaginations **147**

or strumming with one hand. Move a finger from the other hand along the length of the string to change pitch.

▶ Harp: Make a simple square frame, put in eye bolts on two opposite sides, and string nylon strings across. Tighten them to tune them. Play by plucking.

▶ Bleach bottle banjo, spike fiddle, and washtub bass: Common household items and ingenuity combine to create simple yet surprisingly musical instruments. You can find plans for each of these instruments online.

IMPROVISING AND COMPOSING

Once children have explored instrument sounds freely (see Chapter 7), they are ready to move into the more formal processes of improvisation and composition. Improvised music is invented spontaneously. It is performed by the improviser(s), and it is not formalized, refined, or repeated. Beginner-level improvisation allows children to play with sounds and musical syntax (putting those sounds together)—a most appropriate process for children in the elementary grades. Children who improvise are learning to manipulate the language of music. Frequent improvisation encourages children to converse in music in the same way they converse using words—freely and spontaneously, with meaning.

CREATING TO MEET MUSIC STANDARDS

1. Singing. When children create songs, either individually or with a group, encourage the entire class to learn them. Once learned, invite children to sing the songs more expressively by changing the phrasing, dynamics, and tempo as needed to make the song truly interesting to listen to, and share their songs with others. Singing expressively helps children read with expression.

2. Playing. As children create pieces for various instruments, guide them to use effective playing techniques, such as holding mallets correctly, strumming correctly, etc. At the same time, encourage them to experiment with other playing techniques, such as strumming, plucking, or bowing stringed instruments, or playing a cymbal with a wooden mallet, soft mallet, or brush. Children need to be free to explore new ways of making sounds (as long as instruments are not damaged).

3. Improvising. Offer many opportunities for children to invent hand jives, chants, raps, or spontaneous songs.

4. Composing and arranging. Make a range of sound sources available in the classroom to facilitate composing and arranging, including student-created instruments and electronic keyboards with headphones. Also lead children to computer programs that can be used for composing.

5. Reading and notating. Encourage children to represent their compositions with standard music notation or invented notations using shapes, lines, colors, designs, or pictures. Invite them to share their notation with another group of children to see how others interpret that notation.

6. Listening. Invite children to listen to a wide variety of music to stimulate their composing and improvising, including folk songs, world music, and popular music of various styles. Use the online resources provided at the end of this chapter to stimulate their creative imaginations.

7. Evaluating. Use questions offered in this chapter to help students learn to critique their own work and the work of others, including professional recordings. Help students articulate what musical ideas they think work and what could be more effective.

8. Connecting to other arts and curriculum areas. Use ideas from this chapter to connect composing with other arts and physical education. Give children the opportunity to use musical creativity to demonstrate their understanding in all curricular areas.

9. Connecting to culture and history. Compose music in styles from cultures they are studying. Create a musical using songs and instrumental music from the historical period they are studying in social studies.

> **EXAMPLE 8.5**
>
> Examples of question and answer form
>
> | | Question | | | | Answer | | | |
> |---|---|---|---|---|---|---|---|---|
> | | Beat 1 | Beat 2 | Beat 3 | Beat 4 | Beat 1 | Beat 2 | Beat 3 | Beat 4 |
> | 1 | X | X X | X | X | X X | X X | X | X |
> | 2 | X X | X | X X X X | X | X X X X | X X | X | X |
> | 3 | X X | X X | X X | X | X X | X X X X | X X | X |
>
> In boxes with more than one X, divide the beat evenly among the Xs.

One of the easiest ways to encourage children to improvise is to have musical "conversations." These conversations can use clapping, body percussion, standard instruments, mouth sounds, or found sounds (such as a pencil tapping on a desk). A leader creates a short pattern over four beats in a question and answer form (see Example 8.5). One or more children respond to that pattern with their own four-beat pattern, using the same combination of sounds. Over time, the patterns can grow longer, expanding to eight beats. These improvised musical conversations are an excellent use of free time, and older children who have had a few years of these experiences will find themselves at ease in improvising rhythms and melodies.

Children in preschool through second grade often enjoy improvising short songs. Teachers can hold a regular song circle, where children sit in a circle and one child in the middle volunteers to create a song. The teacher can suggest a theme or a story, or the volunteers can come up with their own ideas. These early childhood exercises teach children to express themselves, so that in third through sixth grades they can work in small groups to improvise songs vocally and on musical instruments. Children who improvise regularly gain fluency in both thinking and expression—skills that readily transfer to language arts and other areas of learning.

Children can learn the differences between consonants and vowels by improvising using only one or the other. Choose two or three vowel sounds, such as oo, ee, ah, oh, ay, eye, yay, yah, yo, you, etc., pair children, and have them improvise for each other in short phrases, taking turns. Invite children to choose two consonants, such as B, T, K, or P, to improvise voicing consonants, as in lines 1 and 2 in Example 8.6.

Children improvising short conversations with musical sounds.

EXAMPLE 8.6

Improvisation with consonants and vowels

	Beat 1	Beat 2	Beat 3	Beat 4	Beat 1	Beat 2	Beat 3	Beat 4
1	B	B B	B	B	T	T	T	T
2	K T	K T	K T	K	T	T	T K	
3	Foo	Foo Foo	Fee	Fay	Foo Fee	Foo Fee	Fay	
4	Fee	Fi	Fo	Fum	Fo		Fum	

Finally, have children combine consonants with vowels, as in lines 3 and 4. Clapping or snapping the beat can keep their vocal improvisations on rhythm.

In a second level of improvisation, called "planned improvisation," children work together in groups of four or five and spend about twenty minutes planning a short piece of music (they may use words from the current week's spelling list, math operation terms, or any other collection of information). To provide accompaniment or a "groove" for the words, they can use mouth, body, or found sounds, or invented or standard instruments. Teachers can help guide them initially, but children will soon become quite sophisticated in deciding what sounds will work best for their improvisation. Children will need time to plan and rehearse before they are ready to perform. A planned improvisation is performed one time only and is not refined. Teachers can record the performance and everyone can listen to the results. Such activities allow children to own the improvised material, and the spelling or math test that comes after is likely to reveal amazing results.

At the end of the process, teachers can ask and students can reflect on the following questions:

- What did you like about the piece?
- If you were going to change anything, what would you change?
- Did it achieve the intent of the assignment?
- How well did your group work together?

Composing, the fourth National Standard for Music Education, involves crafting a piece over a period of time. It requires more reflective thought than improvising does; children work over several days or even weeks to develop their pieces. Box 8.1 gives some starting ideas for composition, but children may come up with their own ideas, too.

Students plan improvisations to accompany words from the weekly spelling list.

BOX 8.1 MOTIVATIONS FOR PLANNED IMPROVISATIONS AND COMPOSITIONS

Themes: "Clouds," "A Day in a Factory," "Life and Death of a Mosquito"

Emotions or moods: angry, happy, sad, excited, proud, regal, frustrated, mysterious

Pictures or images: photographs from magazines, paintings, designs, maps, scores

Stories: picture books, children's own stories, fairy tales

Poetry: children's own poems, poetry for children, other well-known and evocative poetry

Sounds: families of sounds, individual sounds, contrasting sounds

Patterns or cycles: "The Seasons," "A Day," "A Storm," "The Butterfly," "The Water Cycle," "The Life Cycle of a Salmon"

Musical elements: melody, rhythm, harmony, tone color, tempo, dynamics

Aesthetic ideas: density, texture, tension and release, repetition and contrast (see Appendix 1)

Musical structures: ostinato, phrase, motive, phrase sequences (AB, ABA, rondo), layered parts, theme and variations, twelve-bar blues, free form (through-composed) (see Appendix 1).

Recorded music: any music can evoke creative responses; works need to be selected carefully for various age levels based on complexity.

Children may work in pairs, or in small groups of three or four. From third grade on, they can also compose independently. They may decide to refine something that started with a planned improvisation, or they may simply start with a new idea. Composition plans can be written down in words, or notated using regular musical notation or invented pictorial notation as shown in Examples 8.7 and 8.8. Or children can use an aural plan that they simply remember. Composition synthesizes learning in every area of the curriculum, as demonstrated in the opening classroom vignettes. Teachers can support composition by providing materials, time, and ideas as well as structuring groups if necessary. See suggestions for online composition resources at the end of this chapter.

Arranging music, also part of the fourth National Standard for Music Education, invites children to take a familiar piece of music and to create their own arrangements of that piece. Children enjoy creating parodies of familiar songs and writing their own words to a known tune, such as a nursery rhyme. This is another effective way to integrate music into other classroom content, as children synthesize what they've learned by writing new lyrics to an old song and performing it in class. Another way to arrange music is for children to take a familiar piece and add their own accompaniment to it using any of the sound sources listed in this chapter.

INVENTING CHANTS AND RAPS

Children are surrounded with chants, and most are well acquainted with rap as a the practice of rhythmic speech within the more expansive culture of hip hop. Chants and raps can be invented about any aspect of the curriculum and help make material that is important to remember, such as spelling words, math facts,

EXAMPLE 8.7

Invented notation using abstract symbols. This piece is notated with teardrops to show that it is in a minor key. Other symbols are used as well, but it is not possible to reproduce the piece from the notation alone.

or the names of states, playful and delightful. The popular Broadway musical *Hamilton* is an example of successfully using rap to tell the story of a period of American history.

Chants are performed in fairly strict rhythm and usually rhyme. Often they accompany activities such as rope-jumping, or they are accompanied by hand-clapping or body percussion. Children might practice spelling by establishing a steady beat and chanting their spelling words over that beat. Adding dynamic shaping to their chant makes the creative product that much more musical (see Example 8.9). Chant composition is another opportunity for group work, allowing children to demonstrate their spelling prowess musically.

Raps usually tell a story, describe people's interactions, relationships, and daily lives, featuring rhymed words in rhythmic presentation. They are often set against a track of "scratching," achieved by a DJ scratching a record rhythmically by moving it back and forth with his hands. Children can use mouth sounds to replicate the sound of scratching, setting up a rhythm for the rapper. Rappers are solo artists, yet children enjoy composing raps in large and small groups on a topic or concept they have learned. Some children can set up the scratching sound (or provide beatboxing mouth sounds) while others rap in rhythm. Teachers can assign a rap in any area of study.

EXAMPLE 8.8

Invented notation using letter names of pitches. The backward 2 (upper left) means "with two hands and two times." The knife next to the F indicates the note is sharp. ("It is a pirate's knife, and a pirate's knife is *very sharp*.")

EXAMPLE 8.9

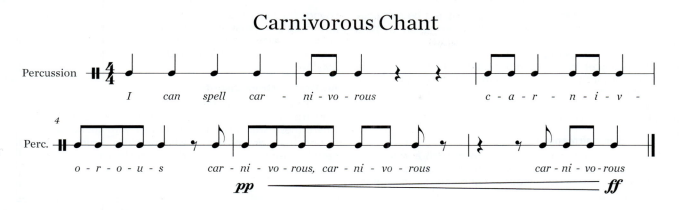

COMPOSING SONGS

Children in elementary school (and all the way through high school) create songs informally in many places.[2] Whether self-composed, family favorites, playground songs, or popular music, songs seem to be constant companions for children. In *The World in Six Songs*, Daniel Levitin develops a convincing case for the important cultural, spiritual, and psychological need for song.[3] He recognizes singing, song creating, and song sharing as essential to our humanity.

Collective song circles and songwriting stations can meet children's interests and needs to create their own songs. Classroom stations are especially enticing as places where children can record songs they have created.

Teachers can work more formally with children to create a song with the entire class or in small groups by using the following procedures:

1. Select a topic. Create a bank of descriptive words the children suggest. Invite them to work from the word bank to suggest phrases for a poem, and transcribe the poem on the board.

2. After the children chant the poem together, getting a feel for its rhyme and rhythm, play a home key (tonic) chord on an autoharp, keyboard, or guitar and ask different children to sing an original melody for the first line of the poem.

3. Have the class vote on their favorite melody for that line, and learn to sing it together. Then record the melody.

4. Continue the process for each line of the poem, supplying underlying chords to support the harmonic structure of the melody. (Alternatively, provide a harmonic structure in which children create the melodies.) Common underlying chords are I, IV, and V[7] (in the key of C: C, F, and G[7]; in the key of D: D, G, and A[7]). See page 136 for guitar and autoharp chords in various keys, and experiment until you find a chord or chords that fit the melody. Of course, melodies can also be sung without chords.

ADAPTING INSTRUCTION FOR VARIOUS NEEDS

Intellectually gifted children may or may not be musically gifted, but they will often enjoy the challenge of creating music. Some may already read music or play instruments proficiently. Encourage them to use their instruments as sound sources in their compositions. If they want to notate their music, encourage them to develop systems for notation. Many are natural leaders and may want to lead the group; encourage them to listen to ideas from all of the students to develop a true group composition.

Mobility Impairments

Because sounds can be chosen from such a wide variety of sources, including mouth, body, vocal, found, and instrumental sounds, encourage children to incorporate

sounds they can easily manage to produce. If necessary, pair mobility-impaired students with others who can help them play an instrument, or use adaptive devices, such as a glove with Velcro strips to hold mallets for playing.

Autism Spectrum Disorders

Lots of sounds at once may feel like chaos and overwhelm students on the autism spectrum. Find a quiet space where these students can experiment with sounds while helped by a group leader, who provides structure and security. Use very clear directions and simplify the task, if necessary.

---

5. For evaluative purposes, children should listen to the entire song and suggest changes. They can then sing the song in its final form and record it in its entirety. The teacher (or music teacher) might notate later and share it with the class in that form.

Finally, as children mature, they often enjoy writing poetry that they could then turn into a song. An electronic keyboard with headphones is a place for children to experiment with building their song. This process of song construction and refinement occurs over time as children craft what sounds good to them. Other children may invent songs in their heads and then try recording or refining them by adding other instruments along with the voice.

OTHER ARTS AND COMPOSING

Virtually anything can stimulate composition: a theme, an image, a sound, a pattern, or a task to be practiced, such as spelling or multiplication tables. One of the most exciting inspiration for composition over the centuries, however, comes from artists, musicians, poets, and dancers encountering each other's work and developing projects that combine those works in some way. The following composing ideas are arts-inspired.

MUSIC FOR PLAYS AND VIDEOS

As a part of their language arts curriculum, many creative teachers challenge children to write or produce their own plays or videos, with children or puppets serving as actors. Regardless of which form they choose, each involves telling a story.

Once the story structure is determined, invite children compose music that will enhance the story in their play or film. As they plan their music, they may ask themselves:

▶ What moods shall we create in different parts of our story?
▶ What sort of music will create the moods we want—happy, sad, scary, excited, etc.?
▶ Do we want to have theme music throughout?

- ► Should a theme or short motive represent the different characters in the story?
- ► Shall we create music that precedes the story, preparing the audience for what is coming? What about music at the end?
- ► What instruments and sounds will best achieve the effects we want?
- ► How will we time the music to fit the play or film?
- ► Will we have a live accompaniment or a prerecorded one?

Children will need to discuss, experiment with, and refine their music to achieve a satisfying result. They will also need to learn to balance the music with the voices, so that the music does not overwhelm the script itself. All of this takes time but can be very rewarding for children (and it has the benefit of involving some children in roles other than acting).

MUSIC FOR OPERAS AND MUSICALS

The Metropolitan Opera of New York City, as well as many other opera companies throughout the country, has developed programs that train music specialists and classroom teachers to create and produce operas collaboratively with their students. Some companies come to schools to teach teachers and students how to create an opera.

An opera is a story set to music, with singers who act and an orchestra of instrumentalists who accompany the solos, duets, trios, and choruses of singers. Operas are staged with scenery, costumes, and lighting. Participants may sing, play an instrument, act, dance, fence, juggle, direct, design, or produce. Children may be familiar with the idea of a musical play (similar to an opera) from such shows as *The Lion King*, *Annie*, or *Matilda*. Musicals feature acting and discrete songs, while operas contain continuous music from the opening scene to the end.

Classroom teachers wishing to create operas or musicals can work with their children to prepare the story line and script, as well as on costuming, set design, direction, and production. The music specialist teacher is well suited to composing the music, arranging it for available instruments, and shepherding children through learning the songs and instrumental accompaniments. Parents may join in for rehearsals and the final production.

Although making an opera is a complex process, the wide range of experiences allows individual children to explore their particular interests and gifts. Teachers may want to check with a local opera company for assistance (and inspiration).

MUSIC AND POETRY

When words are set to melodies, they become song lyrics, a special kind of poetry. The best melodies make the words more expressive. Teachers can encourage poetry writing that children later turn into song—individually, in a group, or with the help of the music specialist or other knowledgeable adult. Children can also compose instrumental accompaniments for their sung melodies, whether on piano, guitar or other chording instrument, or a group of xylophones.

BOX 8.2 THE POETRY RECIPE

What: the subject of the poem.

How: describe the subject, drawing on images, word pictures, feelings, emotions, memories, and experiences.

Children can also set preexisting poetry (their own or that of published poets) to music. The Japanese haiku, with its syllabic structure of 5–7–5, is a miniature form that usually depicts a season of the year or an intense impression of something in nature. Children enjoy adding simple accompaniments to their spoken haiku, using sounds suggestive of Japanese music, such as woodblocks, drums played with mallets, finger cymbals, flutes, xylophones, or metallophones playing notes from a pentatonic scale (five notes, for example the black keys of the piano). The music creates a setting that enhances the emotion and imagery of the poem, which of course will vary from one poem to the next and for different styles of poetry. Key to a music and poetry experience is reading the poem carefully, analyzing the mood of the poem, and paying close attention to the rhythm of the words. The music will need to match the words and phrases to support the essence of the poem fully.

Katz and Thomas[4] use the Poetry Recipe for writing poetry with children. They help children generate words that describe each of the senses (sight, sound, touch, smell, and taste) and the overall emotion. The resulting poems are generated from such subjects as colors, moods, places in nature, or personal experiences. The following poem was written by third graders:

White

White feels like two people
getting married.
White smells like peppermint
candy getting ready
to be eaten.
White looks like fluffy
clouds in the blue sky,
feels like roses growing in a garden,
white tastes like
vanilla ice cream cones.
White feels comfortable.

VISUAL ARTS AND COMPOSING

Paintings have often inspired great composers. The Russian composer Modest Musorgsky wrote an entire suite of pieces called *Pictures at an Exhibition*, each movement representing the emotions, movement, and color he felt as he viewed an art exhibition. The main piece that binds the work together is called "Promenade," a slow and rather stately piece that symbolizes visitors moving through the exhibit. At various points Musorgsky represents other painted scenes, including "The Ballet of the Unhatched Chicks in their Shells," and "The Hut on Fowl's Legs (Baba Yagá)," who is a witch in Russian lore. Predictably, these two pieces are quite different from each other in character. The first is bright and playful, with many short sounds as the chicks scurry around pecking the ground. The second is dark and ominous, suggesting the fear one might feel at discovering the hut of a witch in a dark forest.

As we learned in Chapter 5, children can draw or paint in response to music. Likewise, they can also compose in response to pictures (just as Musorgsky did). Some of the best art in the world is available online through such major art museums as New York's Metropolitan Museum of Art, or Paris's Louvre. Many schools have enlarged prints of famous artworks for teachers to use with children, and books and magazines are also credible sources. Children should explore images until they find one that inspires them to compose, and then discuss the moods, colors, and story evoked by the painting. Using language from art that also applies to music, such as theme, color, line, shape, texture, density, pattern, repetition, and contrast, will help children make appropriate choices in timbre (color), melody (line and shape), texture and density (number of lines and thickness of sound), repetition and pattern (pitch and rhythm), and contrast (among forms or sections of the music).

Paintings such as *The Great Gate of Kiev* inspired Musorgsky to compose music representing his impressions.

Summary

Music is a powerful language for humans. Listening to, composing, and making music stimulates the entire brain, creating neural pathways that help all learning. Creating music develops imaginative thinking and brings playfulness and joy to the lives of children. It builds the confidence they need to continue to invent in the future, regardless of the subject or setting. The possibilities are unlimited.

Review

1. What is one key characteristic of creative thinking? How might creative thinking develop through music?

2. What is the difference between improvisation and composition?

3. How should teachers set up the composition or planned improvisation processes?

4. What are some categories of instruments that parents, teachers, and children could construct together?

5. What is one way to stimulate children to improvise musically?

6. Name four ideas to stimulate composition.

Critical Thinking

1. What might be impediments to having children compose or invent music in your classroom?

2. How would you work around those impediments?

3. What are some occasions you might find to have children create a chant or a rap?

4. How do you think composing on a regular basis might contribute to different dimensions of children's thinking? What are those dimensions?

Projects

1. Build several simple rhythm instruments or one string or wind instrument. When you are satisfied with the sound, bring it to class and use it with others to compose or improvise.

2. With a child you know well, try improvising back and forth, using a call-and-response form and any sounds that the two of you enjoy. Improvise a rhythm pattern by patting on your lap and have the child create a new pattern over yours. Gradually shift your pattern to a new pattern with another part of your body and see what the child does. Reflect on how it felt to improvise.

3. Collect a set of images (maybe photographs from magazines or art prints) that suggest a place, mood, or pattern of some sort. Mount them on construction paper. Use them as a basis for small-group composition with children.

4. Listen carefully to the music that accompanies a film you enjoy. Analyze what the composer does to create mood, tension, excitement, and a sense of place. Use your knowledge to help guide children in creating a soundtrack for a film of their own. Reflect on that process.

5. Develop a poetry writing project with children. Once the poems are written and refined, encourage them to work alone or in small groups to set selected poems to music.

Additional Resources for Teaching

Creating Music: www.creatingmusic.com

Creating music for children: Classics for Kids: www.classicsforkids.com/composers

Composing Children on Pinterest: www.pinterest.com/mlbailey/composing-children

Composition software for children:

Subotnick, Morton. (1995). *Making Music* [computer software]. Available from https://www.amazon.com/Making-Music-Morton-Subotnick/dp/1581250088

Music Ace by Harmonic Vision: https://www.harmonicvision.com

Online resources for building instruments:

Bleach Bottle Banjo: http://www.kids.ct.gov/kids/cwp/view.asp?Q=314088

Bongos, Banjos, Fiddles and More: http://mudcat.org/kids/bongos.cfm

Building Musical Instruments: http://www.wannalearn.com/Crafts_and_Hobbies/Woodworking/Building_Musical_Instruments

How to Build Your Own Slit Drum: http://www.drummercafe.com/education/articles/how-to-build-your-own-slit-drum.html

The Washtub Bass: http://www.jugstore.com/washtub.html

Online Resources: Audio and Songbook

digital.wwnorton.com/classroom

PART III
MUSIC THROUGHOUT THE DAY

Just as live and recorded music permeates our lives, it also finds its way into the nooks and crannies of daily classroom activity. Beyond instruction with the specialist music teacher, children can encounter music in the general classroom throughout the day. Music captures children's attention, maintains their focus, and provides repetition without drudgery, helping them learn more than in lessons presented without music. Lessons in language arts, social studies, math and science, and the other arts that allow children to sing, play, listen, and move rhythmically are more fun, and thus more effective. The chapters ahead are full of enticing ways to enliven the classroom with joyful, enthusiastic learning.

These final six chapters show how music can enhance the general classroom climate and help children learn important concepts, principles, and skills in other subjects. Many of the core standards adopted by the National Council of Teachers of English and the International Reading Association (NCTE/IRA), the National Council of Teachers of Mathematics (NCTM), and the National Science Teachers Association (NSTA) can be met and enhanced through music. The National Council for the Social Studies (NCSS) spells out two standards advocating the use of music and other arts to further learning in social studies. Each of the following chapters presents a plethora of ideas and techniques for using music to learn other subjects through experiences that children will enjoy and remember.

> Music belongs in lessons in language arts, social studies, math, science, and the other arts.

IN THIS CHAPTER

In the Classroom

Musical Openers and Closers

Music at Classroom Listening Centers

Music at Camp and on Field Trips

Music for Holidays, the Seasons, and Special Events

Summary

Review

Critical Thinking

Projects

Additional Resources for Teaching

Additional Songs for Teaching

9

MUSIC FOR THE JOY OF IT

"Ah, music," he said, wiping his eyes. "A magic beyond all we do here!"

—J. K. Rowling, *Harry Potter and the Sorcerer's Stone*

Music activities make classroom learning joyful.

IN THE CLASSROOM

Well-chosen music makes classroom experiences vibrant, deep, and joyful, from the time children gather together to the time they leave for home. Music helps children focus attention, think creatively, retain information, transition from one subject to the next, energize and get excited, calm down after recess or rousing activity, find peace after moments of emotional turmoil, and empathize with others. Music enriches individual learning in classroom music centers; makes holiday celebrations more expressive, communal, and genuine; and enhances schoolwide assemblies. Music transforms a plain, dull, and uninspiring classroom, adding magic and motivation that targets children's attention to learning.[1]

VIGNETTE ONE

Ever since she began teaching, Ms. Booth has used music in her kindergarten curriculum. She sings and chants rhythms and rhymes with her five- and six-year-olds, and they dance to recordings in freestyle and in short routines in lines and circles. She plays music recordings while children cut, color, paint, do puzzles, and practice writing their numbers and letters. The music is not constant (she does not want it to become background noise easily tuned out), but something children enjoy and react differently to as its moods change. She uses songs and chants to welcome children at the start of the day, call them to circle time, distribute worksheets and snacks, form a line for the bathroom break, and wait for the closing bell at the end of the day. Her children sing at birthdays and holidays, and every other day, too. She sometimes sings instructions or questions, and encourages her children to make up their own songs in response.

VIGNETTE TWO

Mrs. Williams insists, "I'm not a musician. I never played an instrument, never sang in a choir, and if you heard me sing, you'd know why." But anyone visiting her second-grade classroom would think otherwise, when she confidently claps out rhythms that the children joyfully echo. On one particular day, children bunch together in threesomes at computer screens, working animatedly on their language arts assignment: creating new fables for new times. After observing several groups at work, Mrs. Williams focuses the children's attention by clapping the rhythm (♩ ♩ ♫ ♫ ♩) at which point the children immediately clap the pattern back to her and stop talking. She asks leading questions that elicit volunteers to restate the storywriting criteria, and then she claps the pattern again, which the children repeat and then go right back to work. After ten more minutes of storywriting, Mrs. Williams signals the children back into a large group with a chant she taught them while she pats and claps a steady beat:

You Will Learn

- several ways to use music to open and close the school day

- techniques for using music to transition between class activities

- how listening centers can benefit learning

- where to find song resources for field trips and camps

- a beginning repertoire of songs for seasons, holidays, and celebrations

Ask Yourself

- Do you ever find yourself singing, dancing, or tapping your toes or patting your hands to the beat of music you are hearing or imagining? How do you feel when you are doing this?

- When you were a child in school, did music ever open or close the school day?

- Did you sing songs or chants at school assemblies, or when you were getting ready for lunch or recess?

- Was ever music playing while your class was engaged in other activities (an art project, computer time, small-group collaboration)? How did it make you feel?

- Do you remember music you made on the bus, on field trips, or at camp?

- Did you sing songs at school to celebrate Thanksgiving, the winter holidays, Martin Luther King, Cinco de Mayo, or other special days?

Time		to		close	it	up	
pat		*clap*		*pat*		*clap*	

Time		to		put	a-	way	
pat		*clap*		*pat*		*clap*	

Clean	up	all	your	work-	ing	sta-	tions
pat		*clap*		*pat*		*clap*	

for	a-	noth-	er	day.			
pat		*clap*		*pat*		*clap*	

The children join her in the chant, quickly saving their files, closing their notebooks, pushing chairs under computer tables, and returning to their seats, ready for the next activity. Music makes transitions smooth, orderly, predictable, and joyous with no time wasted in extraneous talking or horseplay.

VIGNETTE THREE

Every year Mr. D'Angelo's fourth-grade children sing their way through the calendar of seasons and holidays. He believes the arts bring a special vibrancy to the social studies standards embedded in the reading core standards. The songs associated with religious and cultural holidays, such as Rosh Hashanah (Jewish New Year), Diwali (Hindu festival of lights), Chinese New Year, Black History Month, Christmas, and Cinco de Mayo, embody and convey core beliefs and practices of their cultures. Mr. D'Angelo stocks his listening center with recordings of world music for individual- and small-group listening, sends home to parents a playlist of online recordings of "fourth-grade world music favorites," and encourages children to view recommended videos in the listening center and at home that illustrate cultural identities through festivals, displays of visual arts and crafts, and performances of music, dance, and drama. It's no wonder parents and students request placement in Mr. D'Angelo's classroom: his students don't just learn facts, they *feel* them through the arts.

VIGNETTE FOUR

One of Mrs. Kwan's year-long goals for her sixth graders, in their last year of elementary school, is to broaden their understanding of their community. She knows that many of her children do not come from families with the interest or time to visit museums, monuments, parks, and other major markers of the large metropolitan area in which they reside. So one Friday each month, after studying particular city sites through assigned readings, Internet searches, and Mrs. Kwan's own in-class presentations, the students board buses to explore their world. Any trip of ten minutes or more can seem long to children, so Mrs. Kwan encourages them to sing. In fact, she has helped them build a repertoire of traditional camp songs, school songs, silly songs, and hand-clapping songs for just these occasions, to stem boredom and build camaraderie. She sings these songs with the children about once a week, usually in the last 15–20 minutes of a day. Some songs are sung without accompaniment, but others are accompanied by downloaded recordings or by chords on the guitar or portable keyboard, which she or students play. Because she sang as a child and enjoys these songs some 20 years later, she wants to give children the same opportunities to know songs they can sing anytime (including on field trips) just for the fun of it.

MUSICAL OPENERS AND CLOSERS

Music entices learning and social interaction.

Strong and effective teachers know that children's emotions affect their concentration and learning, and that music influences emotions powerfully. They have long used music to welcome children, open the day's activities, build a classroom community, and provide predictable patterns throughout the day that comfort children. Music starts the day on a positive note, and helps children feel that they belong to a group that works together to make or experience something beautiful.

MUSICAL WAYS TO START THE DAY

- Sing national heritage songs about spirit, pride, or the people of the nation, such as "America (My Country, 'Tis of Thee)," "America, the Beautiful," "This Land Is Your Land," and "The Star-Spangled Banner." Project the lyrics on a screen for songs children may not know well, or for songs with many words. Sing these songs daily so that children become familiar with them. Vary the activity by singing as a class, in small groups, unaccompanied, and with accompaniment on guitar, keyboard, or recordings.
- Move rhythmically to music. Invite children to enter the classroom with a vigorous march playing on the sound system. Model different ways to show the beat, e.g., clapping, snapping, stamping, hopping, blinking eyelids, nodding head, lifting shoulders alternately, or tapping head, shoulders, knees, and toes. (For children in the intermediate grades, combine two or more movements into a repeating pattern, such as clap-snap or stamp-hop.) Children can imitate these movements as soon as their coats and lunches are stored and they move toward their desks. The energy ratchets up in this experience, and children focus their attention.
- Direct children to "enter the classroom as the drum says." Play a steady marching rhythm (heavy-light-heavy-light) on a hand drum, at a moderate walking tempo and medium dynamic level for a while, then change: slower (children should slow their steps), faster, softer (children tiptoe), louder (children stomp), or a skipping rhythm (long-short-long-short). Come to a complete musical stop occasionally, during which the children freeze in

place. You might also choose a child to play the drum to direct how other students come into the room.

▶ When children are fairly acquainted with left and right, offer an entrance activity that pairs a drum sound for the left foot with a metallic percussion sound (cymbal, triangle, or agogô bells) for the right foot. Thus you can direct marching on alternate feet (drum-cymbal-drum-cymbal), hopping on the left foot alone (drum-drum-drum), hopping right foot alone (cymbal-cymbal-cymbal), or hopping on both feet (play both instruments at the same time).

▶ Play recordings of gentle music to set a calm tone, or of more rigorous music to set an upbeat tone. Children can listen while they get ready for the day, talk quietly with friends, or draw. They might engage directly with the music: moving rhythmically, dancing alone or mirroring the movement of a partner, making puppets dance, or moving ribbons or scarves in the air.

▶ Open the class as though it were an opera or musical. Sing or chant instructions or questions in musical ways, and have students respond by singing or chanting answers or follow-up questions.

Just as music can set the mood at the beginning of the day, it can also modulate moods during the day. Teachers may engage children in rousing and rhythmic ways, with or without recorded music, to work off excess energy or enliven them during the after-lunch lull. When school days are stressful from testing or academic challenges, music (especially with vigorous movement or dance) can help children relax, wind down, release emotional energy in safe ways, and center their thinking.

MUSICAL WAYS TO END THE DAY

▶ Sing a song. Repeat the day's opening song, or sing a farewell song. Sing a selected song of the week, or assign a song to each day of the week. Invite children to form small groups to sing for the class a song they know or wrote themselves. (See Chapter 4 for song suggestions grouped by grade level, or Chapter 8 for creating songs.)

▶ Invite students who are learning band or orchestral instruments, or piano, to play music for their classmates. The performance need not be polished; it is merely an opportunity to share what they have been learning.

▶ Play recordings of soothing music at the end of particularly stressful days, and have the children listen quietly as they read, complete their worksheets, or get a head start on their homework. (See Chapter 5 for listening suggestions.)

▶ Play recordings for directed listening, allowing students to relax with their heads resting on their arms or desks. Focus their attention by asking, "What image does the music bring to mind?" or "What do you feel when listening to this music?"

▶ Play a rhythmic follow-the-leader game using body percussion (clapping, snapping, patting, stamping), a few drums and other percussion instruments, or boxes, pencils, and trash cans. The teacher or a student leader plays a rhythmic phrase, and children echo it. Begin with four-beat rhythm patterns, and lengthen to eight-beat patterns once children become familiar with the activity. Invite individual students to lead, spontaneously creating rhythmic phrases. Some possible rhythms are:

Beat 1		Beat 2	Beat 3	Beat 4	Beat 5		Beat 6	Beat 7		Beat 8

SIGNALS AND ATTENTION-GETTERS

Musical signals save the teacher's voice while catching the attention of talkative children, and remind them to pay attention, listen, or focus on the assigned activity. The simplest and least intrusive signal is one chime by a finger cymbal or small brass bell. The high tone cuts through the sound of children talking and can be set as the teacher's reminder for silence, during reading for example. It should only be rung once. If the silence breaker continues to talk, the teacher will need to take other measures, although this signal has perennially proven effective.

Teachers often clap a short rhythm pattern to get their children's attention. When children hear it, they typically echo it, stop what they are doing, and look at the teacher for instructions. Percussion instruments can represent common recurring actions during the day (a triangle roll for lunchtime, or C-A-F pitches played on tone bars for the end of silent reading or other subjects). Weekly student leaders may play these instrumental signals. Recorded music can also signal time to put things away and get ready to go home.

MUSICAL BREAKS AND TRANSITIONS BETWEEN SUBJECTS

Transitions from one subject or activity to the next are necessary parts of the school day, and, if not handled properly, can turn into chaotic time-wasters. Music provides a pleasant and relaxing change of pace during transitions, maximizing efficiency. Music between activities energizes, provides an emotional break from intellectual focus, and stimulates muscular exercise that gets the blood moving through bodies and brains. Following are some specific suggestions for using music in transition periods.

- ▶ Kindergarten, first-, and second-grade teachers can see when children are losing attention to an assignment. When you observe restlessness and waning concentration, it's time for a wiggle song. Have children stand up and sing a song with movements, such as "My Dog Rags," "The Hokey Pokey," or "She'll Be Comin' 'Round the Mountain."
- ▶ Inform children that they will have 30 seconds to be ready for the next subject, then play a recording of the theme from the television show *Jeopardy!*, which runs exactly 30 seconds.
- ▶ Announce the end of a period for one subject and have children estimate how many seconds it will take them to put away current learning materials and ready themselves for the next activity. Note their estimate on the

board, then play recorded music for the estimated time. If children do not complete the transition by the end of the music, discuss how to accelerate the activity.

► Set up the transition as above, but this time ask the children to sing a song of an appropriate length, at the end of which all should be ready to begin the next subject. One verse of "The Star Spangled Banner" runs 70 seconds, one verse of "America (My Country, 'Tis of Thee)" runs 30 seconds, and one verse of "We Shall Overcome" runs 45 seconds. Ask the children to suggest favorite songs for these transitions, time them, and select them. (If a song is too short, sing it two, three, or four times; if too long, reduce it to one verse).

► Invite children who are studying instruments to play songs while the rest of the class sings or hums the melody. "Mary Had a Little Lamb" takes about 15 seconds to play; "Twinkle, Twinkle Little Star," "Clementine," "Hop, Old Squirrel," "Jubilee," and "Sing Together" can be performed in 15 to 30 seconds. Repeat or combine these song melodies for longer transitions. Teachers who play instruments may also play during transitions.

► However the music is made, suggest that children move in the character of the music as they put away books or bring out pencils, paper, or laptops. Children would march to marching music, step softly and slowly to a lullaby, or dance in the character of a selection from ballet (such as *The Nutcracker*; see Appendix 3) or popular music, bringing joy, excitement, and sometimes humor, to the transitions. Music transforms boring tasks into times for community-building and amusement.

MUSIC AT CLASSROOM LISTENING CENTERS

In many classrooms teachers create spaces where students can explore topics of particular interest to them, or find information directed by the teacher. A classroom listening center may consist of a nook or corner in the room where children can listen to recorded music, view music videos, and explore the Internet for information on musicians, musical styles, instruments, historical eras, and cultural expressions. With headphones on, they can pursue independent listening and viewing, or be guided by a worksheet with questions that direct their search. They can collaborate in pairs or trios with multiple headphones, in music listening or searching for information on music and musicians. Listening centers provide instruction and skill development, but also solace and safe havens for children who need a break or emotional release. With nothing more than a table, a chair, and a computer, a classroom listening center can transport children to another, more beautiful world.

MUSIC AT CAMP AND ON FIELD TRIPS

Many fifth- and sixth-grade curricula include outdoor education and environmental science units that take place at a camp. Children may go during the day or stay overnight with their classmates in cabins as they learn about nature and the

CHAPTER 9 | Music for the Joy of It

> **CELEBRATING HOLIDAYS AND SEASONS TO MEET MUSIC STANDARDS**
>
> 1. Singing. Most holidays come with a number of songs. Encourage singing in tune and in time, with good tone and breath support.
>
> 2. Playing. Many holidays specific to particular countries are associated with folk instruments. Bring them into the classroom to let children explore them, and invite children who have been studying these instruments to play and demonstrate for others.
>
> 3. Improvising. Encourage children to create instrumental riffs to accompany holiday songs, rhymed chants, or instrumental melodies.
>
> 4. Composing and arranging. Have children compose poetry about a holiday and arrange it into a rap with a steady beat and rhythmic accompaniment, or add pitches to the rap to turn it into a melody.
>
> 5. Reading and notating. Encourage children to invent their own graphic icons to represent holiday music they invent or perform, and have them exchange their graphs with another group to realize and interpret.
>
> 6. Listening. Listen to a number of holiday songs, noticing the formal structure of musical phrases, which are often one of the following:
>
>   - Phrase A/Phrase A/Phrase B/Phrase A (AABA) (Example: "Deck the Halls")
>   - Verse 1/Refrain/Verse 2/Refrain, etc. (ABAB) (Example: "Cielito lindo")
>
>   Holiday songs are also excellent for listening and discerning the song's meter.
>
> 7. Evaluating. Play two different recorded performances of a holiday song and invite the children to state qualities of each. Ask whether each quality belongs only to one version or to both, then write it on a Venn diagram, with shared qualities in the overlapped section. When finished, have children vote on which version they prefer, based on the qualities.
>
> 8. Connecting to other arts and curricular areas. Have students write new, discipline-specific lyrics (language arts) to a familiar holiday song, substituting humorous events where appropriate (example for health education: "Over the liver and through the tum, my food goes a-rollin' down. / The vitamins help, and minerals, too, to make my body strong. / Over the liver and through the tum, my food goes a-rollin' down. / I eat the food that's good for me, and then I can't go wrong").
>
> 9. Connecting to culture and history. Help children connect holiday songs with historical events through stories and dramatizations.

environment along with regular academic subjects. Camps employ counselors who are also trained to teach. They may lead camp-themed songs, which are often catchy, funny, and light-hearted to reflect the joy of being at camp. Counselors often visit the school weeks ahead to prepare children for their camp experience. They may teach a song or two during this visit and leave song sheets (and sometimes recordings) so that the teacher and children may preview and practice the songs they will sing at camp. Children sing these songs enthusiastically long after the camp has ended. Classroom teachers can help children learn these songs before camp, and use them for various purposes throughout the day after camp.

Most schools provide transportation for one field trip per year per class. This is an ideal time for children to sing songs together that they have learned in the classroom or music class. Children enjoy the communal feeling and emotional expression of singing together, as do teachers, parent chaperones, bus drivers, and passersby, who may join the children on familiar songs. Songs add to

Singing adds to the joy of discovering new things on field trips and at camp.

the joy of discovering new things on a field trip and help pass the time on long bus rides. Classroom teachers can prepare students for field trips by teaching them songs about where they are going, such as:

- The zoo: "Kookaburra," "I Bought Me a Cat," "Five Little Monkeys," "Who Built the Ark?" and other songs about animals, birds, and reptiles.
- A museum: Choose songs corresponding to the content of a particular museum, including "I've Been Working on the Railroad," "We Shall Overcome," and "When Johnny Comes Marching Home."
- City Hall or state capitol: Official city or state songs, or songs of regions, rivers, mountains, and lakes such as "Erie Canal," "Rocky Mountain," and "This Land Is Your Land."

MUSIC FOR HOLIDAYS, THE SEASONS, AND SPECIAL EVENTS

Songs that celebrate special days and seasons reinforce what is taught and learned in language arts, math, science, and social studies. Table 9.1 offers a summary of the songs detailed below, which celebrate holidays and seasons throughout the year and around the world.

AUTUMN HOLIDAYS: SEPTEMBER–NOVEMBER

Chuseok

Date: September

Occasion: Chuseok is the Korean harvest festival, celebrated at the autumnal equinox, as summer passes into fall. The holiday may be rooted in ancient celebrations of the harvest moon, when harvested foods were offered to family ancestors and deities, or may have grown out of a month-long weaving competition during the Silla kingdom (57 B.C.E.–935 C.E.). During Chuseok, South Koreans return to their hometowns to visit the graves of their ancestors, offering them harvest crops and food. Children and adults alike play folk games, some dress in cow and turtle costumes, and a dance called nongak is performed to the percussion music of *p'ung mul* or *samulnori*, a farmers' ensemble of outdoor instruments. The holiday food includes *songpyeon*, a crescent-shaped, steamed rice cake. Chuseok is a three-day legal holiday in South Korea.

Song: "K'wejina ch'ing ch'ing" is a Korean harvest song that celebrates the sound of the gong: "k'wejina ch'ing ch'ing nane." The gong is played alone or in a percussion ensemble such as *nongak*, along with drums, woodblocks, and bells.

Nongak (farmer's dance) accompanied by pungmul musicians is a traditional part of the South Korean autumn holiday of Chuseok.

CHAPTER 9 | Music for the Joy of It **171**

TABLE 9.1 HOLIDAY AND SEASONAL MUSIC FOR THE SCHOOL YEAR

DATE	HOLIDAY OR SEASON	COUNTRY OR REGION	MUSIC
September	Chuseok (Autumnal equinox)	Korea	K'wejina ch'ing ch'ing
September–October	Eid al-Fitr	Muslim communities worldwide	Ramadan el sana di
October	Rosh Hashanah	Jewish communities worldwide	Hava nashira
October 31	Halloween	Worldwide	Ghost of Tom
November 11	Veterans Day	Worldwide	Taps
Late November	Thanksgiving	United States	Over the River and through the Wood
October–November	Diwali	Hindu communities worldwide	Oru kallu
Late November–December	Hanukkah	Jewish communities worldwide	The Hanukkah Song
December	Loy Krathong	Thailand	Loy krathong
December 25	Christmas	Christian communities worldwide	Children, Go Where I Send Thee
Last week of December	Kwanzaa	African-American communities worldwide	Lift Every Voice and Sing
Third Monday in January	Martin Luther King Day	African-American communities worldwide	We Shall Overcome
January–February	Chinese New Year	Chinese communities worldwide	Gong xi-fa cai
February	Black History Month	United States, United Kingdom, Canada	Keep Your Hand on That Plow
February–March	Carnival	Christian (especially Catholic) communities worldwide	Roda pião
February 14	Valentine's Day	Worldwide	Valentine's Day Greeting
Third Monday in February	President's Day	United States	Presidents for Their Time
March 17	St. Patrick's Day	Irish communities worldwide	Dúlamán
May 5	Cinco de Mayo	Mexican communities worldwide	Cielito lindo

Eid al-Fitr

Date: September–October

Occasion: In the ninth month of the Islamic calendar, known as Ramadan, Muslims fast and pray for 30 days. By not eating or drinking during daylight hours, they demonstrate patience and spirituality. Even by the age of 10 or 11 children read the Quran and concentrate on prayer, self-control, and developing greater sensitivity toward others. After sunset, family members share a meal together. Eid al-Fitr is the holiday at the end of Ramadan, when people dress in their best clothes, pray, offer food to the poor, give presents to one another, and enjoy a feast with family and friends. The lantern symbolizes Ramadan, and is hung in houses and mosques.

Song: "Ramadan el sana di" was produced by the youth-oriented Hadeer Organization but is enjoyed by adults and children alike. Online music videos of the song show children singing, dancing, and engaging in typical childhood activities like basketball, bicycling, painting, and studying. The verses speak to the importance of fasting and praying (five times a day), and the recurring chorus is "Ramadan, Ramadan, Ramadan el sana di" ("Ramadan this year").

Jewish New Year

Date: September–October

Occasion: Rosh Hashanah celebrates the first day of the new year in the Hebrew calendar, a reminder of the creation of the world. It occurs between mid-September and mid-October, and is the first of the ten High Holidays. Religious poems and prayers are shared, and the shofar (horn) is blown at religious services. Meals include apples and honey to symbolize the sweetness of the new year, and challah (braided bread with sesame seeds). "Shana Tova" ("A good year") is the traditional greeting.

Song: "Hava nashira" ("Come, let us sing, Alleluia") is a song of Jewish communal celebrations. It celebrates life itself, and the joy of participating in a community of families, friends, and neighbors. It is sung in unison or as a canon (or round), and is often danced in a circle, moving to the right, hands held, arms swinging in and out, stepping on every beat. A grapevine step is typical, with the left foot stepping in front of and then behind the right foot (right step, left in front, right step, left behind). The group sings and dances their love and care for one another.

Halloween

Date: October 31

Occasion: Costumes, pumpkins, ghost stories, and trick-or-treating are common on Halloween, a holiday celebrated on the last day of October. The holiday dates from at least several centuries ago, when the English and Scots commemorated All Hallow's Eve, the evening before All Saint's Day. In the northern hemisphere, the holiday's chilling air, falling leaves, and blowing wind have inspired stories of ghosts, goblins, witches, and characters such as Frankenstein's monster, Dracula, mummies, and Ichabod Crane of *The Legend of Sleepy Hollow*. Trick-or-treating dates to the early twentieth century; children in costumes of spooky characters, heroes, and heroines go door to door and receive sweets and candies.

Song: "Ghost of Tom" is a traditional Halloween round. Like most folk songs in the oral tradition, the song is sung with some variation. Some people know it with these lyrics: "Have you seen the ghost of John? Long white bones with the flesh all gone. Oooh, wouldn't it be chilly with no skin on?." while another variation is "Have you seen the ghost of Tom? Sharp, pointed teeth and a nose so long, Oooh, only one cheek to keep his tongue in." Sometimes, the lyrics of one version mix with the other. The song can be sung in a four-part canon or in just two parts, or played or sung and played, all in a quiet and mysterious way as children discuss how in the world John turned out so ghastly!

Veteran's Day

Date: November 11

Occasion: Every year, Americans honor and celebrate military veterans in what is also called Remembrance Day or Armistice Day (when World War I ended); Canadians celebrate their own Remembrance Day on the same date. President Woodrow Wilson established the holiday in 1919 as a time to reflect upon the heroism of those who died serving their country as well as to celebrate peace time. Schools and government offices close, and programs on or around that date honor living and deceased American veterans.

Song: "Taps" is a musical signal that used to mean "lights out" in the U.S. military. It is typically played by a solo bugle or trumpet, and was used as far back as the American Civil War by the Union and Confederate forces.

Americans honor and celebrate military veterans on Veterans Day, or Armistice Day.

It is heard at military funerals, on Memorial Day and Veterans Day, and several times daily at the Tomb of the Unknown Soldier in Arlington National Cemetery. Occasionally it is sung with these words: "Day is done, gone the sun, from the lake, from the hills, from sky; All is well, safely rest, God is nigh." Children enjoy gesturing the words with American Sign Language, which is easy enough for first graders to learn.

Thanksgiving

Date: Late November

Occasion: Citizens of the United States and Canada celebrate Thanksgiving, about seven weeks apart; Canadians celebrates on the second Monday of October and Americans on the fourth Thursday of November. The holiday can be traced to European harvest festivals and Native American celebrations of the end of the harvest season. Americans recall the feast in the Plymouth, Massachusetts colony in 1621, when the Wampanoag Indians taught them about fishing, planting, and harvesting, while Canadians are reminded of the safe return of a lost explorer, Martin Frobisher, who had been in search of the Northwest Passage, and his formal giving of thanks in Newfoundland for having survived. Nowadays, Thanksgiving brings families together to share such holiday foods as turkey, a bread dressing, cranberries, and pumpkin pie, and to be thankful for good health and blessings.

Song: "Over the River and through the Wood" was written as a poem and song for Thanksgiving by Lydia Child in 1844. A prominent abolitionist (her home was a stop on the Underground Railroad), she was also a teacher, journalist, poet, and staunch feminist; however, her fond memories of Thanksgiving at her grandfather's house were first published as "A Boy's Thanksgiving Day."

WINTER HOLIDAYS: NOVEMBER–DECEMBER

Diwali

Date: October–November

Occasion: Also called "Deepavali," Diwali is the Hindu festival of lights marking the end of the harvest season and the triumph of good over evil. Indian families celebrate Diwali for five days, sharing sweets and snacks and dressing up, and recalling the traditional epic story in which Rama returns to Sita following his victory over the demonic Ravana. Lights decorate shops and homes, traditional clay lamps hang in the streets, and fireworks stream through the air. Music is sung, played, and danced to everywhere, and children enjoy folk and traditional songs they learn from their elders. For devout Hindus, it is a significant time for recognizing the inner light of peace, harmony, and spirituality.

Song: "Oru kallu" is a children's folk song in the Tamil language, from southern India. The song accompanies a children's game of picking up stones and flapping the arms like a parrot, played in a circle. The words translate as "One stone, we shall pick it up. One stone, we shall throw it away. One thousand flying parrots, dancing, singing, and flying the temple, flying to the sky." The song can be accompanied on simple classroom instruments such as hand drums, xylophones, and recorders, and can be danced by children in a circle facing center and moving thusly:

1. Bend and pretend to pick up stones and throw them outside the circle (eight beats)

2. Turn in a circle, flapping arms like parrot wings (four beats turning right, four beats turning left)

3. Repeat step two

4. Repeat step one

5. Hold hands and step forward (four beats)

6. Hold hands and step backward (four beats)

7. Repeat steps five and six

Hanukkah

Date: Late November–December

Occasion: Hanukkah, or Chanukah, is the eight-day Jewish festival of lights It is symbolized by the menorah, a set of eight candles or lights with one raised light at center; one additional light is lit every day of the Hanukkah season. Jews sing songs, pray, and share latkes (potato pancakes), dairy, and fried foods. Children play the dreidel, a four-sided spinning top, with rewards of nuts, raisins, candies, and coins. Often, families exchange small gifts each day of the Hanukkah season.

Song: "The Hanukkah Song" is sung during the joyful celebration of a menorah burning miraculously for eight days despite having oil for only one day. Another Hanukkah song is the well-known "Ma'oz tzur" ("Rock of Ages"), a Hebrew song dating back nearly a millennium. Hanukkah songs are often danced in a basic eight-beat grapevine pattern: step right, left in front, step right, left behind, step right, lift left, step left, lift right).

Loy Kratong

Date: December

Occasion: In Thailand, Loy Krathong celebrates the full moon of the twelfth month in the Thai lunar calendar. The holiday dates to the mid-nineteenth century as a tribute to the Buddha, Siddhārtha Gautama. Loy Krathong is a thanksgiving for an abundant supply of water, when people float (*loy*) little boats (*krathong*) made of banana leaves, with candles or other devices of light attached, in lakes and rivers. Large boats and rafts, too, are decorated for the occasion and paraded in a grand procession. The Thai let go of their anger, fear, and sorrow on this holiday, and float away all their bad traits. Fireworks and music fill the air on this festive occasion.

Song: Children and adults sing "Loy krathong" everywhere during the festival, and it is broadcast on radio and television. The melody is played on every imaginable instrument, from traditional xylophones, tuned gongs, flutes, and oboes to keyboards and guitars. The song is also danced by partners in a circle with small, shuffling steps as they move their hands gracefully, with upturned fingers, in a distinctive Thai style.

Christmas

Date: December 25

Occasion: One of the most popular holidays in much of the world, Christmas celebrates the birth of Jesus, the central figure of Christianity. Non-Christians also celebrate, giving gifts, singing carols, sending cards, and eating holiday meals with family and friends. Many Christmas celebrations today are more secular than sacred, but church ceremonies remain important to many who adhere to the religious significance of the holiday.

Song: "Children, Go Where I Send Thee" is one of many songs associated with Christmas. Built into the song is a call-and-response device (Direction: "Children, go where I send thee," Call: "How shall I send thee?," Response: "I'm gonna send thee one by one," etc.). The verses draw from biblical references.

Kwanzaa

Date: Last week of December

Occasion: From December 26 to January 1, African Americans celebrate seven principles of an African-based philosophy of their heritage during Kwanzaa: unity, self-determination, collective work and responsibility, cooperative economics, purpose, creativity, faith. Based on the efforts of Maulana Karenga and the black nationalist movement of the 1960s, Kwanzaa provides a unique and separate holiday which typically does not replace Christmas but adds African- and African-American dimensions.

Song: "Lift Every Voice and Sing" is an anthem to African-American identity, and has been referred to as "The Black American National Anthem." It was composed by two brothers, the poet and school principal James Weldon Johnson and the composer John Rosamund Johnson, in honor of a prestigious visitor to James Johnson's school, the author and educator Booker T. Washington. The poem came first, in 1900, followed by the song in 1905. The song rings of freedom, patriotism, and identity, and has been recorded by such notable artists and groups as Stevie Wonder, Leontyne Price, Take 6, and the Women of the Calabash (on *The Kwanzaa Album*).

WINTER INTO SPRING HOLIDAYS: JANUARY–MAY

Martin Luther King Day

Date: Third Monday in January

Occasion: Martin Luther King day was first observed in 1986, eighteen years after the Rev. Dr. Martin Luther King was assassinated during the civil rights movement. Dr. King was born on January 15, 1929, and quickly rose as a Baptist minister who endorsed nonviolent methods, inspired by Mahatma Gandhi, to secure fair and equitable treatment, including voting rights, for all American citizens. He led the Southern Christian Leadership Conference and maintained that peaceful protesting and powerful black churches were the antidote to racial discrimination. Dr. King inspired thought and action by pursuing justice orally and in print, notably with his "I Have a Dream" speech and his "Letter from Birmingham Jail." He was awarded the Nobel Peace Prize in 1964.

Song: "We Shall Not Be Moved" is a spiritual that took hold in the civil rights movement as early as the 1930s. It became a theme song in reference to Rosa Parks, who chose to disobey the unjust law that African Americans must sit at the back of the bus; she refused to be moved from her front seat in protest. Along with "We Shall Overcome" and other African-American spirituals, "We Shall Not Be Moved" galvanized the efforts of those who fought for equal rights for all people in the middle of the twentieth century.

Chinese New Year

Date: January–February

Occasion: By far the most important Chinese holiday is the Chinese New Year, celebrated not only in China, but in Chinese communities in Hong Kong, Taiwan, Singapore, Malaysia, and around the world. It marks the end of winter, beginning on the first day of the traditional Chinese calendar. That evening, families gather to feast, and over the next fifteen days, families sweep the house of the bad luck and make room for the good luck to come in the spring, offering children *hong bao* (red paper envelopes with money inside), setting off firecrackers, and enjoying roast pig, duck, and various sweets. Chinese New Year follows the lunar calendar, landing sometime between January 21 and February 20 and influencing festivals in the region, including Tet (in Vietnam).

Song: "Gong xi-fa cai" is based on the common greeting of the Chinese New Year, which translates as "Congratulations! May your wealth and prosperity increase!" In response to this wish for a happy new year, children may respond playfully, "Hong bao na lai," or "Red envelope, please!"

Black History Month

Date: February

Occasion: Three nations share in the celebration of Black History Month: Canada, the United Kingdom, and the United States. The month was designated to raise awareness of African Americans' history, heritage, and contributions to the world. Music, the arts, literature, poetry, science, and the social sciences all owe debts to highly accomplished individuals who struggled on the long journey toward recognition and respect.

People of Chinese descent celebrate the New Year with parades all over the world.

The broader goal of Black History Month is to emphasize how efforts by African Americans enrich the overall fabric of our lives.

Song: "Keep Your Hand on That Plow" is a classic African-American spiritual, emanating from a time when most African Americans lived in rural areas on large working plantations and farms. It is a song of giving one's all, staying on course, and holding to one's convictions. One text variant is "Got my hand on the gospel plow, wouldn't take nothing for my journey now." During the civil rights movement, "Keep your eyes on the prize" was substituted for the refrain. The song affirms that hard work will pay off: with education, a good job, a good life, and salvation.

Carnival

Date: February–March

Occasion: In Brazil and elsewhere in South America, the Caribbean, and the New Orleans, Carnival precedes the coming of Lent. For Roman Catholics in particular, Lent once was a harsh time of fasting and abstinence, thus the period preceding it is one of great celebration. Although Carnival begins the weekend before, Mardi Gras, also called Fat Tuesday, is the peak party day, when revelers bid farewell to bad things before heading into a time of meditation and repentance. In Brazil, parades of dancers and drummers organized by samba schools stream through Rio de Janeiro, São Paulo, and Recife. Costumed and energetic, musicians and dancers cavort through the streets on foot and on fantasy floats on large motorized wagons. African-based rhythms preside, and the music-making and feasting continues all day and night.

Song: "Roda pião" is a Brazilian children's song about a teetotum, a top that is spun on an axis once a string is pulled and released from it. The words translate roughly as: "The teetotum has joined the circle; roll the teetotum and let it loose. Stamp your feet in the backyard. Give your hat to a chosen friend." Children form a circle, holding hands, singing, and clapping, as they walk around the child at the center of the circle who spins and shakes in imitation of the top, improvising on the rhythms that are sung and clapped.

Valentine's Day

Date: February 14

Occasion: Valentine's Day, a widely-observed commemoration of love, is a cultural and commercial phenomenon. People profess love for spouses, significant others, friends, classmates, and family members, usually through commercial or handmade cards, flowers, and chocolate candies.

Chant: The "Valentine's Day Greeting" rhyme refers to the customary practice of sending greeting cards on Valentine's Day with expressions of love and kind words. It can be rhythmically chanted and moved in several ways:

1. In an ostinato of gestures over eight beats (pat, clap, snap/clap, clap, pat, clap, snap, rest)

2. In an invented mixture of body percussion that gives a sound to every syllable

3. In a hand-clapping pattern invented, practiced, and performed with a partner

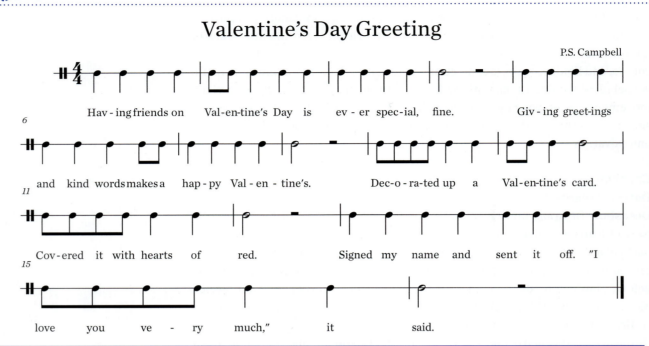

Presidents' Day

Date: Third Monday in February

Occasion: A federal holiday, Presidents' Day falls on the third Monday in February and was originally designated to celebrate George Washington's birthday, but now honors all American presidents. It offers a day off from federal (and many state) government jobs, and from school—a respite in a North American winter—and its appearance on the calendar argues for focused study of the lives and works of American statesmen, including George Washington, Abraham Lincoln, Franklin D. Roosevelt, John F. Kennedy, and others.

Rap: "Presidents for Their Time" is a children's rhyme about two historic American presidents. Just as children enjoy vocal expressions with rhythm and rhyme, they will enjoy accompanying the chant with an eight-beat pattern for drums and cowbells. Once the voices and instruments are underway, children may develop new rhythmic improvisations all their own on various other non-pitched percussion instruments (e.g., sticks and claves, wood blocks, güiros, or sand blocks).

St. Patrick's Day

Date: March 17

Occasion: St. Patrick, the patron saint of Ireland, has his own national holiday there, and is celebrated by those who claim Irish ancestry in North America, the United Kingdom, Australia, New Zealand, and elsewhere. A bishop, he brought his faith to Ireland in the fifth century and converted the island to Christianity. The three-leafed shamrock was purportedly his way of teaching the Holy Trinity, and thus today the green shamrock symbolizes him. Irish traditional music and dance, corned beef and cabbage, and wearing green are standard features of a St. Patrick's Day celebration.

EXAMPLE 9.2

People of Irish descent everywhere celebrate St. Patrick's Day with parades, music, singing, and dancing.

Song: "Dúlamán" is a traditional Irish song about the seaweed that hangs over the rocky cliffs of the western end of Ireland. Like so much of the traditional Irish music played on fiddles, flutes, bagpipes, harp, guitar, and bodhrán (a hand drum with stick), it moves in the skipping rhythm of a single jig. It can be sung in Gaelic, on a neutral syllable like "doo," or in an English translation. (The words refer to dúlamán, a type of edible seaweed, and the verse translates as "Dúlamán, the weeds are hangin' on the rocks of Ireland. From the sea the weeds are comin', Dúlamán of Ireland.") The melody can also be played on recorders, flutes, violins, piano, and other melody instruments.

Cinco de Mayo
Date: May 5
Occasion: The fifth of May is celebrated by Mexican Americans and also regionally in the state of Puebla, Mexico, where it is referred to as the Day of the Battle of

---

ADAPTING INSTRUCTION FOR VARIOUS NEEDS

Blind or Visual Impairments
Children with no or partial sight enjoy singing, playing, listening, dancing, and creating perhaps more than sighted children. Support all these interactions, but take proper precautions for safety and provide appropriate substitute instruction and materials for this population. Teach songs by rote, rather than from written notation; assign a sighted partner guide for transition periods and other activities involving movement.

Deaf or Hearing Impairments
Children with no or limited hearing can find music deeply meaningful. Many children with limited hearing have hearing aids or listening devices and can perceive music almost as well as children with normal hearing, as long as the music is not loud enough to cause distortion. Completely deaf children can still feel vibrations on their skin and from wooden floors (as does the deaf percussionist, Evelyn Glennie). Deaf children can sing with their hands, along with hearing children, using American Sign Language to express the lyrics.

Behavioral Disorders with Externalizing Behaviors
State clear parameters of acceptable behavior for all musical experiences, so that all children can enjoy participating in music within acceptable limits of expression. Ask students to repeat the instructions, or even write the instructions in a notebook. Use any number of behavior-modification techniques, from giving limited choices (are you able to sing with us nicely today, or do you need some time out?) to more formal and intensive interventions (such as a behavior contract with set consequences).

Behavioral Disorders with Internalizing Behaviors
Some children may enjoy music even though they may not appear to respond to it. Offer gentle encouragement, or a few friendly words expressing interest in a child's musical response (but without undue pressure to join in). Children with moderate or profound autism may not react to music at all, or may be overloaded with sensory input when the class makes music. Check the child's cumulative record for suggestions by experts of ways to overcome problems. Parents will also have good ideas.

Mobility Impairments
Adjust instruments for children's involvement. Model ways for an assistant to help guide the child's involvement, or partner children such that one can gently assist a child who may require some help in playing an instrument or moving to the music.

Puebla (El Día de la Batalla de Puebla), when in 1862, the Mexicans first defeated the French during their occupation of Mexico. Cinco de Mayo in the United States is primarily a celebration by Americans of Mexican ancestry, akin to the Irish St. Patrick's Day, the German Oktoberfest, and the Chinese New Year. Revelers play mariachi music, perform baile folklórico (folkloric dance), and enjoy homemade tortillas, tacos, burritos, and tamales .

Song: "Cielito lindo," a love song that resonates as a serenade to a young lady by her suitor, is one of the best-known of all Mexican melodies. It is sung solo and with guitar accompaniment, and it is performed by full-size mariachi bands of violins, vihuela, guitar, guitarrón, harp, and trumpets. It was popularized in Mexican films in the 1940s and 1950s, and may have been based on a traditional melody.

Summary

Children and their teachers need and deserve joy every day throughout the year. Music lifts the spirit, lightens the workload, brings joy to mundane tasks, promotes community, and celebrates special events. Teachers who regularly use music in their classrooms promote joyful learning and well-being in their students, and give themselves the gift of knowing they are providing enlightened, holistic education to their children.

Review

1. Discuss several ways to use music to open the school day.

2. Discuss several ways to use music in transitions.

3. How can a listening center in your classroom facilitate learning?

4. Where can teachers find song resources for field trips?

5. Name some songs to help children celebrate particular seasons or holidays.

Critical Thinking

1. Compare and contrast the benefit and drawbacks of using music vs. words as a signal or attention-getter.

2. Describe your preferred way of using music to set the mood at opening of the day and explain why you prefer it.

3. Evaluate the pros or cons of infusing music into an elementary classroom.

Projects

1. Call the principal of a local elementary school, identify yourself as a student of Elementary Music Methods, and ask which teacher uses the most music in his or her classroom. Set an appointment to interview that teacher and take notes on how they use music. If time allows, observe the teacher in the classroom.

2. Design a classroom music center of your own imagination. Diagram its physical space, and describe its contents and activities.

3. With a colleague, learn a holiday song and develop at least one additional activity that would help children to celebrate that holiday (storytelling, food preparation, craft-making, etc.). Present the song and selected activity to the class.

Additional Resources for Teaching

Bjørkvold, Jon-Roar. (1992). *The Muse Within: Creativity and Communication, Song and Play from Childhood through Maturity.* (William H. Halverson, Trans.). Oslo, Norway: Peer Gynt Press.

Dillon, Susan. (2003). *The Scholastic Big Book of Holidays Around the Year.* New York, NY: Scholastic Teaching Resources.

Matthew, Kathryn I., and Joy L. Lowe. (2004). *Neal-Schuman Guide to Celebrations and Holidays Around the World: The Best Books, Media, and Multicultural Learning Activities.* New York, NY: Neal Schuman Publications.

Wallin, Nils J., Bjorn Merker, and Steven Brown (Eds.). (2000). *The Origins of Music.* Cambridge, MA: MIT Press.

Additional Songs for Teaching

Autumn's Here	Hop, Old Squirrel	I Went to California
Hey, Ho, Nobody Home	How Many Miles to Babylon?	Oh, John the Rabbit
Hill an' Gully Rider		

Online Resources: Audio and Songbook

digital.wwnorton.com/classroom

10
MUSIC AND LANGUAGE ARTS

All the words that come out of our mouths (as well as the lines that emerge from our pens and word processors) ride upon a stream of music. To help individuals achieve literacy, it seems critically important that we acknowledge this important connection between words and music and use it as fully as we can to help our students read and write more effectively.

—Thomas Armstrong, *The Multiple Intelligences of Reading and Writing*[1]

IN THIS CHAPTER

In the Classroom

Relationships between Language Arts and Music

Music Helps Children Learn Language Arts

Integrating with Integrity: Engaging the National Standards for Music Education

The National Standards in this Chapter's Vignettes

Music and Children's Literature

Developing Reading and Thinking Skills through Music

Phonological (Phonemic) Awareness

Building Comprehension

Writing About Music

Summary

Review

Critical Thinking

Projects

Additional Resources for Teaching

Children point to each letter as they sing the alphabet.

183

You Will Learn

- more about the relationships between language arts and music
- how music can be used to enhance literature
- how music can help teach basic reading skills and build fluency, inflection, and comprehension
- how music can help with various kinds of writing

Ask Yourself

- As a child, did you ever read story books based on music?
- As a child, did a classroom teacher use music to help you learn to read?
- How do you feel about using music to help teach reading and language arts?
- Have you ever written a poem or prose piece in response to music?

IN THE CLASSROOM

VIGNETTE ONE

The children in Ms. Gayle's kindergarten class love to sing "The Itsy Bitsy Spider" with hand motions. Over time, Ms. Gayle has helped the children to discover the rhyming words (spout/out and rain/again). The children focus on those words by singing the song silently in their heads, then singing the rhyming words out loud. Later they add a woodblock to "spout" and "out," and a cymbal to "rain" and "again," to emphasize the rhymes.

Ms. Gayle's children especially enjoy inventing a spider dance to Little Richard's recording of "The Itsy Bitsy Spider," moving their bodies up and down with the spider and feeling the funky rhythms. Finally, Ms. Gayle puts copies of the book *The Itsy Bitsy Spider* in the reading corner so children can follow the pictures and words as they sing or read the song—moving from familiar lyrics into the visual representations of those words. Ms. Gayle reinforces the words during various pre-reading activities such as chanting words that rhyme with itsy-bitsy (mitsy-witsy) and spider (glider, wider, cider).

VIGNETTE TWO

The second graders in Mrs. Thompson's class are listening to her read *Abiyoyo*, Pete Seeger's book based on a South African folktale. As she reads, they sing the simple lullaby each time it appears in the story. Later, they discuss the story and retell it using their own words. Once they feel comfortable with the story line, they dramatize the story, singing the song and improvising accompaniment on drums and rattles, playing gently on the strong pulses, demonstrating their comprehension of the story as well as aspects of its cultural origins.

VIGNETTE THREE

Mr. Garcia's fifth graders are researching and reporting on their favorite musician or musical group. He allows them to work alone in a team of no more than four students, and encourages them to consult a variety of print and web-based resources to gather their information. Mr. Garcia has provided guiding questions for the children to consider regarding the development of the musician or group; the focus and style of the music; and what draws them to this music. His students will respond to the questions in an oral report that presents images and sampled sounds from the artists with presentation software. The students will critique the clear communication of their own work and reflect on the challenges of making it in the music industry.

RELATIONSHIPS BETWEEN LANGUAGE ARTS AND MUSIC

Language arts and music are closely related in several ways. They both:

▶ communicate between and connect individuals and groups;
▶ combine small elements into larger structures: words or musical motifs into phrases or sentences;

- concern the elements of rhythm, pitch, and accent;
- convey direct and implied meanings;
- create imagery and affect the emotions;
- convey important cultural information;
- integrate time and sound as part of the artwork;
- tell stories—specifically with words or abstractly in sound—such as *The Little Train of the Caipira* by Villa Lobos or *In the Hall of the Mountain King* by Grieg.
- combine to tell a story in a more complete and interesting way, such as Prokofiev's *Peter and the Wolf* (see Appendix 3);
- can represent natural sounds (language through onomatopoeic words—splash, rickety-rackety, meow, and so on—and music through instruments, vocal colorings, or sound effects).

Poetry and music combine in songs, which offer not only individual but also communal forms of expression. As literary forms, songs convey history, myth, inspiration, celebration, and cultural comment. Songs embody particular moments in time and place, ultimately transcending time and place.

MUSIC HELPS CHILDREN LEARN LANGUAGE ARTS

To read effectively, children must do more than just decode: they must be sensitive to visual imagery, emotional correlations of sound and rhythm, how words are used for more than just their direct meanings.[2] Effective teachers understand the importance of these higher-level language skills and how they can be mastered through music.

Because children are inherently musical, music provides a motivational bridge to learning the mechanics and higher-level skills of language arts. Studying song texts can reinforce phonemic awareness; rhyming; sensitivity to alliteration, assonance, and consonance; response to graphemes; understanding of syllable identification and word segmentation; and expression and flow.[3, 4] Song texts can also hone students' higher-level thinking skills, such as paraphrasing and summarizing, inferring information, comparing and contrasting, identifying the moral of the story, identifying mood, predicting outcomes, and sequencing the events in a story. Songs may be used for word analysis, vocabulary building, and spelling lists. Some songs provide rich and evocative sources for learning social context and historical significance. Children can sing songs from other languages before they are able to speak or read the language, and thus songs bridge cultural gaps.

INTEGRATING WITH INTEGRITY: ENGAGING THE NATIONAL STANDARDS FOR MUSIC EDUCATION

Music is fun and engaging when it reinforces language arts education in a low-level way, such as singing "The Alphabet Song" to teach the alphabet, but more effective teaching strategies can invoke the full power of music. When teachers employ the most significant content of each discipline, learning becomes more meaningful and complete. Each academic subject has a set of national learning standards. The K–12 standards for music and for English language arts are presented here at their broadest level; specific details are available in the publications written to support their implementation). Outstanding teachers use these standards to help their students achieve goals across disciplines.

NATIONAL STANDARDS FOR MUSIC EDUCATION

1. Singing, alone and with others, a varied repertoire of songs

2. Performing on instruments, alone and with others, a varied repertoire of music

3. Improvising melodies, variations, and accompaniments

4. Composing and arranging music within specified guidelines

5. Reading and notating music

6. Listening to, analyzing, and describing music

7. Evaluating music and music performances

8. Understanding relationships between music, the other arts, and disciplines outside the arts

9. Understanding music in relation to history and culture

Source: Music Educators National Conference. (1994). *National Standards for Arts Education.* Reston, VA: Rowman and Littlefield.

NATIONAL STANDARDS FOR THE ENGLISH LANGUAGE ARTS

1. Students read a wide range of print and non-print texts to build an understanding of texts, of themselves, and of the cultures of the United States and the world; to acquire new information; to respond to the needs and demands of society and the workplace; and for personal fulfillment. Among these texts are fiction, nonfiction, classic, and contemporary works.

2. Students read a wide range of literature from different periods in a variety of genres to understand the many dimensions (e.g., philosophical, ethical, aesthetic) of human experience.

3. Students apply a wide range of strategies to comprehend, interpret, evaluate, and appreciate texts. They draw on their prior experience, their interactions with other readers and writers, their knowledge of word meaning and of other texts, their strategies for word identification, and their understanding of textual features (e.g. sound-letter correspondence, sentence structure, context, graphics).

4. Students adjust their spoken, written, and visual language (e.g., conventions, style, vocabulary) to communicate effectively with a variety of audiences and for different purposes.

5. Students employ a wide range of strategies as they write and use different writing process elements appropriately to communicate with different audiences and for different purposes.

6. Students apply knowledge of language structure, language conventions (e.g., spelling and punctuation), media techniques, figurative language, and genre to create, critique, and discuss print and non-print texts.

7. Students research issues and interests by generating ideas and questions, and by posing problems. They gather, evaluate, and synthesize data from a variety of sources (e.g., print and non-print texts, artifacts, people) to communicate their discoveries in ways that suit their purpose and audience.

8. Students use a variety of technological and information resources (e.g., libraries, databases, computer networks, video) to gather and synthesize information and to create and communicate knowledge.

9. Students understand and respect diversity in language use, patterns, and dialects across cultures, ethnic groups, geographic regions, and social roles.

10. Students whose first language is not English make use of their first language to learn the English language arts and to understand content across the curriculum.

11. Students participate as knowledgeable, reflective, creative, and critical members of a variety of literacy communities.

12. Students use spoken, written, and visual language to accomplish their own purposes (e.g., for learning, enjoyment, persuasion, and the exchange of information).

Source: National Council of Teachers of English. (1996). *The Standards for the English Language Arts.*

TABLE 10.1 THE NATIONAL STANDARDS IN THE VIGNETTES

VIGNETTE	MUSIC STANDARDS	ENGLISH LANGUAGE ARTS STANDARDS
Ms. Gayle's "The Itsy Bitsy Spider"	I. Singing 6. Listening and describing	1. Reading 3. Comprehension 4. Expression
Mrs. Thompson's *Abiyoyo*	1. Singing 2. Playing instruments 3. Improvising accompaniments 4. History and culture	1. Reading 3. Comprehension 4. Adjust communication 9. Diversity across cultures
Mr. Garcia's reporting on favorite musicians	6. Analyzing and describing 8. Music and disciplines outside the arts 9. History and culture	4. Adjust communication 5. Diverse strategies 7. Research 8. Use technology

THE NATIONAL STANDARDS IN THIS CHAPTER'S VIGNETTES

The vignettes that open this chapter combine elements of the Common Core Learning Standards in both music and language arts, as listed in Table 10.1.

By singing, listening and dancing to recordings, and reading printed copies of "The Itsy Bitsy Spider," Ms. Gayle's kindergarteners have engaged with myriad aspects of the song: the poetry and its rhymes, various interpretations of the music, and even pictorial representations of the story. Mrs. Thompson's second graders sing a song within a larger framework; they learn how the music furthers the story, how to improvise an appropriate accompaniment, and the cultural significance of the music. Mr. Garcia's fifth graders are using technology to research and report on musicians, and arguing persuasively to defend their choices. The best projects, lessons, or series of lessons offer students several ways to demonstrate their learning.

MUSIC AND CHILDREN'S LITERATURE

When creative teachers combine children's literature with music, their classrooms come alive with literacy and imaginative thinking.

MUSICAL PLAY

Many picture books invite musical play because they incorporate chants, musical sounds, or rhythms. Reading the books aloud to hear the *melopoeia*, or the music of the language, is the place to start. As children become familiar with the story and even able to read the book, they can then retell the story by rhythmically chanting

USING READING TO MEET MUSIC STANDARDS

1. Singing. Sing a range of songs that tell stories about people's lives. Learn to sing them with expression. Divide each story into characters (such as men, women, children, soldiers, and narrator). Invite children to sing different parts of the song that relate to specific characters.

2. Playing. Chant the week's spelling words in rhythm. Clap the syllabic rhythms of the various words. Use wooden percussion instruments to play the rhythms and have children identify which words fit the particular rhythms. Order the words from short to long and play their rhythms in that order. Finally, try combining some of the rhythms into a percussion piece.

3. Improvising. Divide older elementary children into groups of four or five. Review the meaning of an adjective. Give each group a "secret" noun. Have them improvise a short vocal piece using only adjectives to describe that noun. Encourage them to use loud/soft and high/low sounds in their improvisation. Invite the other groups to try to guess the noun from the adjectives.

4. Composing and arranging. Select a favorite simple story. Work in small groups to tell that story through musical sounds, including vocal sounds, body sounds, and instrumental sounds. Have children practice their pieces until they are satisfied with the results.

5. Reading and notating. Have children notate their story pieces using various shapes, words, and numbers. Ask them to try playing their pieces from their musical scores.

6. Listening. Listen to a piece of music with a narrator in which the instruments of the orchestra help tell the story, such as *Peter and the Wolf* by Prokofiev. Discuss what instruments go with each character and how effective or ineffective those choices are. Listen again and generate lists of words to describe each character, such as "bassoon," "low," "slow," and "plodding" for the grandfather. Share your words with others.

7. Evaluating. Use music vocabulary to describe and critique your own and others' musical creations suggested in this chapter.

8. Connecting to other arts and curriculum areas. Select a favorite story and choose art forms—music, dance, visual arts, or drama—to help bring that story to life. Work with others to add your creative ideas to the story. Share it with others and invite their feedback for refining your ideas.

9. Connecting to culture and history. Read a story from a particular culture or time. Find what instruments people in that culture or time used. Listen to recordings of those instruments if possible. Learn a song from that culture or time and add the sounds of traditional instruments as accompaniment.

it or adding instrumental or body percussion accompaniments. Adding sounds and gestures to stories not only brings them to life, it leads to greater understanding and offers additional practice with oral expression.

When combining musical play and children's literature, ask yourself:[5]

Questions About the Music

▶ Are there repeating phrases or a refrain?

▶ Does the text lend itself to an ostinato?

▶ Can you add rhythm?

▶ Can you add sounds for characters, moods, or objects?

▶ Can you add instruments or a song while reading the book?

▶ What other possible learning extensions and opportunities exist?

Questions About the Literature

▶ Is the book enjoyable and the right length?

▶ Is the book age-appropriate?

▶ Are the illustrations engaging?

▶ Are the illustrations large enough for the children to see them?

▶ Does the book lend itself to expressive reading aloud?

The following books illustrate some possibilities, and you can transfer suggested strategies to other books. *We're Going on a Bear Hunt* illustrates the traditional children's chant and invites vocal sound play from the outset. Repeated words at each new stage of the adventure encourage children to enter the story quickly and

CHAPTER 10 | Music and Language Arts **189**

find familiar places to read and speak: We're going on a bear hunt. / We're going to catch a big one. / What a beautiful day! / We're not scared. Other sets of repeated words suggest not only vocal play with onomatopoetic sounds, but also dynamic expression from soft to loud, conveyed by type size:

Squelch squerch!

Squelch squerch!

Squelch squerch!

As the children participate in telling the story, encourage them to use expressive sounds and dynamic change to heighten the suspense. Retellings can include body percussion such as finger snapping, rubbing palms together, and patting laps to suggest many of the sounds in the story. Eventually, body percussion can be replaced with instrumental sounds (for example, sand blocks to suggest the swishing of the grass) to build excitement and replicate the tone colors suggested by the words.

Max Found Two Sticks uses music to engage children in reading. In this story, a young boy improvises musical patterns represented by onomatopoetic word sounds (see Box 10.1). Read the story aloud, then write these words on a screen or board in the order they appear in the book.

Encourage individual children to read each sound pattern aloud in whatever rhythms they think best fit the story. If they suggest more than one rhythm for a sound pattern, the class can experiment and choose which one to use when reading aloud together. The type size changes to suggest dynamics, so children can stretch their expressive capacities. By reading the sound patterns aloud several times, they learn the associated rhythms and dynamic levels.

Once the children master the sound patterns, they can decide which sounds could be played on wood, metal, or glass and find objects in the classroom like those Max used to play the rhythms. One child or a chorus of children can read the story while others play their instruments at the appropriate time, substituting their instrumental sounds for the vocal sounds listed in order on the chart or

BOX 10.1 MAX'S ONOMATOPOEIC WORDS

Pat ... pat-tat

Putter-putter ... pat-tat

Tap-tap-tap

Tippy-tip ... tat-tat

Dum ... dum-de-dum

Di-di-di-di. Dum-dum.

Dong ... dang ... dung.

Ding ... dong ... ding!

Cling ... clang ... da-BANG!

A-cling-clang ... DA-BANGGGG!

Thump-di-di-tump. THUMP-DI-DI-THUMP!

EXAMPLE 10.1

combining instruments with the words. Children can take turns being the leader, pointing to each sound pattern when it occurs in the story. Although no sound words are featured at the story's end, Max is still playing his music. Allow the children to experiment with combining the sounds and sound patterns in sequence or simultaneously.

Some books, such as *Twist with a Burger, Jitter with a Bug*, immediately suggest a rhythmic response (see Example 10.1). Once children know the rhymes, they can keep a steady beat while the teacher chants the words in rhythm. Younger children can pat the beat on their laps. Older children (beginning in second or third grade) can accompany the chant with a hand jive pattern, such as pat-clap or pat-clap-snap-clap. Once children can say the chant in time, half the class can clap or tap the rhythm pattern of the words while the other half keeps the beat going.

Children may also add creative movements to the rhythmic and rhymed phrases or invent vocal ostinatos to accompany the chant, such as "polka (rest) (rest) (rest)," or "(rest) (rest) mambo (rest)." The children might also list the rhyming words in order and add musical sounds to accompany them as they occur in the chant.

CREATING SOUNDSCAPES

Soundscapes are musical backgrounds for stories. When children read books (including picture books, which fascinate learners from preschool through the sixth grade), they enter imaginative spaces, transcending their daily routines and immersing themselves in new worlds. This imagining helps children master the very important reading goal of comprehension, or understanding meaning. They can construct a sense of place by imagining the sights, tastes, and smells that bring that place to life. Children can also imagine sound, and may turn their ideas into soundscapes.

Soundscapes are not sound effects. Sound effects, which children know from movies, TV shows, and video games, are specifically tied to events in a story, such as a cow mooing or a window breaking, while soundscapes provide a musical setting for the story, like background music. Generally soundscapes are continuous or semicontinuous with occasional breaks.

Soundscapes are a dramatic way to enhance the oral reading of a familiar story, and they motivate children to present stories in an interesting fashion. From second grade through their elementary school years, children are able and eager to make musical decisions on their own. Younger children can begin by using vocal sounds, and then consider other instruments with some teacher guidance. Children in the upper elementary can apply their imaginations and considerable instrumental skills to create colorful soundscapes that enrich their favorite stories, book chapters, and scenarios.

To create a soundscape, children will need to know the story well (what a great motivation for rereading a book!), and then use their imaginations to create the musical setting for the story. This requires experimentation and discovery, until they arrive at a satisfactory setting. Children with strong voices may be assigned the roles of narrator and various characters within the story, while others may play the music they have created.

Maurice Sendak's *Where the Wild Things Are* is a fitting story to set with a soundscape. Children can read through the book alone or together as a class and imagine the various moods as the story unfolds (angry, dreamy, excited and wild, lonely, calm and quiet, happy). Children can work in small groups to create a soundscape for a section of the book, working up to a performance featuring narrators, characters, and musical soundscapes.

Many children's books naturally elicit rhythmic responses with repeated ideas and rhymes (see Box 10.2). Encourage children to invent repeating patterns and sounds to accompany the words. Often the book will lead naturally from words to music to movement, all of which are possible given time and space. There is no age limit to the reading aloud of children's books and imagining their musical possibilities, and children in the intermediate grades are genuinely enthusiastic to perform stories with musical components for children in kindergarten and the primary grades.

SONGS AND LITERATURE

Picture books illustrating children's songs connect children's literature and music through sung lyrics, written words, and illustrative images. Once children have heard a song, a matching picture book provides a bridge to reading, where they will recognize and understand written words within the illustrated context. Lyrics, words, and images combine to stimulate children who are struggling to read, because each dimension cues the others. Having so many cues helps students decode and comprehend the text's meaning (English language arts standard number 3).

BOX 10.2 BOOKS RECOMMENDED FOR SOUNDSCAPES

Pre-Kindergarten through First Grade

Guide the children to use vocal sounds. They can explore on their own using instruments at a later time.

Barnyard Banter by Denise Fleming

Bear's Day Out by Michael Rosen

Emily's House by Niko Scharer

Dinosaur Roar! by Paul and Henrietta Stickland

Max Found Two Sticks by Brian Pinkney

Nini Here and There by Anita Lobel

Old Macdonald Had a Farm illustrated by Pam Adams

The Quiet Noisy Book by Margaret Wise Brown

The Very Quiet Cricket by Eric Carle

Root-A-Toot-Toot by Anne Rockwell

Twist with a Burger, Jitter with a Bug, by Linda Lowery

Second and Third Grade

Many of these may stimulate younger children's imaginations and vocabularies.

Six Snowy Sheep by Judith Ross Enderle and Stephanie Gordon Tessler

The Maestro Plays by Bill Martin, Jr. and Vladimir Radunsky

I See a Song by Eric Carle

The Little Old Lady Who Was Not Afraid of Anything by Linda Williams

Listen to the Rain by Bill Martin, Jr. and John Archambault

Drumheller Dinosaur Dance by Robert Heidbreder

Saturday Night At the Dinosaur Stomp by Carol Diggory Shields

Rain Song by Lezlie Evans

Where the Wild Things Are by Maurice Sendak

Night Noises by Mem Fox

The Happy Hedgehog Band by Martin Waddell and Jill Barton

Train Song by Diane Siebert

Fourth through Sixth Grade

Older children could also set some of the preceding books, then share them with younger children.

My Many Colored Days by Dr. Seuss

Possum Come a-Knockin' by Nancy Van Laan

The Rainbow Fish by Marcus Pfister

Yo, Hungry Wolf!: A Nursery Rap by David Vozar

Where the Wild Things Are by Maurice Sendak

Learning to read song lyrics provides a strong motivation for learning to read words.

Teach children the songs in class, work collaboratively with a music specialist to design experiences that combine music with literature. Store picture books and song recordings side by side in a classroom library, so children might explore on their own during individual reading time. Some classic literary works are available online for children to enjoy the songs, stories, and images all together. Introduce the book and song to children, and encourage them to read the book again on their own. Invite the school librarian to display the selected book for a week or two, so that many children may view it on their own.

Use words from the song as vocabulary and spelling words for the class. Invite children to write additional verses to various songs to practice their understanding of rhyming, rhythmic flow, and phrase structure. Encourage them to create their own books, illustrating the songs that they love to sing. Children take particular delight in creating shape books, such as a star-shaped book for "Twinkle, Twinkle Little Star," a boat for "Who Built the Ark?," or a train engine for "Wabash Cannonball" (see Barkley and Walwer[6] for more ideas).

Box 10.3 offers illustrated books of songs in a wide range of genres, from patriotic and folk to nursery rhymes and popular song.

CHAPTER 10 | Music and Language Arts

BOX 10.3 SELECTED CHILDREN'S LITERATURE OF ILLUSTRATED SONGS AND CHANTS

Pre-Kindergarten through First Grade

All the Pretty Horses by Susan Jeffers

Baby Beluga by Raffi, illustrated by Ashley Wolff

Hush Little Baby illustrated by Aliki

Hush Little Baby by Sylvia Long

Hush, Little Baby by Margot Zemach

I'm a Little Teapot illustrated by Moira Kemp

It's Raining, It's Pouring by Kin Eagle

The Itsy Bitsy Spider by Iza Trapani

Little Rabbit Foo Foo by Michael Rosen

Ms. MacDonald Has a Class by Jan Ormerod

Old MacDonald Had a Farm illustrated by Pam Adams

Peanut Butter and Jelly by Nadine Bernard Westcott

Row Your Boat by Pippa Goodhart

Shake My Sillies Out by Raffi, illustrated by David Allender

10 in the Bed by Anne Geddes

Tingalayo illustrated by Kate Duke

Twinkle, Twinkle, Little Star illustrated by Michael Hague

What Will You Wear, Jenny Jenkins? illustrated by Bruce Whatley

What Shall We Do When We All Go Out? illustrated by Shari Halpern

Wheels On The Bus illustrated by Sylvie Kantorovitz Wickstrom

Second and Third Grades

Abiyoyo by Pete Seeger

All God's Critters Got a Place in the Choir by Bill Staines

Aunt Harriet's Underground Railroad in the Sky by Faith Ringgold

Frank and Ernest Play Ball by Alexandra Day

Frog Went A-Courtin' by John Langstaff

Mama Don't Allow by Thacher Hurd

O Beautiful for Spacious Skies illustrated by Wayne Thiebaud

One Wide River to Cross by Barbara and Ed Emberley

Proud to Be An American by Lee Greenwood

Puff, the Magic Dragon by Peter Yarrow and Lenny Lipton

The Star-Spangled Banner illustrated by Peter Spier

There's a Hole in the Bucket illustrated by Nadine Bernard Westcott

There Was an Old Lady Who Swallowed a Fly illustrated by Pam Adams

There Was an Old Lady Who Swallowed a Fly by Simms Taback

There Was an Old Lady Who Swallowed a Trout! by Teri Sloat

Who Built the Ark? illustrated by Rick Brown

Yankee Doodle by Mary Ann Hoberman and Nadine Bernard Westcott

Fourth and Fifth Grades

From A Distance by Julie Gold

Follow the Drinking Gourd by Jeanette Winter

John Henry by Julius Lester

Joseph Had a Little Overcoat by Simms Taback

Lift Every Voice and Sing by James Weldon Johnson, illustrated by Bryan Collier

Lift Ev'ry Voice and Sing by James Weldon Johnson, illustrated by Jan Spivey Gilchrist

Simple Gifts by Chris Raschka

To Every Thing There Is a Season by Leo and Diane Dillon

The Fox Went Out on a Chilly Night by Peter Spier

ADDING SONGS AND OTHER ART FORMS INTO STORIES

Inserting songs into stories is another way to make the learning process multi-artistic. Invite children to act out stories, dance them (as in a ballet, with or without scarves or other props), play instruments at designated times, or bring stories to life through puppetry and artwork. *Abiyoyo,* by Pete Seeger, comes with a ready-made lullaby that appears throughout the book (see Example 10.2 and Lesson Plan 10.1).

Many folktales invite songs. Particularly appropriate are repetitive stories, such as *Chicken Little.* Her repeated refrain, "the sky is falling," can be chanted in

Abiyoyo

rhythm or set to a melody that it is sung each time the phrase appears. *Goldilocks and the Three Bears* is another story that lends itself to song. The phrases "Who's been eating my porridge," "sitting in my chair," and "sleeping in my bed?" are quite lyrical, and you could even assign musical motives to each of the characters to be played or sung every time they enter the story. Children may also enjoy creating musical motives for fractured fairy tales, such as *Yo! Hungry Wolf: A Nursery Rap.*

Preexisting songs can enrich story experiences as well. Older children with a greater song repertoire might consider adding songs such as "Yankee Doodle" to a Revolutionary War story, or "Clementine," "Goodbye, Old Paint," or "Oh! Susanna" to stories of westward expansion. "Follow the Drinking Gourd" ties in with the secret escape of slaves to the North along the Underground Railroad.

LESSON PLAN 10.1

Abiyoyo

1. Introduce children to the book *Abiyoyo*, by Pete Seeger. Show them the picture of the giant, Abiyoyo, and tell them that this story is about singing a lullaby to that giant.

2. Encourage the children to notice times when singing a lullaby to Abiyoyo would be appropriate, then read the story aloud.

3. Teach the children to sing the lullaby, rocking gently from side to side as you sing. Add the lullaby the next time you read the story.

4. Explain that *Abiyoyo* is a story-song of the African Bantu people, who are traditionally farmers. Using a globe, explain that the Bantu people live across sub-Saharan Africa, including Botswana, the Congo, Malawi, Namibia, Rwanda, Tanzania, and Uganda.

5. Invite children to accompany their singing with simple rattles and drums, in a style that would put a giant to sleep.

6. Have children tell the story in their own words and then dramatize it with the song and the instrumental accompaniment.

DEVELOPING READING AND THINKING SKILLS THROUGH MUSIC

Reading is an extremely complex activity involving many skills and layers of thought. As such, reading presents many challenges for children, who may not understand how to use one or more of the processes. Children struggle similarly with learning to read music. Fortunately, learning songs not only gives children additional practice with their reading skills, it also allows teachers to tap into music's appealing nature to enrich the learning process.

BASIC READING SKILLS

Music researcher Jayne Standley has studied reading problems and how auditory discrimination and visual recognition combine in the process of reading.[7] Among her conclusions are the following elements:

- ► Reading problems occur at the level of the single word, when a reader fails to quickly decode visual information.
- ► Decoding depends on sensitivity to the sound structure of language, rather than on comprehension. In other words, recognizing that words rhyme or don't rhyme is separate from recognizing the word's meaning.
- ► To decode language information, readers must recognize alphabet letters and pair them with phonetic sound patterns, thus learning to blend sounds and segment words.
- ► This process of decoding builds attention, memory, and comprehension skills.
- ► Hansen et al. suggest that reading words and reading music require parallel basic skills (see Box 10.4). The two disciplines build aural and visual awareness and skills quite similarly, and classroom teachers can use one to teach the other.

Songs and chants comprise much of the music children encounter in preschool and through the elementary grades, and offer natural practice for various reading skills. The following strategies use music as a vehicle for language development, but at the same time, children will develop the important musical skills of singing, listening, and rhythmic competence.

PHONOLOGICAL (PHONEMIC) AWARENESS

Phonological awareness (often called phonemic awareness) is the ability to discriminate between and identify the characteristics of sounds. Some specific phonological skills are awareness of beginning, middle, and ending sounds; rhymes and speech rhythms; sound similarities; and syllables and phonemes. All these skills are important for reading. Songs and chants help children practice these important perceptual skills. When children know the songs or chants well and produce the words accurately, they can begin to identify the various parts—words, syllables, rhythms, and pitches.

BOX 10.4 COMPARATIVE SKILLS FOR READING TEXT, MUSIC SYMBOLS, AND MUSIC TEXT

Phonological Awareness

Text Reading Skills: Sensitivity to all units of sound. Generating and recognizing rhyming words, counting syllables, and separating the beginning sound of a word from its ending sound.

Music Symbol Reading Skills: Sensitivity to all elements of musical sound. Recognizing repeated or imitated sound patterns, ostinatos, sequence, matching pitches, etc. Attention to texture, timbre, stylistic nuances.

Music Text Reading Skills: Learning how to produce the sounds of language in a musical setting. Generating and recognizing how the sound elements of text and the sound elements of music coordinate within a musical setting (e.g. pairing rhymed text with like phrases, cadences, or repeated rhythmic passages.)

Phonemic Awareness

Text Reading Skills: A special kind of phonological awareness involving letter-sound correspondence in the smallest units of oral language: phonemes (e.g., stop = s/t/o/p). Identifying and manipulating the smallest sound units within the written symbol.

Music Symbol Reading Skills: How notation is related to the smallest units of musical sounds in systematic ways, or music symbol-sound correspondence (e.g., pitches within a phrase, rhythmic subdivisions within a metered measure). Articulation, phrasing, tonguing, performance practice.

Music Text Reading Skills: In a choral setting, identifying and manipulating sounds as they relate to music symbols, including articulation of pure vowel sounds, diphthongs, elisions, and consonants (plosives, fricatives, and affricates). Vocally forming the smallest sound units so that the listener can comprehend the lyrics.

Sight Identification

Text Reading Skills: Identifying high-utility words that appear most often in print (sight words such as *the*, *of*, *it*, or *and*).

Music Symbol Reading Skills: Identifying and playing high-utility notes, types, rests, lines, spaces, rhythm symbols, dynamic markings, fingerings, etc.

Music Text Reading Skills: Learning the proper vocal enunciation of high-utility words in music lyrics and performing them consistently from song to song.

Orthographic or Graphophonemic Awareness

Text Reading Skills: Knowing that letters and diacritics represent the spoken language. Understanding the writing system of a language and specific connections between sequences of letters, characters, and symbols, including spelling patterns that are used to recognize familiar chunks in words. Spelling includes variable and complex but mostly predictable rules.

Music Symbol Reading Skills: Knowing that music symbols represent musical language. Understanding that scales are series of patterns that are the tools for melody. In western culture, a notational system with rules governing the sequences of pitches and organization of rhythms that occur in predictable ways. Knowing that pitched and unpitched instruments are scored differently.

Music Text Reading Skills: Combining alphabetic knowledge (as described in text skills column) and music symbol reading knowledge. Knowing rules for the use and placement of music and text symbols to write music.

Hansen, Dee, Elaine Bernstorf, and Gayle M. Stuber. (2007). *The Music and Literacy Connection.* New York, NY: Rowman & Littlefield Education/National Association for Music Education (NAfME).

Young children rhythmically chanting "Teddy Bear, Teddy Bear" with their favorite stuffed animal.

INITIAL SOUNDS

"Teddy Bear, Teddy Bear" is appropriate for children from preschool through first grade. Children can sing it while using simple motions to mime the action words, such as "turn around" and "touch the ground." Once the children know the song well, write the letter "t" on the board. Have children say the "t" sound. Sing the first verse together, listening carefully to find "t" sounds at the beginning of various words. Invite children to sing the song and tap their desks every time they hear a word that starts with a "t." Monitor their progress: they should identify "t"s on "Teddy," "turn,"

EXAMPLE 10.3

EXAMPLE 10.4

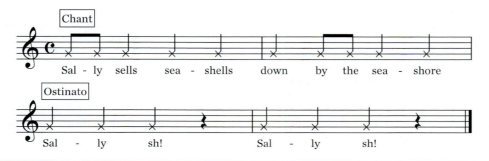

"touch," and "tie" (the "t" on "that" is a blend, which creates a different sound than the hard "t").

Once children can easily identify the "t" sound in the beginning position of words in "Teddy Bear, Teddy Bear," discuss the quality of the "t" sound (short and sharp). Direct children to find an instrument with a short, sharp sound (such as a rhythm stick or wood block) and play the instrument every time the "t" sound begins a word. Repeat the exercise to give all children a chance to play the instrument, and assess their comprehension

This basic exercise can be applied to other chants or songs with repeated sounds. Focus children's attention on consonant and vowel sounds in the initial position, then move to sounds in the final position, and finally to sounds in the middle. Tongue twisters are another useful resource for these activities. Older children might take the tongue twister "Sally Sells Seashells" and offer an aural analysis of where the "s" and "sh" blend sounds occur. They can clap on the "s" and move their arms in an arc on the "sh" sounds. Finally, they can create an ostinato, such as "Sally, sh" (see Example 10.4) for half the class to chant in the background with patterned movement while the other half chants the entire tongue twister with their accompanying movements.

 EXAMPLE 10.5

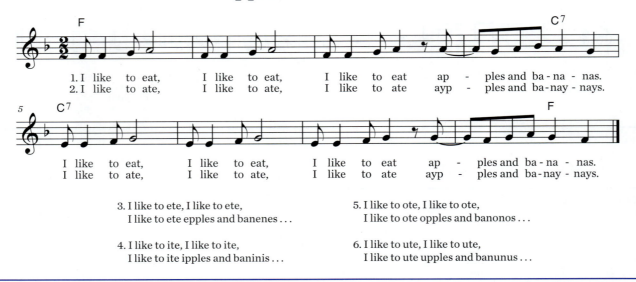

3. I like to ete, I like to ete,
    I like to ete epples and banenes . . .

4. I like to ite, I like to ite,
    I like to ite ipples and baninis . . .

5. I like to ote, I like to ote,
    I like to ote opples and banonos . . .

6. I like to ute, I like to ute,
    I like to ute upples and banunus . . .

MIDDLE VOWEL SOUNDS

"Apples and Bananas" is a song that substitutes vowel sounds to make ordinary words into silly words. By playing with vowels, children build their phonological awareness.

Teachers can work with young children to review the names and long and short sounds of each vowel. Once they learn the song, children can substitute the vowel sounds in "eat," "apples," and "bananas" with either the long or short version of each vowel. Children delight in the silliness of this song and its phonological changes.

RHYMING SOUNDS

"Teddy Bear, Teddy Bear" is also useful for focusing on rhyming words. Encourage children to identify all of the song's rhyming words: around/ground; shoe/do; stairs/prayers; light/night. Then have them choose four contrasting instrument timbres, such as sounds that scrape, ring, rattle, and thump, decide which pair of rhyming words each sound will represent. As they sing the song, children can play their instruments when the rhyming words appear.

"Skip to My Lou" provides an opportunity for children in second, third, and fourth grades to play with rhyming words and improvise phrases to fit the rhyme and rhythm of the song. Once they learn several verses of the song and become familiar with the song's rhythmic flow and rhyme scheme, they can invent their own verses, such as, "Cows in the meadow go moo, moo, moo" or "Stubbed my toe, oh boo, hoo, hoo." They can write the invented phrases on note cards, then trade the cards among themselves and take turns singing the new phrases in solo voice. Adding in some blank note cards can encourage recipients to invent a new rhyming phrase.

EXAMPLE 10.6

Dance Sequence:
Form a circle, all join hands.

Verse 1:
Phrases 1 and 2: *circle right for eight beats.*
Phrases 3 and 4: *circle left for eight beats.*
Chorus: *hook your right elbow with your partner's right elbow and skip around in a small circle for eight beats.*

Verse 2:
Phrases 1 and 2: *break formation and search for another partner.*
Phrases 3 and 4: *find a new partner; hold both hands and swing side to side.*
Chorus: *hook your right elbow with your partner's right elbow and skip around in a small circle for eight beats.*

Verse 3 (same motions as Verse 1):
"There's a red wagon, paint it blue."
Chorus: same motions as above

Repeat Verse 2

Verse 4 (same motions as Verse 1):
"Can't get a red bird, jay bird'll do."
Chorus: same motions as above

Repeat Verse 2

"Skip to My Lou" can also help children develop phonemic awareness of vowel and consonant sounds, and blended diphthong sounds. Encourage them to:
- isolate and name the first sound in a song word, such as "s" in skip or "l" in Lou.
- recognize the same sound in different words, such as "m" in meadow and moo.
- isolate the sounds in a word, such as "s," "k," "i," and "p" in skip, then put them together gradually, such as "s," "sk," "ski," "skip." Children can hold up

a finger for each sound they pronounce, and link fingers together as sounds are combined; blends, such as "sh," "ch," or "th," count as one sound.

▶ shift from oral pronunciations to writing and reading the words and syllables.

See also the work of Yopp and Yopp[8] for further activities and songs for phonemic awareness.

BUILDING COMPREHENSION

Reading comprehension is at the core of the National Standards for English Language Arts. Songs contain texts that run the gamut from simple nursery chants—like "Row, Row, Row Your Boat," "Bounce High, Bounce Low," and "One, Two, Three Alary" to extended story songs that detail adventures—such as "Froggie Went A-Courtin'," "Michael Finnegan," and "Skye Boat Song." Song lyrics invite children to play, introduce them to historical periods, and call forth wide range of emotions. Like poetry, lyrics can transmit many layers of meaning, and thus songs make natural entry points for children to build and test their reading comprehension.

ADDING MOVEMENT

For many beginning readers and for English language learners at any level, game songs with movements help to reinforce word meanings. Many songs in this textbook encourage children to express their understanding of the words through gestures and full-body movements, including "Hey, Betty Martin," "London Bridge Is Falling Down," "Ring around the Rosie," "Mouse, Mousie," "This Old Man," "Lucy Locket," "Little Sally Walker," "Draw Me a Bucket of Water," "Weevily Wheat," "Just from the Kitchen," "Jubilee," and "Skip to My Lou," and in Spanish "A la rueda de San Miguel" and "San Sereni."

Other songs, such as "Paddling Song," "Row, Row, Row Your Boat," "Here Comes Uncle Jesse," and "Rig-a-Jig-Jig" do not offer word-by-word gestures but do feature movements that reinforce the meaning of the words. Chants such as "Peanut Butter and Jelly" can also employ movements to build comprehension (see Lesson Plan 10.2).

USING AMERICAN SIGN LANGUAGE

Singing while signing songs with American Sign Language (ASL) offers a powerful way to build comprehension through movement. ASL gestures focus children on the meaning of the words, keep the attention of both singers and listeners, and help the teacher assess each child's understanding of the words. A quick Internet search yields several websites that allow users to call up words from a dictionary and see the hand signs performed.

Not all songs can be signed easily. The best songs for signing are slower in tempo, with several repeated sections or words, or sections where only a few words are changed (a good example is "We Shall Overcome"). Not every word needs to be signed; signs can emphasize important words that are prominently featured in each phrase of the song. The flow of the signs' movements should match the rhythmic flow of the song's lyrics. Children in the intermediate grades can learn

LESSON PLAN 10.2

"Peanut Butter and Jelly"

1. Model singing and chanting small chunks of the song, have students repeat, then everyone sings or chants the entire song.

2. Using magnetic strips or clips, affix index cards to the board, with one action word (spread, bite, dig, crush, munch, pick, swallow) written on each.

3. Point to each card and invite children to read them aloud together.

4. Invite children to invent motions for each action word, and assign each index card to a different student, who stands beneath the card and becomes the leader for that word.

5. Everyone sings the chant again, and follows the motions of each leader. Repeat with different leaders until everyone has had a turn.

Children love to sing songs that can be dramatized with specific motions. Children singing "Peanut Butter and Jelly" and acting out the motion, "spread it on some bread."

Signing while singing helps build comprehension and keeps attention focused.

to sign more difficult songs, such as traditional freedom, peace, and protest songs as well as popular songs with deeply meaningful texts. Classroom teachers may collaborate with music specialists to find songs that lend themselves to signing.

SEQUENCING AND CUMULATIVE SONGS

Many songs tell stories with a particular sequence of characters and actions using multiple verses. "The Farmer in the Dell" and "Little Cabin in the Wood" are ideal for young children. "Who Built the Ark?" and "Froggie Went A-Courtin'" are appropriate sequence songs for second through fourth graders, and fifth- and sixth-grade children can follow the sequence of events in songs such as "Barb'ry Allen," "Matty Groves," and "Qua Cầu Gió Bay." Help children learn the songs by giving them movement or pictorial cues to remember the sequence. Some of these songs

BOX 10.5 AMERICAN SIGN LANGUAGE FOR "WE SHALL OVERCOME"

We	The right index finger touches the right shoulder then the left shoulder.
shall	The open right hand with the fingers together moves forward and downward from the side of the head (the forward movement indicates that something will occur in the future).
overcome	Both hands in fists, one fist starts behind the other and rolls over to the front.
some	The side of the right open hand (fingers together) slices across the open upward palm of the left hand.
day	Left arm held horizontal in front of the chest (representing the surface of the earth), the right arm's elbow "hinges" on the left finger tips and points vertically. The right arm moves downward in an arc (as if pointing to the sun as it crosses the sky during the day).
Oh	The hand sign for "O" (fingers curled to touch thumb in a round shape) slowly rising from stomach to head.
deep	Left arm held horizontal in front of the chest (representing a surface), the right hand starts above the horizontal arm, fingers point down and move downward below the horizontal arm.
in	Left hand holding an imaginary glass in front of the chest, the right hand, with fingertips touching each other, moves down into the "glass."
my	Right open hand, fingers together, moves from a short way in front of the chest to touching the chest.
heart	ASL: *right fingers tap the chest over the heart area. More dramatic sign: each index finger simultaneously draws half the heart shape on the chest.*
I	Right index finger points to center of the chest.
do believe	*Right index finger touches the forehead, then claps the upward palm of the left hand in front of the stomach.*

CHAPTER 10 | Music and Language Arts **203**

ADAPTING INSTRUCTION FOR VARIOUS NEEDS

Learning Disabilities

Children with learning disabilities often have trouble hearing certain sounds, and may omit or reverse letters, impairing their fluency. Highlighting certain letters with instrumental sounds and chanting spelling words musically may help these children. Tracing fine sandpaper letters or imaginary letters on the wall can also help. Vocal sounds can reinforce the shape of the letters. Multimodal strategies using vision, movement of large and small muscles, and hearing provides many ways to reach and teach these children. Speak slowly, repeat directions, and ask children to rephrase assignments to make sure they understand the task to be done.

Blind or Visual Impairments

Use assistive devices to help visually impaired children see picture books used in assignments. When incorporating instruments, team visually impaired or blind children with sighted children who are trained to ask them what instrument they want and give them to them.

Deaf or Hearing Impairments

Use assistive devices for story reading for children who are hard of hearing. Use signing for children who are deaf. (If you are not skilled in American Sign Language, ask for a teaching aide who is to attend class with deaf students). If they are using instruments, encourage them to play large instruments with slow vibrations they can feel, or handheld instruments whose vibrations can be sensed through bone conduction.

---

may be dramatized, and any associated gestures will exercise the brain and help children remember the sequence—even as they bring the story alive.

Children enjoy singing cumulative songs that add one word, phrase, or motion with each verse and repeat previous parts in reverse order as the song progresses, such as "She'll Be Comin' 'Round the Mountain" and "The Twelve Days of Christmas." Cumulative songs are challenging to remember, especially for children who are working to developing language skills, and should be introduced after children master songs that simply go forward in a sequence. To help children remember the reverse sequence, work with them to name each element in the song, such as (in "The Twelve Days of Christmas") a partridge in a pear tree, two calling birds, three French hens, and so on, and direct them to draw pictures of the elements on full-page cardstock. On completion, place the cards in order as visual cues to help the children remember the verses. Designate one child to point to the images as they occur in the song, helping to cue the singers. For additional challenge, sing the song backwards as well as forwards, using the cards as cues. Mix up the cards and sing the song in that order, or have the children put them in the correct order and then sing. "Old MacDonald," "I Bought Me a Cat," and "An Austrian Went Yodeling" also teach sequencing in a playful way.

Many of the songs named in this section can be found in illustrated picture books listed earlier in this chapter, and in the song collections of music teachers and librarians. While these books may be intended for children in the earlier grades, those in the upper elementary grades may find them useful in preparing a program of songs to share with their buddies or partners in kindergarten and the primary grades. Sharing books before or after children learn the songs will help enhance comprehension and word recognition.

USING CHANTS AND CHORAL READING TO BUILD FLUENCY AND INFLECTION

Fluency and expressiveness in reading aloud is fundamental to the fourth Standard for the English Language Arts, and happens only when children are able to decode the words instantly as they read. Achieving this fluency starts with simple chants containing only a few words and repeated patterns performed in time and with inflection. "Rain Chant" is one such chant.

Hansen et al. suggests that teachers place new or difficult words on the wall and draw children's attention to the sounds of the words by creating chants or rhymes.[5] Word walls can be set to rhythms and ostinato patterns much like "Rain Chant."

Similar to chanting, but less defined rhythmically, choral reading also builds fluency, vocabulary, self-confidence, and enjoyment of literature. Struggling readers throughout the elementary grades can join with more fluent readers to move the text along as a group, as musicians do in ensemble singing and playing. Regular

LESSON PLAN 10.3

"Rain Chant"

1. Print the words on a chart without the hyphens separating the syllables.
2. Invite students to read the words aloud.
3. Have students speak each word separately, then provide a steady beat while students chant all the words in the rhythm indicated. Repeat this process with the ostinatos.
4. Invite students to think about the sounds rain makes and how those sounds might inform the articulation of the alliterative word pairs (pitter patter, sprinkle splatter, drip drop).
5. Experiment with changing dynamics (loud/soft), durations (long/short), and pitch (high/medium/low) of the sounds.
6. Experiment with applying those qualities to each line of the chant, creating distinct differences between them.
7. Read the entire chant and the two ostinatos expressively.
8. Divide the class into three groups for the main chant, ostinato 1, and ostinato 2.
9. Begin chanting ostinato 1, add ostinato 2, then add the chant.
10. Speak the chant four times, then drop ostinato 2, then drop ostinato 1.
11. Later, experiment with adding instruments such as sticks and rattles to accompany the chant.
12. Alternate speaking the chant with singing, "Rain, Rain, Go Away."
13. Once the children are confident with the chant and satisfied that they've made it interesting using inflection, record it (audio or video).
14. Then record the group speaking the piece without any inflection.
15. Have students listen to the two versions and note how reading with expression is more interesting.
16. Use this lesson in expressive reading to inform children's efforts reading aloud from familiar texts.

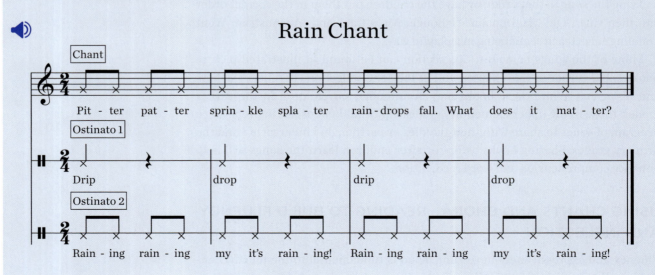

CHAPTER 10 | Music and Language Arts   **205**

BOX 10.6 TYPES OF CHORAL READING

Antiphonal

Divide the class into groups and assign parts of the text to each group. Allow students to practice reading before bringing them back together to read their assigned parts chorally.

Dialogue

Select a text that contains different speaking parts. Assign the part of the narrator to one group and each character to other groups.

Cumulative Choral Reading

The number of students reading builds gradually as the text is read. An individual or small group reads the first line or section, then they are joined by another group. By the end of the passage, the whole group is reading. (This can also be done in reverse, starting with whole group and ending with just one person or group.)

Impromptu Choral Reading

Students choose ahead of time what section(s) of a text they will read. As the text is read, they join in or fade out as they choose. Some students may choose to read certain words or sections, every other line, or the whole selection. (If no one selects a section, someone usually jumps in!)

If you like these ideas, Timothy Rasinski includes more ideas for choral reading in his book *The Fluent Reader*.[10]

---

choral reading helps struggling readers to read fluently in a safe context without being singled out for errors or long hesitations. With repeated choral reading, a text can become more expressive through variations in pitch, speed, and emphasis. The ideas in Box 10.6 make choral reading even more interesting.

Another possibility for choral reading is hocketing, a medieval musical technique in which different musicians alternate notes of a melody, sharing it in a turn-taking progress of utterances. For a hocketing choral reading, prepare the text by underlining every other word in a different color, such as red/blue/red/blue. Designate one group to speak only the red words and another group only the blue words. A hocketing performance using three groups and colors is even more challenging and highly motivating.

WRITING ABOUT MUSIC

Classroom teachers looking to motivate various kinds of writing can take advantage of children's engagement with music and musicians by assigning writing projects on musical topics. Listening to, performing, or creating music can inspire writing in response to the sounds and processes of the music. Students may also choose to write about music in historical periods and cultural contexts, various instruments, or the musicians themselves.

There are many genres of writing, each inviting children to invent unique responses to the writing task. Some are appropriate for older elementary children who have developed abstract thinking, critical reasoning, and analytical skills. Others, such as creative, descriptive, and expository writing, can be assigned to all ages in elementary school, from pictures and simple sentences in kindergarten right up to sophisticated vocabulary, exact spelling, colorful and impressionistic language, linking multiple paragraphs on a topic, and developing a personal authorial style in the fifth and sixth grades. Regardless of the writing genre, classroom teachers will need to develop children's prewriting, critiquing, and revising skills, as well as their understanding of writing conventions.

CREATIVE WRITING ABOUT MUSIC

Creative writing conveys meaning through imagery, narrative, and drama. Creative writing takes many forms, including poetry, playwriting, fiction, screenplays, and creative nonfiction. Narrative writing and descriptive writing are types of creative writing, too. The following music-related prompts stimulate creative writing:

- ▶ Write a title and imaginative story that fits with a short piece of recorded instrumental music.
- ▶ Write a playground chant.
- ▶ Write a rap.
- ▶ Write lyrics for a nonsense song.
- ▶ Write new lyrics for a preexisting melody.
- ▶ Write a haiku or other poem in response to recorded instrumental music.
- ▶ Write a rhymed verse to be set to a melody.

NARRATIVE WRITING ABOUT MUSIC

Narrative writing is creative writing that tells a story. Narrative writing requires a theme, a plot, characters, a storyline that unfolds, and some kind of resolution. Effective narratives often contain some sort of conflict that builds tension, culminates, and then resolves. Narrative writers need to be able to develop the setting, characters and their emotions and moods, and a storyline or plot that pulls the reader in. Narrative stories can come from the writer's own life experience or imagination. Dialogue can be included as well as the writer's first-person voice. Several music-related prompts for narrative writing follow:

- ▶ In small groups, write a short story or play about a musician.
- ▶ Write a short story in which a character takes a music lesson on a particular instrument.
- ▶ Write a musical tall tale, e.g., *The Town Musicians of Bremen*.
- ▶ Write a series of imaginative journal entries for a famous musician.
- ▶ Write a fable about how music came into the world.

DESCRIPTIVE WRITING ABOUT MUSIC

Descriptive writing can be incorporated into various genres, including narrative and expository writing. Descriptions help the reader imagine a place or feeling, and can be expressed in poetry or through metaphor in creative or narrative writing. Music-related prompts for descriptive writing include:

- ▶ Write a poem to describe a piece of recorded music.
- ▶ Write a poem to describe how a piece of music makes you feel. Include the music's title in the poem.
- ▶ Write a descriptive paragraph about the best musical experience you've ever had.

Write a descriptive paragraph about how a particular piece of music sounds to you, using at least four adjectives and three musical terms.

► Write a letter to a friend describing a concert you have attended.

EXPOSITORY WRITING ABOUT MUSIC

Expository writing is the most common form of writing used in school. It involves researching a topic, such as an historical event or scientific process, and writing about it in a logical and organized fashion. Expository writing typically begins with a main idea out of which flows a series of clearly organized ideas that logically support the points the writer is making. It is based in fact rather than the writer's creative imagination. There are many music-related prompts for expository writing, including:

► Write a report on a favorite living musician or musical group.
► Choose a renowned classical composer and write about a key aspect of his or her life, including specific historical details.
► Review a concert held at your school.
► Critique a group or individual whose music is currently popular.
► Write a biography of a well-known and much-admired musician.
► Compare and contrast two different recordings of the same musical piece.
► Write about the invention and evolution of a musical instrument.
► Students should include recorded music and photographic or video images if any of these activities are presented as oral reports. Sources of the music should be included in written reports.

PERSUASIVE WRITING ABOUT MUSIC

Persuasive writers begin with an opinion, support that opinion with facts, and present arguments to convince the reader to agree. Children need to think analytically and synthesize information in order to make a persuasive argument. Several music-related prompts for persuasive writing follow:

► Write a letter persuading your parents to buy a piano, violin, guitar, trumpet, drums, or other instrument.
► Write a short essay persuading people to attend a concert or recital by you or your friends.
► Write a short essay to persuade someone else to listen to a piece of music you enjoy.
► Write a persuasive essay on why one style of music is more fun to listen to than another.
► Write a letter to a newspaper editor persuading readers to vote for extra funding for local music education.

TECHNICAL WRITING ABOUT MUSIC

Technical writing is the standard writing style for technical reports, directions, memos, and graphs. It conveys important details about processes and techniques. In order to write technically, one must clearly understand the topic and be able to use words precisely and develop ideas sequentially or in a graphic form.

Music-related prompts for technical writing include:

- ► Write a description of how to hold and play a familiar instrument properly.
- ► Write a description of how to produce an effective vocal sound as a singer.
- ► Develop a graph or chart to describe a favorite group's record sales over a four-year period.

These prompts to stimulate various kinds of writing about music are just a beginning. Creative classroom teachers will develop many other possibilities that use music to build their students' writing skills.

Summary

Teachers who bring music and musical activities into the reading and language arts curriculum enliven children's interest, involvement, and focus so that they can learn the diverse skills required. Music pulls children into learning in ways that words alone cannot; it touches the human spirit verbally and nonverbally. Music is motivating and invites playfulness, imagination, and reflective thought. Infusing music into the language arts curriculum helps children accomplish important learning standards in the two fields.

Review

1. List four different ways music can be combined with children's literature and what the outcomes of those engagements might be.

2. Name several ways to make children aware of sounds using music activities.

3. How can singing and chanting help children's word comprehension?

4. What are some practical techniques for using music to help children develop critical thinking and analysis skills?

5. Name several ways children can write about music.

Critical Thinking

1. Why is it important for children to master sequential songs before singing cumulative songs?

2. Why might writing about music be motivating for children? What ideas might you have for such assignments that go beyond the suggestions in this book?

Projects

1. Find a children's book that elicits some kind of sound play, using mouth, body, or found sounds. Develop a plan for engaging the children musically as they read the book. Try out the plan with a group of children and reflect on the experience. Interview the children to learn their responses, and make any modifications that may improve the plan for the next opportunity.

2. Find a book that would be appropriate to set to a soundscape. Assess the reading level of the book and determine the age at which children would enjoy setting this story to a soundscape. Gather a range of found sounds or instruments and introduce the idea of a soundscape to the children. While reading the book out loud, invite children to imagine the musical possibilities. Have them share ideas and then encourage them to experiment on their own and to set the story to music. Have one or more children read the story while others play instruments to accompany the story. Record the experience and have the children critique the results. Did the sounds assist in creating a backdrop for the story or did they get in the

way? What did you like about the sound choices? What would you change to make the soundscape more effective? Once children are satisfied with their soundscape, encourage them to share it with others.

3. Find a book that illustrates a song, keeping in mind the reading level of the children. Share the book with a child or children. Sing it as a song while you turn the pages to illustrate the text. Read the book again, inviting the children join you in singing. Check to determine whether they can read the book without singing. If not, leave the book with them for a while, then check with them later to see if they can identify words in the song. Discover whether they know the words through reading or through singing (or both). Talk to them about that process.

4. Find a story with characters who appear repeatedly and often say the same thing (fairy tales are often a good source). Compose a simple musical theme for each character, or ask children to invent a short tune for each character. Sing these themes as the story is read aloud. Teach them to others and see what suggestions they might have.

5. Create a collection of poetry, chants, stories, and songs that would be good to for choral reading. Try various choral reading strategies with a group of children and reflect on how it influenced their ability to read with fluency.

Additional Resources for Teachers

Common Core State Standards Initiative. (2010). *Common Core State Standards in English and Language Arts.* http://www.corestandards.org/ELA-Literacy/

Biggs, Marie C., Susan P. Homan, and Robert Dedrick. (2005). *Does Singing Improve Reading Skills?* Monograph from the Childhood Education Department, College of Education, Tampa, FL: University of South Florida.

Cooper, David. (1997). *Literacy: Helping Children Construct Meaning* (3rd ed.). New York, NY: Houghton Mifflin.

Hansen, Dee, Elaine Bernstorf, and Gayle M. Stuber. (2007). *The Music and Literacy Connection.* New York, NY: Rowman & Littlefield Education/ National Association for Music Education (NAfME).

Music Educators National Conference. (1994). *National Standards in Arts Education.* Reston, VA: Rowman and Littlefield.

Rasinski, Timothy. (2010). *The Fluent Reader: Oral & Silent Reading Strategies for Building Fluency, Word Recognition, and Comprehension* (2nd ed.). New York, NY: Scholastic.

Rasinski, Timothy, Nancy D. Padak, and Gay Fawcett. (2009). *Teaching Children Who Find Reading Difficult* (4th ed.). Columbus, OH: Pearson.

Yopp, Hallie Kay and Ruth Helen Yopp. (1997). *Oo-pples and Boo-noo-noos: Songs and Activities for Phonemic Awareness.* New York, NY: Harcourt Brace.

Online Resources: Audio and Songbook

digital.wwnorton.com/classroom

11
MUSIC AND SOCIAL STUDIES

Music is not separated from culture: it is culture.

—Bruno Nettl[1]

IN THIS CHAPTER

In the Classroom

Musical Connections to Time and Place

Illuminating History through Music and the Arts

Sample Lessons for Music and Social Studies

Valuing Culture through Music and the Arts

Summary

Review

Critical Thinking

Projects

Additional Resources for Teaching

Additional Songs for Teaching

Singing songs, listening, dancing, and studying instruments deepen lessons in the social studies and bring to life important social values and holidays.

Music gives pleasure to children and teachers any time of day, but music can also provide much more: meaningful insights to the study of history and culture. Singing songs, listening, dancing, and studying instruments all add depth to lessons in the social studies and bring to life important social values and holidays of people around the world. Music teaches children to know themselves, one another, each other's families, the local community, and myriad communities around the world and throughout history.

The National Council for the Social Studies (NCSS) has established standards for Social Studies curricula, in which music is an important consideration. One standard requires students to "describe ways in which language, stories, folktales, music, and artistic creations serve as expressions of culture and influence behavior of people living in a particular culture," while another asks students to "describe instances in which language, art, music, belief systems, and other cultural elements can facilitate global understanding."[2] Many social studies textbook publishers as well as state and local departments of education have established similar standards of curricular scope and content sequences at various grade levels. Most move from the self in early years, to families, communities, and cultures, and on to state, national, and world history as students' understanding of the world expands.

IN THE CLASSROOM

VIGNETTE ONE

Throughout the year, Mrs. Priestley's second-grade students learn about holidays and festivals around the world through music. She invites parents and community members from different cultures to visit on festival days and share authentic stories, songs, and musical instruments. For the Korean harvest festival of Chuseok, the children sing "K'wejina ch'ing ch'ing" (about memories of ringing the gong in childhood and youth). They play classroom gongs and drums in traditional Samul nori style and then listen to and view performances of Korean percussion music.

In October the children sing "Ramadan el sana di" to observe the Muslim fasting of Ramadan. In November they sing "Over the River and through the Wood" for Thanksgiving and accompany their singing with jingle bells. As the school year continues, Mrs. Priestley's children learn about people from other parts of the world through their holiday and festival music, and in April and May they sing "Blue Bird, Blue Bird."

VIGNETTE TWO

Mrs. Cohen's third-grade students are learning about communities near and far by studying the beautiful music, architecture, paintings, weavings, masks, sculptures, and (translated) poetry produced around the world. Her students search the Internet and download interesting songs, poems, folktales, and photos of intriguing art objects. For these students, learning in social studies means active engagement with history and culture through the arts. They use what they've seen to create

You Will Learn

- many resources for adding music to the study of major historical eras.

- how to sing and play many songs from different cultures of the world.

- how to teach authentic cultural dances.

- how to present two complete model lesson plans included in this chapter.

Ask Yourself

- How familiar are you with music from around the world?

- Did you ever learn about a historical or cultural event through a musical experience (e.g., the emotional toll of war through Tchaikovsky's *1812 Overture*, or American rural life through Copland's *Appalachian Spring*)?

- When you listen to music from a certain place or time, such as dance music from the Renaissance, an eighteenth-century piano sonata by Mozart or Beethoven, a rag by Scott Joplin, or salsa by Eddie Palmieri, what does the music tell you about the cultural place and the historical time?

- What do you need to know in order to teach children about a musical culture?

- How can music enhance the social studies curriculum?

211

USING SOCIAL STUDIES TO MEET MUSIC STANDARDS

1. Singing. Choose songs for children to sing that relate to the history, culture, or geography lesson.

2. Playing. Include instruments in lessons on particular places and times, such as maracas in a unit on the Caribbean, gongs and drums in a unit on China, or recorders in a study of colonial America.

3. Improvising. Perform a story set in a particular context, inviting children to choose instruments that evoke the setting and reinforce a character, mood, or event. For pitched instruments, determine which pitches will be used, such pentatonic pitches (C, D, E, G, and A) that blend well.

4. Composing and arranging. In one large group, or in small groups, have children create a short poem about a historical event or cultural value. Have children set the poem to a melody and play simple accompaniments on instruments such as xylophones, guitars, or recorders. Using improvised icons or standard music notation, have children write down their music.

5. Reading and notating. Children can read notation and perform music on historic and cultural topics (ask the music specialist if you need help reading notation).

6. Listening. In lessons about neighborhoods and different cultures, play recordings of music from cultures within local communities (receive suggestions from children and their families). Whenever possible, invite folk musicians from the community to come in and perform, especially on authentic instruments.

7. Evaluating. After children learn to sing or play a song from a particular culture or historical period, ask them to compare their performance with authentic models and indicate how authentic they think their own performance was by holding up fingers: ten fingers = completely authentic, zero fingers = not authentic at all, etc. Discuss why they gave the rating they did.

8. Connecting to other arts and curricular areas. Explore dance, drama, and the visual arts of historical times and cultures.

9. Connecting to culture and history. This entire chapter is about this standard.

similar art, poetry, and music in the style of particular cultures, immersing themselves in their studies.

VIGNETTE THREE

Mr. Gray's sixth-grade class studies geography lessons designed to bring the world into their ears, voices, and bodies. In addition to map work and assigned readings, children sing songs of each region they study, such as "Sansa kroma" during the unit on Ghana, "Guru ndiani" (Zimbabwe), "Roda pião" and "Bambu" (Brazil), "Arirang" (Korea), "Mos', mos'!" (the Navajo-Hopi), and "Ala De'lona" (Jordan and Lebanon). Where there are dances associated with the songs, Mr. Gray teaches them. He is as curious about instruments as his students are, and he borrows a *mbira* (a metal-pronged thumb piano) and a beaded *hosho* (a gourd for shaking) for the unit on Zimbabwe. He also plays musical recordings and videos from the Internet. These cultural experiences give his students an engaging, multisensory education of the world and its people.

Korean students playing Samul nori instruments.

MUSICAL CONNECTIONS TO TIME AND PLACE

From kindergarten onward, elementary school teachers deepen children's understandings of themselves, their families, their friends, and their neighbors. Curricular studies in history and geography teach students about the early and evolving years of their nation and about the wider world beyond national borders. To help children remember the myriad abstract facts they read, effective teachers engage children with hands-on activities, school and homework projects, visitors to the classroom, and occasional field trips to a museum, government site, or community center where they can experience culture in action.

Many teachers explore history and culture through music because music motivates, reinforces, and deepens learning of social-historical facts. When children sing a song, dance a folk dance, and play musical instruments from a particular culture, they absorb that culture's artistic, social, and cultural expressions. Music transcends the here and now, helping students imagine and emotionally connect with other times and places.

ILLUMINATING HISTORY THROUGH MUSIC AND THE ARTS

Much of history has been determined by music, dance, drama, and the visual arts. The study of historical culture asks questions about how people lived: What did they eat? What did they wear? What language did they speak? What did the children learn in school? What did they value? What did people do for fun and entertainment? Histories and timelines provide factual information, but music and the arts allow students to feel what others felt. Listening to music of the late eighteenth century evokes what it meant to live in the time of the American Revolution, a time of transition between the old and new, a period of reshaping European traditions in colonial America, an era fiercely focused on all that could lead to an independent America.

Social-historical values come to life in music, dances, plays, and the visual arts. The popular, folk, and art music of a historical period illustrate how people in different socioeconomic classes approached life, from rituals and worship to birth and death, parades and processionals, courtship and weddings, entertainment, etc. Music and the arts put human faces on the people of a specific time and place, and convey feelings and sentiments that words alone never could. Following are some

History and geography broaden students' understanding of their country and the wider world beyond their national borders.

Music and the arts put human faces on the people of a specific time and place, which words alone cannot do.

musical highlights of human history that enhance children's understanding of particular people and events.

MUSIC IN ANCIENT GREECE

Social studies standards in many states specify the study of ancient civilizations, including Greece, in sixth grade. After introducing students to the wars, politics, epic poems, architecture, and sculpture of the civilization, teachers can illuminate the important roles that Greek music and instruments played. Music was a fundamental part of community life, and Plato thought it vital to the stability of the state. Music was the first cornerstone of education, and played important roles at marriages, funerals, political gatherings, religious ceremonies, theatrical productions, and recitations of epic poems. The Pythian Games, precursor to the Olympics, began at Delphi with competitive hymn singing. The word *music* derives from the Muses, the daughters of Zeus (father of all other Greek gods) who preside over the arts and sciences.

Music of ancient Greece was played on panpipes, *lyre* and *kithara* (two strummed, harplike instruments), *aulos* (two double-reed pipes banded together), *hydraulis* (a water-powered organ), conch shells, and brass trumpets. Most Greek music consisted of a single melody line within a mode, each of which offered extramusical meaning, such as the Phrygian mode (E to E on the piano's white keys), which communicated sensuality, or the Dorian mode (D to D), which was characterized as harsh-sounding.

Ancient Greeks passed on their history and amused themselves by reciting long epic poems, such as the *Iliad*, that could take many hours to perform. To add interest, storytellers often accompanied themselves with a lyre, kithara, or other instrument listed above. In some ways, today's rap music is similar to epic poetry; the words tell a story, are rhymed, strongly rhythmic, and are usually accompanied by background instruments. Ask children to create and perform rhythmic raps using material from their study of ancient Greece—a rap about Olympic sports or Greek city-states, for example. End this activity with a rapping contest among groups in the class, judged in ancient Greek Olympic fashion by children from another class. This culminating activity is could even take place among the wider community of students at a school assembly.

Musical instruments of ancient Greece

MUSIC IN ANCIENT ROME

In the Roman world, music was used in military exercises, theater, religious rites, civic ceremonies, and entertainments (including Roman festivals). The Romans adopted many aspects of Greek culture, including their musical ideas and instruments. Drums, tambourines, cymbals, and castanets were featured, along with horns and trumpets, especially in military and hunting contexts. A three-stringed lute, possibly from Egypt or the Near East, was also prominent in Roman music. But singing was probably the most common form of music-making, especially with the growing Christian population. Monophonic chants became prominent by the third century C.E., and are still sung today in monasteries and convents.

Expose children to ancient Roman pageantry and music by showing them the Academy Award–winning 1959 movie *Ben-Hur*, with its views of old Rome, the Colosseum, chariots, and gladiators in the time of the Roman Emperor Tiberius, around 30 C.E. Listen for and identify instruments prominent in this period, including bugle, trumpet, large brass instruments, drums, and cymbals. Write the instruments on the board, and find words to describe their sound or effect ("bright," "clear," "powerful," "grand," "triumphant," "victorious"). Encourage students to write a paragraph describing the music and how it evokes ancient Rome.

MUSIC IN MEDIEVAL EUROPE

Social studies curricular standards specify the study of communities—large and small, near and far, then and now. The elementary social studies curriculum aims to develop the intellectual processes that enable children to participate actively in classrooms and in the world around them. Studying history and geography builds a foundation for understanding cultural diversity; music brings to life the cultures, people, places, and times. Lessons in music from medieval Europe can help students understand some of the foundations of Western civilization.

The Middle Ages began with the fall of the Roman Empire in the fifth century and ended with the Renaissance in the fifteenth century. During this period, Islam spread through Eastern Europe and Northern Africa, while Christianity established itself in central, Western, and Northern Europe. Each region developed distinctive artistic styles. Chivalry and courtly love were in vogue, and royal courts and churches governed social activities. Mathematics, philosophy, painting, and poetry were just some of the outstanding achievements of this period, sparked by geniuses such as Fibonacci, Thomas Aquinas, Giotto, Dante, and Chaucer.

Sacred music resounded in medieval cathedrals at Chartres, Reims, Cologne, Salisbury, and elsewhere. Plainchant, similar to Roman hymns, gave way to polyphonic choral music, particularly motets, which were often sung with instrumental accompaniment. Itinerant poet-musicians sang secular songs and choral madrigals about religion, love, chivalry, and other topics. Instruments of the Middle Ages included the wood flute, recorder, rebec and rebab (violins), sackbut (a trombone), organ, bagpipes, hurdy-gurdy (a mechanical violin), and various string instruments (lute, psaltery, dulcimer). All were used in dance and ceremonial music for the theatre and the noble courts.

Introduce children to English fourteenth-century life by reading a modern-English excerpt from one of Geoffrey

Musical instruments of the Middle Ages

Chaucer's *Canterbury Tales*.[3] The stories illustrate people's lives, roles, and relationships. Find the General Prologue on www.luminarium.org to give students an example of Middle English (listen to the first stanza while projecting the written words on a screen). Choose several phrases and compare them to current English expressions.

Listen to music of the Middle Ages, including the popular Middle English song, "Sumer is icumen in." Give students the notation, and sing the song with a light and bouncing quality. Challenge students to decode some of the Middle English words (the opening phrase translates to "summer is coming," and "lhude sing cuccu" translates to "loudly sings the cuckoo bird"). Draw student's attention to the fact that the coming of summer was as much a delight in the Middle Ages as it is now.

Introduce children to dance music in medieval England by playing a recording of the Abbots Bromley Horn Dance (see Appendix 3). Encourage them to learn this historic melody on recorders or other wind or string instruments they may be learning in their music class. Ever since the sixteenth century, this tune has accompanied twelve dancers with antler horns in the village of Abbots Bromley. Performed on Christmas Day, New Year's Day, and other holidays, this dance depicts how medieval English villagers searched and foraged for food.

EXAMPLE 11.1

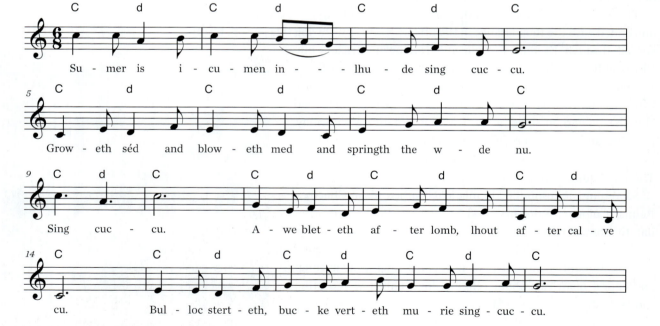

MUSIC IN THE AGE OF DISCOVERY

United States history, from the arrival of the British through the precolonial period until American independence, is typically taught in fifth grade. A complete curriculum would include facts of history, language and literature, geography, music, and dance. In the fifteenth, sixteenth, and seventeenth centuries, Europeans went out to map the planet, exploring Africa, the Americas, and Asia. This Age of Discovery featured explorers like Christopher Columbus, Vasco da Gama, and Ferdinand Magellan, who traced routes to Asia, the Americas, and around the tip of southern Africa to India. Spanish conquistadores, including Hernán Cortés, set off for Mexico, Peru, and the empires of indigenous Aztecs and Incans; Dutch explorers delved into Australia, New Zealand, and the Southeast Asian islands; and Russians ventured into Siberia and over the Bering Sea to Alaska. The British explored and then established colonies in North America. Some stayed on, or were followed by shiploads of people from Europe seeking adventure and freedom. Explorers returned to their European homelands with silver, gold, and exotic spices and foods that entered the local markets as highly desirable commodities.

Meanwhile, European art music became increasingly complex, with intricately ornamented melodic lines and many parts performed simultaneously. Many compositions were also written for church services, and commoners joined together to sing, dance, and play instruments of the period—including recorders, flutes, lutes, violins (fiddles), drums, and concertinas. In the palaces that financed explorers' journeys, instrumental and vocal music was performed regularly for royalty and their guests.

Listening to some of the styles known to explorers and the people and cultures they were encountering during the Age of Discovery can help children make connections to various aspects of European global exploration. Consider the soundscapes of these European explorers as they made their way across unknown Atlantic waters to the Americas by listening to old and new world examples.

Find examples of instrumental music that would have been played at court in countries from which explorers were sent on their journeys to the Americas. Listen to instrumental and choral music by composers like Guerrero, Morales, and Vittoria. For example, two Spanish lutes, called vihuelas, provide the musical ambiance for studying this Age of Discovery in a featured performance of Francisco Guerrero love songs (see Appendix 3). Seek out examples of court dances such as the pavane and galliard, which were performed in the castles of Spain, France, and England. A collection of these dances by English Renaissance composer Anthony Holborne, as performed by the Dowland Consort, provides a suitable entry point to the music that would have been popular in this era of discovering the new world (see Appendix 3). Reflect on the music

Recorders of the Baroque era: sopranino, soprano, alto, tenor, bass

and dance of the time against the backdrop of visits by explorers like Christopher Columbus, whose expedition was funded by the court of Spain.

When Hernán Cortés arrived in Mexico from Spain, he would have heard and seen performances by Aztec musicians on ocarinas (round flutes of hardened clay), wood flutes, drums, and gourds full of dried seeds. Seek out photos and videos to hear and see these instruments and their reproductions. Find or make examples of these instruments that were popular among the Aztecs at least five hundred years ago.

As British adventurer John Smith arrived in Virginia in the seventeenth century, and waves of British settlers followed in the next century, they brought with them songs like "Barb'ry Allen," "The Golden Vanity," "Matty Groves," "Early One Morning," and "Greensleeves." Provide recordings and notation for these songs, and teach children to sing them. Discuss how these songs express British interests in seventeenth- and eighteenth-century America.

British explorers in Canada encountered the Mi'kmaq (Micmac) people and may have heard them sing "Kwanu'te'," a song intended to honor the animals that gave their lives to provide food. Teach children to sing the song by listening and following the notation. Note that the song features vocables, meaningful but untranslatable syllables often found in Native American songs. Over many centuries, cross-cultural encounters have inspired and shaped music, allowing culture-specific expressions to flourish even as further riches emerge from the cultural blends.

MUSIC OF THE AMERICAN REVOLUTION

Curricular programs call for the study of United States history from the colonial period through independence, typically in fifth and sixth grades, and curricular experiences in singing, playing, and listening to music can shed special light on the quest for American independence. Eighteenth-century patriots yearning to escape British rule gained courage to fight by marching to drum and fife music and

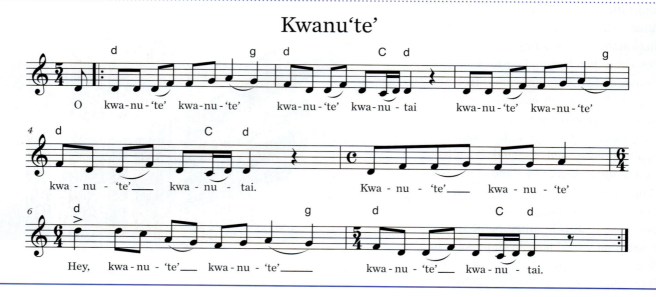

singing songs of everyday life and love, work and worship, and growing nationalism. In Europe, the art music of Bach, Handel, Mozart, Haydn, and Beethoven was drawing audiences to concert halls, courtyards, and churches, but Americans were involved in congregational church singing, dancing to small consorts of fiddles and viols, and playing marches for assemblies and in wartime.

Lead children in singing patriotic songs popular in this formative period of the new American republic. Songs such as "Yankee Doodle," "When I First Came to This Land," "Soldier, Soldier, Will You Marry Me?" and "Hail, Columbia" reveal in their poetry the development of an American identity. More than two centuries later, these songs are still sung in schools, communities, and civic centers, some on patriotic holidays. Sing along with recordings or live accompaniment on guitar, piano, or other chording instrument.

Listening, small-group research projects, and even small-scale performance activities can help students discover instrumentals of the time, including fifes (small, high-pitched flutes), bugles (trumpets without valves), and drums. These instruments were used to signal or wake up soldiers, call them to meals, and direct them to camp chores. Fife and drum bands are still active today for the joy of playing old American tunes and to participate in reenactments of the Revolutionary War. Encourage students to search the Internet for hornpipes, jigs, and marches that were popular in the eighteenth century. Challenge children who already play an instrument (particularly recorder, violin, trumpet, clarinet, or other melody instruments) to learn a hornpipe by ear, to play "Taps" or "Yankee Doodle," or to explore and invent a signal that might function as a call to dinner. Ask children to use popular song texts of the era to reflect on historical events, criticisms of political figures, and calls for resistance and revolution.

MUSIC OF THE INDUSTRIAL AGE

In the upper elementary grades, the social studies curriculum calls for students to understand the importance of the industrial age in United States and world history. Machines replaced much manual farming, manufacturing, mining, and transportation labor in nineteenth-century Europe and North America. As a result, productivity increased dramatically, and socioeconomic and cultural conditions changed profoundly. Coal-powered steam engines allowed manufacturing in factories without water-powered mills, ships to move quickly and independently of the vagaries of the wind, and railways to provide cheap, fast transportation for people and products. The scientific method led to discoveries of new products and processes, including chemical and electrical products and the mass manufacturing of steel. Interchangeable parts led to the drudgery of assembly lines, abuse of child labor, malnutrition, and poor living conditions at first, but wealth gradually increased across all classes, and work hours and poor conditions eventually improved.

Many brass and other metal instruments were modified or invented in the Industrial Age, including the modern-day flute, clarinet, trumpet, tuba, and saxophone. This era

The pianola, or player piano

corresponded to the Romantic era in music, which favored expansive musical forms with highly expressive ornamentation and colorful timbres. Wealthy industrialists supported the arts (including symphony concerts), the upper and middle classes played pianos (grand, upright, and even player pianos) in their parlors, and Americans in small towns and rural areas made music on guitars, banjos, fiddles, mandolins, harmonicas, dulcimers, button concertinas, and keyboard accordions.

Much music of the nineteenth century speaks to the era's history and culture. Consider popular songs of the era, including the work of the American composer Stephen Foster, whose songs depict everyday life on the expansive plantations of the Deep South, or explore the "ragged" and syncopated rhythms of the Louisiana pianist and composer Louis Gottschalk. Search online for pianola or player-piano performances to understand why they were so popular in American parlors. Teach children to sing "My Grandfather's Clock," a well-known song about the mechanical clocks that often stood in grand entry halls of affluent Americans of the period. Consider the importance of music and musical innovation to Americans living in the Industrial Age.

MUSIC IN THE TWENTIETH CENTURY

Social change accelerated dramatically from 1900 to 2000, with empires dissolving (including the British, Austro-Hungarian, and Ottoman empires); the United States, all of Europe, Russia, and Japan involved in global wars; and ideologies like communism and capitalism were pitted against one another. Transportation underwent drastic change, moving from horses and carts to the automobile and finally to airliners and the space shuttle. Telecommunications and the mass media joined transportation in shrinking the world to a global village. An interdependent global economy evolved, which strongly influenced politics, the environment, education, the arts, and entertainment.

Music changed rapidly in the twentieth century as well, when experimentation with styles and techniques prevailed. In art music, there were colorful orchestral works by Debussy and Mahler, experimental forms by Schoenberg (*Verklärte Nacht*) and Stravinsky (*Petrushka*), nationalist and folkloric works (Copland's *Rodeo*), electronic works by Stockhausen and Varèse, and minimalist compositions with repeating musical ideas by Philip Glass and Steve Reich. In popular realms, a revival of blues and American folk music in midcentury was followed by interest in music from world cultures such as India, South Africa, Brazil, and Ireland. Jazz went from blues-based expressions to swing to free improvisation, and popular music intended for mass consumption took many guises, from rock and roll to soul, funk, disco, hip-hop, country, techno, and many more. Technology offered composers new tools, while listeners could enjoy every favorite style at any place or time. From the invention of the Victor Talking Machine, to radio,

Victor Talking Machine

TV, home (and car) stereo systems, computers, and iPods, nearly all music—current, historical, world-wide—became accessible.

SAMPLE LESSONS FOR MUSIC AND SOCIAL STUDIES

The following lesson plans focus on important moments in American history and culture: the journey from slavery to freedom, and how our transportation system built our nation. Each plan reinforces historical coverage through a lively discussion of the art, music, and culture of the period.

iPod

LESSON PLAN 11.1

From Slavery to Freedom

Grades:
Third–sixth

National Standards for Social Studies addressed in this lesson:

- Describe ways that music expresses culture.
- Identify how stories contribute to our understanding of the past.
- Construct maps of locales and regions.
- Recognize issues of equity and justice.
- Investigate concerns related to universal human rights.
- Identify key ideals of human dignity and liberty.

National Standards for Music Education addressed in this lesson:

- Sing a varied repertoire of songs from diverse cultures.
- Perform easy rhythmic, melodic, and chordal patterns on classroom instruments.
- Identify relationships between music and other subjects and fields.
- Identify by style music from various historical period and cultures.

Objectives:
Students will

- sing songs of nineteenth-century African-American slaves;
- learn to play simple chordal accompaniments on classroom instruments;
- understand why these songs were sung, and the meanings of the symbolic phrases embedded within the song texts; and
- understand song as an emotional outlet for enslaved African Americans.

Continued on next page

Materials:

- "Oh Freedom" (notation and recordings)
- "Follow the Drinking Gourd" (notation and recordings)
- Book or website rendering of the Drinking Gourd tale
- One or more of the following instruments: guitar, autoharp, ukulele, bass and alto metallophone, glockenspiel, recorder
- Map of the United States

Procedure:

1. After children learn about the plight of enslaved Africans who were transported from West Africa to the United States, discuss how nineteenth-century slaves expressed their yearning for freedom in songs (note that living conditions were difficult and there was no real hope of becoming free). Often after a hard day of working in hot cotton fields, slaves would gather around campfires and sing songs, such as "Oh Freedom."

2. Sing "Oh Freedom," and learn to play the melody and accompanying parts on piano, guitar, ukulele, autoharp, or other chording instruments.

Note to guitar players: capo at the first fret in order to substitute easier chords: E for F, A for B♭, and B7 for C7.

3. Read or listen to the story of the Drinking Gourd to understand the meaning of the song by that name, and for an explanation of the Underground Railroad.

4. Review symbolic phrases in the lyrics of "Follow the Drinking Gourd" by asking children to tell the meaning of "when the sun comes back" (just after winter solstice), "the first quail calls" (early in the spring), "the drinking gourd" (the Big Dipper constellation of stars), "follow the drinking gourd" (head for the North star in the sky), "the old man" (Peg Leg Joe, a conductor on the Underground Railroad), "dead trees will show you the way" (trees marked by Peg Leg Joe with a left footprint and a round mark in place of a right foot), and "when the great big river meets the little river" (when the Tennessee and Ohio rivers come together).

5. Sing "Follow the Drinking Gourd" by following the notation or learning it aurally. Add chords on the autoharp, guitar, or ukulele, or offer students an opportunity to learn an instrumental accompaniment on bass or alto metallophones, glockenspiel, and recorder.

6. Ask children why singing was important to slaves (it made them feel better, gave them hope, and helped them escape their harsh reality). Trace on the map the route described in the song, and discuss whether they think it was fair to keep people in slavery, whether anyone would want to be a slave, and whether there is slavery right now in other parts of the world.

Assessment:
Children sing in tune and in time the songs "Oh Freedom" and "Follow the Drinking Gourd," play instrumental accompaniments, and understand the meaning of these songs for nineteenth-century African-American slaves prior to the Civil War. You may wish to record video of the class singing, playing, and discussing the songs, so the children can watch and evaluate their performance and so the recording can be shared with parents in conferences or added to each child's portfolio of musical accomplishments.

Continued on next page

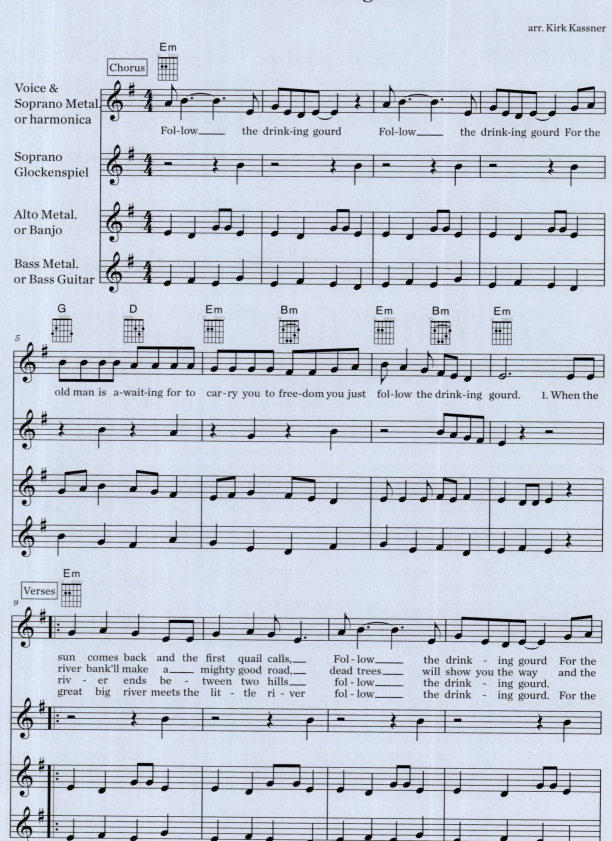

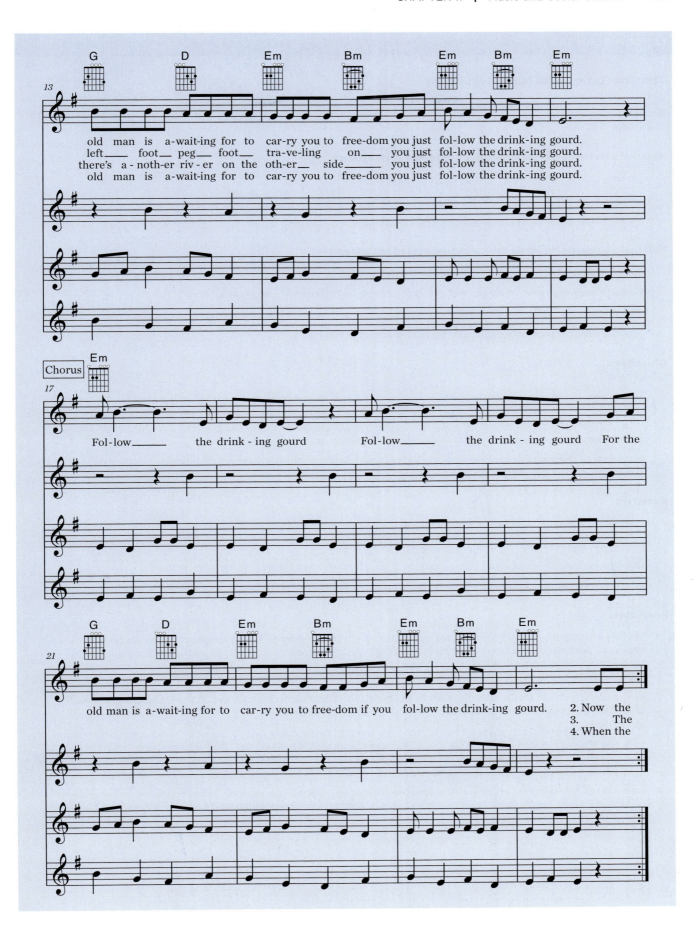

226 PART III | Music throughout the Day

LESSON PLAN 11.2

Transportation and Nation-Building

Grades:
Third–fifth

National Standards for Social Studies addressed in this lesson:

- Describe ways in which music expresses culture.
- Identify how stories contribute to our understanding of the past.
- Identify how science and technology have changed the environment.

National Standards for Music Education addressed in this lesson:

- Sing a varied repertoire of songs from diverse cultures.
- Perform easy rhythmic, melodic, and chordal patterns on classroom instruments.
- Read whole, half, dotted half, quarter, and eighth notes and rests in $\frac{2}{4}$, $\frac{3}{4}$, and $\frac{4}{4}$ meter.
- Identify relationships between music and other subjects and fields.

Objectives:
Students will

- sing songs about trains as important means of transport in the nineteenth and twentieth centuries;
- add simple chordal accompaniments on classroom instruments;
- understand trains as symbolic of American industrialization; and
- learn how settlements expanded from the eastern seaboard, the Great Lakes, and the south to points west of the Mississippi all the way to the Pacific Ocean.

Materials:

- "Wabash Cannonball" (notation and recording)
- "I've Been Working on the Railroad" (notation and recording)
- Book or website description of trains, such as *Train: The Definitive Visual History*[4]
- One or more guitars, autoharps, or ukuleles

Procedure:

1. Discuss nineteenth-century forms of transportation and remind children that transportation speed became critical to commerce and industry. With the completion of the transcontinental railroad in 1869, people and cargo could move from small towns to cities with remarkable ease, and horse-drawn wagons and riverboat barges began to fall out of use.

2. Find books or online materials to present illustrations and information about trains in the United States. Read and share pictures from the book *Train: The Definitive Visual History*.

3. Research and explore songs about trains. Consider ballads, blues, country, and popular (rock) songs about not only train travel but also life in the various cities and towns on the train routes. Discuss why trains have figured so prominently in songs. Is it the sound and rhythms of the steel wheels on the tracks? Or could the travelers' colorful adventures inspire the poetry to which the songs are set?

4. Listening or following notation, learn to sing the train song "Wabash Cannonball," about a mythical high-speed train that follows the Wabash River in Indiana. Play a harmonic accompaniment on guitar, autoharp, or ukulele.

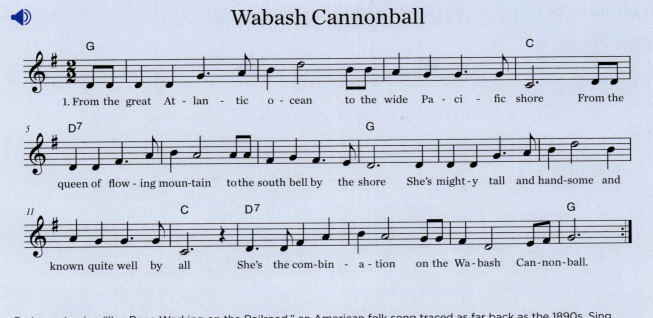

5. Learn to sing "I've Been Working on the Railroad," an American folk song traced as far back as the 1890s. Sing the song with chordal accompaniment on guitar, autoharp, or ukulele.

6. Discuss how trains facilitated the westward expansion of the United States, as Americans moved from small settlements, villages, and towns in the east to places west of the Mississippi in the nineteenth and twentieth centuries.

Continued on next page

VALUING CULTURE THROUGH MUSIC AND THE ARTS

The broad goal of social studies is to create effective young citizens who are sensitive to global affairs as well as to the perspectives of diverse communities living locally. The National Council for the Social Studies recommends that children explore how groups, societies, and cultures address human needs similarly and differently, and be able to describe how language, stories, folktales, music, and artistic creations express culture and human behavior. Most children will experience a wide variety of languages and dialects, holidays and cultural events, and customs firsthand in their own communities, neighborhoods, and schools. Television, the Internet, books, and songs give children secondhand knowledge of distant peoples.

Children as young as second grade are learning about communities near and far. By studying music of the world, children learn that some rhythmic and melodic elements, forms, and functions are universal, while others differ from place to place. As children sing, dance, play instruments, or listen to music, they experience subtle differences of how other groups of people think. They learn to value different musical expressions, and to respect the people who make them. The sample lessons below give children opportunities to learn how others think and feel.

I've Been Working on the Railroad

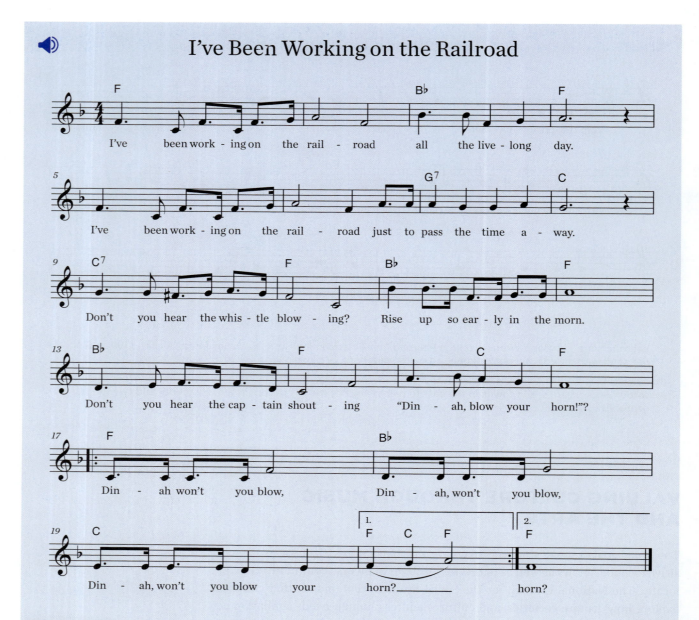

Assessment:
Students sing the train songs with melodic and rhythmic accuracy, playing accompaniments on chordal instruments, and understanding how trains changed America.

CHAPTER 11 | Music and Social Studies **229**

LESSON PLAN 11.3

Out of Africa: Rhythm!

Grades:
First–third

Objectives:
Students will

- sing two songs commonly sung by children in Ghana (in Akan);
- perform movements of singing games;
- learn about how the Ghanaian people value community; and
- understand that children in Ghana enjoy socializing through song and singing games.

Materials:

- "Sansa kroma" (notation and recordings)
- "Kye kye kule" (notation and recordings)
- Pebbles (or other small objects, like marbles or plastic cups), one for each child
- Photographs of Ghanaian children, or online video examples of children's singing games of Ghana

Procedure:

1. Tell students that children around the world enjoy singing games, and that the Akan-speaking children of Ghana sing while dancing, clapping, and passing stones to one another. Find Ghana on a world map, and search online for images of Ghanaian children at play.

2. Tell the story behind the singing game, "Sansa kroma." The Akan words mean "Sansa, the hawk. You are an orphan, and so you snatch up baby chicks." The song reminds Akan children that if they were ever orphaned (or something tragic happened to their parents), they would not need to worry or wander alone but would be cared for by the people of their village. In Ghana, community is important, and people look out for each other in and beyond their immediate family.

3. Learn the song by listening to the recording and reading the notation, with children gradually joining in as they feel comfortable. The song is sung repeatedly while the game is played.

4. To play the game, sit in a tight circle on the floor. Distribute the pebbles (or other small objects), one to each child. Hold the pebble in the right hand, and practice this movement pattern, counting "1, 2, 3, 4." Note that the movements form a triangle as the right hand extends forward in front, then left, then right.

   - Movement 1: *tap the pebble on the floor directly in front*.
   - Movement 2: *tap the pebble on the floor to the left of center*.
   - Movement 3: *tap the pebble on the floor to the right of center and release it there*.
   - Movement 4: *pick up the pebble that has been released by your neighbor to the left*.

   Practice the movement first without releasing the pebble, to master the rhythmic flow of the repeated pattern. Then, release the pebble and pick up the next one as it is released without pause. Start at a slow speed, and gradually increase the tempo.

Continued on next page

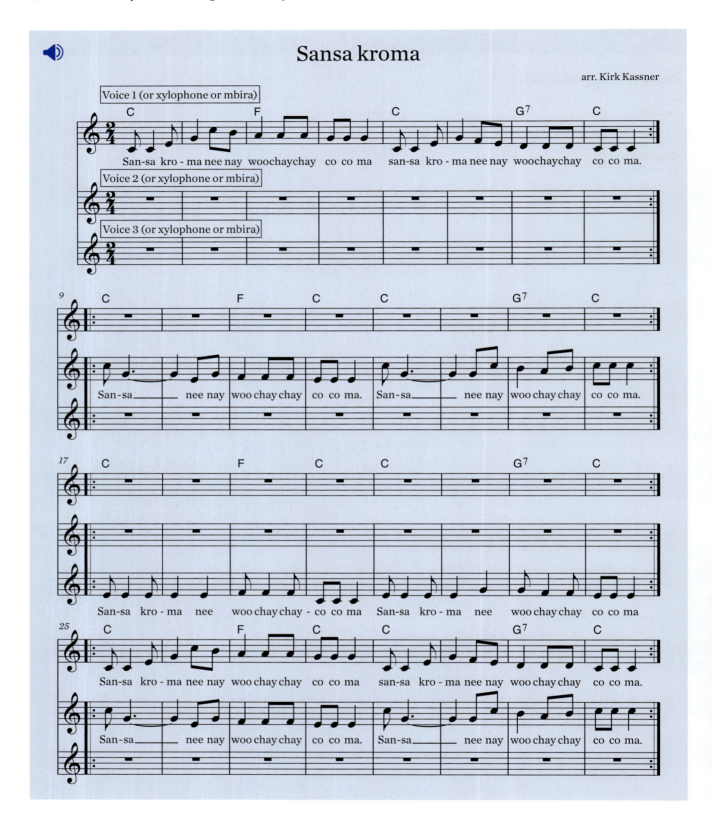

Performance suggestions:
1. One or more instruments play the music first time through phrases 1–5, on repeat voices join in.
2. On phrase 6, all instruments stop the first time through, leaving voices singing alone, then join back in on the repeat. Continue playing phrase 6 another time or two with everyone performing.
3. Begin the performance only with polyrhythms on African percussion instruments below and keep playing throughout song.

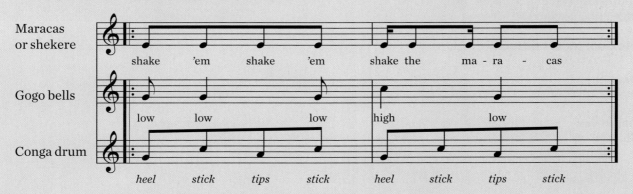

heel = strike the center of the drum head with the heel of the hand.
stick = hit the side of the drum with a stick.
tips = strike the edge of the drum head with the finger tips.

5. Share another children's song of Ghana, "Kye kye kule." Tell students that children in many parts of Africa know it as the "head, shoulders, knees, and toes" song.

6. Learn the song by listening to the recording, or through call-and-response, in which the teacher sings a phrase and is immediately imitated by the students in words, melody, and movement.

7. Practice the movements while singing the phrases, noting that the leader sings first and the group immediately follows. The last phrase is sung together.

Continued on next page

8. Search the Internet for cultural practices in Ghana, including music, dance, and other children's singing games.

9. Encourage children to share singing games that they know, and discuss why these songs are important to them and why children around the world enjoy singing games.

Kye kye kule

Assessment:
Students sing the children's songs of Ghana with melodic and rhythmic accuracy, performing game and dance movements in unison to the rhythm of the song and understanding that children in Ghana and elsewhere in the world enjoy singing games.

LESSON PLAN 11.4

Mexico: ¡Ole! Mariachi

Grades:
First–third

Objectives:
Students will

- sing and play a Mexican children's singing game (in Spanish);
- learn aspects of Mexican culture, including selected Spanish words; and
- listen to selected instruments of Mexico's mariachi.

Materials:

- "A la rueda de San Miguel" (notation and recording)
- World map or globe
- Online examples of Mexican music (especially mariachi) and culture
- *¡Viva el Mariachi!: Nati Cano's Mariachi Los Camperos* (this recording is available from Smithsonian Folkways Recordings; see Appendix 3)

Procedures:

1. Ask children to find Mexico on a map or globe and note its proximity to the United States. Ask children what images come to mind when thinking of Mexico (sunshine and warm climates, cities and coastal towns, piñatas, tacos and burritos, Spanish language, guitars). Search the Internet to find and share images of Mexico, its people, and its culture.

2. Describe one of the best-known musical ensembles in Mexico, the mariachi band. Share examples of mariachi music on film or recordings, such as Nati Cano's Mariachi Los Camperos, Mariachi Vargas de Tecalitlán, and Mariachi Divas, or search online. Explain that mariachi is popular in restaurants for listening, is often used to mark special occasions such as weddings and birthday parties, and is used in church services.

3. Listen to and identify instruments of the mariachi, including guitars, violins, the bass sound of the large guitarrón, and trumpets, and encourage students to "air play" what they hear as they listen to such standard mariachi songs as "El rey," "La Adelita," "La malagueña," "Volver volver," "Si nos dejan," "Guadalajara," and "El cascabel."

4. Listen to "A la rueda de San Miguel," and learn to sing the song with or without the notation as a visual aid.

5. Share the translation of the song: "To the circle, to the circle of St. Miguel / Everyone brings their carton of honey / When it's ripe, when it's ripe / Let the donkey (name of child) turn around." Learn the Spanish words for "circle" ("la rueda"), "everyone" ("todos"), "ripe" ("maduro"), and "donkey" ("burro").

A la rueda de San Miguel

Translated by Kirk Kassner

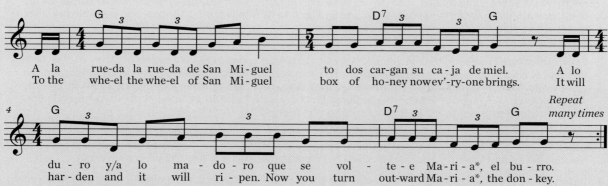

*Change Maria to a different child's name each time.

6. Play the game, with children in a circle holding hands. One child stands in the middle, while the other children step counterclockwise while singing. The center child's name is sung in the last phrase, "Que se voltee (name) de burro" ("Let the donkey (name) turn around"). The singing stops and the center child chooses a new child to stand in the center, then joins the circle facing outward like a donkey (an animal famous for being stubborn and uncooperative). The song is sung again with the name of the new center child, who then chooses the next child and joins the circle facing outward. The singing game repeats until all children's names have been called and the entire circle of students is moving with backs to the center.

7. Discuss with children how great and varied the span of Mexico's music is, from simple children's singing games to the brilliant and sophisticated sounds of mariachi.

Assessment:
Children demonstrate a Spanish-language singing game of Mexico with melodic and rhythmic accuracy, performing the movements of the game to the rhythm of the song, identifying traditional Mexican instruments of the mariachi, and understanding the importance of music to the people of Mexico.

LESSON PLAN 11.5

Native America: Music the Navajo Way

Grades:
Third–fifth

Objectives:
Students will

- sing and dance a Navajo song (in Navajo language);
- learn selected cultural interests and values of the Navajo people; and
- listen to and understand the importance of song at work (grinding corn).

Materials:

- "Jo ashila" (notation and recording)
- One or more drums with soft felt- or cloth-covered mallets
- Scarves (optional)

Procedures:

1. Encourage students to share their knowledge of Native Americans, the first residents of North America. Who are they? What are some tribal group names? Where do they live? Do they share mainstream American values and customs? What Native American values and customs do they maintain? On a map, find places in the United States where Native American communities are located. Note especially the location of the Navajo people in Arizona, New Mexico, and Utah.

2. Share aspects of Navajo culture, including its music. Note that songs in all cultures reflect the cultures' activities and values. The Navajo have songs about their families, their land, horses, coyotes and wolves, and the spirit world. They sing about their surroundings, including mountains and canyons, rivers, the wind, and the sky. The Navajo sing songs to lessen the tedium of manual work (such as planting, harvesting, and grinding corn), and to amuse, entertain, and foster social interaction.

3. Listen to "Jo ashila" and learn to sing this traditional Navajo song about walking together in beauty, and in celebration of all the people and places that are beautiful to see and hear. Pick out the word "hozho," which means beauty, and listen for vocables that are not translatable, such as "hey nay yung ay yunga."

4. Listen to the song multiple times, and encourage children to find the phrases that repeat and sing whatever phrases they can, gradually adding to the phrases. Seek out other recordings of Navajo music, such "Corn Grinding Song" (*Navajo Songs* on Smithsonian Folkways).

5. Play a steady pulse on hand drums (or other drums) with a soft felt- or cloth-covered mallet. Children form a circle around the drummer, face left, and shuffle one step forward to every pulse of the drum while singing the song.

6. The Navajo way of dancing the "Jo ashila" varies. Have children choose a partner (women and girls do the choosing in the Navajo tradition). Everyone makes a circle, facing clockwise, with partners holding hands, hooking elbows, or holding scarves. Step forward to the pulse of the drum while singing the song, with feet close to the ground in a shuffle step.

Jo ashila

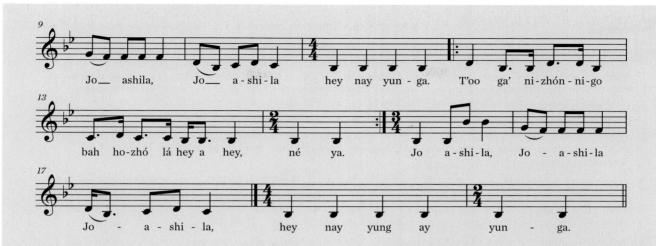

Dance Instructions:

Perform this simple variant of the Navajo Two-step with this song.
   The Navajo women always choose their partners, because this is a matrilineal society.

- Partners stand in a circle, with the male on the outside.
- The man holds his right arm up and the woman places her left arm on the top (like walking down the aisle in a wedding), or they just join hands, or the woman places her hand on the man's shirt, jacket, or sash
- Dancers move in a clockwise direction with the drummer in the center of the circle.
- Start on any foot, moving forward with a slight bounce to the rhythm.

When the dance has ended, the man traditionally gives the woman something as a token of appreciation—a small coin (a penny or dime, for example), or object of clothing (hat, scarf) if he has no small honoring token.

Assessment:

Children sing the social song "Jo ashila" with melodic and rhythmic accuracy, shuffle-stepping the dance to the rhythm of the song, playing a steady pulse on the drum, and understanding the purpose and content of a Navajo song celebrating beauty.

LESSON PLAN 11.6

Vietnam: Traditions and Change

Grades:
Third–fifth

Objectives:
Students will

- sing a Vietnamese song (in Vietnamese);
- learn aspects of Vietnamese culture; and
- listen to selected traditional Vietnamese instruments.

Materials:

- "Qua Cầu Gió Bay" (notation and recording)
- Selected Vietnamese stories such as *The Lotus Seed* and *The Walking Stick*

Continued on next page

Procedures:

1. Initiate a conversation about Vietnam, and invite children to discuss their impressions. Encourage them to describe the land of Vietnam, a long and narrow country of seacoasts, mountains, and rivers, and the Vietnamese people who are fond of rice, noodles and fish sauce, silk and bamboo, lotuses, and áo dài tunics with slits in the side that are worn over trousers. Search online for glimpses of these and other images of Vietnam. Display a map of Southeast Asia and point out Vietnam and its proximity to China, Laos, Cambodia, and Thailand.

2. Find traditional Vietnamese stories, such as *The Lotus Seed*[5] and *The Walking Stick*,[6] in books or online. Read them aloud, talk about the morals of the stories, consider their function as folk tales to teach Vietnamese values.

3. Listen to the traditional song, "Qua Cầu Gió Bay" ("The Wind on the Bridge"). The verses are sung solo and the chorus by a group. Listen to the sound of the wind in the phrase, "tinh tinh tinh gio bay," and have children sing softly on this refrain after each of the three verses (the song of the wind is pronounced "teen teen teen zhaw-oh bye").

4. Tell children that this song is about the traditional old Vietnamese practice of arranged marriages, in which parents and extended family decide whom their children will marry with little input from the children themselves. Explain that Vietnamese children so respected their elders that they would trust completely in the elders' choice of their marriage partner. Note that the story behind the song is that a boy fell in love with a girl at school, and each day he would go to school with an item to give to his beloved—his pointed straw hat, his jacket, and his grandmother's ring, meant to be given to his bride. Coming home without these items, he would say that the wind on the bridge took them from him, for he could never tell his parents that he'd given them as presents to the girl with whom he'd fallen in love.

5. Practice singing the sound of the wind on the bridge. Learn the verses if time allows, or sing just the refrain between the verses along with the recorded version of the song. Pantomime the giving of the hat, shirt, and ring in each verse.

Assessment:
Students sing "Qua Cầu Gió Bay" in Vietnamese with melodic and rhythmic accuracy, identify one or more Vietnamese icons or cultural practices, and understand the traditional practice of arranged marriage in old Vietnam.

ADAPTING INSTRUCTION FOR VARIOUS NEEDS

Blind or Visual Impairments

Find songs and instrumental works online that tell of historical people and places and cultures near and far, such as oral histories (search for the Smithsonian Archives of American Art oral-history interviews as well as StoryCorps). For children with some vision, provide music and lyrics in large, bold type.

Deaf or Hearing Impairments

Provide earphones of sufficient quality to enable hard-of-hearing children to hear the music and lyrics. Have children read and study song lyrics (either provided by the teacher or that they find online) that express the values of particular groups of people then and now, here and far.

Behavior Disorders with Externalizing Behaviors

Guide children to focus on a music-based social science project, giving them specific tasks to accomplish—such as filling out a worksheet or answering specific questions while listening to folk music, such as sea shanties or mariachi music.

Behavior Disorders with Internalizing Behaviors

Some withdrawn children respond well when paired with gregarious and outgoing children for certain tasks, such as searching for music and presenting it to the class with its historical or cultural background information.

Mobility Impairments

It is possible for wheelchair users to roll through most folk-dance motions (sometimes with help from the teacher). Many folk dances can also be adapted to chair dancing with motions in the upper body only.

Autism Spectrum Disorders

Visit frequently with children in class, or set aside some individual time, to clarify and reinforce various tasks of seeking connections between music, history, or culture. Ask direct questions about the music, time, place, and people, and find ways that autistic children can comfortably express their understanding by selecting from among several options presented to them, or by matching photographic images with what they hear.

Summary

When children study history and culture, they forge their own identities based on models of civic responsibility, leadership, and conscious and careful decision making. As children learn about social development and change, they better understand themselves and others. When they discover that some aspects of history should never be repeated, they learn from the mistakes and collective wisdom of others. In learning something of how people lived, what work they did, and how they spent their leisure, they come to understand the human need for making music for camaraderie, amusement, work, and worship. The works of composers in their own times, or in reflection of earlier historical events, help children imagine the sentiments of real people in each historical era. Music may set the scene for the study of history and culture, or cap this study.

A strong social studies curriculum brings children in touch with the world. Each lesson hones their understanding of history, continuity and change, and human culture as a group of shared understandings and values. Throughout history, music has been an important expression of cultural identity, so it offers unique opportunities for examining human perspectives within societies. Teachers can choose songs, singing games, dances, or instrumental pieces to enhance children's understanding of people of a particular time or place and reinforce social studies concepts. Music helps children understand customs and values of local and global cultures, and make connections among cultures and societies of every time and place.

Review

1. Explore how the Lesson Plans in this chapter integrate and blend music and history through their materials and procedures.

2. What arguments can be made for and against the statement, "Music is a universal language?"

3. How can music help us know people and their patterns of behavior?

Critical Thinking

1. Do you agree that one of the primary goals of American schools should be to develop in students of a sense of American (and eventually, world) heritage, history, and culture? Why or why not?

2. Choose one of the historical periods (ancient Greece, ancient Rome, medieval Europe, etc.) and explain how music, dance, theatre, and the visual arts can deepen understanding of the people of that time.

3. Explain how studying historical and cultural events and figures, including experiences in music and the arts, helps children forge their identities.

Projects

1. Consider how music can help meet aims for teaching social studies. Examine social studies textbooks and curricular materials, extract key concepts and aims, and match them to musical materials and methods that could enhance and promote an understanding of society and culture.

2. How might music help children to understand the African American struggle for freedom, the influence of trains on the American economy, and the identities of people in Ghana, Mexico, the Navajo nation, and Vietnam?

3. Call a local school principal or the district music supervisor and tell them you are studying to be a teacher and have been assigned to interview an elementary teacher who uses music to teach social studies. Ask the principal or music supervisor to recommend a teacher who could provide you with good information. Interview the teacher and take good notes, including a list of the resources that the teacher uses.

4. With four other students from your class, select a culture to study through the arts. Work together to find visual arts, music, dance, poetry, theater, and other arts from that culture. Learn what materials are used to create or perform these arts; why are were created; what they represent; what meaning they have for people; and how and when they are used. Develop child-centered activities to help students engage creatively with these materials. Present your ideas to the rest of your class.

Additional Resources for Teaching

Anderson, William M. and Patricia Shehan Campbell. (2011). *Multicultural Perspectives in Music Education* (Vols. 1–3) (3rd ed.). Lanham, MD: Rowman & Littlefield.

Association for Cultural Equity. www.culturalequity.org

Campbell, Patricia Shehan. (2004). *Teaching Music Globally: Experiencing Music, Expressing Culture*. New York, NY: Oxford University Press.

Carlson, Laurie. (1998). *Classical Kids: An Activity Guide to Life in Ancient Greece and Rome*. Chicago, IL: Chicago Review Press.

National Council for the Social Studies. (2010). *National Curriculum Standards for Social Studies*. http://www.socialstudies.org/standards

Smithsonian Folkways. www.folkways.si.edu

Additional Songs for Teaching

Ambozado	Hashewie	Pleeng chaang
De colores	La raspa	Sakura
Haere, Haere	Lak gei moli	Savalivalah
Doraji	Las mañanitas	Tinikling
Feng Yang	Leak kanseng	Yo mamana, yo!
Gerakina	Mbube (The Lion Sleeps Tonight)	Zum gali gali

Online Resources: Audio and Songbook

digital.wwnorton.com/classroom

12

MUSIC AND MATH

IN THIS CHAPTER

In the Classroom

Getting in the Music Groove with Basic Math

NCTM Goal #1: Understand Numbers, Ways of Representing Numbers, Relationships among Numbers, and Number Systems

NCTM Goal #2: Understand Meanings of Operations and How They Relate to One Another

NCTM Goal #3: Compute Fluently and Make Reasonable Estimates

Algebra, Geometry, and Music

Summary

Review

Critical Thinking

Projects

Additional Resources for Teaching

Music is the pleasure the human soul experiences from counting without being aware that it is counting.

—Gottfried Wilhelm von Leibniz

Singing songs about math is an engaging way to achieve goals of the National Council of Teachers of Mathematics (NCTM).

240

One often hears the adage, "If you're good in music, you're good in math." This connection may or may not be supported in empirical studies, but the thinking processes of both disciplines are strikingly similar. Just as music enhances other curricular subjects—social studies, history, and language arts—music can illuminate and concretize abstract mathematic principles and processes. The artful combining of music and math can produce amazing gains in children's learning, but care must be taken that the best music and musical practices be used.

Math and music have many natural parallels: both are concerned with patterns; both have complex relationships between parts, divisions, subdivisions, and prolongations; and both pay close attention to groupings and sequences. Music, math, and science overlap in studies of vibration frequency (pitch), wave complexity (timbre), intensity levels (decibels and dynamics), and attack, decay, sustain, and release (timbre synthesis), to name a few. The sum of music, however, is greater than its elemental parts: music transcends mathematics and sound elements by its artistic intentions and power of communication. Maximizing music's power to teach math depends on music's ability to fully engage and delight students, and that only happens when high-quality music is used in artistic ways.

IN THE CLASSROOM

VIGNETTE ONE

Ms. Kohler teaches her kindergartners many simple counting songs and chants (see Table 12.1). When the children are able to chant the rhyme in time to the beat, she invites them to count the numbers up to ten using their fingers. Another time, she selects ten children to form a number line from one to ten and gives each child a number card that matches his or her place in line. The children squat down and pop up when their number is sung. These activities help children develop physical, visual, and intellectual understanding of our base ten (decimal) number system, number sequence, and matching the number symbol with the corresponding number of people. It also gives them practice with chanting in time. Ms. Kohler repeats this activity until every child has had a turn in the number line.

You Will Learn

- how to use music to help children understand numbers, ways of representing numbers, relationships among numbers, and number systems

- how to use music to help children understand meanings of operations and how they relate to one another

- how to use music to help children compute fluently and make reasonable estimates

Ask Yourself

- Have you ever used chants or songs to practice mathematics facts, such as multiplication tables or number sequences? Did it improve your performance in math?

- Do you know of great mathematicians, other than Leibniz and Einstein, who wrote about links between mathematics and music?

- What musical concepts relate to the concept of patterns in mathematics?

TABLE 12.1 ONE, TWO, THREE, FOUR, FIVE, ONCE I CAUGHT A FISH ALIVE

BEAT 1	BEAT 2	BEAT 3	BEAT 4	BEAT 5	BEAT 6	BEAT 7	BEAT 8
One	two	three four	five	once I	caught a	fish a-	live,
Six	seven	eight nine	ten	then I	let it	go a-	gain.
Why	did_ you	let it	go?__ Be-	cause it	bit my	finger	so.
Which	finger	did it	bite?__ The	little	one up-	on the	right.

241

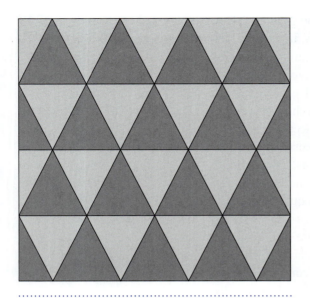
A basic tessellation

VIGNETTE TWO

Mr. Gant introduces his fifth graders to the geometric concept of tessellations, the covering of a surface with shape patterns with no overlaps or gaps. He explains that a regular tessellation is a repeating pattern of the same polygon, and a semi-regular tessellation is a repeating pattern of two or more regular polygons. He encourages them to draw their own patterns using different colored pens. Once the patterns are complete, Mr. Gant invites his students to turn those patterns into music with each shape and color representing a sound or group of sounds. Children then get together in small groups with various instruments and "play" each other's tessellations, using them as a musical score.

The tessellation shown left has upright and inverted triangles in alternating shades. Children in this group create a three-note melody for the dark triangles and invert that melody for the light triangles, alternating the melodies. They perform it with one student conducting by pointing to each polygon in sequence. The other students evaluate how well the composition represented the pattern by holding up anywhere from one finger (not very well) to ten fingers (very well).

GETTING IN THE MUSIC GROOVE WITH BASIC MATH

The National Council of Teachers of Mathematics (NCTM) lists three overriding goals for all math instruction from kindergarten through 12th grade regarding numbers and their operations:

Student art inspired by mathematical principles

1. Understand numbers, ways of representing numbers, relationships among numbers, and number systems.
2. Understand meanings of operations and how they relate to one another.
3. Compute fluently and make reasonable estimates.

These are the basic goals that students need to accomplish at age-appropriate levels in each grade. Additional goals exist for algebra, geometry, data management and probability, and process. The NCTM encourages music, art, and dramatic play as ways of making these abstract concepts more concrete and lively for children. Adding movement is another way to make the abstract more concrete. The following strategies provide a variety of ways to use music to engage children in selected mathematical concepts and processes at age-appropriate levels.

USING MATH TO MEET MUSIC STANDARDS

1. Singing. Encourage children to sing with appropriate tone and support, even though most math songs are quite simple.

2. Playing. Use proper playing techniques when performing the African drumming patterns in Examples 12.4 and 12.5. Use a flat hand slap against the edge of the drum head and a cupped hand toward the center. Strike bells on their edges to let them ring. Strike the sticks in a short, clear motion.

3. Improvising. Once children learn to use instruments or body percussion to represent math problems, invite them to invent their own problems and illustrate them with instruments or body percussion.

4. Composing and arranging. Work in a small group to compose a math rap of multiplication facts in various sets from 1 to 10. Add a movement or instrumental sound each time a product is reached, then make up a sentence that rhymes with the product (e.g.

"Two times four is eight, get that right and you'll be great").

5. Reading and notating. Develop a way to notate the math rap with actual musical notes or pictographs.

6. Listening. Listen to a variety of recorded music, tapping the beat of the music. Work to determine the strong beats and weak beats, then how the beats are grouped in sets. Which set is the most common in most of the music we listen to?

7. Evaluating. Evaluate how successful you were in correctly showing sums through playing instruments. Connecting to other arts and curricular areas. Using colors and shapes, create tessellations and then use them as a musical score.

8. Connecting to culture and history. Research how math informs music technology such as digital recording, synthesizers, speakers, etc.

NCTM GOAL #1: UNDERSTAND NUMBERS, WAYS OF REPRESENTING NUMBERS, RELATIONSHIPS AMONG NUMBERS, AND NUMBER SYSTEMS

COUNT WITH UNDERSTANDING

Strategy one

Preschool–second grade: Sing and dramatize or add motions to simple counting songs: "The Counting Song (Uno dos y tres)," "One Little Elephant," "This Old Man," "Johnny Works with One Hammer," or "Children, Go Where I Send Thee." Count objects as you sing or chant. Create puppets or stick figures to fit the characters in the songs. Have the puppets dance or march to the beat.

UNDERSTANDING PLACE VALUE AND NUMBER ORDER IN THE BASE TEN SYSTEM

Strategy two

Preschool–second grade: Lead children in chanting counting rhymes in rhythm over a steady beat (e.g., "One potato, two potato, three potato, four; five potato, six potato, seven potato, more" or "One, two, buckle my shoe; three, four, shut the door; five, six, pick up sticks; seven, eight, lay them straight; nine, ten, a big fat hen"). Invite ten children to stand in a row. Each child invents a unique movement for their number and performs the movement when it occurs in the song or chant. Other children copy each movement. Follow these chants with the song "This Old Man" (see Example 12.1). Invite one student to tally the

 **EXAMPLE 12.1**

This Old Man

1. This old man, he played one, He played knick-knack on my thumb, With a knick-knack pad-dy whack, give a dog a bone, This old man came rol-ling home.

2. This old man, he played two, he played knick-knack on my shoe … (*touch shoe*)
3. This old man, he played three, he played knick-knack on my knee … (*touch knee*)
4. This old man, he played four, he played knick-knack on the floor … (*touch floor*)
5. This old man, he played five, he played knick-knack on my hive … (*touch forehead*)
6. This old man, he played six, he played knick-knack on my sticks … (*tap fingers*)
7. This old man, he played seven, he played knick-knack up in heaven … (*raise hands*)
8. This old man, he played eight, he played knick-knack on my pate … (*touch head*)
9. This old man, he played nine, he played knick-knack on my spine … (*touch spine*)
10. This old man, he played ten, he played knick-knack over again … (*twirl hands around*)

numbers on the board while the other children make the following movements for each verse:

- on "knick-knack paddy whack," tap index fingers together on each syllable;
- on "give a dog a bone," point thumb back over shoulder;
- on "this old man came rolling," roll forearms around each other;
- on "home," pat lap.

Strategy three

Preschool–first grade: Lead children in singing "Five Green and Speckled Frogs" (see Example 12.2). When children have learned to sing the song, five children become five green and speckled frogs. Each child is given a number. The "frogs" sit on a "log" and jump into the "pond" when their number is sung. When the song is finished, the five frogs choose children to take their places as frogs and the song is repeated until every child has had a turn.

Follow "Five Green and Speckled Frogs" with "Ten Little Alligators" (see Example 12.3). Lead children in learning the song, and invite ten children to stand in front of the class. Distribute alligator stick puppets, numbered one to ten, to each child. (If the children are old enough to read numbers, pass out the numbers randomly and have them put themselves in the right order. If they don't know their numbers well, pass out the numbers in order and tell each child their number.) The class sings the song, and on the first verse the ten children hold the alligators behind their backs, pulling them out front when their number is sung.

Five Green and Speckled Frogs

2. Four green and speckled frogs ... Now there are three ...
3. Three ... Now there are two ...
4. Two ... Now there is one ...
5. One ... Now there are no more speckled frogs.

Ten Little Alligators

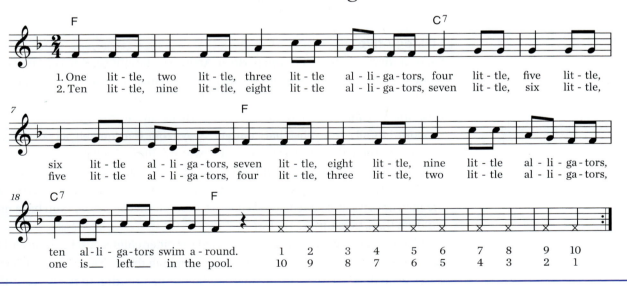

Between the verses, all children count from one to ten while the alligators swim around in the air. On the second verse, children hide their alligators behind their backs when their number is sung. Repeat until every child has had a turn with an alligator.

Strategy four

First–third grades: Give each of ten children a number card labeled one to ten and have them arrange themselves in numerical order. Chant "One potato, two potato" or "One, two, buckle my shoe." The child whose number is chanted jumps up to a standing position. By the end of each sequence, all of the number line children should be standing. Instruct children to pass their number cards to children who have not yet participated in the exercise, and repeat the process until every child has had a turn holding a card.

Extend this activity by distributing cards labeled in tens—10, 20, 30 and on up to 100. Ask children the difference between the 1–10 number set and the 10–100 number set (the bigger numbers all end in zero), then ask what is similar (the bigger numbers start the same as the little numbers). Teach children the rhyme below and repeat the process of holding up cards.

Ten		**twen-**	ty	**thir-**	ty	**for-**	ty
Wear	a	**jer-**	sey and	**you'll**	look	**spor-**	ty
Fif-	ty	**six-**	ty	**se-ven-**	ty	**eight-**	y
Wear	a	**dress,**	to	**look**	like a	**la-**	dy
Nine-	ty, a	**hun-**	dred, if	**you're**	a	**ba-**	by
Wear	a	**dia-per,**	and I	**don't**	mean	**may-**	be!

Strategy five

Second–fifth grades: Children perform African drumming patterns using a cycle of eight beats, playing accurately when each number occurs and maintaining a steady tempo (see Examples 12.4 and 12.5). Use instruments typical in African ensembles: drums, rattles, double iron agogô bells, and sticks.

Work initially from the chart but get away from it as quickly as possible, internalizing the patterns as sets of either twos or threes (except for the bell part in Example 12.5). Practice each pattern separately, using body percussion. Take care to maintain a steady beat for all patterns. When ready, transfer patterns to the instruments indicated (several children can play each part). If you have more children than, take turns as before.

When performing the complex designed for older children, select one child to serve as master, or lead, drummer to play on a high drum. The master drummer raises a hand to strike the drum once loudly to call attention to the players, then plays a starting sequence of six straight beats in tempo, after which the pattern begins. Pattern 1 is played once through, then repeats as pattern 2 joins in. Each part enters after the previous part has completed one 12-beat sequence, until all parts are playing together. To stop the group, the master drummer plays the six-beat starting sequence as an ending. All players stop together on the sixth beat.

CHAPTER 12 | Music and Math — 247

Once children are comfortable with their parts, all parts can start at the same time following the master drummer's starting sequence.

Children may even create their own drum patterns. Copy the rhythm template in Example 12.6 and give one to each group of three to five children to record their rhythm decisions.

EXAMPLE 12.4

African rhythm complex for younger children

Pattern 1	*pat on lap* (shaker)	D	U	D	U	D	U	D	U
Pattern 2	*flat-hand clap* (medium drum)	1	2	3	X	5	6	7	X
Pattern 3	*finger snap* (woodblock or sticks)	X	2	X	4	X	6	X	8
Pattern 4	*cupped-hand clap* (large drum)	1	X	3	4	X	6	7	X

D = down on lap, U = up in other hand, number = make sound, X = rest

1. Establish the beat with Pattern 1 in lap pats.
2. Add Pattern 2: flat-hand claps.
3. Add Pattern 3: finger snaps.
4. Add Pattern 4: cupped-hand claps.
5. Repeat the patterns until children master the most complex, then choose some students to transfer each pattern to an instrument to perform while the others continue their body percussion. (Use multiple instruments on each part, if you have them, so more children get a chance to play.)
6. After playing the complex a short while, ask those with instruments to give them to someone who has not yet had a turn to play an instrument.
7. Repeat until every child has had a chance to play at least one instrument.

Note: this is a great demonstration piece to do with parents on back-to-school night.

EXAMPLE 12.5

African rhythm complex for older children

Pattern 1	*pat on lap* (medium drum)	1	X	3	X	5	X	7	X	9	X	11	X
Pattern 2	*flat-hand clap* (sticks or woodblock)	X	2	X	4	X	6	X	8	X	10	X	12
Pattern 3	*tap lap/slap** (rattles)	D	U	D	U	X	X	D	U	D	U	X	X
Pattern 4	*cupped-hand clap* (high drum) (master drummer)	1	X	X	X	5	6	7	X	X	X	11	12
Pattern 5	*foot tap* (low drum)	X	2	3	X	5	6	X	8	9	X	11	12
Pattern 6	*pat/shoulder pat*† (two-headed drum)	L	L	S	L	L	S	L	L	S	L	L	S
Pattern 7	*pat/shoulder pat*† (double agogô bells)	L	X	S	X	S	S	X	S	X	S	X	S

D = down on lap, U = up to slap hand, number = make sound, X = rest, L = lap, S = shoulder

*Hold one hand palm down about a foot above thigh; with other hand, pat lap, then raise to slap the back of the hand to the palm of the stationary hand.

†Pat one hand on lap (L) and other hand on shoulder (S).

EXAMPLE 12.6

Rhythm grid template

	Student name	*body percussion* (instrument)	1	2	3	4	5	6	7	8
Pattern 1		*foot tap* (low drum)								
Pattern 2		*flat-hand clap* (sticks or woodblock)								
Pattern 3		*lap pat/shoulder pat* (double agogô bells)								
Pattern 4		*cupped-hand clap* (high drum)								
Pattern 5		*pat on lap* (medium drum)								
Pattern 6		other:								

Instructions: using a pencil or erasable pen, write the number of the column in each cell where you want a sound. Write an "X" in or leave blank cells where you don't want a sound. Practice your complex until everyone can play it perfectly five times in a row. You may revise rhythm patterns to make it easier to play or more interesting to hear.

CONNECT NUMBER WORDS AND NUMERALS TO THE AMOUNTS THEY REPRESENT

Strategy six

Preschool–second grade: Perform any of the songs or chants listed previously, using words or numbers printed on cards along with the corresponding number of any particular item (icons from the Wingdings font, such as in Figure 12.4, work well for this purpose). Children hold up the correct card when the number is sung or chanted.

RECOGNIZE "HOW MANY" IN A SET

Strategy seven

First–sixth grades: Play beats on a drum in various meter patterns (which function as sets): two-beat duple meter = loud-soft, three-beat triple meter = loud-soft-soft, and four-beat quadruple meter = loud-soft-medium-soft. Children respond by stamping on the loud (strong) beats, clapping on the soft (weak) beats, and snapping fingers on the medium beats.

To add visual interest, select two to four children to stand in a line and act out the patterns as follows: represent loud (strong) beats by standing in a body-builder pose, soft (weak) beats by sitting on the floor, and medium beats by kneeling. Children can practice pose patterns for each meter when the teacher plays two-, three- and four-beat

1 One	2 Two	3 Three	4 Four	5 Five
6 Six	7 Seven	8 Eight	9 Nine	10 Ten

Number cards and the amount of things they represent

patterns. Allow the posers to choose replacements for their task and repeat the process. Extend this exercise by having children draw or place objects, such as math manipulatives, in a row to represent the patterns.

Strategy eight

Third–sixth grades: Choose one child at a time to be the leader, who plays a drum in duple, triple, or quadruple meter while the other children hold up the number of fingers in the set being performed. When enough practice has made this an easy task, the leader alternates playing between two different sets, and the other children hold up both hands with fingers representing the two different sets. Finally, write the meter (set) patterns on the board as follows:

On the top line (for two-beat, duple meter): **1** 2 (note the size difference)

On the second line (for three-beat, triple meter): **1** 2 3

On the third line (for four-beat, quadruple meter): **1** 2 3 4

Invite one child at a time to point to each number in the set being improvised.

Strategy nine

Second–sixth grades: Guide the children in identifying phrases in short songs, such as "Twinkle, Twinkle Little Star." Once they identify a phrase, they clap or step the number of beats in each phrase (which represents a set), and find ways to show that relationship through drawing or manipulating objects (such as one large block for a strong beat and three small blocks for the weak beats, multiplied by the number of beats in the song).

Strategy ten

Second–sixth grades: Play recordings of music in duple meter (such as a march), triple meter (such as a waltz), and quadruple meter (such as most familiar songs or popular tunes), and have children indicate how many beats are in each set by holding up the corresponding number of fingers. Alternately, have children hold hands with enough friends to create the correct number in the set, then each set marches in a circle to the beat. Children can also represent the meter by moving, drawing, manipulating blocks or other math materials, or using standard musical notation.

UNDERSTAND AND REPRESENT COMMONLY USED FRACTIONS

Strategy eleven

Fourth–sixth grades: Explain that children can make more than one sound per beat, and demonstrate this by walking a steady beat and clapping twice per step (model the first clap as the foot goes down, and the second clap up as the foot lifts up). Have children imitate this movement. Then model three claps per footstep, with the first clap low, the second clap of medium height, and the third clap high, and have children imitate the movement. Finally, model four claps per footstep, and have children imitate. (Clapping a number different from a beat is not easy for some children—even in the upper intermediate grades—but they will succeed given enough practice. Often children who have trouble with this activity are the ones who struggle to understand how fractions relate to the whole, so

Children playing complex rhythms in a bucket brigade

this activity is great for reinforcing this math concept.)

Strategy twelve

First–sixth grades: Teach children to sing "Hey, Betty Martin" (see Example 12.7), and then have them think the song while clapping its rhythm. Clap the song's rhythm while walking a steady beat. Identify places where the rhythm is shorter than the beat (every time the word "Betty" occurs). Look at the notation of the song and learn to anticipate and perform these subdivisions. (Experiment with other songs, too, such as "When Johnny Comes Marching Home" and "Little Johnny Brown," focusing each time on "Johnny.")

Strategy thirteen

Third–sixth grades: Form small ensembles with simple percussion instruments in which some children play a slow and steady beat and others play various subdivisions (overturned buckets with dowel sticks can serve as makeshift drums). A conductor (first the teacher for the whole class, then selected children from each group) indicates the level of subdivision by holding up two, three, or four fingers. Generally, older students will be able to master divisions into three and four faster than younger students. Example 12.8 gives two versions of this exercise.

Search the Internet for "bucket brigade percussion" and share the complex rhythmic pieces with your students.

 **EXAMPLE 12.7**

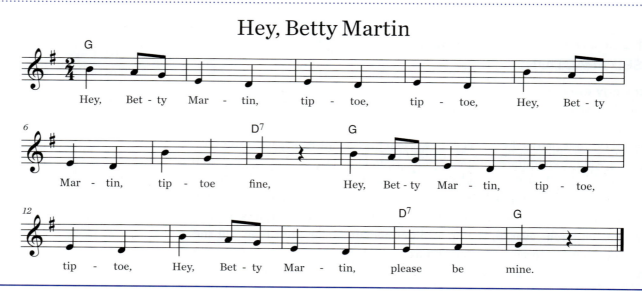

EXAMPLE 12.8

NCTM GOAL #2: UNDERSTAND MEANINGS OF OPERATIONS AND HOW THEY RELATE TO ONE ANOTHER

As children gain confidence with the meaning of basic numbers, they can begin to perform operations such as addition, subtraction, multiplication, and division. Physical movement and music-making can make each of these concepts concrete, as exemplified in several strategies below.

UNDERSTAND VARIOUS MEANINGS OF ADDITION AND SUBTRACTION OF WHOLE NUMBERS AND THE RELATIONSHIP BETWEEN THE TWO OPERATIONS

Strategy one

Preschool–second grade: Sing simple songs that use addition ("This Old Man," "One, Two, Three Alary," "Children, Go Where I Send Thee") or subtraction ("Ten in the Bed," "Five Green and Speckled Frogs," "Five Little Monkeys"). Add or subtract all of the numbers as they are mentioned in each song to get to a total. Represent these on fingers, on a board, with lines, or with math manipulatives. Have children dramatize the songs by moving to the actions of the song. For example, with "Ten in the Bed," have ten children lie on a pretend bed on the floor. Give each child a number from 1 to 10. As the other children sing the song, each "number" rolls out of bed on cue. Over time, have a board with ten numbers on it and each time a number is taken away, have a child erase one figure. Eventually, represent this action by using a minus sign; do the opposite with the songs named above that focus on addition.

UNDERSTAND THE EFFECTS OF ADDING AND SUBTRACTING WHOLE NUMBERS

Strategy two

First–fourth grades: Ten children stand in a number line, each holding a different classroom percussion instrument. A student conductor signals children to enter in order, one at a time. Each instrument continues playing as numbers are added, leading to a complex of sounds with everyone playing. The student conductor then signals instruments to drop out one at a time for subtraction. Another child could represent the addition and subtraction on the board by writing "+1" each time an instrument enters, then erasing them one by one as the sounds disappear.

Older children can make a longer number line and add or subtract more than one number. Children with instruments will need to know which number they are in the number line so that they (and all the children before them) can begin playing at once. In an addition problem such as 3 + 3, the first three people will begin to play and then the second three, which will lead to the sum of six. The opposite occurs for subtraction. Children not in the number line can represent the computations on paper and check that the number line children have the correct answers.

Strategy three

Second–sixth grades: Children create a piece that begins with one 4-beat pattern that repeats on one percussion instrument, then adds another 4-beat repeating pattern on a different percussion instrument, going up to six layered patterns. Remove the patterns, one by one. On paper, represent visually the addition or subtraction of patterns as the children perform the piece.

Strategy four

Second–sixth grades: Referring to Table 12.2, allow children to experience the concept of adding notes visually, aurally, and kinesthetically through body movement and sound. Use the quarter note as the beat and invite children to extend sounds by tying two quarter notes together to create a half note; three quarter notes to create a dotted half; and four quarter notes to create a whole note. Keep an underlying beat as children clap on the initial beat and move the hand or arm in

CHAPTER 12 | Music and Math **253**

TABLE 12.2 SUBDIVISIONS AND EXTENSIONS OF THE BEAT

Subdivisions of the beat		4 in 1 (sixteenth notes)
		3 in 1 (triplet eighth notes)
		2 in 1 (eighth notes)
Beat note		1 on 1 (quarter note)
Extensions of the beat		2 beats (half note)
		3 beats (dotted half note)
		4 beats (whole note)

a flowing motion to the beat to show the length of the note. Help children learn to read and perform those note values accurately from notation.

Once children are comfortable reading different notes for different durations, invite children to show how many beats are in each duration by clapping and then representing them with numbers on paper.

UNDERSTAND THE EFFECTS OF MULTIPLYING AND DIVIDING WHOLE NUMBERS

Strategy five

Third–sixth grades: Arrange children into small groups, and challenge them to invent a rap based on the multiplication table such as 2 x 1 = 2, 2 x 2 = 4, 2 x 3 = 6, and so on (see Example 12.9; you may choose to distribute this grid to children, and supply lists of rhymes from Table 12.3 from which they may choose). When children have finished writing their raps, play a funky ostinato with a strong beat on percussion instruments, giving children time to practice the rap to this rhythm track. Add body percussion that coordinates with the rap, such as a pats, claps, or clap-snaps, and suggest that each group feature some students "scratching" behind the chanted rap. Use the rap to practice the multiplication table, and teach the rap to other groups.

At first, students may wish to use their printed grids to remember the rap, but encourage them to gradually move away from the printed version, just remembering the aural. Perform timed practices of the multiplication tables, returning to the raps to help struggling children.

Strategy six

Third–sixth grades: Sing "Frère Jacques," "Three Blind Mice," and "Row, Row, Row Your Boat." Tell the children that each song has four parts and challenge them to figure out how to divide the class into four groups, as equal as possible, to sing the songs as rounds.

Once children can sing the rounds, ask them how many groups would be needed to sing both rounds at the same time (2 x 4 = 8). Challenge them to divide the class into eight groups as evenly as possible. Start the first four groups in singing

254 PART III | Music throughout the Day

EXAMPLE 12.9

Sample rap on multiplication tables

2	times	1	is	2:	that's	cool.	(rest)	2	times	2	is	4	not	more.	(rest)
2	times	3	is	6:	nice	mix!	(rest)	2	times	4	is	8	I	state.	(rest)
2	times	5	is	10:			(rest)	2	times	6	is				(rest)
2	times	7	is				(rest)	2	times	8	is				(rest)
2	times	9	is				(rest)	2	times	10	is				(rest)
2	times	11	is				(rest)	2	times	12	is				(rest)

TABLE 12.3 SAMPLE RHYMING WORDS FOR NUMBERS

NUMBER	RHYMING WORDS, NEAR-RHYMING WORDS, AND RHYMING PHRASES
10	Ben, den, friend, glen, Jen, Ken, men, mend, pen, rend, then, trend, wend, Zen
12	delve, shelve
14	door team, drawer team, floor team, more team, roar team, score team, shore team, s'mores team, snorting, thwarting, cavorting
16	fix team, hicks team, kicks team, mix team, nix team, Nick's team, pics team, tricks team, Vic's team, wicks team
18	bait team, crate team, date team, fate team, freight team, gate team, great team, Kate's team, mate team, Nate's team, plate steam, skate team, slate team, state team, wait team, weight team
20	punty, grunty, runty, muddy
22	I see you, no can do, trendy you, voulez-vous
24	in the core, apple core, heavy chore, close the door, on the floor, filled with gore, mystic lore, want some more, can't ignore, help the poor, let it pour, make a roar, that feels sore, in the store, time to soar, hear him snore, fight a war

"Frère Jacques" as a four-part round. Once the singing is solid and they are creating harmony together, direct four more groups in singing "Row, Row, Row Your Boat." The two songs (eight groups) blend together as a double round.

Extend the double round with a triple round, adding four more groups i singing "Three Blind Mice." Children can experience a multiplication concept firsthand, noting the number of groups needed to sing three four-part rounds simultaneously (3 x 4 = 12), and then deciding how to divide the class into 12 groups as evenly as possible.

CHAPTER 12 | Music and Math **255**

Strategy seven

Third–sixth grades: Moving to the beat is a great way to start class in the morning or after a recess: it's energetic, it exercises the body and brain, it gets the blood flowing, and it builds community as everyone focuses on a movement that looks, sounds, and feels in sync with one another.

Play a recorded instrumental march (such as *The Stars and Stripes Forever* in Appendix 3) and models a repeating pattern in duple meter (patting lap on the strong beat, clapping hands on the weak beat) for the children to imitate. Stop the music and tell children the march is in duple meter, with one strong beat and one weak beat. Play the music again, modeling the pat-clap movements (with children imitating), but at the end of the first phrase (either 16 or 32 beats), change the movements to foot-stamping on strong beats and finger-snapping on weak beats. Change movements for each subsequent phrase (e.g., touch stomach/touch forehead, touch knee/touch nose, raise right shoulder/raise left shoulder, blink right eye/blink left eye). Stop the music and ask the children if they noticed that the music changed when the movement pattern changed. Ask how many beats were in each phrase. Play the piece again and count aloud, starting the counting over when new movements signal the new phrase. Once children have identified the number of beats in a phrase, write the number on the board and the words "beats in a phrase."

Extend this exercise for children in fourth–sixth grades by asking them to determine the number of phrases in the piece. Play the piece again, changing movements with every phrase and calling out the phrase number at the beginning of each phrase. When the piece is finished, write the number on the board under the number of beats in a phrase, and follow with the words "phrases in the piece." (Marches often follow a pattern of repeated phrases that can total 16–24 phrases in all.)

Ask children how they might determine the number of beats in the piece (aside from counting every beat). Lead them to understanding that they can multiply the number of beats in a phrase by the number of phrases in the piece. Invite a student to perform the multiplication at the board, while other children work on the problem at their seats. Children can then hold thumbs up if their answer agrees with the answer on the board.

NCTM GOAL #3: COMPUTE FLUENTLY AND MAKE REASONABLE ESTIMATES

As children gain confidence with computing numbers, they can begin to estimate results in various situations involving numbers. Singing games and musical activities provide a delightful way for children to demonstrate their mathematical prowess.

COMPUTE FLUENTLY

Strategy one

First–fourth grades: For this math-music game, choose three children, each of whom selects a different classroom instrument. Child #3 sits in a chair and puts on a blindfold.

Write an addition or subtraction problem on the board (do not write subtraction problems that result in negative numbers). Child #1 plays beats equal to the number before the operation sign, all children speak the operation sign aloud, and then Child #2 plays beats equal to the number after the operation sign. Child #3 (blindfolded) counts the number of beats, hears the operation sign, then calculates the answer and plays that number of beats on the instrument. Each set of children performs three problems before choosing other children to take their places.

Strategy two

Third–sixth grades: To build fluency with number place values, have children use body percussion to answer math questions by slapping the chest for each number in the hundreds column, clapping hands for each number in the tens column, and snapping fingers for each number in the ones column.

Begin by writing several numbers on the board and realizing each number with corresponding body percussion. For example, the number 325 is played with three chest slaps, two hand claps, and five finger snaps. Model this realization and have children echo it. Once children understand the system, ask them addition, subtraction, multiplication, and division questions, to which they respond with body percussion: "what is 2 x 4?" (8 snaps), "what is 7 + 7?" (1 clap, 4 snaps), "what is 50 + 67?" (1 slap, 1 clap, 7 snaps).

To increase student interest, invite one child to play the answer on instruments: gong or low drum for the hundreds, high drum for the tens, and rhythm sticks for the ones. Other students continue with body percussion, practicing the process while awaiting their turn with the instruments. Offer each instrumentalist three math questions, and give more children a turn at the instruments by setting up two or three sets. To involve the entire class, divide the class into three groups, line up each group behind an instrument set, and have them compete in a math bee. Rotate math questions across the three groups. One child plays at a time, then goes to the end of the group's line. Correct answers earn a point for the group.

Children may enjoy composing body or instrumental math questions, performing them with sounds for numbers and speaking only the operation and the word "equals" (for example, slap-clap-clap-snap-snap-snap "plus" slap-slap-snap "equals" represents the question of 123 + 201 = ?). Other children may listen to the sounds, write the math question on the board or at their desks, and then calculate the answer (in this example, 324). The instrumental version of this activity has one student play the first number, speak the operation, play the second number, and speak "equals." Another student answers with body percussion or instruments.

DEVELOP AND USE STRATEGIES TO ESTIMATE THE RESULTS OF WHOLE-NUMBER COMPUTATIONS AND JUDGE THE REASONABLENESS OF THE RESULTS

Strategy three

Third–sixth grades: Direct children to sit in a circle, each with a drum or rhythm sticks. Explain that each child will make up a two-beat pattern, using one or two sounds per beat, and demonstrate the four possibilities by chanting: 1) "pear pear," 2) "pear, ap-ple" 3) "ap-ple pear," and 4) "ap-ple ap-ple" (see Example 12.8). All children begin patting a steady beat on their laps. Appoint one child to begin a

CHAPTER 12 | Music and Math 257

LESSON PLAN 12.1

"Five Fat Turkeys"

Grades:
Second–fourth

Objectives:

- Sing and play the chase game song, "Five Fat Turkeys."
- Use estimation to guess how many turkeys are left after some have been captured.
- Use subtraction to check accuracy of the estimation.

Materials:

- White board and pen
- Open space for movement

Procedures:

1. Establish boundaries for movement in the classroom:

2. Explain the boundaries of the turkey "yard" and the space for the "oven." Going out of bounds means going straight to the oven, and no running is allowed—turkeys can only wobble on their short legs. Appoint one child to be the cook, who puts on an "apron" and estimates the number of turkeys in the yard, then leads everyone in counting how many turkeys are present and writes the number on the board.

3. Teach everyone to sing the song (Example 12.10), beginning with the number of turkeys in the yard (the number of children playing the game). Once everyone knows the song, ask the cook how many people are coming to dinner, and then tell the cook how many turkeys are needed for the day's meal.

4. The turkeys sing the song again as they waddle around the yard, and the cook comes out to catch the required number of turkeys, tapping them to go in the oven.

5. Ask the cook to estimate the number of turkeys left in the yard, then have the children count to clarify, and write that number as the remaining number of turkeys.

6. Ask the children to subtract the remaining turkeys from the starting number of turkeys, and writes the answer on the board. Children check the math is correct by counting the turkeys in the oven.

7. The children sing the song again, starting with the new number of turkeys in the yard. Send the cook out for a new number of turkeys for the next meal (improvise if necessary: "wouldn't it be nice to feed the mayor's family?" "shouldn't we invite some people caught in snowstorms?" "how about making a thank-you dinner for the town's firefighters?"), and continue the cycle until only one turkey remains. That person becomes the new cook and the game can start again.

Assessment:
Note how successful children were in following directions and in solving and representing the math problems visually and with their bodies.

Continued on next page

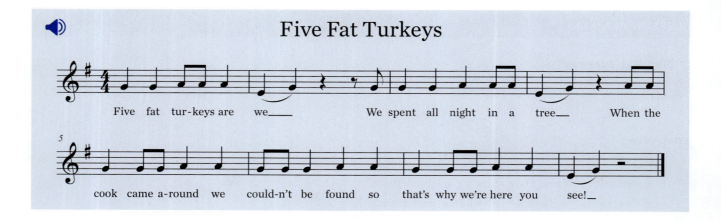

two-beat pattern, and all children echo. Without missing a beat, the next child repeats the first pattern and adds another two-beat pattern, the entirety of which is echoed by all. This process continues, accumulating rhythms, until a player cannot play the previous accumulation of patterns or add a new pattern correctly. On the board, write the number of children who played correctly, then asks the children to predict how long the next round will last and write a consensus number on the board. The playing cycle begins anew with the child who ended the previous round. When the pattern breaks, again write the number of children who played correctly and compares this number with the prediction, then ask for another prediction. The process resumes; point out whether the predictions are becoming more accurate or not. Vary this exercise by asking a specific child for the next prediction.

ALGEBRA, GEOMETRY, AND MUSIC

Algebra deals with number relationships, and geometry with line and shape relationships. Music deals with both (number relationships in rhythms and pitches, and with shapes in patterns and form). Music can teach both algebra and geometry, and children who have had rich musical experiences reap benefits when it comes time to learn math. Long before children are able to understand abstract problems of algebra and geometry, their brains can apply mathematical principles to rhythmic and melodic patterns. Children can perceive when patterns are similar and different. They can replicate short four-beat patterns in AA form, or listen to one four-beat pattern and improvise a contrasting four-beat pattern to create AB form. They can identify sequences in music, when a pattern of pitches repeats but starts lower or higher than the previous pattern. They notice when larger music sections repeat and contrast, as in verse-chorus song structures (ABABAB, as in "Erie Canal"). They perceive the phrase structure of simple songs, such as "Twinkle, Twinkle Little Star" (ABBA), "Bow Wow Wow" (ABCA), and "Scotland's Burning" (ABCA). They understand and follow larger forms from recorded music, such as the rondo form in Beethoven's Rondo in C Major, Op. 51, No. 1 (ABACABA). Using patterns that repeat and contrast, children can invent their own music structures and play them on instruments they have made or on classroom instruments. They can represent these patterns and shapes visually with colors, icons, or symbols.

Two computer programs, Making Music[1] and Making More Music,[2] help children hear, see, and create musical patterns and relationships. These programs are ideally suited to classroom music centers with computers and headphones. In Making Music, younger children can draw geometric lines and shapes and listen to how the program turns them into sound patterns. Children in fourth–sixth grades can use Making Music to create short melodies, then experiment with playing them backwards (retrograde), upside down with the same pitch intervals (inversion), or backwards and upside down at the same time (retrograde inversion). Manipulating sound translates naturally to manipulating shapes in geometry.

ADAPTING INSTRUCTION FOR VARIOUS NEEDS

Blind or Visual Impairments
Use adaptive technology to help children perceive the numbers. Give them blocks, figures, or puppets to manipulate with the chants and songs involving counting. Have number shapes 1–10 made of fine sandpaper or yarn pasted on cardboard for children to trace. Include raised dots at the bottom for them to count the number.

Hearing Impaired
Add gestures and puppets to songs and counting rhymes to help children feel and see the numbers. Engage them physically as much as possible to represent various numbers and number processes. Use charts and number cards to reinforce concepts visually.

Mobility Impairments
Involve children in actual movements as much as possible, for example, rolling their wheelchair forward or backward to indicate addition or subtraction. They could also move their head upward for addition or downward for subtraction. Invite them to make a clicking or tapping sound to show the answer to a problem.

Behavior Disorders with Externalizing Behaviors
Set clear parameters for all children when acting out counting games such as "Ten in the Bed." Outline the "bed" space and a clear place to land when they "roll out" of the bed. Assign individual tasks to children who struggle with controlling behaviors, such as showing on the board what number is left each time a child rolls out.

Behavior Disorders with Internalizing Behaviors and Children on the Autism Spectrum
Invite children into counting games by having them hold a puppet, manipulate blocks, or play an instrument if they don't want to be as involved as other children in acting out the words of a song. If a particular child is highly sensitive to sound, have them play a soft-sounding instrument.

Summary

For many students, mathematics can be frustratingly abstract. Music offers myriad ways to explore mathematical concepts, from simple counting songs to multiple divisions of the beat. When students engage with concrete examples of mathematics in music, both subjects become clearer to them, and everyone wins.

Review

1. What are some authentic connections between math and music?

2. What does it mean to make math concrete for children and how can music help to do that?

Critical Thinking

1. How might singing songs about math operations help children to learn? How might it not be effective?

2. What are some of the potential benefits of thinking similarly about math and music?

3. What are the advantages to learning math through singing, moving, visualizing, and counting over sitting at desks and doing more math worksheets?

Projects

1. Try one or more of the strategies in this chapter with children at an appropriate age level. If you think it can be adapted to another age level, give it a try and reflect on what happened in terms of children's engagement and learning.

2. Work with one other person to look at the NCTM website. Find another math concept or skill you think could be taught through music. Collaborate to develop a strategy, and test it on children to see if it works. Reflect on the success of your idea(s).

3. Collect songs that you believe will help children learn math concepts and develop appropriate skills. Rehearse those songs as many times as you need to in order to memorize them and be able to use them as a teacher.

4. Try several of the strategies outlined in this chapter with children and determine how well they help children to concretely understand abstract mathematical concepts.

5. Invent a chant or rap to learn the multiplication tables. Teach it to friends and have them add a musical accompaniment to your chant or rap.

Additional Resources for Teaching

An, Song A. and Mary M. Capraro. (2011). *Music-Math: Integrated Activities for Elementary and Middle School Students*. Irvine, CA: Education for All.

Subotnick, Morton. (1995). Making Music [computer software]. Irvington, NY: Voyager. Available from http://www.creatingmusic.com/

Subotnick, Morton. (1999). Making More Music [computer software]. Irvington, NY: Voyager. Available from http://www.creatingmusic.com/

Online Resources: Audio and Songbook

digital.wwnorton.com/classroom

13

MUSIC AND SCIENCE

The theory of relativity occurred to me by intuition, and music is the driving force behind this intuition.... My new discovery is the result of musical perception.

—Albert Einstein

IN THIS CHAPTER

In the Classroom

The Science of Sound

Basic Concepts and Experiments in the Science of Sound

Other Intersections of Music and Science

Summary

Review

Critical Thinking

Projects

Additional Resources for Teaching

Additional Resources for Listening

Music connects in many ways to physics, earth and space sciences, engineering, and technology.

You Will Learn

- many techniques for using music to help children achieve National Science Teachers Association (NSTA) Standards in physical science

- several ways to use music to meet NSTA Standards in life sciences; earth and space sciences; and engineering, technology, and applications of science

Ask Yourself

- What about music is related to the science of physics?

- How might music be meaningfully integrated into studies of technology?

- How might combining music and science enliven the study of science?

- How did you learn about how sounds are created and what relation they have to vibrating surfaces?

- What have you noticed about the acoustics of rooms from listening to sounds in noisy restaurants vs. quiet restaurants?

- If you play an instrument, how is the sound activated and how does the sound resonate?

- Have you ever imagined ways deaf people might perceive sounds?

The National Science Teachers Association (NSTA) provides detailed national standards in four core areas: physical sciences, life sciences, earth and space sciences, and engineering, technology, and applications of science. The NSTA's goals range from recognizing patterns and formulating answers to questions about the world, to demonstrating proficiencies in gathering, describing, and using information about the world. Music relates most obviously to the physical sciences, especially in the physics of sound, but there are also ways music can build children's understanding in the other three areas.

IN THE CLASSROOM

VIGNETTE ONE

Ms. Mallory and her second graders are studying birds. From a list of 30 categories of birds, the children have selected the types that are most common in their region. They've researched each of those types and what learned about their similarities and differences. The children work cooperatively in groups, focusing on different types and reporting on the qualities of that type to the rest of the class. They draw and paint pictures of their bird, find out the sound of its call, and learn about its habitat and food. As a part of their final report, they write a short poem describing their bird and then turn that poem into a song, integrating the shape and pattern of the bird's call into the song's introduction and ending.

VIGNETTE TWO

Mr. Cardoza is teaching a project on instrument building to his fourth graders, so they will have sound resources to use in the classroom to compose, improvise, and accompany songs and stories. In the process he teaches them important scientific principles of sound wave vibration, resonance, timbre, tuning, and the relationship of pitch to string length, thickness, and tension. He uses an oscilloscope to show students the different complex wave forms their instrument vibrations create.

THE SCIENCE OF SOUND

Scientists seek to understand the properties of sound and represent physical phenomena in mathematical terms. Musicians seek to use sound for artistic expression and emotional effect. Because the two subjects are so closely related, music can be used in many ways to support children's learning in science.

Scientists since the Greek philosopher Pythagoras have been fascinated with the challenge of measuring sound, with the relative values of pitches alone and pitches combined into harmony, and with how humans perceive all of these things. Pythagoras developed a complex mathematical system for describing the relationship between the length of a vibrating object, such as a string, and its subdivision into various pitches. For instance, a string pressed at its midpoint, when plucked, vibrates twice as fast as the full-length string, creating a pitch one octave higher than the whole string's frequency. He also developed theories about what pitch relationships are perceived as agreeable (consonant) or disagreeable (dissonant), although much of what seems agreeable or disagreeable musically depends on the culture in which one has been raised, not on mathematical relationships. Pythagoras believed that both music and mathematics could make order in the world.

Building on the work of Pythagoras and others, physicists have devised ways to measure several characteristics of sound waves and represent them numerically. Frequency, perceived by the ear as pitch, can be measured and expressed as cycles per second, or hertz (abbreviated Hz). For comparison, the human ear perceives frequencies from 20 to 20,000 Hz, and the piano produces frequencies from 27 to 4,186 Hz.

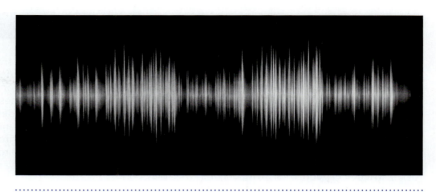

An oscilloscope detects and represents complex sound waves, which can be expressed mathematically as functions in Fourier analysis.

Amplitude (the amount of energy that sound waves contain, which the ear perceives as loudness) can be measured and expressed numerically as decibels (dB). A whisper registers at 30 dB, a chainsaw at 110 dB, a jet taking off at 120 dB.

Wave complexity, perceived as timbre or tone color of voices and musical instruments, can also be measured. Every instrument and voice produces a unique, complex sound wave consisting of the fundamental pitch and various overtones. Electronic instruments (synthesizers) sound like acoustic instruments to the extent they can put together (synthesize) the same mix of fundamental pitches and overtones. Complex sound waves can be represented on a device called an oscilloscope and expressed mathematically as functions in Fourier analysis.

BASIC CONCEPTS AND EXPERIMENTS IN THE SCIENCE OF SOUND

Throughout the elementary years, science experiments can help students discover important principles of the science of sound, from musical sound and speech to natural sounds of birds and animals; environmental sounds such as the hum of a refrigerator, the rumble of car and truck engines, and train whistles; to the mediated sounds of TV, radio, and the Internet. The study of science is rooted in experimenting, discovering, and reflecting.

VIBRATION

Sounds travel through vibrations in the air. The sounds create waves that move back and forth, and expand and contract. When the sound waves reach our ears they make our eardrums vibrate, which sends a message to our brains. Since everything that makes sound vibrates in a different way, we learn to identify what is making the sound that we are hearing.

Sound can travel through air, solids, and liquids, but not through a compression chamber (where there is no air to vibrate). Many sounds are now digitally produced to travel electronically through wire, air, or liquid.

264 PART III | Music throughout the Day

USING SCIENCE TO MEET MUSIC STANDARDS

1. Singing. To teach the concept of resonance, invite children to cup their hands over their mouths and sing with an "ah" sound, then remove their hands and sing with an "ah" sound. Discuss the difference. Extend this experiment by having them sing into increasingly larger containers, such as soup cans, coffee cans, and gallon-sized cans.

2. Playing. Once children have conducted several science experiments, invite children who play band or orchestral instruments to bring them to class. Have students look at the instruments before they are played and predict how the principles of resonance, pitch, and vibration might operate in each instrument. Check their predictions against what actually happens once the instruments are played.

3. Improvising. Group students in threes to improvise a short piece based on one of the principles of the science of sound: resonance, vibration, or pitch. Once each improvisation is finished, invite the rest of the class to guess which principle the group was trying to illustrate and why. Discuss their ideas with them.

4. Composing and arranging. Group students in threes or fours to compose a piece for a given pitched instrument that includes all of the following pitch variation possibilities: repeating high or low sounds, scalar sounds stepping upward or downward, sweeping sounds upward or downward, leaps from high to low, and four-note patterns that repeat or vary.

5. Reading and notating. Once students have worked out their compositions in number 4 above to your satisfaction, have them figure out a way to notate their pieces using actual notes or lines and patterns. Have students play the piece many times to see if they can interpret it as intended. Give the notation to another group of children and see how they interpret it using pitched instruments.

6. Listening. Listen to *Boléro*, by Maurice Ravel (see Appendix 3). Have students describe the ways he uses pitch in that piece and use movements to represent the direction of the melody in the opening section of the piece.

7. Evaluating. Have students listen to the compositions and improvisations that result from suggestions made in numbers 3 and 4, above. Ask them to analyze what happened musically and comment on how effective it was and why.

8. Connecting to other arts and subject areas. This entire chapter is devoted to this standard.

9. Connecting to culture and history. Have students research an instrument type across many cultures, such as a lute, flute, or drums. Determine what materials were used to construct these instruments and compare them to contemporary versions of similar instruments. Predict the differences in sound based on the materials used for construction. They can check their predictions by finding performances of the various instruments online.

Experiment 1: A Long-Distance Call

Materials: Two plastic cups or containers, 10 feet of string.

Method: Punch a hole in the bottom of each cup. Push the string through the holes. Tie a knot in both ends of the string. Have two children stand apart so the string is taut. One child whispers, speaks, or sings into their cup while the other listens. Take turns. Ask students: how did the sound travel? What made it loud enough to hear? (A: It traveled along the string, which vibrated with the pulses of the sounds, and was amplified by the cup or container.)

Experiment 2: Ringing Ears

Materials: A fork and a spoon, five feet of string.

Method: Tie the handle of the fork in the center of the string. Have one child wrap the ends of the string around each pointer finger and place their fingers in their ears. Have another child strike the fork with the spoon. Ask students: what did they hear? How did the sound travel? What would happen if you used a metal grate from a stove? What would happen if you used a plastic fork instead? Why does metal ring so clearly? What instruments are made of metal? (A: The sound traveled from the fork through the string to the eardrum. Metal vibrates and then sustains when struck. Plastic does not sustain a vibration.)

Musical enhancement: Invite children to experiment with metallic objects and simple instruments (finger cymbals, hanging cymbals, gongs) and notice how long the sounds ring. Measure the length of the sound with a stopwatch. Contrast those sounds with the sound of a wood block or rhythm sticks being struck once by measuring how long that sound lasts. Compose a short piece for long and short sounds.

Experiment 3: A Comb Kazoo
Materials: Small hair comb, wax paper.
Method: Cut a piece of wax paper to fit over both sides of the comb. Hold the comb up to your lips and buzz or hum on one pitch, several pitches, or even a full melody. Create a larger version by covering one end of a paper towel or toilet paper tube with wax paper, attached with a rubber band. Ask students: what do you hear? What is vibrating? What do the vibrations feel like? How did the sound reach your ears? (A: The lips or voice is vibrating and the wax paper is vibrating. The lips feel a buzz. The sound reached your ears through bone conduction in the body and by traveling through the air to your ears.)

Music enhancement: Using the instruments created, form a kazoo band. Play familiar pieces together by humming into the instruments.

Experiment 4: See the Vibration
Materials: A bowl, plastic wrap, sugar or rice, metal tray, wooden spoon.
Method: Stretch the plastic wrap tightly over the bowl. Place a small amount of rice or sugar on the plastic wrap. Hold the metal tray over the bowl and strike it with a wooden spoon. Ask students: what happens to the sugar or rice? Why? (A: When the tray is struck, it vibrates, and the sound waves travel through the air and make the plastic wrap vibrate, causing the sugar or rice to jump.)
Musical enhancement: Invite children to stand next to an acoustic piano and place their hands on the back of the instrument. Play the piano slowly from low to high and have them feel the vibrations. Then allow them to look inside and see the strings as you play. Ask students: how is this experiment similar to the experiment with the plastic wrap? What on the piano is vibrating? (A: The strings and soundboard vibrate like the plastic in the earlier experiment. This time striking the keys activated the sound.) Which pitches were easiest to feel? (A: The lowest, because the sound wave is slower and lasts longer.)

Experiment 5: Balloon Vibrations
Materials: Balloons, a radio.
Method: Blow up a balloon. Stand three to four inches away from the radio. Hold the balloon and note what you feel when the radio plays at a moderate volume. Try it again at a louder volume. Ask students: what was different about the louder volume? Why might people who are deaf or hard of hearing be able to hear concerts if they hold balloons up to their heads? (A: The balloon amplifies vibrations from the music, which travel by bone conduction through the body to enhance hearing.)

In each of the preceding experiments, have children discuss whether the vibrations are traveling through air, solids, liquid, or a combination. Ask them what other experiments they might create that would show how vibrations travel.

Feeling vibrations can be the best way to learn about them.

RESONANCE

Our ability to perceive sounds, including the sounds of music, speech, and our environment, depends on the volume and strength of the sounds' vibrations. Resonance is how long something continues to vibrate after it has been activated. In music, the resonance of the sound is determined by the size of the body of the instrument and the material that is vibrating. For example, the wooden body of a string bass will vibrate longer than the wooden body of a violin. The following experiments will help children discover how resonance helps us perceive sounds.

Experiment 1: Rubber Band Box Sounds

Materials: Rubber bands, small boxes of various sizes.

Method: Tighten the rubber band and pluck it in the air. Ask students: is it easy or hard to hear? Why might it be hard to hear? Stretch the rubber band over the smallest box and pluck it. Is it easier or harder to hear? Why? Continue to experiment with boxes of different sizes. Which boxes make it easiest to hear? (A: The string plucked in the air has no amplification. The larger the box, the greater the area of resonance and the louder the sound.)

Musical enhancement: View pictures of the string instruments from the orchestra (violin, viola, cello, and bass). Discuss the sizes of the instruments. Have students postulate why those instruments are the same shape but in such different sizes. Ask students: how will the resonance vary from one instrument to another? Invite a string teacher to bring string instruments in and play them for the children. What is the difference in the instruments' resonances? (A: The larger the body of the instrument, the greater the resonance. The sound has more time to bounce around the cavity of the instrument.)

Experiment 2: A Mighty Ruler

Materials: A wooden or plastic ruler, a desk.

Method: Hold the ruler by one end in the air above the desk and snap it. Ask students: what do you hear? Anchor the ruler on a desk with one hand, with about half of the ruler on the desk and half overhanging. Now snap the ruler against the desk. What is the difference in sound? Why do you think that happened? (A: The desk is amplifying the vibration of the ruler by providing resonance.) Slide the ruler back and forth, extending it over the edge of the desk as you snap it, then moving more of it back over desk. Does the sound change? How? (A: The longer the ruler overhangs, the lower the sound. The shorter the ruler overhangs, the higher the sound. The shorter the length of the vibrating object, the higher the sound.)

Musical enhancement: Improvise a short piece for desk and ruler with the entire class. Choose one child to conduct and have them develop one signal for rulers on the desk and another for rulers up in the air. When the conductor signals the down position, students snap the rulers against the top of their desks, moving backwards and forwards to change the pitch. When the conductor signals the up position, rulers are off the desk and held in the air. Extend this by having half the class keep their rulers on their desks in one position, snapping to a steady beat, while the other half snaps their rulers as they slide backwards and forwards across the desks in unison, changing the pitch together.

Experiment 3: Your Body as a Resonator

Materials: Children's own bodies.

Method: Ask children to pat their legs, arms, and chests. Have them form their mouths into a cave shape with their lips tightly closed, then slide the forefinger into the mouth against one cheek and flip it out, making a popping sound. Ask students: which part of your body has the most resonance? Why? Now hum the lowest sound you can. Place one hand on your chest. Can you feel the resonance there? Touch your throat. Is there a feeling of resonance there? Now hum a high sound. Suggest that children touch their chests, throats, and faces as they hum. Where do the high sounds resonate?

Musical enhancement: Sing a song in a low range. Feel it vibrating in the chest. Sing the song in a normal range. Feel it vibrating in the throat and face. Sing the song in a high range. Feel it vibrating in the upper face. Which sounds the best? Why? Work to sing all songs in the head voice (as described in Chapter 4) with an open mouth, keeping the chin dropped and loose.

Experiment 4: Groove with Galileo

Materials: Four feet of string, a weight or small rock.

Method: Tie one end of the string around the rock. Tie the other end to a rod or a dowel. One child holds it away from the body; another child pulls the rock back and releases it. Notice what happens to the arc of the string over time. Ask students: does the arc get bigger or smaller? How might this compare to the resonance of a sound in a chamber? (Galileo discovered how resonance works using a pendulum.) What happens to the resonance when a musician continues to activate the sound of an instrument? (A: The instrument keeps vibrating.) What happens when the musician stops? (A: The sound dies when the vibrations stop.)

Musical enhancement: Invite a brass player to come to your class. Ask the musician to play an instrument (trumpet, trombone, tuba) and then stop for silent listening. Ask students: how long does the sound last? Play the instrument in a tiled bathroom or into a metal garbage can. How is the sound different? How long does the sound last? Attend a band or orchestra concert in a hall (auditoriums have resonance and are carefully designed and constructed to control how spoken or musical sound continues to vibrate). How big is the sound? What factors make it so? (A: The size of the auditorium, the surfaces and angles of the walls and ceilings, and the size and type of the group that is playing.)

Experiment 5: Instrument Experimentation

Materials: A range of self-constructed or classroom percussion instruments.

Method: Experiment with a variety of instruments. Ask students: which instruments have the most resonance? Why? Put them in order from least to most resonant. What do you notice about the instruments when they are arranged this way? (A: Generally, the bigger the instrument, the greater the resonance.)

Musical enhancement: Choose a variety of instruments and, in small groups, compose a short piece for more resonant sounds and less resonant sounds. Try to keep the volume the same in all of the sounds by plucking, striking, blowing at the same energy level.

Experiment 6: Searching for the Sound

Materials: A music box mechanism without a resonator, wooden tables or boxes, metal tables or boxes, cardboard boxes.

Method: Play the music box in the air. Notice the quality of the sound. Experiment with playing the music box while resting it on wooden, cardboard, and metal boxes. Ask students: how does the sound change? Which containers have the most resonance? Why? (A: The size and material of the box determine the resonance. The denser containers will vibrate more because sound travels more readily through those surfaces.)

Musical enhancement: Have children construct two different stringed instruments, one with a metal can resonator and one with a wooden box resonator. Play both of them. Compare the quality of the sound. Improvise some music for the stringed instruments, sometimes plucking the strings and sometimes tapping on the resonators (see Chapters 7 and 8 for more ideas).

PITCH

Pitch is the relative highness or lowness of a sound. Lower pitches create slower vibrations and higher pitches create faster vibrations. There are two kinds of pitch qualities. The first is exact pitch, which is a pitched sound that can be matched precisely by another instrument or voice. When exact pitches are not matched, they are said to be out of tune, and clashing sound waves create a beating or pulsing sense that does not exist when the sound waves match. This is why it is important for instrumental groups to tune up before they play. They tune to the pitch A440, the A above middle C, which has a frequency of 440 Hz. Choirs must also sing in tune to create pleasant music. Slightly out of tune sounds can be irritating, and it is challenging to listen to untuned music.

The second kind of pitch is indefinite pitch. All objects that vibrate do so relatively high or low, although they may not generate exact pitches. A passing bus generates a lower relative pitch than a passing car. A large cardboard box will sound lower when struck than a small cardboard box. Yet none of those sounds can be matched precisely.

Experiment 1: Exact or Indefinite?

Materials: A wide range of self-made or classroom percussion instruments.

Method: Distribute one percussion instrument to each child and invite children to experiment with striking, shaking, or scraping their instruments. Direct them to notice whether the sound is relatively high or low. Have them compare the sounds and divide into groups of exact pitch and indefinite pitch. Once grouped, have them stand in order from relatively low to relatively high. Have each group check the other's decisions by listening to their pitches in order.

Musical enhancement: Divide children into groups of four or five. Have them compose a short piece for instruments of both definite and indefinite pitch contrasting low and high sounds. Encourage them to practice their piece several times, and then to invent a system for notating it, using various colors and symbols. Perform the piece for others.

Experiment 2: Create a Monochord

Materials: A two-foot length of two-by-four wood, two small eyebolts, nylon string.

Method: Screw the eyebolts onto the top of the board at either end. String the nylon string securely between them and tighten so that it feels taut. Pluck the string and notice the pitch. Press the string down to the board in various places, plucking with the other hand. Ask students: what happens when you press the string to the board? how does the pitch change? How long was the vibrating string for the lowest pitch? How long was the vibrating string for the highest pitch? How is this like what a guitar or violin player does when they are playing? (A: Pressing the finger on the string shortens the vibrating length of the string, resulting in a higher pitch.)

Musical enhancement: Learn to play simple tunes on your monochord by figuring out where to place your finger for each note of a major scale. Mark those placements with a pen, then glue a toothpick on each place to slightly raise the pressure point. Play a simple song such as "Twinkle, Twinkle Little Star" by ear.

Experiment 3: A Straw Oboe

Materials: A plastic straw, scissors.

Method: Press one end of the straw flat and cut off each corner at an angle, leaving a flat section in the middle. Pinch the cut end of the straw between your lips, curling the lips over the straw. Blow into the straw, trying different amounts of pressure until a sound emerges. Once you can produce a continuous sound, gradually cut off the other end of the straw and notice what happens to the pitch as the straw gets shorter. Ask students: how does this relate to the way panpipes are designed? (A: Panpipes are like straws of various lengths joined together. The shorter pipes are the higher notes and the longer pipes are the lower notes.) How does this relate to the pitches of wind instruments? (A: The longer the instrument body, the lower the sound. The piccolo is the shortest and highest woodwind instrument; the contrabassoon is the longest and lowest.)

Musical enhancement: Have students build their own panpipes out of straws or plastic tubing (search the Internet for detailed instructions). Have them play simple songs together or make up some of their own.

Experiment 4: Feeling Tension

Materials: Rubber bands.

Method: Grip one end of a rubber band in your teeth and hold the other end out in front of your mouth. Hold your mouth slightly open and pluck the rubber band. Tighten the rubber band and pluck again. Ask students: what happens to the pitch of the sound? Can you play a simple tune by tightening and loosening the rubber band? How does this relate to the tuning of stringed instruments or timpani? (A: The tighter the string or drum head, the higher the pitch.)

Experiment 5: A Bottle Scale

Materials: Eight identical glass bottles or drinking glasses, water, a wooden mallet.

Method: Leave one bottle empty. Strike it gently and hear its basic pitch. Pour a small amount of water in the next bottle and strike it. Ask students: is it higher or lower? Pour slightly more water into each successive bottle, increasing or decreasing the amount to get a scale. Why does the pitch change? What would happen if you blew across the tops of the bottles? How would the pitch change? Why does it change? (A: The higher the water level, the higher the pitch when struck or blown. The pitch when struck will vary depending on the shape and thickness of the bottle or glass.)

Musical enhancement: Play familiar songs on the bottle scale by ear. Add color coding to each bottle and use it to develop a notation system. Find jug band music on the Internet (Jim Kweskin is a famous jug-band musician). What other instruments are in a jug band? Form your own jug band with simple instruments including a jug.

Experiment 6: Singing Together
Materials: CantOvation Sing and See[1] computer program.
Method: Ask children to sing a familiar song together, as in tune and in time as they can. Record their singing with CantOvation Sing and See, which samples sound many times per second and plots the samples as a line, similar to an oscilloscope. Children can see while they are singing how accurate their pitches are.

Experiment 7: In-tune Instruments
Materials: Digital tuning device or app.
Method: Play any pitched instrument and review the feedback from the electronic tuning device. Experiment with playing flat, sharp, and in tune using visual feedback.

These experiments are a small sample of many that children can do to discover principles of the science of sound. The Additional Resources for Teaching at the end of this chapter contains many resources that support such science of sound units. Building instruments (see Chapters 7 and 8) also leads to experimentation and discovery of the principles of sound. Select experiments that seem appropriate for the children with whom you work. After each experiment, invite children to discuss and write about the principle they have discovered.

OTHER INTERSECTIONS OF MUSIC AND SCIENCE

Music has its place in areas of science other than physics, including the life sciences, earth and space sciences, and engineering, technology, and applications of science. Children may sing a song, write a rhythmic chant or rap, create a new musical expression featuring voices and instruments, or listen to an existing piece of music to enhance learning in many science areas.

When teachers present topical information from several academic disciplines, students stay interested longer and can more easily connect and integrate the knowledge into a fuller understanding of the topic. You may wish to consult the school-music specialist to borrow recordings, instruments, and other resources to enhance scientific lessons. Music adds lively interest and memorable depth to what is sometimes little more than a list of facts and figures.

WHALE COMMUNICATION

The following activities suggest ways that key content from music, math, acoustics, ecology, history, and geography might be integrated into an entire unit on whales.

Listen to recorded vocalizations of whales communicating in "Solo Whale" from *Songs of the Humpback Whale*[2] (see Appendix 3), or search the Internet for audio examples of singing whales. Scientists have used hydrophones to discover that whales communicate with many different sounds. Each sound has a unique purpose: high-frequency clicks and buzzes locate food at close ranges, lower-frequency sounds use echolocation for navigation, whistling sounds send messages between whales, and signature whistles distinguish each individual whale from others in the pod. Scientists are concerned that noise pollution, particularly sonar signals from ships and submarines, interferes with whale communication to such an extent that whales become disoriented, get lost, and sometimes even run aground.

Find a space in the classroom to move while imagining how a whale might move in the ocean. Listen again to "Solo Whale" from *Songs of the Humpback Whale* and try to imitate the whale sounds.

Listen to excerpts from the beginning and end of *And God Created Great Whales*,[3] by Alan Hovhaness. A first excerpt (0:00–3:48) paints a musical picture of a very large creature moving through calm water, and incorporates actual whale sounds. A second excerpt (9:55 to the end) suggests an event involving the whale. Ask students: what do you think happens in the second excerpt? (A: The whale is hunted and harpooned.) Imagine what it would be like to be a whale. How does this music depict whales and how they communicate? Play more of the Hovhaness composition and also George Crumb's *Vox Balaenae (Voice of the Whale)*[4] after recess, at quiet time, during silent reading, while children draw whales at art time, and in transitions between subjects. Make the recording available for individual listening at the classroom listening center.

On a world map, trace the migratory routes of various whale species (including humpbacks, grays, orcas, and belugas) and explain why they migrate. Point out regions where whaling took place. Have students research the work of the International Whaling Commission and respond to the following questions: how is that commission trying to protect whales? Which countries have outlawed whaling? Which countries are still whaling and why? What are some arguments for and against continuing to hunt whales?

Ask students: what were the physical and technical challenges of whaling in the 1800s? What are they now? How might those challenges have affected sailors? In the heyday of whaling (the eighteenth and nineteenth centuries), sailors spent from weeks to years at sea with little entertainment, except telling stories and singing songs, called sea shanties, such as "Haul Away Joe" (see Example 13.1).

Listen to recordings of sailors singing sea shanties. Notice their energy and style. What can you infer about the sailors' lives from the lyrics of the songs? (For more whale-related activities, see Chapter 14.)

Music can teach much about the humpback whale.

EXAMPLE 13.1

PLANETS

Children in the intermediate grades enjoy studying astronomy, especially the planets—their physical characteristics, how they compare with Earth, and the myths and legends connected with them. An integrated series of activities on the planets, which could become part of a larger unit, might contain the following elements from astronomy, music, art, math, language arts, and philosophy:

Read about planets in a science textbook or on the Internet, and watch multimedia presentations, such as *Nova*'s "Tour the Solar System." Then draw two or three planets (one planet per page), or the full order of the planets in the solar system, using illustrations from these sources as models. Label the planets.

Listen to excerpts from each movement of Gustav Holst's orchestral suite, *The Planets*.[5] Write each planet's name on the board, and list descriptive words that children associate with each movement in the suite, such as "mysterious" (Neptune), "loud" or "exciting" (Mars), "peaceful" (Venus), and "playful" (Jupiter).

Hang a picture of the sun in one upper corner of the classroom and construct a scale model of the solar system by hanging one student drawing of each planet at its proportionate distance from the sun. Have students calculate how far each planet should be placed from the sun.

Help children construct papier mâché globes over balloon bases approximating the proportional sizes of the sun and planets and paint the globes to match photographs of the planets. Children may take turns holding planets and orbiting the sun at proportional distances and speeds. Tell children about the concept of *musica universalis* (also called "music of the spheres"), the ancient philosophical idea that celestial bodies moved in harmonic proportions in a kind of heavenly dance.

Use students' knowledge about planets to prompt creative writing assignments, e.g., "The minute my spaceship landed on _____ (choose a planet), I knew I was in trouble because _____."

Encourage children to represent the planets with their own musical creations in independent study projects, or collaborate with the music specialist to have children compose descriptive pieces for recorders, xylophones, guitars, and various unpitched percussion. Student compositions could be combined into a suite of movements similar to Holst's orchestral piece, and recorded or performed for other classes.

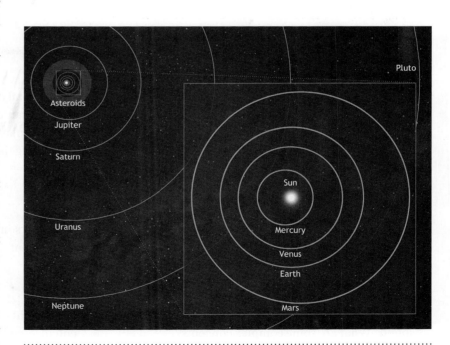

A basic illustration of the solar system

ADAPTING INSTRUCTION FOR VARIOUS NEEDS

Autism Spectrum Disorder

Set up several experiments on the science of sound in various parts of the classroom. Encourage children to explore which might be the most interesting for them and have them stand or sit next to that experiment. Encourage a team solution to the experiment wherein children of various levels of ability and communication can collaborate. Problem solving through experimentation can be engaging for all children.

Mobility Impairments

When possible, use adaptive equipment for children with mobility impairments to play instruments or conduct science experiments. When needed, assign an aid or "buddy" to hold objects so the child with limited mobility can still participate: by grasping a mallet in their teeth through an adaptive device and nodding their head to play an instrument; by blowing into a straw while another child cuts the length shorter; etc.

Deaf or Hearing Impairments

If children with hearing limitations cannot perceive the sounds in the science experiments, have them place their hands on the vibrating surfaces, such as the back of a piano, to feel the vibrations while others play the instruments. As much as possible, use bone conduction by having them blow (conducting the sound through the teeth and jaw, as in the comb kazoo experiment) or touch (conducting the sound through the hands or bare feet). Holding an inflated balloon against the side of the head while external sounds are played will also help perception through bone conduction.

Externalizing Behavior Disorders

Establish clear guidelines for all children when experimenting in small groups with the science of sound materials. Also establish clear consequences for children if they don't follow the guidelines. Build those consequences into a contract with children who struggle to behave. Check with them to make sure they understand both the guidelines and the consequences.

Internalizing Behavior Disorders

Pair a child who is withdrawn with a friend or another child who could gently encourage and guide the child to participate. Create conditions of safety. If necessary, limit teamwork to only one other child, rather than a whole team of five or six children.

Blind or Visually Impaired

Have an aide or another child give auditory directions for experiments. Keep the materials for each experiment on different desks or tables, so that children will not be confused about what they are to use for a particular experiment. When moving a sight-impaired student from place to place, gently steer them by holding their elbow. Do not push or pull.

Summary

Although it may seem difficult to imagine combining music with some areas of science, many wonderful possibilities exist for doing so. The most natural connections occur in the science of sound. Awareness of these principles can form future engineers, acousticians, and environmental designers. Teachers presenting other science units can enliven the learning by having children sing, move, play instruments, compose, draw, film, and write to bring the learning home in exciting ways.

Review

1. What principles of the science of sound are appropriate for elementary children to explore?

2. What are some effective ways to integrate music into the study of science?

Critical Thinking

1. What are some simple concepts of the science of sound? What are some complex concepts?

2. Why might creative engagement in science learning enhance children's retention of important scientific concepts?

Projects

1. Conduct at least one science of sound experiment from each of the three categories listed above (vibration, resonance, and pitch). After you've completed the experiment, write down the principle that you've discovered. Then, extend that experiment into a music experience if possible.

2. Experiment with homemade or commercial instruments to see how they illustrate principles of the science of sound.

3. Working in groups of four to five, choose a science topic you would like to teach to elementary-aged children. Develop a unit to teach basic understandings through arts strategies. Present portions of that unit to your class.

4. Explore CantOvation Sing and See to discover how this technology helps people learn to sing accurately. Note the scientific principles that are relevant here.

Additional Resources for Teaching

Kohl, MaryAnn F. and Jean Potter. (1993). *Science Arts: Discovering Science Through Art Experiences*. Bellingham, WA: Bright Ring Publishing.

Madgwick, Wendy. (2014). *First Science Library: Sound Magic*. Helotes, TX: Armadillo Children's Publishing.

Parker, Steve. (2013). *Tabletop Scientist: The Science of Sound*. Mineola, NY: Dover Publications.

Additional Resources for Listening

Crumb, George. (1974). *Vox Balaenae (Voice of the Whale)* [CD]. Los Angeles, CA: Sony Corporation.

Holst, Gustav. (2009). *The Planets* [London Symphony Orchestra, conducted by Geoffrey Simon]. [CD]. London, UK: Cobra Entertainment, LLC.

Hovhaness, Alan. (1989). *And God Created Great Whales* [Philharmonia Orchestra, conducted by David Amos]. [CD]. Seattle, WA: Crystal Records, Inc.

Payne, Roger (Ed.). (1991). *Songs of the Humpback Whale* [CD]. Litchfield, CT: Earth Music Productions, LLC.

Special thanks for help with this chapter goes to the late Dr. Patricia Costa Kim of the EMP Museum in Seattle.

Online Resources: Audio and Songbook

digital.wwnorton.com/classroom

IN THIS CHAPTER

Considering the Arts

In the Classroom

Roles of the Arts

The Arts in Learning

What Makes Something Artistic?

Music and Other Arts

Connecting the Arts

Summary

Review

Critical Thinking

Projects

Additional Resources for Teaching

14

ALL OF THE ARTS

I believe arts education in music, theater, dance, and the visual arts is one of the most creative ways we have to find the gold that is buried just beneath the surface. They (children) have an enthusiasm for life, a spark of creativity, and vivid imaginations that need training—training that prepares them to become confident young men and women.

—Richard W. Riley, Former US Secretary of Education

Multiple-arts experiences prepare children to be creative thinkers and problem solvers.

CONSIDERING THE ARTS

Our current educational climate is highly politicized, driven by testing with an emphasis on literacy, numeracy, and science and technology. Where does this leave the arts? Those who believe that public education should prepare children to be productive workers may think arts education is superfluous and a waste of time and resources. But those who believe that education should prepare children to be creative thinkers and problem solvers, fully functioning citizens, and capable of happy and meaningful relationships and careers may regard the arts as crucial to balance the continuous stream of literacy and numeracy exercises. Because children are complete and complex human beings, education needs to include substantive learning in all ways of knowing. These multiple ways of knowing interact with and support one another as children learn how the world works.

IN THE CLASSROOM

VIGNETTE ONE

Ms. Bartholomew draws ideas from several art forms when she plans her lessons. After she introduces a new storybook to her second graders, she invites them to discuss how the illustrations enhance the story, guiding them to use the vocabulary of the visual arts. They also discuss the artistic style of the illustrations. Children then choose a favorite character in the book and create their own artwork in the style of the book's illustrations, using similar lines, colors, and designs. Once their art is complete, children think of words to describe the character they chose and write them on a piece of paper. The children then use their characters to dramatize some of the qualities of that character, such as Ferdinand the bull (whose sits peacefully under a tree rather than engaging in bull fights), or Winnie-the-Pooh (who enjoys not only honey but also creating poems and songs), or James (acclaimed as a hero for saving New York City from being destroyed by a giant peach), or Mr. Toad of *The Wind in the Willows* (who finally learns quiet humility and how to make up for his wrongdoings). The children reflect on each dramatization. Later, the class works together to dramatize the entire story with children in different roles, including the parts of objects in the story, such as a tree, a rock, or a bucket. Ms. Bartholomew has found that exploring a story at this level helps children to write their own stories, develop characters, and illustrate what they have written. By the end of the school year, every child in the room has a portfolio of stories they have written and illustrated to show their progress.

VIGNETTE TWO

Mr. Bond wants his fifth-grade students to develop their own play based on their year-long study of American History. They've broken the play into five acts: 1) Colonial America and the American Revolution; 2) The Civil War and Emancipation; 3) Westward Expansion; 4) The Industrial Revolution; and 5) The Twentieth Century and the Rise of Technology and Diversity. He has divided his class of

You Will Learn

- the myriad roles that the arts can play in the classroom

- the uniqueness of each art form, but also how to combine them

- how to design and implement strategies in various arts to support lessons on other subjects

- about a range of resources for planning effective arts experiences for children

Ask Yourself

- Which of the following arts have you produced or created: music, visual arts, theater, dance, literary arts, media arts?

- Which art form are you most comfortable doing?

- Which of the arts do you regularly enjoy as participant or consumer? Reflect on what they mean to you.

- Which art form would you be most comfortable teaching to children? Which would you be least comfortable teaching?

- What roles should the arts should play in education?

- What roles do you expect the arts to play in your own classroom?

- Why might engaging in all of the arts be important for children?

- Do you think all children have the potential to learn in and through the arts? Why or why not?

30 students into groups of six, assigning a different act to each group. They work across many weeks identifying key ideas of each period and determining how to show those ideas through narration, period costume, simple sets, music, and dance. Once each group has crafted a script, they present to the other groups for critiquing and constructive suggestions. Mr. Bond uses class time for building the sets, which requires children's mathematical thinking and application. Parents and the costume department of the nearby children's theater help with the costuming. The music specialist helps children prepare relevant songs and dances from each of the periods. Mr. Bond takes time to ensure that each group of children has the content and skills to offer a coherent presentation. After weeks of rehearsal, the children present their American History play as a school assembly and in an evening performance for parents and families. The fifth graders learned much from the comprehensive project, internalizing concepts and contexts in the unfolding events of their nation's history.

VIGNETTE THREE

A K–12 private school spent six weeks every winter studying a particular region or culture. One year it was France, another year it was India, and still another year it was South Africa. During that time, musicians, artists, and dancers as well as other cultural informants visited the school to share their art with the students. At each grade level, teachers taught developmentally appropriate content concerning that culture in language arts, math, science, and the social sciences. The unit culminated in a school-wide festival in which every classroom displayed artwork that summarized key learning. Children made brief presentations on the festival stage. They and their families sampled authentic foods from the region, prepared by parents and children working with community experts. Children's paintings, prints, and graphic designs representing the culture were displayed in the cafeteria. The end of the evening featured a music and dance performance by artists in residence and the children.

VIGNETTE FOUR

The teachers and principal of a public elementary school met at the beginning of the school year to establish writing as a school-wide, year-long goal, culminating in a fair focused on writing across the curriculum. They invited parents, the superintendent, school board members, and community leaders to attend the fair and see what students had accomplished at each grade level. Children who worked with the reading specialist displayed their story writing. In another room, children shared books they had written and then bound with special fabric bindings with the help of a resident visual artist. A third-grade class performed a story-song they had written with the help of a guest musician, playing ukuleles to accompany their singing. Sixth-grade students shared scripts they had written and short plays they had produced with the help of a visiting playwright. A videographer worked with other children to record performances of their poetry. Children learned to write by drafting, critiquing, rewriting, and finally presenting their work. Incorporating the arts inspired them to write and present their ideas in a range of exciting ways.

ROLES OF THE ARTS

The arts are central to what it means to be human. They are how we express our innermost thoughts and most profound perceptions and insights. They represent the world ineffably, often transcending the capacity of words to express deepest human meaning. The arts both express emotion and evoke emotional responses. They invite intellectual engagement through both their structures of expression and their meanings. When we respond both emotionally and intellectually, we are responding aesthetically. The more we experience and the better we understand various art forms, the more developed our aesthetic response. The American psychologist Abraham Maslow[1] considered the aesthetic response to be our greatest capacity for transcendence. Most people who have responded with chills to great beauty in nature, or to the sublime artistic expression within a painting, a piece of music, or a dance or theater performance, know the power of an aesthetic experience.

Archaeologists have found evidence of art-making and aesthetics in human cultures from around 200,000 years ago. Masks, cave paintings, metal arts, figurines, jewelry, and simple musical instruments, such as flutes, have been found in ancient caves and digs throughout the world. Preliterate people understood symmetry, design, and beauty as they shaped their tools and symbolically represented their physical and spiritual worlds. The humanist Ellen Dissanayake identified the human need for elaboration as central to artistic expression from the earliest times.[2] Humans strive to go beyond the ordinary to make things beautiful.

The arts are also entertaining. They lead us to feel intensely, to laugh and cry, and to step out of our everyday experiences and imagine other worlds and other possibilities. They tell the stories of our culture and other cultures, and they stimulate our imaginations, taking us to places we've never been. In some places in the world there is no word for music, or for art, because the arts are inseparable from the everyday and special events of society. The Balinese say that "we have no art, we do everything as well as we can."[3]

The arts mirror the culture from which they emerge. They reflect people's values, interests, and experiences within any given culture at any given time. They are highly influenced by time and place as well as by the availability of materials. They both reflect and affect societies. With knowledge that comes from an education in the arts, we can quickly identify artistic images or musical masterworks as emanating from cultures as disparate as the Hindustani North Indians, the Japanese, the Wolof (of Senegal), or the Samoans (of the South Pacific). When we study the arts, we gain a meta-view of cultures, and we come to understand the artistic similarities that bind all humans together.

THE ARTS IN LEARNING

The arts are disciplines in their own right, each requiring important understandings, ways of thinking, and unique skills for its development. But they are also part of a comprehensive curriculum that encourages and enables children and young adults to grow in their artistic expressions and understandings. The arts enliven learning in all subject areas.

The arts allow children to discover their own multiple intelligences (visual–spatial, musical–rhythmic, bodily–kinesthetic, verbal–linguistic, logical–mathematical, interpersonal, intrapersonal, naturalistic, existential, and moral), and they provide important entry points for children's learning of all subjects. The arts develop creative and imaginative thinking, and are crucial to the development of children's intellectual capacities.[4] When combined with verbal, mathematical, and kinesthetic literacies, the arts bolster learning in creative classrooms. The arts help all children, but especially those children in multicultural societies who struggle to learn in a language that is not their first.[5] Because they are both multisensory and concrete, the arts reach children with a variety of learning styles. As a means of personal expression that calls on children's emotions and intellect, the arts add emotional meaning and significance to learning.

The arts strengthen children's community membership, as they express their personal ideas and also consider the ideas of others when producing a concert, play, or dance performance. The arts are a source of joy, entertainment, and sharing for children within the larger community.

WHAT MAKES SOMETHING ARTISTIC?

Usually the intent of art is to express ideas in ways that provoke responses from others, whether these ideas convey great beauty or horror. Sometimes, art is simply for self-expression, and may or may not be valued by others. Creating art involves technical skill, creative imagination, and deep understanding.

Craft differs from art, in that it involves the skillful copying of an artistic creation. Often, crafting a poem, a painting, or a percussion piece does not require original ideas and elements, but pays tribute to present art. Artists may copy others' ideas to gain technique and craft for themselves, but these techniques prepare them to create original artistic expressions. With opportunities to engage in both arts and crafts, children develop the understanding and skills that inform artistic and creative expressions. This chapter is intended to familiarize teachers with individual art forms and learn how to incorporate the arts into their curriculum and classroom culture.

MUSIC AND OTHER ARTS

The eighth National Standard for Music Education aims for children to understand relationships among music, the other arts, and disciplines outside the arts. The National Association for Music Education published a guide for standards in all of the arts, entitled *National Standards for Arts Education: What Every Young American Should Know and Be Able to Do in the Arts*,[6] that offers ways to integrate significant content from each of the art forms.

Even though each art form has its own language, expressive medium, set of symbols, and technical demands, the arts remain deeply connected. In working with multiple arts, teachers need to be sensitive both to the commonalities among the arts and to the unique qualities of each art.

MUSIC AND DANCE

Dance probably is the art form most analogous to music. Dance involves the movement of the body through time, just as music involves sound through time. Both music and dance cease to exist after the performance (unless they are recorded). The artistic experience is in the moment of performance. Dance is usually performed in time to music, and any musical style or genre can stimulate artistic movement in dance. Choreographers usually begin their work by listening analytically to the music in order to determine dance steps in relationship to the music's flow, rhythm, dynamics, texture, and other qualities. Box 14.1 outlines the elements of dance.

Time, flow, space, force, and shape are the elements of dance.

Expressive experiences in the art of dance begin with exploring everyday movement. Chapter 6 suggests ways to combine music and movement: eurhythmic movement, free movement, patterned folk and popular dances, singing games, and songs and chants that can be gestured and danced. You can also incorporate dance elements with music in the following movement activities to build children's movement vocabularies and make any choreography they invent more interesting. These movements are best accomplished in a large open space. Children need

BOX 14.1 ELEMENTS OF DANCE

Time

- Tempo: fast, medium, slow, stillness
- Duration: long, short
- Beat: steady, even
- Accent: stressing a beat
- Rhythm: patterns of different durations

Flow

- Sustained: smooth, flowing, connected
- Percussive: jerky, segmented
- Vibratory: shaking, swinging

Space
Personal

- Size: large, small, wide, narrow
- Nonlocomotor movements: stretch, shake, twist, curl, bend
- Force field: protective bubble that surrounds you so that you do not bump other things or people

General Space

- Directions: up or down, front or back, right or left, diagonal
- Pathways: curved, straight, angular
- Locomotor: walk, run, leap, skip, hop, jump, slide, crawl, scoot

Force

Strong or gentle

Shape

- Individual: curved, straight, twisted, balanced, symmetrical, asymmetrical
- Group: lines, clumps, touching, not touching, balanced
- Thematic: animal, sports, emotions

to be aware of personal space and general space, and able to move through space without touching each other, objects, or the perimeter of the room.

Play slow-moving instrumental music. Use the body to create shapes: high shapes, low shapes, wide shapes, and narrow shapes. Change shapes, observing how you move in slow motion from one shape to the next. Prompt with specific suggestions if necessary (e.g., become an interesting statue, then change to another statue).

Play upbeat instrumental music. Walk to the music through general space in a straight line, a zigzag line, or a curved line. Walk forward, backward, sideways, or in some combination of these directions. Shift from walking to running to stopping and standing still.

In personal space, use one arm to make a smooth movement, then switch to a jerky movement. Expand the two movements to the entire body. Make a fast movement with one arm, then a slow movement. Make a slow jerky movement and then a fast jerky movement. Make a slow and smooth movement and then a fast and smooth movement.

Play instrumental music in a moderate tempo. Stand and face a partner. Use just one hand to dance with the person opposite you. Choose from slow and smooth movements or fast and jerky movements, but do not imitate each other and do not let your hands touch. High, low, wide, and narrow movements are possible. Carve different pathways of movement.

Imagine the body as a giant paintbrush. Using straight lines and curved lines, move from high to low to "paint" the letters of the alphabet, numbers, math sums, geometric shapes, or spelling words. When children experience familiar patterns kinesthetically, they more readily learn and retain ideas and concepts.

Use the body to create geometric shapes such as a square, triangle, or circle. Find another person with whom to create a shape, and change the shape when the teacher says "switch." In groups of four, create more complicated shapes, such as a trapezoid.

Find and face a partner, designating one as dancer A and the other as dancer B. When the music starts, dancer A leads by moving in personal space, using high or low, wide or narrow, big or little, fast or slow, straight or curved, and strong or gentle movements. Dancer B mirrors the movements of dancer A. At the teacher's cue to switch, dancer B leads. Shift the leadership throughout the mirroring dance several times. Mirroring takes tremendous concentration and focus and builds patterns in the brain. Smooth the flow of this activity by substituting a triangle or bell for the verbal cue to switch.

Work in a group of five children and identify a favorite sport you can suggest through movement. Practice your movements. Perform the short sports movement pieces, and invite others to identify the sport from the movements.

Provide a list of movement vocabulary words, including walk, run, hop, step, skip, shuffle, spin, bounce, glide, twist, turn, lope, stretch, expand, and contract. Play recorded music and encourage children in small groups to create a movement piece in response that expresses at least four of the movement words.

These exercises of basic dance movements become the vocabulary children can use to create their own expressive dance forms alone or together with others. Once a movement vocabulary has been established, bring in a variety of recorded music and invite children to choreograph their own dances based on the qualities they hear in the music.

MUSIC AND VISUAL ARTS

The visual arts and music often go hand in hand, even sharing terminology; however, because the visual arts function in space rather than time, some of the shared terms (e.g., "line" or "texture") take on distinctive meanings within each art form. Box 14.2 highlights the basic elements of the visual arts.

Art docents are volunteers trained by local art museums to guide children in the visual or fine arts. Docents often supply prints of paintings and sculptures for the classroom, as well as biographies of artists and explanations of an artwork's historical meaning. Seek docents from local museums to visit your classroom and expand children's artistic understandings, and offer children the following activities combining music with the visual arts.

Give each child a long, narrow strip of paper. Discuss various types of lines (straight, broken, curved, angular, thick, thin, and so on). Direct children to draw a line composition using different colors and moving from left to right across the strip. Ask them to use at least three different types of line sequentially, and to realize these lines in sound using their voices or pitched instruments such as keyboards, recorders, or xylophones. Extend this project by having the children work in groups, combining their individual patterns into a collective whole. View works by artists such as Piet Mondrian or Paul Klee and discuss how they used line and color to create their works. Challenge children to realize a painting in

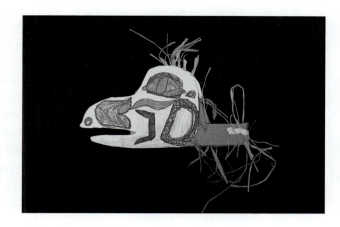

Shape, color, texture, line, and space are elements of the visual arts.

BOX 14.2 ELEMENTS OF THE VISUAL ARTS

Shape

Square, rectangle, triangle, circle, etc. Shapes are created by line and color, and can form patterns that create rhythm and design.

Color

Red, green, yellow, etc. Color creates intensity and contrast, and gives light.

Texture

Smooth, rough, soft, hard, etc. Texture is the feel of the work when touched, and can be created by building up layers, carving into, or weaving.

Line

Straight, curvy, zigzag, thin, thick, broken, connected, soft, loud, echoing, parallel, etc. Lines make patterns, designs, shapes, and objects.

Space

Negative or positive. Space is created by placement of shapes.

sound by studying and finding musical ways to express the painting's features of line, color, texture, and motion.

Use lines, shapes, colors, and patterns to illustrate different musical events as they occur in absolute (nonreferential) music. For example, listen to a Bach two-part invention for piano and use different colored lines to depict two melodic lines that rise, fall, overlap, and pull apart from one another. Draw precisely the same line, one after the other, where the one part imitates the other part. Study art that features interwoven line patterns, some of which appear as abstract geometric patterns, such as works by M. C. Escher, Wassily Kandinsky, and Mark Tobey. Discuss similarities and differences between works by professional artists and those the students have drawn. The Goldberg Variations in Chapter 5 exemplify this kind of work.

Find examples of art from various periods and cultures (often available through school art docent programs or art teachers) to introduce children to stylistic characteristics that are reflected in both art and music. For example, compare Monet's *Water Lilies* (paintings) to Debussy's *La mer* (symphonic poem), looking and listening for blurred lines (melodies) and muted colors (instrumental timbres), and contrast the reflected light of the Monet paintings with the shimmering, dreamy, blurred quality of Debussy's music. Research the lives of Monet and Debussy to discover what inspired them, and to understand the impressionist style of visual art of their time. Paint in the impressionist style using various watercolor techniques, and play music that shimmers, blurs, and blends on a piano with the sustain pedal down or on ringing metallophones. Play a recording of a musical work. Then, from a range of visual art works, have children select the style that most closely matches the style of the music. Have them justify their choices using vocabulary from the two art forms.

Play recorded works of music that were composed in response to paintings and sculptures, such as Modest Musorgsky's *Pictures at an Exhibition* or Gunther Schuller's *Twittering Machine*. Bring in prints of the works that inspired the compositions (in this example, *The Hut on Hen's Legs (Baba Yaga)* by Victor Hartmann and *Twittering Machine* by Paul Klee). Discuss the connections between the music and the visual art. (These and future works are all cited in Appendix 3, with links to quality recordings that can be purchased and downloaded easily.)

Inspire painting, drawing, or puppetry with program music, such as Paul Dukas's *Sorcerer's Apprentice*, Ferde Grofé's *Grand Canyon Suite*, Arnold Schoenberg's *Verklärte Nacht*, William Grant Still's Symphony No. 1 (*Afro-American*), or Ralph Vaughn Williams's *Lark Ascending*. Encourage children to create finger or hand puppets to dramatize works that tell stories, such as Gioachino Rossini's *William Tell* Overture or Pyotr Il'yich Tchaikovsky's *Nutcracker*. Guide children to demonstrate a sense of style and to employ balance, design, color, and line in their works.

Finally, try to avoid vague assignments, such as telling students to "draw the music." If children don't know how to draw in a way that reflects their analytical understanding of musical and visual art structures, they will miss opportunities for intellectual and emotional (aesthetic) development. Create true multiple-arts experiences by encouraging children to draw images that convey visually what the music contains in line, color, and pattern. As they represent musical patterns and moods visually, and musically interpret the features of paintings and sculptures, they learn the relationships between these arts just as they learn each art form.

MUSIC AND MEDIA ARTS

Children enjoy making videos and taking photos with cellphones, cameras, and tablets. They can edit these images in a number of ways: removing or reordering sections, photoshopping to alter colors and designs, setting the subjects against various backgrounds, and cropping, enlarging, or reducing the images. Children can create montages of pictures or draw their own images. Constantly evolving technology makes electronic media arts accessible to all children. The simple mechanics of making a video or taking a photo is seldom art, but becomes so when children process the images cleverly and creatively.

Invite individual or small groups of children to create a video or photo montage on a topic they are studying in school. They may wish to include artistic renderings and realistic representations of seasons, communities, landscapes, shapes, rivers, weather, or machinery. Finally, have them select appropriate music to underscore a mood or sentiment. If this is a culmination of a unit, children can include the video in their portfolio and also share it with others.

Children can use instruments and voices to compose their own soundtrack, synchronizing the music in time with the video images. Encourage them to assess and revise their composition until the music fits well with the video's images, timing, and overall effect.

Share a segment of video from a film, television show, or documentary with the sound turned off, then view the segment with the volume up. Invite children to discuss how music and sound contribute to the excitement and drama of the video. Share another segment of the video without sound, and invite children to compose or improvise their own music to accompany it. Listen to and view the results, and compare the students' soundtrack to those of professional film and video composers.

MUSIC AND THEATER

Creative drama and theater lend themselves to the elementary school curriculum. Any lesson involving dramatic characterizations can teach children to focus and concentrate on words and meanings, facial and body movements, and respect for space. Teachers can sensitize children to other elements of a drama or story line by asking questions:

- ▶ Setting: Where does the drama take place? What is the mood of this place?
- ▶ Characters: Who is involved in the drama? How do they relate to each other?
- ▶ Theme: What is the main idea or message of the drama?
- ▶ Action: What is happening in the plot? What is the sequence of events? Where is tension created? How is it resolved?
- ▶ Dialogue: How do the actors convey moods and emotions through words and movement?
- ▶ Spectacle: What helps convey the setting, characters, theme, action, dialogue, and mood? Consider how costumes, props, lights, music, sounds, and scenery contribute to the theater piece.

Elements of creative drama and theater are at home in the elementary classroom.

These elements can be incorporated into any dramatization, although dialogue and spectacle are not necessary as often as setting, characters, and action. Consider the following suggestions for combining music and theater.

Sing songs, preexisting or newly created, that describe characters or tell stories, including ballads and story songs from assorted cultures. Discuss the characters, their motivations, and their actions. Experiment with creating characters and conveying the dramatic action described in the song. Work with concentration and focus and avoid stereotypical responses. (Carefully create a system in which all children have opportunities to playact the characters. Avoid assigning roles before children understand the plots and characters.)

Learn the stories of programmatic works such as Prokofiev's *Peter and the Wolf*, or operas such as Seymour Barab's *Little Red Riding Hood*, Rossini's *La Cenerentola* (*Cinderella*), or Mozart's *Magic Flute*. (The Metropolitan Opera offers educator guides, workshops, and a program called *HD Live in Schools*, all of which are useful for introducing children to opera as a form.) Listen to these musical selections and discuss how music heightens the experience of the drama. How do particular instruments paint a picture, character, or mood? How do rhythm, tempo, or dynamics express elements of the story? Experiment with ways to dramatize the story using mime or dialogue, characterization, and simple props. Puppetry is another way to dramatize operas and programmatic works.

Create an opera by singing the dialogue of a familiar children's story, adding instrumental music for mood or transitions, and dramatic actions to tell the story. Collaborate with a music teacher to help children write their own opera, including a script, melodic and rhythmic renderings of the dialogue, and instrumental accompaniment. (See Chapter 8 for further opera ideas.)

Create a musical around a theme, such as rain, animals of the forest (or prairie, mountain, desert, or coastal areas), freedom, or friendship. Integrate traditional folk songs or popular songs and dances into the production, or develop parodies to fit the selected theme. Invite children to write a story line to tie components together. Incorporate all the elements of drama in shaping the musical.

MUSIC AND LITERATURE

Both literature and music are arts of time, with gradually unfolding ideas and expressions. Both can evoke images and tell stories. Both are based on sounds, especially as stories and poems are read aloud, and they share many sound possibilities. Children can learn to tell stories using sound expressions, and instruments can produce the sounds of onomatopoetic words such as swish, whirr, slosh, beep, crackle, twang, rickety-rackety, plunk, honk, pitter-patter, and hiss. The following ideas extend ideas found in Chapter 10.

Use fine children's literature to connect students with music. Many beautiful books illustrate folk, patriotic, and children's songs; tell the stories behind works of program music, ballets, or operas; tell the stories of composers and musicians; and set the cultural context for songs or listening experiences. School librarians are eager to help find children's literature that enhances musical experiences. Such books can stimulate children's own creative writing, musical creativity, and visual arts.

Use books, stories, and poetry to inspire musical play. Read wordless books and familiar fairy tales using sounds instead of words, or with a combination of sounds and words.

Have children generate banks of descriptive words in response to recorded music and then use them to write stories or poetry to describe the music. The poems might include the title of the music and the name of the composer or performer.

Seek out poetry or literature that uses onomatopoetic sounds or particularly strong imagery and have children set it to music. Encourage students to speak or sing the poem expressively; try single and combined voices for different effects.

Read books about the lives of famous composers or musicians. Develop a story or play about a composer's life, incorporating some of the music performed by classmates or played on recordings.

Have children write the lyrics for an original song or work together as a class to write the lyrics for a class song. Invite a music teacher or composer in residence to help with the melody or encourage children to compose their own melody.

USING ART TO MEET MUSIC STANDARDS

1. Singing. Sing a round with others. Add creative movement or dance, also in the form of a round, and perform the piece as a round, singing and moving simultaneously.

2. Playing. Learn to play a piece with different instruments playing different layers. Alternate sections of this piece with sections of a spoken piece, where different voices reading different lines begin and end at various times, also creating layers.

3. Improvising. Create a visual artwork using dots of various sizes and colors. Improvise a vocal piece in response to that work using different pitches, volume levels, and vocal colors as the dots change on the page.

4. Composing and arranging. Move your body through personal space, changing levels from high to low, making smooth movements with your arms. Create a series of those movements. Practice that series until it is memorized. Invite someone else to select a pitched instrument and compose a piece to accompany those movements, matching the energy, height, and flow of the movements. Practice the two together until a set piece is established. Share it with others.

5. Reading and notating. Use images and shapes to map a piece of music. Perform that music from your map. Share the map with someone else to see how they might interpret it.

6. Listening. Draw in response to a piece of symphonic music, particularly one with a programmed intent. Reflect on what images emerge. Are these the images the composer was trying to evoke? Discuss what parts of the music suggested the images.

7. Evaluating. Use artistic vocabulary to describe and critique your own creations or the creations of others.

8. Connecting to other arts and curriculum areas. Select a favorite story and choose an art form—music, dance, visual arts, or drama—to bring that story to life. Work with others to add creative ideas to the story. Share it with others and invite their feedback for refining your ideas.

9. Connecting to culture and history. After learning about the stories, music, dances, instruments, and visual arts of another culture or era, try to create art works in the same style. Articulate what studying the arts has taught you.

CONNECTING THE ARTS

All the preceding ideas suggest ways to connect music with individual art forms. It can also be exciting and engaging to connect other art forms with each other. Interdisciplinary thinking within the arts begins with exploring aesthetic principles common to the arts, such as tension and release, repetition and contrast, rhythm, texture, patterns, motives, theme and variation, density and sparseness, balance, symmetry, asymmetry, and foreground and background. Encourage children to notice repetition and contrast in nature, a song or instrumental work, a poem, a painting, or a dance. Discuss how repetition creates a sense of rhythm, fulfills expectations, and creates unity, but can be boring if used too much. Discuss how contrast can be used to hold interest, to defy expectations, to surprise, and to create complexity.

Listen to Prelude, Op. 28, No. 15, by Chopin (see Appendix 3). Discuss why it was given its "raindrop" nickname. Discuss the effect of the repeated notes. What if the whole piece had been a single repeated note? Would the listener be bored? What did Chopin do to make it interesting? Listen to Ravel's *Boléro*. How does repetition figure in important ways, and what is its effect? How does Ravel create interest, freshness, and tension in spite of the repetition? Bring in or project images of paintings by contemporary artists. Notice what is repeated. Identify contrasts. Sing "Hava nagila" and dance the Israeli circle dance, the hora (discussed in Chapter 6). How is repetition used in both the song and the folk dance? What does that repetition accomplish? How is contrast created? How does that contrast make the dance more interesting?

Explore repetition and contrast across multiple art forms. Invite children to create their own music, dance, poetry, play, painting, or sculpture of clay or blocks based on the principles of repetition and contrast. Invite them to share their creative products and the thinking processes that led to the creative work. Ask children to comment on the repetition and contrast in their art. Examining multiple art forms simultaneously helps children expand their aesthetic vocabulary and their awareness of concepts that permeate all the arts as well as life itself.

Sound Ways of Knowing: Music in the Interdisciplinary Classroom explores another model for interdisciplinary thinking in the arts—the jeweled faceted model.[7] In this model, interdisciplinary questions surround the art work or experience like multiple facets of a diamond jewel. In the center of the model is the name of the work of music, visual art, dance, drama, or other artistic work, and in the facets are the following questions about the art:

- ► Who created it?
- ► When and where was it created?
- ► Why and for whom was it created?
- ► What does it sound or look like?
- ► What kind of structure or form does it have?
- ► What is its subject?
- ► What is being expressed?
- ► What techniques did its creator use to help people understand what is being expressed?

The answers to these questions integrate history, culture, the arts, and other disciplines. They stimulate children to explore art in greater depth. Figures 14.5 and 14.6 illustrate this model of jeweled facets as applied to the Shaker hymn, "Simple Gifts," and to American composer Aaron Copland's variations on that hymn in his ballet, *Appalachian Spring*. Copland's orchestral music is set in the form of a theme (the melody of "Simple Gifts") and variations.

Classroom teachers work closely with children through most of the day and week, and thus are at an advantage to integrate the arts into children's experiences. They can design and deliver curricular experiences that spin a thread through the arts, connecting multiple arts via a common topic or theme (see Lesson Plan 14.1).

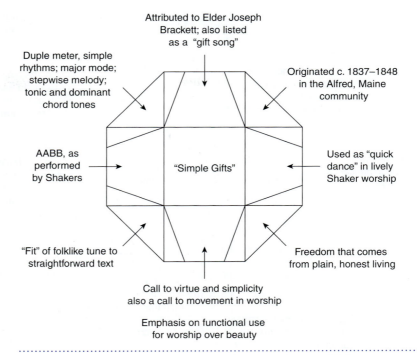

The facet model asks questions that integrate history, culture, and other arts. Here, the model as applied to "Simple Gifts."

Source: Barrett, Janet R., Claire W. McCoy and Kari K. Veblen. (1997). *Sound Ways of Knowing: Music in the Interdisciplinary Curriculum*. New York, NY: Schirmer.

 **EXAMPLE 14.1**

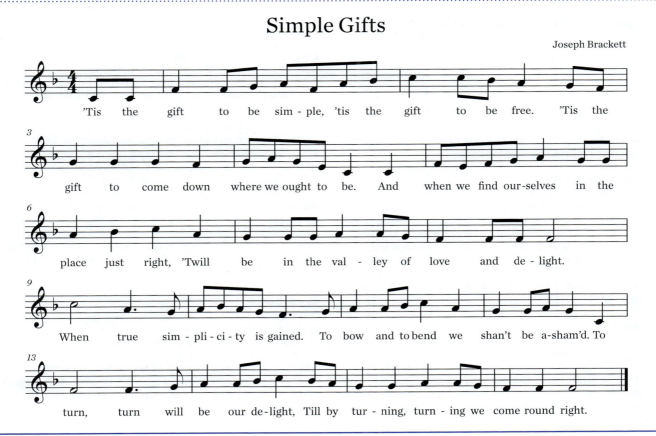

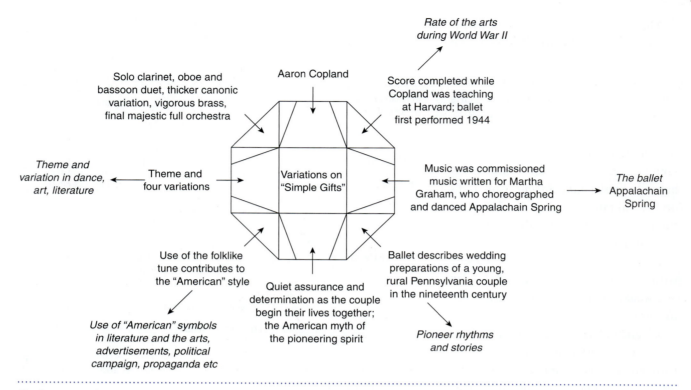

The facet model as applied to the variations on "Simple Gifts" in Aaron Copland's *Appalachian Spring*.

Source: Barrett, Janet R., Claire W. McCoy and Kari K. Veblen. (1997). *Sound Ways of Knowing: Music in the Interdisciplinary Curriculum*. New York, NY: Schirmer.

LESSON PLAN 14.1

Spinning a Thread through the Arts

Grades:
Second–fourth

Day 1: Literature
Read *The Rainbow Fish*, by Marcus Pfister, to the children. Discuss the plot and the characters. Invite children speculate on the moral of the story. Discuss how that moral might pertain to them.

Day 2: Visual Arts
View photos of tropical fish. Discuss their shapes, colors, and lines. Look at the illustrations in *The Rainbow Fish*. How might real tropical fish have inspired the artist? What about the rainbow fish seems exaggerated? Have children use colored paper, crayons or markers, glitter, scissors, foil, and glue to create their own fish puppets inspired by the rainbow fish and real tropical fish. Keep it small enough to tape to a straw or stick. If possible, make it two-sided.

Day 3: Music
Reread *The Rainbow Fish*, imagining what kinds of sounds might be used to create a sense of water and floating in water. Have children suggest sounds and list them on the board. Listen to "The Aquarium" from *The Carnival of the Animals* by Camille Saint-Saëns. Discuss what sounds Saint-Saëns used to create a sense of floating in water and moving upward and downward. Listen again and trace the motion of the melody with a hand in the air. Draw a map of the melody. Play the music a third time and trace the melody in the air with the stick puppets.

Day 4: Media Arts and Music
View Bill Patterson's video of "The Aquarium" by Saint-Saëns on www.tropicalsweets.com.[8] Discuss how the videographer and editor were able to coordinate the natural movement of the tropical fish with the music. Invite small groups of children to use their own music maps to create an underwater piece for instruments. If they use pitched percussion such as bells or a xylophone, encourage them to use notes from a whole-tone scale: C, D, E, F♯, G♯, A♯, C. Have them practice, refine, share, and critique their pieces. What effects did they use to create a sense of floating or drifting? Of changes levels? Of water?

Day 5: Dance
Discuss how fish move through the water both individually and in schools (review the video if necessary). Invite children to move through general space with the flowing movements of fish through water. Have them work in small groups to choreograph either "The Aquarium" or their own compositions and perform it for others. Scarves could serve as fish costumes, or the fish puppets could participate to add to the effect.

ADAPTING INSTRUCTION FOR VARIOUS NEEDS

English Language Learners (ELL)

Artistic strategies are ideal for children who are learning to speak English. Drawing, writing, dancing, and singing what they are learning will help them understand what words and ideas mean.

Physical Disabilities

Children who struggle with coordination or who have limited mobility can still be invited to move whatever parts of their bodies can move, such as heads, eyelids, or mouths. They can also get a sense of dancing when someone else moves their wheelchair to the beat and patterns of a dance, if they are unable to do so themselves. Large pens they can hold with a claw or hand will help them do art, as will holding a paintbrush in their mouth or painting with their feet.

Blind or Visual Impairments

These children need to move within a prescribed space, such standing in a hula hoop or holding onto a parachute, activities commonly done in elementary schools with sighted classmates Using clay or other tactile materials to create visual arts gives people with no or limited sight a chance to use their sense of touch more meaningfully.

Children with visual impairments can be paired with sighted children who can describe to them scenes from an opera as the story unfolds. They can also participate in dramatizations with others if they use a cane or sighted person to assist their mobility.

Autism Spectrum Disorders

Adjust to the unique needs of each child by finding which art forms they are most comfortable using to express their ideas: moving, painting, drawing, singing, playing instruments, listening, filming, etc. Plan strategies that encourage their involvement and build on their strengths.

Behavior Disorders

Set clear boundaries for use of art materials, instruments, technology, and movement with children who have a difficult time controlling their responses.

Give them positive recognition for following directions. If necessary, remove them from an activity if their behavior is inappropriate or dangerous. Have them reflect on what they need to do differently to be able to participate again.

Summary

Culminating events at the end of the school year, but also throughout the year to mark children's achievements, engage parents and children meaningfully in the school's broader embrace of community values. Schoolwide concerts, festivals, and arts fairs, competently and confidently performed and presented, are long-remembered for their magic, both imaginative and full of deep personal and collective feelings. The arts are uniquely powerful in helping to convey what children have learned, through images, music, theater, poetry, film, stories, and dance, and they entertain as well as inform.

The arts are powerful learning avenues for children. They can and should be taught as disciplines in their own right, but they can also be integrated with each other, taught in an interdisciplinary fashion, and integrated with other curricular subjects. The arts provide rich and stimulating ways for children to acquire and reflect learning. They engage children deeply in creating and in exercising the imagination, and they make learning interesting and more meaningful. Above all, the arts feed both mind and spirit at a learning banquet.

Review

1. List four reasons for including the arts in the general curriculum.

2. What makes something artistic?

3. What is the art form most analogous to music?

4. List one way each to connect music to visual arts, movement, literary arts, media arts, and theater.

5. Why are festivals or fairs important to the life of a school?

Critical thinking

1. What challenges might you face in integrating the arts into your curriculum?

2. What skills do you have that may help you integrate the arts into your curriculum?

292 PART III | Music throughout the Day

3. What challenges might you might face in encouraging teachers to collaborate with you on an arts-integrated project?

4. What are the potential advantages for you, the other teachers, the children, and the school in planning and implementing carefully constructed arts-integrated projects?

5. What is one large theme you think would be appropriate for an entire school to focus on for a year or for a shorter unit of study? Why is that theme valuable? Would it be able to incorporate the arts in significant ways?

Projects

1. Teach one of the music and visual arts activities to a group of children. Reflect on the project, their success, and your success. If you were to implement that project again, how would you change it and why?

2. Find several recordings of instrumental music in different moods and tempos to accompany creative music and dance. Implement some of the initial dance activities with elementary-aged children, choosing appropriate music for different activities. How successful were the children? How successful were you?

3. Develop a rationale you would present to a principal and other teachers to justify having an arts-integrated grade-level or school-wide unit of study around a theme. Include your vision for a culminating festival or fair. Use some of the resources in the bibliography to help you develop your rationale.

4. Meet with a group of your peers who are training to become teachers. Brainstorm a series of themes that would include important learning in a variety of disciplines including the arts. Brainstorm motives that you might use to develop those themes. Finally, brainstorm important concepts and skills in several disciplines (including the arts) that you might accomplish in this unit of study, and ways to achieve them. Diagram your plans. Share them with others in your class.

5. Interview visual or performing artists. Ask them what excites them about their work; what processes they go through to create; what impulses and inspirations drove them to be artists; and how they've grown over the years. Summarize your interviews and reflect on what you've learned from them.

6. Develop a series of arts experiences for children in which you connect relevant themes to spin a thread through the arts. Reflect on what children might learn by engaging in those experiences.

Additional Resources for Teaching

Barrett, Janet R., Claire W. McCoy, and Kari K. Veblen. (1997). *Sound Ways of Knowing: Music in the Interdisciplinary Curriculum*. New York, NY: Schirmer.

Goldberg, Merryl. (2006). *Integrating the Arts: An Approach to Teaching and Learning in Multicultural and Multilingual Settings* (3rd ed.). Boston, MA: Allyn & Bacon.

Kase-Polisini, Judith and Carol Scott-Kassner (Eds.). (1996). *Interconnecting Pathways to Human Experience: Teaching the Arts Across the Disciplines*. Tallahassee, FL: Arts for a Complete Education/Florida Alliance for Arts Education.

Music Educators National Conference. (1994). *National Standards for Arts Education*. Reston, VA: Rowman and Littlefield.

Patterson, William. (2015). *Tropical Sweets: Classical Music Video Adventure* [DVD]. (Available from www.tropicalsweets.com)

Online Resources: Audio and Songbook

digital.wwnorton.com/classroom

APPENDIX 1: MUSIC FUNDAMENTALS

Notes are just one aspect of music, the aspect that can be written down. A shadow of the real thing, and an imperfect shadow at that.

—David Rothenberg[1]

IN THIS APPENDIX

Visualizing Sounds with Symbols and Icons

Musical Elements

Review

Critical Thinking

Projects

Suggestions for Further Reading

Music notation is meant to depict sound in symbols, and to assist transmission and memory.

You Will Learn

- the basic elements of and vocabulary commonly used in music

- basic symbols used to notate musical elements

- to read music notation well enough to sing and play the music in this book and other simple music.

- about several websites and computer programs to use for practicing reading music

Ask Yourself

- How comfortable are you reading musical notation? Can you look at notation and hear the song in your head, does notation look like a foreign language, or are you somewhere in between?

- As a child, did you learn to play an orchestra or band instrument, recorder, guitar, piano, or other instrument? Did you learn to read some notation for that instrument? What do you remember about those experiences?

- As a child, did your general music teacher ever help you read notation?

VISUALIZING SOUNDS WITH SYMBOLS AND ICONS

Sounds and their complex relationships are the essence of music, and what we write on paper about music can only suggest its full meaning. Most of the world's music is received aurally, that is, by ear, and is never written in notation. Western (European) music is in the distinct minority, where many systems for notating music evolved over hundreds of years. Nothing seen by the eyes, however, can capture what our ears perceive and how it affects our psyche. If actual sounds are the territory, music notation is merely the map, a shorthand to indicate how music is performed and to assist transmission and memory.

As the Roman Empire collapsed, the early Christian church in Rome struggled to maintain control of Christian theology and sought to standardize chants so that believers could stay united spiritually, if not politically, throughout the known world. At first, the church relied on iconic neumes to indicate relative pitch and direction of melodies.

Later, more complex music demanded more than just indications of melodic direction—it required precise pitch and durational values. Western music notation evolved over many centuries to its present form, and now precisely indicates pitches, rhythmic durations, meters, and tempos, and suggests various expressive elements of musical sound. Music notation may be only the imperfect shadow of the real thing, but it's a shadow that gets us close enough to the real thing to allow our innate musicality to realize the rest.

Reading music is like reading words, mathematics, or foreign language symbols, in that such skills are all a matter of degree. Preschoolers who can read and write their own names can claim they know how to read and write. They can say two plus two is four, but of course there is much more to math than that. Yet it is a start—a place to build from. Some college students preparing to become classroom teachers are skilled in music reading and music performance; others are not. This Appendix aims to demystify music notation and help all students feel comfortable enough with it to access the music suggested throughout this book and use notation to incorporate music into all curricula. In focusing on these goals, we will necessarily overlook many more complex aspects of music theory. Just like learning to read words or calculate math, learning to read music requires memorization, decoding skills, strategies. As with any worthwhile endeavor, the more you practice the skills, the more proficient you will become.

MUSICAL ELEMENTS

When we study chemistry, we learn first about chemical elements: basic substances that combine with one another in different ways to form many compounds with radically different properties. Music, like chemistry, has elements, but while there are over 100 chemical elements, music has just four basic elements and a few simple compounds:

1. *Pitch* (vibration frequency). Pitches combine sequentially and with rhythm to form *phrases* and *melodies*, and simultaneously to form *harmony*.

2. *Duration* (time). Sounds and silences occur over time in different combinations of short and long, which the ancient Greeks named *rhythm*, and in different recurring patterns of strong and weak beats, called *meter*.

3. *Timbre* (sound quality; pronounced tam-bər). Sounds have different tone qualities, characteristic of each voice and instrument, formed by complex interactions of overtones with their fundamental pitches and determined by the manner in which they begin, decay, sustain, and release.

4. *Intensity* (loudness). Sounds can be barely perceptible (*soft*) or nearly deafening (*loud*), or anywhere in between and constantly changing.

Melodies often contain distinguishable phrases, which produce *form* in compositions, such as in the song "Twinkle, Twinkle Little Star":

Phrase A (twinkle, twinkle little star)

Phrase B (how I wonder what you are)

Phrase C (up above the world so high)

Phrase C (like a diamond in the sky)

Phrase A (twinkle, twinkle little star)

Phrase B (how I wonder what you are)

Neumes were an early system of music notation that showed relative pitch and the direction of melodies.

The ear easily perceives all these elemental nuances and combinations, and music notation attempts to represent them for the eyes. Few have Mozart's capacities for music or Einstein's capacities for physics and mathematics, but we can all learn to use fundamental ideas in many disciplines to our advantage. Notation preserves music and makes it available to others who can decode it and perform it at another time and place.

NOTATING THE ELEMENT OF PITCH

In the sixth century B.C.E., Pythagoras calculated a system for tuning instruments based on the natural mathematical relationships pitch frequencies have to each other. The result was an *octave* (a span between two pitches, one twice as high as the other) divided into seven pitches in a *scale*, now named A, B, C, D, E, F, and G. Different tuning systems developed in other cultures, but the Pythagorean system evolved into the tempered tuning system we use today. The most commonly used musical pitches can be represented on a *grand staff* of eleven lines separated by ten spaces (see Example A1.1). A note head placed below the lowest line is F2, on the lowest line is G2, in the space above it is A2, and so forth. Originally, the eleven lines of the grand staff were evenly spaced, but because it was difficult to read pitches on eleven lines, the middle line was soon eliminated and a light, short line (called a *ledger line*) was inserted when needed for middle C (C4). Ledger lines are also used to represent pitches below and above the grand staff, as with A5 at the end of Example A1.1.

Most human ears can perceive pitches as low as 20 hertz (cycles per second, abbreviated Hz), and as high as 20,000 Hz, although most music occurs in a far more limited range. For example, the piano's 88 keys play pitches from 27.5 Hz (A0) to 4186 Hz (C8). Most men can sing pitches from 98 Hz (G2) to 784 Hz (G4) (in *falsetto*, their "false" high voices). See these pitches on the grand staff in Example A1.1 and on the keyboard below.

EXAMPLE A1.1

Notes on the grand staff

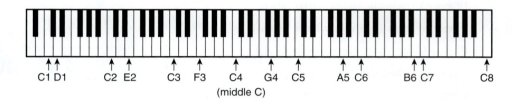

The middle part of the piano keyboard, with pitch letters and octave numbers.

Practical application: On a keyboard, play F2, indicated at the bottom of the bass staff. Men can try to sing that pitch, then play G2 and sing it. Continue up the scale playing and singing. Around middle C (C4) or D4, most men need to change to falsetto and some, but not all, are able to sing up to G5 (three full octaves). Women can find the piano key matching their lowest comfortable singing note (usually around E3) and continue up the scale. Most women can sing up to G5 or even as high as C6, although maybe not comfortably.

For centuries before paper was invented, music and everything else was written on expensive parchment (made from animal skin), so to save money, the *treble staff* was used when only high pitches were needed (treble means high), and the *bass staff* was used when only low pitches were needed (bass means low). To distinguish the two staves, they wrote a giant fancy G at the left edge of the treble staff, which circles around and ends on the G4 line, and a giant fancy F at the left edge of the bass staff, which is anchored on the F3 line. The two dots replaced the fancy F's tines on both sides of the F3 line to prevent ink blots from calligraphy pens.

The two halves of the grand staff are often taught separately. The treble staff lines, named E, G, B, D, and F, can be remembered via any number of mnemonics (Every Good Boy Does Fine, Every Girl Buys Dresses Friday, Empty Garbage Before Dad Flips), and the treble staff spaces spell the word FACE (see Example A1.2).

EXAMPLE A1.2

Lines and spaces of the treble staff

The bass staff lines are named G, B, D, F, and A (mnemonic: Good Boys Do Fine Always) and the spaces are A, C, E, and G (mnemonics: All Cars Eat Gas, All Cows Eat Grass).

EXAMPLE A1.3

The lines and spaces of the bass staff

Practical application: Play the games in the software Music Ace,[2] which most college music libraries have. Game 7 reinforces the treble staff pitches, and Game 13 reinforces bass staff pitches. You can also find many music notation games online.

A complicating factor in notating pitch is that the successive pitches in Pythagoras' octave are not evenly spaced. Most pitches are spaced a whole step apart, but there are two half steps in each octave (between pitches three and four, and between pitches seven and eight, which doubles as the beginning of the next octave). Again, it is the purpose of this Appendix to prepare readers to use the basic notation in this book, so this complication is introduced only to alert readers about symbols collectively known as *accidentals*: *sharps* (♯) raise the pitch one half step, *flats* (♭) lower the pitch one half step, and *naturals* (♮) return sharped or flatted pitches to their normal pitch in the scale. Sharps and flats appear at the beginning of a composition in a *key signature*. If a sharp appears on the F line, it means that all notes called F will be F♯. Similarly, if a flat occurs on the B line, all Bs will be read as B♭s. There is much more to know about key signatures and pitch spacing, but it is beyond the scope of this Appendix to discuss it.

Practical application: Referring to the piano keyboard in Figure A1.3 or using a real piano or keyboard, find the notes in Example A1.4. Sharp notes are played on the black keys immediately to the right of the white key with the same letter name, and flat notes are played on the black keys immediately to the left.

Harmony results from two or more pitches sounding simultaneously. Harmony parts are often notated on one or more additional staves below the melody staff, but simple harmony can be written on the same staff as the melody. Harmony can be produced by several means, such as rounds, countermelodies, partner songs, chords (two or more pitches sounding simultaneously), and ostinatos (short patterns of pitches that repeat over and over). Children's songs accompanied by

EXAMPLE A1.4

Accidentals and key signatures

Accidentals change the pitch of a specific note by a half step. Key signatures change the pitch of all notes on the line or space where an accidental is located.

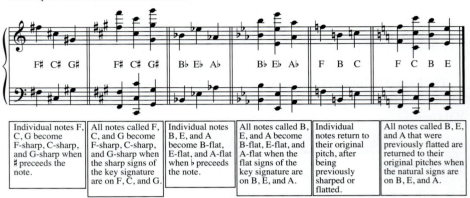

| Individual notes F, C, G become F-sharp, C-sharp, and G-sharp when ♯ preceeds the note. | All notes called F, C, and G become F-sharp, C-sharp, and G-sharp when the sharp signs of the key signature are on F, C, and G. | Individual notes B, E, and A become B-flat, E-flat, and A-flat when ♭ preceeds the note. | All notes called B, E, and A become B-flat, E-flat, and A-flat when the flat signs of the key signature are on B, E, and A. | Individual notes return to their original pitch, after being previously sharped or flatted. | All notes called B, E, and A that were previously flatted are returned to their original pitches when the natural signs are on B, E, and A. |

guitar or autoharp indicate the chord names above the melody staff where the chords change.

NOTATING THE ELEMENT OF TIME

Most, but not all, music has a more or less steady *beat*, which can range from slow to fast. The rate of the beat is called the *tempo* and is expressed as beats per minute, often in the form MM ♩ = #, where MM stands for Maelzel's Metronome (a device that produces steady clicks over a range of different speeds) and # is the number of beats per minute. For example, a song with the tempo of one beat per second would have the tempo marking MM ♩ = 60. There are many online metronomes and metronome apps for smartphones and tablets. (Other music-related apps, for tuning, note reading, and general music theory and ear training, are endlessly useful, as are virtual pianos and other instruments.)

Practical application: Find an online metronome and experiment with setting the clicks to different speeds. Listen to any piece of music or sing a familiar song, then guess its tempo. Check your accuracy with the metronome. Repeat several times until you consistently guess tempos within a few beats per minute. Hint: it helps to keep a favorite song and its tempo in mind. Many marches are 120 beats per minute (twice per second), and many popular and rock songs are faster.

Music compositions are divided into measures (sometimes called bars, especially in American jazz music and in England) marked by vertical measure lines, or bar lines. The number of beats in a measure depends on the *meter*, or recurring pattern of heavy and light beats. A piece in duple meter has one heavy beat and one light beat in each pattern. Triple-meter pieces contain one heavy beat and two light beats. Quadruple-meter pieces are composed of one heavy beat, a light beat, a medium beat, and a light beat. Larger sections of a composition are separated by double bar lines, and the end is indicated with two bar lines, the second twice as thick as the first.

Practical application: Listen to several favorite songs and try to discern the meter. Pat the lap on heavy beats, clap hands on weak beats, and snap fingers on

APPENDIX 1 | Music Fundamentals **A7**

medium beats. The vast majority of modern songs are written in quadruple meter, so this pattern fits them well: pat, clap, snap, clap. Pieces in triple meter need the pattern: pat, clap, clap. Children can use this exercise to guess the meter and come up with different movement patterns to show the three kinds of beats. It boosts energy and gets children involved and mentally focused.

The *time signature* indicates the meter and is written as two numbers (arranged like a fraction, with one number above the other) just after the clef sign or just after the key signature, if there is one. The top number gives the number of beats in a measure (the meter), and the bottom number (read as a denominator with one as the numerator) indicates the type of note that equals one beat. For example, the number two on the bottom means the 1/2 (half) note equals one beat; the number four on the bottom means the 1/4 (quarter) note equals one beat. Most modern music is written with the quarter note equaling one beat, so the bottom number of the time signature is usually four. Examples:

TIME SIGNATURE	MEANING
$\frac{4}{4}$	Top number means: 4 beats per measure
	Bottom number means: quarter note = one beat
$\frac{3}{4}$	Top number means: 3 beats per measure
	Bottom number means: quarter note = one beat
$\frac{6}{8}$	Top number means: 6 beats per measure
	Bottom number means: eighth note = one beat
$\frac{12}{8}$	Top number means: 12 beats per measure
	Bottom number means: eighth note = one beat

Theoretically, the top number can be any number between one and infinity, but most often it is 2, 3, 4, 6, or 12 and occasionally 5, 7, 9, etc. The bottom number must always be a division of the whole note: 2, 4, 8, 16, etc., but is most often 2, 4, or 8. Occasionally $\frac{4}{4}$ time is indicated with a c (meaning common time), and $\frac{2}{2}$ time is indicated with a $\cent$ (meaning cut time).

Some musical sounds last exactly one beat, others last more than one beat, and still others last less than one beat. Collectively, patterns of sound and silence over time are referred to as *rhythm*. Rhythm notation is one of the places where music and math principles coincide. The longest note commonly used today is the whole note: a note head resembling a horizontal zero, with an empty center and without a stem (𝅝). In $\frac{4}{4}$ time, the whole note is equal to four beats, or the whole measure. The half note (𝅗𝅥) looks like a whole note with a stem, and generally equals two beats. The quarter note (𝅘𝅥) looks like a half note, but the note head is filled in, and it generally equals one beat. The eighth note (𝅘𝅥𝅮) looks like a quarter note, but it has one flag attached to the stem and generally equals half a beat. Each additional flag added to the stem cuts the rhythmic value in half, thus two flags = sixteenth note (𝅘𝅥𝅯 one-fourth beat), three flags = thirty-second note (𝅘𝅥𝅰, one-eighth beat), and so forth. The note names are all a fraction of the whole note (generally

A8   APPENDIX 1 | Music Fundamentals

TABLE A1.1 CHART OF RHYTHMIC VALUE NOTES

Whole note		o			4 beats
Half note		♩	♩		2 beats
Quarter note	♩	♩	♩	♩	1 beat
Eighth note	♪ ♪	♪ ♪	♪ ♪	♪ ♪	½ beat
Sixteenth note	♬ ♬ ♬ ♬	♬ ♬ ♬ ♬	♬ ♬ ♬ ♬	♬ ♬ ♬ ♬	¼ beat
Thirty-second note	♬♬♬♬♬♬♬♬	♬♬♬♬♬♬♬♬	♬♬♬♬♬♬♬♬	♬♬♬♬♬♬♬♬	⅛ beat

worth four beats). This can be quite confusing for those who wonder why a whole note should not be worth a whole beat. It helps to think of the whole note as a whole dollar, which divides into two half-dollar coins or four quarter-dollar coins (although the comparison stops there, as there is no coin worth an eighth-dollar and no rhythmic value equal to a dime, nickel, or penny). See Table A1.1 for a chart of each note's rhythmic value in $\frac{4}{4}$ time.

Stems going up are attached to the right side of the note head, and stems going down are attached to the left side of the note head. Flags are always attached to the right side of the stems. Sometimes the flags are exchanged for bars connecting groups of the same note values together, which make the rhythms easier to write and read. You can add note values together (exactly like numbers in math) by drawing a *tie* between note heads (♩‿♩). For example, a quarter note tied to an eighth note (♩‿♪) has 1 and 1/2 beats. Another way to increase note values is to place a dot after the note head. Each dot adds half of the note's original value. Thus, ♩. = 1 + 1/2, ♩. = 2 + 1, and ♪. = 1/2 + 1/4. Each note value has a corresponding symbol for rest (silence); see Example A1.5.

EXAMPLE A1.5

Symbols for rests

Whole rest   Half rests   Quarter rests   Eighth rests   Sixteenth rests

Practical application: Tap your foot to a steady beat (with or without a metronome), count the beat aloud, and clap the rhythmic exercises in Example A1.6.

Many websites and apps offer practice with rhythms and reading rhythmic notation.

In notated rhythm, the total value of all the notes and rests in each measure must equal the top number of the time signature. The exceptions to this rule are the first and last measures of a piece, if the music does not start on the first beat of the measure. The incomplete measure at the beginning is said to

EXAMPLE A1.6

Rhythmic exercises to clap while keeping a steady foot tap to the beat

Tap your foot to a steady beat (with or without a metronome), count aloud the beat of the measures, and clap the rhythmic exercises.

contain *pick-up notes*, or *anacrusis* (meaning "against the point"). Rhythm symbols combine in many different ways to form patterns. Elementary-school children learn to read and clap rhythm patterns such as those in Example A1.7. Triplet patterns are noted with three eighth notes barred together (totaling one beat) and the number 3. A parallel system of note division also exits in time signatures with the number eight in the "denominator," in which each beat divides into three parts, then six, nine, and twelve. Some children's songs, especially from the British Isles, employ this triplet subdivision of the beat, in songs such as **Hick**ory, **dick**ory, **dock**. The **mouse** ran **up** the **clock**. The **clock** struck **one**, the **mouse** ran **down**, **Hick**ory, **dick**ory, **dock**.

EXAMPLE A1.7

Typical rhythm patterns taught in elementary school

Italian words for various tempos (*tempi*) also help to notate time. Musicians all over the world use these terms, because Italian music was in vogue when the Gutenberg printing press first made printed music available worldwide. *Largo* = slow, *andante* = walking speed, *moderato* = medium speed, *allegro* = quick, and *presto* = very fast. There are many more tempo indicators in Italian and other languages. Learn more by searching "Italian tempo words."

NOTATING THE ELEMENT OF TIMBRE

There are fewer terms and symbols for notating timbre. Music scores indicate at the beginning or above each staff the voice type (soprano, mezzo-soprano, alto, tenor, baritone, or bass) or instrument (flute, clarinet, piano, violin, guitar, etc.) that is to perform the music. There are terms for subtle variations in timbre for some instruments, such as *pizzicato* (plucking) or *arco* (bowing) strings of orchestral instruments, or muting brass instruments, but most are too specialized for this Appendix. Guitar timbre is effected by strumming, picking, pull-offs, hammer-ons, and other subtle techniques. Piano timbre can be slightly altered by pressing the keys with different forces and velocities and by pressing the pedals (indicated by *Ped.* in piano scores). Electronic keyboards have a huge selection of different timbres that can be selected from menus. Many drums, such as the conga and the djembe, produce different timbres depending on the striking technique used, e.g., bass, open, slap, or stick. Many classroom instruments can produce more than one timbre: xylophones and metallophones sound different when struck with a soft, medium, or hard mallet; cymbals, triangles, gongs, etc. vary in timbre when struck in different places or with mallets of different materials.

Practical application: Explore different timbres available on an electronic keyboard or omnichord, or find a virtual piano keyboard online. Experiment with several classroom instruments to discover how many different timbres each can produce.

NOTATING THE ELEMENT OF INTENSITY

As with tempo markings, many Italian terms are used in music to indicate relative loudness levels, collectively known as *dynamics*. The two basic terms are *piano* (abbreviated *p*), meaning low or soft, and *forte* (abbreviated *f*), meaning strong or loud. It might help to remember that *piano* literally means floor (the lowest part of a room), and *forte* literally means strong, the way a fort is a stronghold. Students often confuse the dynamic *piano* with the instrument, until they know that the original full name for the instrument was *pianoforte,* or the soft-loud instrument, to distinguish it from earlier keyboard instruments (harpsichord, clavichord, etc.), which could play only loud or soft.

Adding the prefix *mezzo* (abbreviated *m* and pronounced met-so), meaning medium, to *piano* results in the intensity level of *mezzo piano* (medium soft), marked *mp* in scores. Similarly *mezzo forte* (*mf*) means medium loud. The Italian suffix, -*issimo*, means as much as possible, thus *pianissimo* (marked *pp*) means as soft as possible, and *fortissimo* (marked *ff*) means as loud as possible. Two other terms are also commonly used: 1) *crescendo* means to gradually grow louder and is marked by the abbreviation *cresc.* or a hairpin ($<$) and 2) *diminuendo* means to gradually diminish loudness and is marked by the abbreviation *dim.* or a reverse hairpin ($>$). *Diminuendo* is sometimes called *decrescendo* outside Italy. See Table A1.2 for a summary of dynamic markings.

TABLE A1.2 SUMMARY OF BASIC NOTATIONS FOR INTENSITY

soft as possible	soft	medium soft	medium loud	loud	loud as possible
pianissimo	*piano*	*mezzopiano*	*mezzoforte*	*forte*	*fortissimo*
pp	*p*	*mp*	*mf*	*f*	*ff*

Gradually grow louder: *Crescendo cresc.*

Gradually diminish loudness: *Diminuendo dim.*

Many other terms notate intensity, such as *sforzando* (marked *sfz*), which literally means to strain or force in Italian and is interpreted as suddenly louder in music and often compared to a sneeze. You may also see markings above or below a note head that indicate a slight emphasis in intensity, or a short wedge that means to accent or stress the note.

Review

1. Define frequency terms: pitch, phrase, melody, harmony, grand staff, treble, bass, accidentals, sharps, flats, naturals, and key signature.

2. Define timing/duration terms: beat, rhythm, meter, time signature, pick-up beats or anacrusis, tempo, *andante, allegro.*

3. Define sound quality terms: timbre, soprano, alto, tenor, bass, *pizzicato.*

4. Define the terms related to intensity: dynamics, *piano, forte, mezzo, -issimo, crescendo, diminuendo, sforzando.*

5. Name the lines and spaces of the grand staff.

6. Accurately clap the rhythms in Example A1.6.

Critical Thinking

1. Why are Italian terms used in music notation?

2. Explain how learning rhythmic notation reinforces the mathematical operation of division.

Projects

1. Search the Internet for music theory worksheets, download a few covering pitch notation, and fill in the blanks.

2. Search the Internet for music theory worksheets, download a few covering rhythm notation, and fill in the blanks.

Suggestions for Further Reading

Clendinning, Jane Piper, Elizabeth West Marvin, and Joel Phillips. (2014). *The Musician's Guide to Fundamentals* (2nd ed.). New York, NY: W. W. Norton & Company.

Gerou, Tom and Linda Lusk. (1996). *Essential Dictionary of Music Notation: The Most Practical and Concise Source for Music Notation.* Van Nuys, CA: Alfred Music.

APPENDIX 2: THREE COMMON METHODS OF TEACHING MUSIC TO CHILDREN

To be a complete musician, one requires a good ear, imagination, intelligence, and temperament—that is, the faculty of experiencing and communicating artistic emotion.

—Émile Jaques-Dalcroze[1]

Three of the best-known music pedagogues are Émile Jaques-Dalcroze, Zoltán Kodály, and Carl Orff. Their instructional techniques are referred to throughout this book. A comparison of their methods and further discussion on developing a personal method conclude this appendix.

DALCROZE: MOVEMENT WITH A MISSION

"Movement with a mission" is one description of the Dalcroze approach to music instruction, which is characterized by three parts: 1) a unique form of rhythmic movement (eurhythmics), 2) ear training (solfège), and 3) improvisation. Each of these elements requires imagination, perceptive listening, and quick response to musical stimuli. Dalcroze instruction intertwines the three parts to develop mind-body connections that foster musicianship.

The founder of the Dalcroze approach, Émile Jaques-Dalcroze (1865–1950), was a Swiss musician and professor of solfège, harmony, and composition at the Geneva Conservatory. Early in the twentieth century, he noticed that his instrumental students made frequent errors with rhythms, pitches, and intonation: their playing was mechanical, not musical.

Part one of the Dalcroze approach is *eurhythmics* (from the Greek *eu* meaning good and *rythmos* meaning flow), which activates the diaphragm, lungs, and articulation functions of the mouth and tongue. Eurhythmic movements are personal and immediate responses to music played usually on the piano or percussion instruments, and sometimes to recorded music. As students develop coordination of ear, brain, and body, their ability improves to discriminate among subtle changes in tempo, dynamics, texture, structure, and musical style and to react quickly to these changes with their movements. Eurhythmic movement requires a repertory of complex kinesthetic reactions, including many locomotor (moving the body through space) and non-locomotor movements (gestures using the hands, arms, head, and shoulders independently and in combination).

IN THIS APPENDIX

Dalcroze: Movement with a Mission

Kodály: Inner Hearing and Music Literacy

Orff: Schulwerk

Personal Method

Suggestions for Further Reading

| do | re | mi | fa | sol | la | ti | do |

Solfège hand signs identify each pitch of the scale.

Part two of the Dalcroze approach is solfège, a system representing pitches of the scale by names and hand signs (see illustrations above).

Dalcroze includes many solfège exercises:

▶ sing the scale with pitch names and hand signs

▶ sing intervals (*do–mi, do–la, re–sol, ti–mi*, etc.)

▶ learn the difference between whole and half steps and their various sequences in scales and musical passages

▶ sing scales in patterns, such as dichord (*do–re, re–mi, mi–fa*, etc.) and trichord (*do–re–mi, re–mi–fa, mi–fa–sol*, etc.), in increasingly complex combinations: in canon with the teacher, at different speeds, and with alternating silent internal singing and singing aloud on cue

These exercises strengthen pitch pattern memory, and, when transferred to singing, increase accuracy of pitches and intonation. Solfège also reinforces independent singing of song parts, as in rounds, ostinatos, and harmony parts.

Part three, improvisation, allows children freedom of expression through movement, in rhythmic speech, with instruments, or at the keyboard. Beginning by precisely imitating the teacher's or a partner's melodies, rhythms, and movements, children eventually acquire a repertory of movement and musical ideas from which they can draw for improvisation. Eurhythmics and solfège combine to offer a strong musical knowledge base for improvisation.

Many teachers learn techniques for applying Dalcroze Eurhythmics at conferences sponsored by the Dalcroze Society of America or at music teacher conferences at the local, state, or national levels. Search for "Dalcroze Eurhythmics" for more information.

KODÁLY: INNER HEARING AND MUSIC LITERACY

If there is a single underlying philosophy of the Kodály approach to music instruction, it is that "music belongs to everyone." Zoltán Kodály and his Hungarian associates who first evolved this method maintained that music is the right of not only the talented few but of all children, who can and should develop performance, listening, and literacy skills. With music instruction beginning in early childhood, children discover folk and art music through a sequence that begins with singing and results in musically independent individuals who can read and write music with ease. Kodály proponents believe that the content and sequence of the curriculum should be driven by children's musical development and their musical literature. While hand signs and rhythm syllables are closely associated with Kodály, it is far more comprehensive than these techniques suggest, with systematic training that results in musical literacy in children at an early age.

"Music must not be approached from its intellectual, rational side, nor should it be conveyed as a system of algebraic symbols, or as the secret writing of a language with which he has no connection. The way should be paved for direct intuition."

—Zoltán Kodály, 1974

Zoltán Kodály (1882–1967) was a composer, ethnomusicologist, and advocate of music education for children. He and Béla Bartók collected songs in Hungary, Romania, and other parts of southeastern Europe. He lectured on composition, harmony, counterpoint, and orchestration at the Academy of Music in Budapest from 1907 to 1940. His best-known works feature folk songs and folklike melodies for orchestral instruments. His educational ideas crystallized in what has become known as the Kodály method, which was later elaborated and expanded by students and colleagues.

American-style Kodály retains the use of pentatonic (five-tone) folk songs; the solfège approach to sight-reading, with its hand signs; a rhythmic system of mnemonic syllables; and an emphasis on unaccompanied song. As part of the focus on music reading and writing, a preparatory period of ear training emphasizes rhythmic and melodic patterns that are encountered in songs and later in visual form. The development of inner hearing—thinking musical sounds without hearing or necessarily voicing them—is important to Kodály training.

Kodály solfège exercises use relative (movable) *do*, where the tonic of the scale moves: C is *do* in C Major, D is *do* in D Major, and so on. Such a system clarifies the functions of individual scale degrees in various keys by allowing the tonic of the key to anchor dominant, subdominant, and other tonal functions. Kodály adapts the French Chevé system of rhythmic mnemonics to teach younger children rhythmic values and their relationships in a pattern (chanting ta, ti-ti, triplet, etc. helps students at every level master difficult rhythms). Kodály also specifies the sequence by which rhythmic and melodic phrases and fragments are taught (usually using large charts). Many teachers learn Kodály techniques at conferences sponsored by the Organization of American Kodály Educators (OAKE) or at music teacher conferences at the local, state, or national levels. Search for "OAKE" online for more information.

ORFF: SCHULWERK

Orff Schulwerk (literally, "school work") is based on the natural behaviors of childhood—singing, saying, dancing, playing, improvisation, and creative movement closely linked to the child's world of play and fantasy, games, chants, and songs. In its original form, elemental music was pre-intellectual and exploratory, with music, movement, and speech all overlapping. Special-model Orff xylophones of wood and metal have become standard equipment in most school music rooms, but the Orff approach is far richer and more varied in its musical experiences than just instrument playing.

> "Every phase of Schulwerk will always provide stimulation for new independent growth; therefore it is never conclusive and settled, but always developing, always growing, always flowing."
>
> —Carl Orff, 1963

The Schulwerk grew from the ideas of German composer Carl Orff (1895–1982), whose experiments with musicians and dancers in the 1920s planted the seeds for his method's association of music with dance and theater. Together with dancer Dorothee Günther, Carl Orff established an experimental school in Munich, the Güntherschule, for the integration of the performing arts. A Güntherschule ensemble of dancers, players, and singers (many of them preparing to be teachers) performed at educational conferences throughout Europe.

Orff believed children to be naturally musical, uninhibited in their expressive movement. He collaborated with Gunild Keetman to establish the Schulwerk method and publish five volumes of chants, songs, and instrumental pieces called *Musik für Kinder* (Music for Children). Canadian and then American adaptations of Orff and Keetman's work in the 1960s helped to spread their pedagogy around the world.

Principal activities of the Schulwerk, as conceived and practiced in Europe, are the imitation and exploration of music and its components, with opportunities to improvise original pieces. As adapted in the United States, the process is developed in four stages: imitation, exploration, literacy, and improvisation. Imitation may be simultaneous, or it may be canonic—echo-like in the form of an interrupted canon, call-and-response (leader claps, then the group), or overlapping in a continuous canon. Imitation may occur through song, movement, or performance on pitched or unpitched percussion instruments. Exploration challenges children's imaginations to find new ways to apply learned information, such as playing a pattern faster or slower, louder or softer, on a different instrument, or on two alternating pitches. Literacy, or competence in reading and writing music, results from children's earlier musical experiences and progresses toward the skillful use of both graphic and conventional staff notation. The Schulwerk advocates extensive musical experience before literacy can become a truly musical (as opposed to mechanical) tool and a means for children to record the music they create. Rhythmic notation for quarter notes and eighth notes may be introduced in kindergarten and first grade, with melodic notation beginning with limited pitches (*sol–mi* and *mi–re–do*) in the first grade, proceeding to the pentatonic scale by second and third grade, and extending to the reading and writing of the diatonic scale by the fifth grade, similar to the progression of skills in the Kodály approach.

Improvisation, in which musical invention emanates from earlier learning, is the ultimate stage of the Orff process, the culminating experience of extensive musical knowledge and creative thinking. Improvisation is central to many of the world's musical cultures, which makes the Orff process a natural link to these cultures. Children can learn the improvised drumming traditions of Ghana, mbira and xylophone music of Zimbabwe, and percussion music of China through techniques of the Orff Schulwerk.

The Orff process features folk and folklike songs in the pentatonic mode; ostinato patterns that are spoken, sung, played, and moved; tonic drones or pedal tones; and static and moving bourdon (the first and fifth degree of a scale played simultaneously) accompaniments on xylophones and other percussion instruments. These are the more prominent facets of the Schulwerk; the modes of music-making in the four-step process are its pedagogy.

PERSONAL METHOD

Children can learn music by any number of methods, but teachers ultimately choose those pedagogical techniques that harmonize with their personal goals, musical strengths, and preferences in music and instruction. Singers may be inclined to sing more than to move or to play, pianists may choose to accompany songs and movement on the piano, and kinesthetically oriented teachers may center their music instruction on movement experiences. There is no one correct way to teach musical understanding, skills, and values, nor is there only one standard way to approach these goals.

Suggestions for Further Reading

Choksy, Lois, Robert M. Abramson, Avon E. Gillespie, David Woods, and Frank York. (2001). *Teaching Music in the Twenty-First Century* (2nd ed.). Upper Saddle River, NJ: Pearson Education.

Findlay, Elsa. (1999). *Rhythm and Movement: Applications of Dalcroze Eurhythmics*. Van Nuys, CA: Alfred Music.

Houlahan, Micheal and Philip Tacka. (2008). *Kodály Today: A Cognitive Approach to Elementary Music Education*. New York, NY: Oxford University Press.

Frazee, Jane and Kent Kreuter. (1997). *Discovering Orff: A Curriculum for Music Teachers*. London, UK: Schott.

Mead, Virginia Hoge. (1996). *Dalcroze Eurhythmics in Today's Classroom*. London, UK: Schott.

Schnebly-Black, Julia, and Stephen Moore. (1999) *The Rhythm Inside*. London, UK: Sterling.

APPENDIX 3: RESOURCES FOR LISTENING

A20 APPENDIX 3 | Resources for Listening

A. CLASSICAL MUSIC

COMPOSER	TITLE	ARTIST(s)	ALBUM	LABEL	TRACK NUMBER
Bach, Johann Sebastian	Cello Suite No. 3 in C Major	Yo-Yo Ma	*The Cello Suites: Inspired by Bach*	Sony	13–18
	Toccata and Fugue in D Minor	Michael Murray	*Bach*	Telarc	1
	Two-Part Invention No. 1 in C Major	Andras Schiff	*J. S. Bach: Two-Part Inventions/Three-Part Inventions*	Decca	1
	Goldberg Variations	Glenn Gould	*Bach: The Goldberg Variations*	CBS Masterworks	
	Jesu, Joy of Man's Desiring	The Top 100 Solo Guitar Tribute Band	*Jesu, Joy of Man's Desiring*	Pacificcoastmusic. com	1
Bartók, Béla	Concerto for Orchestra, Finale	Fritz Reiner and the Chicago Symphony Orchestra	*Bartók: Concerto for Orchestra; Music for Strings, Percussion and Celesta; Hungarian Sketches*	BMG	5
Beethoven, Ludwig van	Sonata No. 14 in C-sharp Minor ("Moonlight"), I	Jenö Jandó	*Beethoven: Piano Sonatas Nos. 8, 14 and 23*	Naxos	4
	Bagatelle in A Minor, "Für Elise"	Alfred Brendel	*Beethoven: Für Elise/ Eroica-Variationen Op. 35*	Philips Import	16
	Symphony No. 5 in C Minor, I	London Philharmonic	*Beethoven: Symphony No. 5 in C minor, Op. 67, and Symphony No. 6 in F, Op. 68 ("Pastoral")*	Avid	1
	Rondo in C Major	Artur Schnabel and the London Philharmonic	*Beethoven: Piano Concertos Nos. 3 and 4*	Naxos	7
	Symphony No. 6 in F Major, IV ("The Storm")	Vienna Philharmonic	*Beethoven: Symphony No. 5 in C minor, Op. 67, and Symphony No. 6 in F, Op. 68 ("Pastoral")*	Avid	8
Bernstein, Leonard	*West Side Story*	Original Broadway Cast	*West Side Story: Original Broadway Cast*	Hallmark	
Brahms, Johannes	*Hungarian Dances Nos. 17–20*	Herbert von Karajan and the Berlin Philharmonic	*Franz Liszt: Ungarische Fantasie, Ungarische Rhapsodien Nr. 2 & 5; Johannes Brahms: 4 Ungarische Tänze*	Deutsche Grammophon (Musikfest)	4–7
	Variations on a Theme by Haydn, Op. 56	Alexander Rahbari and the Belgian Radio and Television Philharmonic Orchestra	*Johannes Brahms: Symphony No. 1/Haydn Variations*	Naxos	5

APPENDIX 3 | Resources for Listening **A21**

A. CLASSICAL MUSIC (*continued*)

COMPOSER	TITLE	ARTIST(s)	ALBUM	LABEL	TRACK NUMBER
Brahms, Johannes	Serenade No. 1	Claudio Abbado and the Berlin Philharmonic	*Brahms: Serenade No. 1*	Deutsche Grammophon	
Chavez, Carlos	Toccata for Percussion	Eduardo Mata	*Carlos Chavez: Xochipilli, Suite for Double Quartet, Tambuco, Energia, Toccata*	Dorian Recordings	11, 12
Chopin, Frédéric	Prelude, Op. 28, No. 15 ("Raindrop")	Various artists	*Raindrop Prelude: Chopin's Greatest Piano Works*	Deutsche Grammophon	6
Copland, Aaron	"Simple Gifts" from *Appalachian Spring*	John Williams and the Boston Pops Orchestra	*Greatest Hits: Ballet*	Sony Classical	26
	Fanfare for the Common Man	London Symphony Orchestra	*Copland Conducts Copland*	Sony Classical	1
Debussy, Claude	*La mer*	Tiblisi Symphony Orchestra	*Absolutely the Best of Debussy*	Figaro Recording Company	1–3
	Children's Corner Suite	Werner Haas	*Debussy: Complete Piano Music Volume 1*	Philips	Disc 2, tracks 10–15
	Clair de lune	Steve Anderson	*Classics for the Heart*	Domo Records	6
Dukas, Paul	*The Sorcerer's Apprentice*	James Levine and the Berlin Philharmonic	*Saint-Saëns: Orgel-Symphonie/Dukas: L'Apprenti Sorcier*	Deutsche Grammophon	5
Dun, Tan	*Crouching Tiger, Hidden Dragon*	Yo-Yo Ma and Tan Dun	*Crouching Tiger, Hidden Dragon: Original Motion Picture Soundtrack*	Sony Masterworks	1
	Ghost Opera	Kronos Quartet and Wu Man	*Tan Dun: Ghost Opera*	Nonesuch Records	1–5
Dvořák, Antonín	*Slavonic Dances*, Op. 46, No. 5 in A	Lorin Maazel and the Berlin Philharmonic	*Antonín Dvořák: Slavonic Dances, Op. 46 & 72*	Angel Records/ EMI	5
Grofé, Ferde	*Grand Canyon Suite*	Bournemouth Symphony Orchestra	*Ferde Grofé: Grand Canyon Suite, Mississippi Suite, Niagara Falls Suite*	Naxos	5–9
Holst, Gustav	*The Planets*	Simon Rattle and the Berlin Philharmonic	*Holst: The Planets*	Warner Classics	
Maraire, Dumisani	*Mai Nozipo*	Kronos String Quartet	*Pieces of Africa*	Nonesuch	1
Mozart, Wolfgang Amadeus	12 Variations on "Ah, vous dirai-je, Maman"	Jenö Jandó	*Easy Listening Piano Classics: Mozart*	Naxos	Disc 3, track 10

Continued on next page

A. CLASSICAL MUSIC (*continued*)

COMPOSER	TITLE	ARTIST(s)	ALBUM	LABEL	TRACK NUMBER
Mozart, Wolfgang Amadeus	Serenade No. 13 for Strings in G Major ("Eine kleine Nachtmusik")	Ronald Thomas and the New London Soloists Ensemble	*Mozart: Symphony No. 29 / Eine Kleine Nachtmusik/ Serenata Notturna*	CRD Records	1–4
	Concerto for Flute, Harp, and Orchestra in C Major, II and III	Claudio Abbado and the Berlin Philharmonic	*Mozart: Flötenkonzerte 1 & 2/Konzert für Flöte und Harfe*	EMI Classics	2–3
	Symphony No. 40 in G Minor	Claudio Abbado and Orchestra Mozart	*Mozart: Symphonies Nos. 39 & 40*	Deutsche Grammophone/ Archiv	5–8
	Piano Sonata No. 11, III (Turkish March)	Christian Zacharias	*Mozart: Piano Sonatas Nos. 10–12*	EMI Classics	6
Musorgsky, Modest, arr. Maurice Ravel	*Pictures At An Exhibition*	Leonard Bernstein and the New York Philharmonic	*Mussorgsky: Pictures at an Exhibition/Night on Bald Mountain*	Sony Classical	1–15
Prokofiev, Sergei	*Peter and the Wolf*	Arthur Fiedler and the Boston Pops	*Classics for Children: Peter and the Wolf/Carnival of the Animals/Nutcracker Suite*	Sony Masterworks	1–13
	Lieutenant Kijé Suite, Op. 60	Antal Dorati and the Royal Philharmonic	*Prokofiev: Peter And The Wolf/Lieutenant Kijé; Britten: The Young Person's Guide to the Orchestra*	Decca	6–10
Ravel, Maurice	*Boléro*	Valery Gergiev and the London Symphony Orchestra	*Ravel: Daphnis et Chloé/ Boléro/Pavane*	LSO Live	12
Rimsky-Korsakov, Nikolai	*Flight of the Bumblebee*	London Philharmonic	*Three Centuries of the Greatest Hits*	Legacy International	11
Rossini, Gioachino	*William Tell Overture*	London Festival Orchestra	*Rossini: William Tell Overture*	Red Note OMP	1
Saint-Saëns, Camille	*Carnival of the Animals*	Charles Dutoit and the London Sinfonietta	*Saint-Saëns: Carnaval des animaux/Danse macabre*	London/Decca	1–14
Schumann, Robert	*Kinderszenen (Scenes from Childhood)*	Vladimir Ashkenazy	*Schumann: Waldszenen/ Kinderszenen/Sonata No. 1*	Decca	10–22
Schoenberg, Arnold	*Verklärte Nacht, Op. 4*	Herbert von Karajan and the Berlin Philharmonic	*Schoenberg: Verklärte Nacht (Transfigured Night)/Pelleas und Melisande*	Deutsche Grammophon	1–5
Schuller, Gunther	*The Twittering-Machine*	Gunther Schuller	*Schuller: 7 Studies on Themes of Paul Klee; Fetler: Contrasts*	Naxos	4

APPENDIX 3 | Resources for Listening **A23**

A. CLASSICAL MUSIC (continued)

COMPOSER	TITLE	ARTIST(s)	ALBUM	LABEL	TRACK NUMBER
Still, William Grant	Symphony No. 1 ("Afro-American")	Neeme Järvi and the Detroit Symphony Orchestra	*William Grant Still: Symphony No. 1 (Afro-American); Duke Ellington: Suite from "The River"*	Chandos	1–4
Tchaikovsky, Pyotr Ilyich	Symphony No. 4, IV	Herbert von Karajan and the Berlin Philharmonic	*Karajan Conducts Tchaikovsky*	Deutsche Grammophon	Disc 4, track 4
Toch, Ernst	*Geographical Fugue*	Turtle Creek Chorale	*Postcards*	Reference Recordings	11
Vaughan Williams, Ralph	*The Lark Ascending*	Yehudi Menuhin and the English Chamber Orchestra	*Sir Yehudi Menuhin conducts Vaughn Williams: Fantasia on a Theme by Tallis and other works*	Arabesque Recordings	3
Villa-Lobos, Heitor	*The Little Train of the Caipira*	Eugene Goossens and the London Symphony Orchestra	*Heitor Villa-Lobos: The Little Train of the Caipira*	Everest Records	1
Vivaldi, Antonio	*Four Seasons, Spring*	Berlin Philharmonic	*Vivaldi I and II: The Four Seasons* with Nigel Kennedy	EMI Classics	Disc 1, tracks 4–6

B. CLASSICAL MUSIC COMPILATIONS

TITLE	ARTIST(s)	PUBLISHER	MEDIUM
Leonard Bernstein's Young People's Concerts with the New York Philharmonic, Volumes 1 and 2	Leonard Bernstein and the New York Philharmonic	Kultur Video	DVD
Three Centuries of the Greatest Hits	London Philharmonic	Legacy International	CD
Encore! John Williams and the Boston Pops Orchestra	John Williams and the Boston Pops Orchestra	Philips	CD
Fantasia	Leopold Stokowski and the Philadelphia Orchestra	Disney	DVD
Fantasia 2000	James Levine and the Chicago Symphony Orchestra	Disney	DVD
Tropical Sweets Classical Music Video Adventure		William Patterson	DVD or download

A24   APPENDIX 3 | Resources for Listening

C. OPERA

Because opera and ballet are visual media, the selections offered below may best be appreciated on video. Search online for each title.

COMPOSER	TITLE	ARTIST(s)	ALBUM	PUBLISHER	TRACK NUMBER
Barab, Seymour	*Little Red Riding Hood*	Opera on the Go	*Little Red Riding Hood*	CD Baby	
Humperdinck, Engelbert	*Hansel and Gretel: Overture, "Brother Come and Dance with Me," "Evening Prayer"*	Sir Charles Mackaerras and the Philharmonia Orchestra	*Humperdinck: Hansel & Gretel*	Chandos	Disc 1, tracks 1, 4, 15
Menotti, Gian Carlo	*Amahl and the Night Visitors: This Is My Box*	Thomas Schippers and the NBC Symphony Orchestra	*Menotti: Amahl and the Night Visitors, Original Cast of the NBC Telecast, Christmas Eve, 1951*	Sony Classical	11
Mozart, Wolfgang Amadeus	*The Magic Flute*	Otto Klemperer and the Philharmonia Orchestra	*Mozart: Die Zauberflöte*	EMI Classics	
Rossini, Gioachino	*Cinderella*	Opera Australia	*Cinderella*	Kultur Video	

D. BALLET

COMPOSER	TITLE	ARTIST(s)	ALBUM	PUBLISHER	TRACK NUMBER
Copland, Aaron	*Rodeo: Saturday Night Waltz, Hoedown*	Aaron Copland and the London Symphony Orchestra	*Copland Conducts Copland*	Sony Classical/ Legacy	22, 23
Stravinsky, Igor	*Firebird Suite: Infernal Dance, Finale*	Robert Shaw and the Atlanta Symphony Orchestra	*Stravinsky: The Firebird/Borodin: Music from Prince Igor*	Telarc	4, 6
	Petrushka	Leonard Bernstein and the New York Philharmonic	*Bernstein Conducts Stravinsky: Petrushka, Pulcinella*	Sony Classical	1–17
	The Rite of Spring	Leonard Bernstein and the London Symphony Orchestra	*Stravinsky: The Rite of Spring/The Firebird Suite (1919)*	Sony Classical	1–13
Tchaikovsky, Pyotr Ilyich	*The Nutcracker: March, Tea (Chinese Dance), Trepak (Russian Dance), Waltz of the Flowers*	Valery Gergiev and the Kirov Orchestra	*The Nutcracker*	Philips	3, 15, 16, 19

APPENDIX 3 | Resources for Listening **A25**

E. AMERICAN PATRIOTIC MUSIC

COMPOSER	TITLE	ARTIST(s)	ALBUM	PUBLISHER	TRACK NUMBER
Cohan, George	"You're a Grand Old Flag"	Rick Benjamin and the Paragon Ragtime Orchestra	*George M. Cohan: You're A Grand Old Rag*	New World Records	6
Gould, Morton	"American Salute"	"The President's Own" United States Marine Band	*Morton Gould: An American Salute*	Altissimo	1
Sousa, John Philip	*The Stars and Stripes Forever*	Band of the Grenadier Guards	*Sousa Marches: Stirring Marches of the USA Services*	Decca	1
Ward, Samuel A. and Katherine Lee Bates	"America the Beautiful"	Ray Charles	*Ray Charles Sings for America*	Rhino	1

F. JAZZ

COMPOSER	TITLE	ARTIST(s)	ALBUM	PUBLISHER	TRACK NUMBER
Armstrong, Louis	"What a Wonderful World"	Louis Armstrong	*Louis Armstrong: The Ultimate Collection*	Verve	Disc 3, track 15
Desmond, Paul	"Take Five"	The Dave Brubeck Quartet	*Time Out: Take Five/Blue Rondo a la Turk*	Columbia/ Legacy	3
Ellington, Duke	"Take the 'A' Train"	Duke Ellington	*Duke Ellington in Concert*	LRC/Groove	1
Fitzgerald, Ella	"A-Tisket, A-Tasket"	Ella Fitzgerald	*4 by 4: Ella Fitzgerald/ Billie Holiday/Sarah Vaughan/Dinah Washington*	Verve	1
Gershwin, George	"Fascinating Rhythm"	Ella Fitzgerald	*Ella Fitzgerald Sings the George and Ira Gershwin Song Book*	Verve	Disc 3, track 13
Gillespie, Dizzy	"Salt Peanuts"	Dizzy Gillespie	*The Best of Dizzy Gillespie*	AAO Music	Disc 3 track 6
Hancock, Herbie	"Watermelon Man"	Herbie Hancock	*Head Hunters*	Columbia/ Legacy	2
Handy, William Christopher	"St. Louis Blues"	Billie Holiday	*Lady Day: The Complete Billie Holiday on Columbia 1933–1944, Volume 6*	Columbia/ Legacy	21
Joplin, Scott	"Maple Leaf Rag," "The Entertainer"	Scott Joplin	*Scott Joplin: The Entertainer*	Shout Factory	1, 4

Continued on next page

A26   APPENDIX 3 | Resources for Listening

F. JAZZ (continued)

COMPOSER	TITLE	ARTIST(s)	ALBUM	PUBLISHER	TRACK NUMBER
Morton, Jelly Roll	"Kansas City Stomp"	Jelly Roll Morton	*Jelly Roll Morton: The Library of Congress Recordings, Volume 1: Kansas City Stomp*	Rounder	25–26
Marsalis, Branford	"B.B.'s Blues"	Branford Marsalis	*I Heard You Twice the First Time*	Sony	2
Nguyen Le	"Ting Ning"	Nguyen Le	*Jazz: The Smithsonian Anthology*	Smithsonian/ Folkways	Disc 6, track 12
Palmeri, Eddie	"Humpty Dumpty"	Eddie Palmieri	*Sueño*	Intuition	5
Waters, Muddy	"Hard Day Blues"	Muddy Waters	*Plantation Blues*	Suncoast Music	5
Zawinul, Joe	"Birdland"	Weather Report	*Jazz: The Smithsonian Anthology*	Smithsonian/ Folkways	Disc 6, track 2

G. AMERICANA

GENRE/ COMPOSER	TITLE	ARTIST(s)	ALBUM	PUBLISHER	TRACK NUMBER
African-American Folk Music	"The Midnight Special," "Pick a Bale of Cotton," "Bring Me a Little Water, Silvy"	Lead Belly	*Lead Belly: The Smithsonian Folkways Collection*	Smithsonian/ Folkways	Disc 1, tracks 4 and 7; disc 2, track 6
African-American Spirituals	"Joshua Fit the Battle of Jericho," "Wade in the Water"	The Fisk Jubilee Singers	*African American Spirituals: The Concert Tradition. Volume 1: Wade in the Water*	Smithsonian/ Folkways	6, 7
Appalachian Folk Music	"Little Moses," "The Coo Coo Bird"	The Carter Family, Clarence Ashley	*Anthology of American Folk Music*	Smithsonian/ Folkways	Dis 4, track 12; disc 5, track 1
	"Freight Train"	Elizabeth Cotten	*Freight Train and Other North Carolina Folk Songs and Tunes*	Smithsonian/ Folkways	2
	"This Little Light of Mine"	Fannie Lou Hamer	*The Songs My Mother Taught Me*	Smithsonian/ Folkways	13

APPENDIX 3 | Resources for Listening **A27**

G. AMERICANA (*continued*)

GENRE/ COMPOSER	TITLE	ARTIST(s)	ALBUM	PUBLISHER	TRACK NUMBER
Bluegrass Music	"Cumberland Gap," "Rabbit in a Log," "The Rebel Girl," "Get up John"	Snuffy Jenkins, The Stanley Brothers, Hazel Dickens, Bill Monroe	*Classic Bluegrass from Smithsonian Folkways*	Smithsonian/ Folkways	9, 18, 22, 25
	"Big Train (from Memphis)"	The Seldom Scene	*Long Time…Seldom Scene*	Smithsonian/ Folkways	7
Cajun Music	"Madame Boudreaux"	Michael Doucet	*From Now On*	Smithsonian/ Folkways	4
Country-Western Music	"Jambalaya (On the Bayou)"	Hank Williams	*24 of Hank Williams' Greatest Hits*	Polygram	13
Hispanic Music	"Fiesta alegre"	Flaco Jiménez & Max Baca	*Flaco & Max: Legends & Legacies*	Smithsonian/ Folkways	17
Mariachi Music	"La Malagueña"	Nati Cano's Mariachi Los Camperos	*¡Viva el Mariachi!*	Smithsonian/ Folkways	10
Native American Songs	"New Two-Step Dance Song: Enjoy Our Lives Together Forever"	The Turtle Mountain Singers	*Music of New Mexico: Native American Traditions*	Smithsonian/ Folkways	9
Navajo Songs	"Corn Grinding Song"	Joe Lee	*Navajo Songs*	Smithsonian/ Folkways	7–8
Popular Folk-Style Songs of the 50s and 60s	"Oh Freedom"	Joan Baez	*Joan Baez: The First Lady Of Folk 1958–1961*	Jasmine Music	Disc 1, track 4
Dylan, Bob	"Blowin' in the Wind"	Bob Dylan	*The Freewheelin' Bob Dylan*	Columbia	1
Guthrie, Woody	"This Land Is Your Land"	Woody Guthrie	*This Land Is Your Land: The Asch Recordings, Vol. 1*	Smithsonian/ Folkways	1
Odetta	"Deep River"	Odetta	*Odetta Sings Ballads and Blues*	Jasmine Music	Disc 2, track 17
Peter, Paul and Mary	"Early in the Morning"	Peter, Paul and Mary	*Peter, Paul and Mary*	Warner Bros.	1
Seeger, Pete	"If I Had A Hammer," "Where Have All the Flowers Gone?"	Pete Seeger	*If I Had a Hammer: Songs of Hope & Struggle*	Smithsonian/ Folkways	1, 10

APPENDIX 3 | Resources for Listening

H. WORLD MUSIC

REGION	TITLE	ARTIST(s)	ALBUM	PUBLISHER	TRACK NUMBER
Africa	Cameroon: "Lullaby," Central African Republic: "Balibo sasasa," Côte d'Ivoire: "Song of Two Little Girls"	Various	*Lullabies and Children's Songs*	UNESCO/ Smithsonian/ Folkways	1, 7, 4
	"Nzombi"	Various	*Aka Pygmy Music*	UNESCO/ Smithsonian/ Folkways	11
	"Eci ameya," "Music for dancing, gboyo"	Ongo ensemble	*Central African Republic: Banda Polyphony*	UNESCO/ Smithsonian/ Folkways	2, 5
Bolivia	"Kacharpaya Kantu"	Musicians of the Chari community	*Bolivia: Panpipes*	UNESCO/ Smithsonian/ Folkways	4
Britain	"Abbots Bromley Horn Dance"	The Christmas Revels	*In Celebration of the Winter Solstice*	Revel Records	1
Cuba	"Zapateo," "Mi tierra es así"	Horizonte Campesino, Cucalambe Ensemble	*Folk Music of Cuba*	Smithsonian/ Folkways	2, 7
Egypt	"Darabukka solo"	Muhammad El-Arabi	*Egypt: Taqâsîm & Layâlî - Cairo Tradition*	UNESCO/ Smithsonian/ Folkways	6
Greece	"Skaros"	Kyriakos Kosoulas, Georgios Florios, Yorgos Tikos	*Greece: Traditional Music*	UNESCO/ Smithsonian/ Folkways	6
	"Epitaphe de Seikilos"	Gregorio Paniagua and the Atrium Musicæ de Madrid	*Musique de la Grèce Antique*	Harmonia Mundi	11
Korea	"Manpa Jungshi Ji Kok"	Various	*Korea*	UNESCO/ Smithsonian/ Folkways	2
Myanmar (Burmese music)	"The forest of Kanda"	Hsaing Waing Orchestra of Master Sein Tin Htay	*Myanmar: Music by the Hsaing Waing Orchestra: The Burmese Harp*	UNESCO/ Smithsonian/ Folkways	Disc 2, track 4
The Silk Road	"Balbyraun"	Aygul Ulkenbaeva	*The Silk Road: A Musical Caravan*	Smithsonian/ Folkways	Disc 1, track 3

APPENDIX 3 | Resources for Listening   **A29**

I. INCIDENTAL RECORDINGS

PURPOSE/ DESCRIPTION	TITLE	ARTIST(s)	ALBUM	PUBLISHER	TRACK NUMBER
Lullaby	"Hush Little Baby"	Heidi Grant Murphy and Auréole	*Dreamscape: Lullabies from Around the World*	Koch Int'l Classics	2
Lullaby	"Hush Little Baby"	Yo-Yo Ma and Bobby McFerrin	*Hush*	Sony Classical	5
Movement	"Itsy Bitsy Spider"	Little Richard	*Every Child Deserves a Lifetime*	Shout Factory	14
Movement	"Jump for Joy"	Joanie Bartels	*Jump for Joy*	BMG Special Products	1
Movement	"The Swan"	Charles Dutoit and the London Sinfonietta (composed by Camille Saint-Saëns)	*Saint-Saëns: Carnival des animaux*	London/Decca	13
Whales	"Solo Whale"		*Songs of the Humpback Whale*	Living Music	1
Whales	"And God Created Great Whales (for Orchestra and Whales)"	David Amos and the Philharmonia Orchestra (composed by Alan Hovhaness)	*Alan Hovhaness: And God Created Great Whales*	Crystal Records	1
Whales	"Voice of the Whale (Vox Balaenae)— For Three Masked Players"	Aeolian Chamber Players (composed by George Crumb)	*Masterworks of the Twentieth Century*	Sony Classical	Disc 5, track 1

APPENDIX 4: NATIONAL STANDARDS FOR MUSIC EDUCATION

These standards were developed and adopted by the Music Educators National Conference (MENC) in 1994 and were superseded by the National Association for Music Education (NAfME, the new name for MENC) with Common Core Standards in 2014, during the time this book was being written. NAfME and many music educators have not abandoned or rejected the 1994 standards but continue to use them in conjunction with the 2014 standards. The 1994 standards are useful for focusing on specific musical processes, while the 2014 standards focus more on general thinking and feeling processes.

1. Singing, alone and with others, a varied repertoire of music.
2. Performing on instruments, alone and with others, a varied repertoire of music.
3. Improvising melodies, variations, and accompaniments.
4. Composing and arranging music within specified guidelines.
5. Reading and notating music.
6. Listening to, analyzing, and describing music.
7. Evaluating music and music performances.
8. Understanding relationships between music, the other arts, and disciplines outside the arts.
9. Understanding music in relation to history and culture.

GRADES K-4

Performing, creating, and responding to music are the fundamental music processes in which humans engage. Students, particularly in grades K–4, learn by doing. Singing, playing instruments, moving to music, and creating music enable them to acquire musical skills and knowledge that can be developed in no other way. Learning to read and notate music gives them a skill with which to explore music independently and with others. Listening to, analyzing, and evaluating music are important building blocks of musical learning. Further, to participate fully in a diverse, global society, students must understand their own historical and cultural heritage and those of others within their communities and beyond. Because music is a basic expression of human culture, every student should have access to a balanced, comprehensive, and sequential program of study in music.

Terms identified by an asterisk (*) are explained in the glossary. The standards in this section describe the cumulative skills and knowledge expected of all students upon exiting grade 4. Students in the earlier grades should engage in developmentally appropriate learning experiences designed to prepare them to achieve these standards at grade 4. Determining the curriculum and the specific instructional activities necessary to achieve the standards is the responsibility of states, local school districts, and individual teachers.

1. CONTENT STANDARD: SINGING, ALONE AND WITH OTHERS, A VARIED REPERTOIRE OF MUSIC

Achievement Standard:
Students

a. sing independently, on pitch and in rhythm, with appropriate timbre, diction, and posture, and maintain a steady tempo
b. sing *expressively, with appropriate dynamics, phrasing, and interpretation
c. sing from memory a varied repertoire of songs representing *genres and *styles from diverse cultures
d. sing ostinatos, partner songs, and rounds
e. sing in groups, blending vocal timbres, matching dynamic levels, and responding to the cues of a conductor

APPENDIX 4 | National Standards for Music Education **A33**

2. CONTENT STANDARD: PERFORMING ON INSTRUMENTS, ALONE AND WITH OTHERS, A VARIED REPERTOIRE OF MUSIC

Achievement Standard:
Students

a. perform on pitch, in rhythm, with appropriate dynamics and timbre, and maintain a steady tempo

b. perform easy rhythmic, melodic, and chordal patterns accurately and independently on rhythmic, melodic, and harmonic *classroom instruments

c. perform expressively a varied repertoire of music representing diverse genres and styles

d. echo short rhythms and melodic patterns

e. perform in groups, blending instrumental timbres, matching dynamic levels, and responding to the cues of a conductor

f. perform independent instrumental parts[1] while other students sing or play contrasting parts

3. CONTENT STANDARD: IMPROVISING MELODIES, VARIATIONS, AND ACCOMPANIMENTS

Achievement Standard:
Students

a. improvise "answers" in the same style to given rhythmic and melodic phrases

b. improvise simple rhythmic and melodic ostinato accompaniments

c. improvise simple rhythmic variations and simple melodic embellishments on familiar melodies

d. improvise short songs and instrumental pieces, using a variety of sound sources, including traditional sounds, nontraditional sounds available in the classroom, body sounds, and sounds produced by electronic means[2]

4. CONTENT STANDARD: COMPOSING AND ARRANGING MUSIC WITHIN SPECIFIED GUIDELINES

Achievement Standard:
Students

a. create and arrange music to accompany readings or dramatizations

b. create and arrange short songs and instrumental pieces within specified guidelines[3]

c. use a variety of sound sources when composing

5. CONTENT STANDARD: READING AND NOTATING MUSIC

Achievement Standard:
Students

a. read whole, half, dotted half, quarter, and eighth notes and rests in $\frac{2}{4}$, $\frac{3}{4}$, and $\frac{4}{4}$ meter signatures

b. use a system (that is, syllables, numbers, or letters) to read simple pitch notation in the treble clef in major keys

c. identify symbols and traditional terms referring to dynamics, tempo, and articulation and interpret them correctly when performing

d. use standard symbols to notate meter, rhythm, pitch, and dynamics in simple patterns presented by the teacher

6. CONTENT STANDARD: LISTENING TO, ANALYZING, AND DESCRIBING MUSIC

Achievement Standard:
Students

a. identify simple music *forms when presented aurally

b. demonstrate perceptual skills by moving, by answering questions about, and by describing aural examples of music of various styles representing diverse cultures

c. use appropriate terminology in explaining music, music notation, music instruments and voices, and music performances

d. identify the sounds of a variety of instruments, including many orchestra and band instruments, and instruments from various cultures, as well as children's voices and male and female adult voices

e. respond through purposeful movement[4] to selected prominent music characteristics[5] or to specific music events[6] while listening to music

7. CONTENT STANDARD: EVALUATING MUSIC AND MUSIC PERFORMANCES

Achievement Standard:
Students

a. devise criteria for evaluating performances and compositions

b. explain, using appropriate music terminology, their personal preferences for specific musical works and styles

APPENDIX 4 | National Standards for Music Education **A35**

8. CONTENT STANDARD: UNDERSTANDING RELATIONSHIPS BETWEEN MUSIC, THE OTHER ARTS, AND DISCIPLINES OUTSIDE THE ARTS

Achievement Standard:

Students

a. identify similarities and differences in the meanings of common terms[7] used in the various arts

b. identify ways in which the principles and subject matter of other disciplines taught in the school are interrelated with those of music[8]

9. CONTENT STANDARD: UNDERSTANDING MUSIC IN RELATION TO HISTORY AND CULTURE

Achievement Standard:

Students

a. identify by genre or style aural examples of music from various historical periods and cultures

b. describe in simple terms how *elements of music are used in music examples from various cultures of the world[9]

c. identify various uses of music in their daily experiences[10] and describe characteristics that make certain music suitable for each use

d. identify and describe roles of musicians[11] in various music settings and cultures

e. demonstrate audience behavior appropriate for the context and style of music performed

Notes:

1. E.g., simple rhythmic or melodic ostinatos, contrasting rhythmic lines, harmonic progressions and chords

2. E.g., traditional sounds: voices, instruments; nontraditional sounds: paper tearing, pencil tapping; body sounds: hands clapping, fingers snapping; sounds produced by electronic means: personal computers and basic *MIDI devices, including keyboards, sequencers, synthesizers, and drum machines

3. E.g., a particular style, form, instrumentation, compositional technique

4. E.g., swaying, skipping, dramatic play

5. E.g., meter, dynamics, tempo

6. E.g., meter changes, dynamic changes, same/different sections

7. E.g., form, line, contrast

8. E.g., foreign languages: singing songs in various languages; language arts: using the expressive elements of music in interpretive readings; mathematics: mathematical basis of values of notes, rests, and meter signatures; science:

vibration of strings, drum heads, or air columns generating sounds used in music; geography: songs associated with various countries or regions

9. E.g., Navajo, Arabic, Latin American

10. E.g., celebration of special occasions, background music for television, worship

11. E.g., orchestra conductor, folk singer, church organist

GRADES 5–8

The period represented by grades 5–8 is especially critical in students' musical development. The music they perform or study often becomes an integral part of their personal musical repertoire. Composing and improvising provide students with unique insight into the form and structure of music and at the same time help them to develop their creativity. Broad experience with a variety of music is necessary if students are to make informed musical judgments. Similarly, this breadth of background enables them to begin to understand the connections and relationships between music and other disciplines. By understanding the cultural and historical forces that shape social attitudes and behaviors, students are better prepared to live and work in communities that are increasingly multicultural. The role that music will play in students' lives depends in large measure on the level of skills they achieve in creating, performing, and listening to music.

Terms identified by an asterisk (*) are explained in the glossary. Except as noted, the standards in this section describe the cumulative skills and knowledge expected of all students upon exiting grade 8. Students in grades 5–7 should engage in developmentally appropriate learning experiences to prepare them to achieve these standards at grade 8. These standards presume that the students have achieved the standards specified for grades K–4; they assume that the students will demonstrate higher levels of the expected skills and knowledge, will deal with increasingly complex music, and will provide more sophisticated responses to works of music. Every course in music, including performance courses, should provide instruction in creating, performing, listening to, and analyzing music, in addition to focusing on its specific subject matter. Determining the curriculum and the specific instructional activities necessary to achieve the standards is the responsibility of states, local school districts, and individual teachers.

1. CONTENT STANDARD: SINGING, ALONE AND WITH OTHERS, A VARIED REPERTOIRE OF MUSIC

Achievement Standard:
Students

a. sing accurately and with good breath control throughout their singing ranges, alone and in small and large ensembles

b. sing with *expression and *technical accuracy a repertoire of vocal literature with a *level of difficulty of 2, on a scale of 1 to 6, including some songs performed from memory

APPENDIX 4 | National Standards for Music Education **A37**

   c.   sing music representing diverse *genres and cultures, with expression appropriate for the work being performed

   d.   sing music written in two and three parts

Students who participate in a choral ensemble

   e.   sing with expression and technical accuracy a varied repertoire of vocal literature with a level of difficulty of 3, on a scale of 1 to 6, including some songs performed from memory

2. CONTENT STANDARD: PERFORMING ON INSTRUMENTS, ALONE AND WITH OTHERS, A VARIED REPERTOIRE OF MUSIC

Achievement Standard:

Students

   a.   perform on at least one instrument[1] accurately and independently, alone and in small and large ensembles, with good posture, good playing position, and good breath, bow, or stick control

   b.   perform with expression and technical accuracy on at least one string, wind, percussion, or *classroom instrument a repertoire of instrumental literature with a level of difficulty of 2, on a scale of 1 to 6

   c.   perform music representing diverse genres and cultures, with expression appropriate for the work being performed

   d.   play by ear simple melodies on a melodic instrument and simple accompaniments on a harmonic instrument

Students who participate in an instrumental ensemble or class

   e.   perform with expression and technical accuracy a varied repertoire of instrumental literature with a level of difficulty of 3, on a scale of 1 to 6, including some solos performed from memory

3. CONTENT STANDARD: IMPROVISING MELODIES, VARIATIONS, AND ACCOMPANIMENTS

Achievement Standard:

Students

   a.   improvise simple harmonic accompaniments

   b.   improvise melodic embellishments and simple rhythmic and melodic variations on given pentatonic melodies and melodies in major keys

   c.   improvise short melodies, unaccompanied and over given rhythmic accompaniments, each in a consistent *style, meter, and tonality

4. CONTENT STANDARD: COMPOSING AND ARRANGING MUSIC WITHIN SPECIFIED GUIDELINES

Achievement Standard:
Students

    a.   compose short pieces within specified guidelines,[2] demonstrating how the elements of music are used to achieve unity and variety, tension and release, and balance

    b.   arrange simple pieces for voices or instruments other than those for which the pieces were written

    c.   use a variety of traditional and nontraditional sound sources and electronic media when composing and arranging

5. CONTENT STANDARD: READING AND NOTATING MUSIC

Achievement Standard:
Students

    a.   read whole, half, quarter, eighth, sixteenth, and dotted notes and rests in $\frac{2}{4}$, $\frac{3}{4}$, $\frac{4}{4}$, $\frac{6}{8}$, $\frac{3}{8}$, and alla breve meter signatures

    b.   read at sight simple melodies in both the treble and bass clefs

    c.   identify and define standard notation symbols for pitch, rhythm, dynamics, tempo, articulation, and expression

    d.   use standard notation to record their musical ideas and the musical ideas of others

Students who participate in a choral or instrumental ensemble or class

    e.   sight-read, accurately and expressively, music with a level of difficulty of 2, on a scale of 1 to 6

6. CONTENT STANDARD: LISTENING TO, ANALYZING, AND DESCRIBING MUSIC

Achievement Standard:
Students

    a.   describe specific music events[3] in a given aural example, using appropriate terminology

    b.   analyze the uses of *elements of music in aural examples representing diverse genres and cultures

    c.   demonstrate knowledge of the basic principles of meter, rhythm, tonality, intervals, chords, and harmonic progressions in their analyses of music

APPENDIX 4 | National Standards for Music Education **A39**

7. CONTENT STANDARD: EVALUATING MUSIC AND MUSIC PERFORMANCES

Achievement Standard:
Students

    a.   develop criteria for evaluating the quality and effectiveness of music performances and compositions and apply the criteria in their personal listening and performing

    b.   evaluate the quality and effectiveness of their own and others' performances, compositions, arrangements, and improvisations by applying specific criteria appropriate for the style of the music and offer constructive suggestions for improvement

8. CONTENT STANDARD: UNDERSTANDING RELATIONSHIPS BETWEEN MUSIC, THE OTHER ARTS, AND DISCIPLINES OUTSIDE THE ARTS

Achievement Standard:
Students

    a.   compare in two or more arts how the characteristic materials of each art[4] can be used to transform similar events, scenes, emotions, or ideas into works of art

    b.   describe ways in which the principles and subject matter of other disciplines taught in the school are interrelated with those of music[5]

9. CONTENT STANDARD: UNDERSTANDING MUSIC IN RELATION TO HISTORY AND CULTURE

Achievement Standard:
Students

    a.   describe distinguishing characteristics of representative music genres and styles from a variety of cultures[6]

    b.   classify by genre and style (and, if applicable, by historical period, composer, and title) a varied body of exemplary (that is, high-quality and characteristic) musical works and explain the characteristics that cause each work to be considered exemplary

    c.   compare, in several cultures of the world, functions music serves, roles of musicians,[7] and conditions under which music is typically performed

Notes:

    1.   E.g., band or orchestra instrument, keyboard instrument, fretted instrument, electronic instrument

    2.   E.g., a particular style, form, instrumentation, compositional technique

    3.   E.g., entry of oboe, change of meter, return of refrain

    4.   E.g., sound in music, visual stimuli in visual arts, movement in dance, human interrelationships in theatre

5. E.g., language arts: issues to be considered in setting texts to music; mathematics: frequency ratios of intervals; sciences: the human hearing process and hazards to hearing; social studies: historical and social events and movements chronicled in or influenced by musical works

6. E.g., jazz, mariachi, gamelan

7. E.g., lead guitarist in a rock band, composer of jingles for commercials, singer in Peking opera

GLOSSARY

classroom instruments: instruments typically used in the general music classroom, including, for example, recorder-type instruments, chorded zithers, mallet instruments, simple percussion instruments, fretted instruments, keyboard instruments, and electronic instruments.

elements of music: pitch, rhythm, harmony, dynamics, timbre, texture, *form.

expression, expressive, expressively: with appropriate dynamics, phrasing, *style, and interpretation and appropriate variations in dynamics and tempo.

form: the overall structural organization of a music composition (e.g., AB, ABA, call-and-response, rondo, theme and variations, sonata-allegro) and the interrelationships of music events within the overall structure.

genre: a type or category of music (e.g., sonata, opera, oratorio, art song, gospel, suite, jazz, madrigal, march, work song, lullaby, barbershop, Dixieland).

level of difficulty: For purposes of these standards, music is classified into six levels of difficulty:

- ▶ Level 1—Very easy. Easy keys, meters, and rhythms; limited ranges.
- ▶ Level 2—Easy. May include changes of tempo, key, and meter; modest ranges.
- ▶ Level 3—Moderately easy. Contains moderate technical demands, expanded ranges, and varied interpretive requirements.
- ▶ Level 4—Moderately difficult. Requires well-developed *technical skills, attention to phrasing and interpretation, and ability to perform various meters and rhythms in a variety of keys.
- ▶ Level 5—Difficult. Requires advanced technical and interpretive skills; contains key signatures with numerous sharps or flats, unusual meters, complex rhythms, subtle dynamic requirements.
- ▶ Level 6—Very difficult. Suitable for musically mature students of exceptional competence. (Adapted with permission from NYSSMA Manual, Edition XXIII, published by the New York State School Music Association, 1991.)

MIDI (Musical Instrument Digital Interface): standard specifications that enable electronic instruments such as the synthesizer, sampler, sequencer, and drum machine from any manufacturer to communicate with one another and with computers.

style: the distinctive or characteristic manner in which the *elements of music are treated. In practice, the term may be applied to, for example, composers (the style of Copland), periods (Baroque style), media (keyboard style), nations (French style), *form or type of composition (fugal style, contrapuntal style), or *genre (operatic style, bluegrass style).

technical accuracy, technical skills: the ability to perform with appropriate timbre, intonation, and diction and to play or sing the correct pitches and rhythms.

Bibliography

Allegri, Gregorio. (1638.) *Miserere mei, Deus.* Free scores in the Choral Public Domain Library (ChoralWiki).

An, Song A. and Mary M. Capraro. (2011). *Music-Math: Integrated Activities for Elementary and Middle School Students.* Self-published.

An, Song, Mary Margaret Capraro, and Daniel A. Tillman. (2013). Elementary teachers integrate music activities into regular mathematics lessons: Effects on students' mathematical abilities. *Journal for Learning through the Arts, 9*(1).

Ardley, Neil. (1991). *The Science Book of Sound.* New York, NY: Harcourt Children's Books.

Armstrong, Thomas. (2003). *The Multiple Intelligences of Reading and Writing: Making the Words Come Alive.* Alexandria, VA: Association for Supervision and Curriculum Development.

Barrett, Janet R., Claire W. McCoy, and Kari K. Veblen. (1997). *Sound Ways of Knowing: Music in the Interdisciplinary Curriculum.* New York, NY: Schirmer.

Barrett, Joshua. www.musicandhappiness.com

Barkley, Kathy D. and Lynn Walwer. (1992). Linking lyrics and literacy through song picture books. *Young Children, 47*(4), 76–85.

Blacking, John. (1967/1995). *Venda Children's Song.* Chicago, IL: University of Chicago Press.

Blacking, John. (1973). *How Musical Is Man?* Seattle, WA: University of Washington Press.

Buehler, Beverly Harding (Program Director). (1999). *Arts Impact Program.* Retrieved from http://www.arts-impact.org/about

Burnaford, Gail. (2007). *Arts Integration Frameworks, Research & Practice: A Literature Review.* Washington, DC: Arts Education Partnership.

Campbell, L., B. Campbell, and D. Dickinson. (1996). *Teaching and Learning through Multiple Intelligences.* Needham Heights, NH: Allyn & Bacon.

Campbell, Patricia Shehan. (2010). *Songs in Their Heads: Music and Its Meaning in Children's Lives* (2nd ed.). New York, NY: Oxford University Press.

Campbell, Patricia Shehan and Carol Scott-Kassner. (2013). *Music in Childhood* (4th ed.). Boston, MA: Schirmer/Cengage.

CantOvation Sing and See [computer software]. www.singandsee.com

Catterall, James. (2009). *Doing Well and Doing Good by Doing Art: The Effects of Education in the Visual and Performing Arts on the Achievements and Values of Young Adults.* Los Angeles, CA and London, UK: Imagination Group/I-Group Books.

Charlesworth, Rosalind. (2014). *Understanding Child Development* (9th ed.). Belmont, CA: Wadsworth/Cengage.

Chaucer, Geoffrey. (1996). *The Canterbury Tales.* Geraldine McCaughrean (Ed.). London, UK: Puffin Books.

Clift, Stephen, and Ian Morrison. (2011). Group singing fosters mental health and wellbeing: Findings from the East Kent "singing for health" network project. *Mental Health and Social Inclusion, 15*(2), 88–97.

Cogan, Elyse (Associate Director of Programs). (1996–2012). *Handbook for Designing a Learning Community* (part of *Parents as Arts Partners* website). New York, NY: The Center for Arts Education. Retrieved from http://www.cae-nyc.org/teaching_learning/paap

Crumb, George. (1974). *Vox Balaenae (Voice of the Whale)* [CD]. Los Angeles, CA: Sony Corporation.

Cslovjecsek, Markus. (2010). How children teach us to teach math: Impulses for creative sound in math's classrooms. In Lily Chen-Hafteck and Jennifer Chen (Eds.), Proceedings from *Educating the Creative Mind: An International Conference on Arts-Based Education.* Union, NJ.

Culture as Self-Expression. (2002). New York, NY: American Museum of Natural History. www.amnh.org/content/download/50204/763069/file/sc_u09_selfexp.pdf

Dissanayake, Ellen. (1992). *Homo Aestheticus: Where Art Comes From and Why.* New York, NY: Free Press.

Dissanayake, Ellen. (2000). *Art and Intimacy: How the Arts Began.* Seattle, WA: University of Washington Press.

Drake, Susan M. and Rebecca C. Burns. (2004). *Meeting Standards through Integrated Curriculum.* Alexandria, VA: Association for Supervision and Curriculum Development. Retrieved from http://www.ascd.org/publications/books/103011/chapters/What-Is-Integrated-Curriculum%C2%A2.aspx

Dunn, Kenneth and Rita Dunn. (1992a). *Teaching Elementary Students through Their Individual Learning Styles: Practical Approaches for Grades 3–6.* Boston, MA: Allyn & Bacon.

Eisner, Elliot W. (2004). *The Arts and the Creation of Mind.* New Haven, CT: Yale University Press.

Eppink, Joseph A. (2008, September 24). Engaged music learning through children's literature. *General Music Today, 22*(2), 19–23.

Ericsson, K. Anders, Ralf Krampe, and Clemens Tesch-Romer. (1993). The role of deliberate practice in the acquisition of expert performance. *Psychological Review, 100,* 363–406.

Flohr, J. (1985). Young children's improvisations: Emerging creative thought. *The Creative Child and Adult Quarterly, 10*(2), 79–83.

Gardner, Howard. (1983/2011). *Frames of Mind: A Theory of Multiple Intelligences.* New York, NY: Basic Books.

A41

A42 Bibliography

Gardner, Robert and LaBaff, Tom (Illus.). (2006). *Jazzy Science Projects with Sound and Music (Fantastic Physical Science Experiments)*. Berkeley Heights, NJ: Enslow Elementary.

Garland, Sherry and Tatsuro Kiuchi (Illus.). (1997). *The Lotus Seed*. Boston, MA: HMH Books for Young Readers.

Goldberg, Merryl. (2006). *Integrating the Arts: An Approach to Teaching and Learning in Multicultural and Multilingual Settings* (3rd ed.). Boston, MA: Allyn & Bacon.

Gopnik, Alison, Andrew N. Meltzoff, and Patricia K. Kuhl. (2003). *The Scientist in the Crib*. New York, NY: HarperCollins.

Grape, C., M. Sandgren, L. O. Hansson, M. Ericson, and T. Theorell. (2003). Does singing promote well-being? An empirical study of professional and amateur singers during a singing lesson. *Integrated Physiological Behavior Science, 38*(1), 65–74.

Graziano, Amy B., Matthew Peterson, and Gordon L. Shaw. (1999). Enhanced learning of proportional math through music training and spatial-temporal training. *Neurological Research, 21*, 139–152.

Hall, Clare. (2005). Gender and boys' singing in early childhood. *British Journal of Music Education. 22*(1), 5–20.

Hanna, Judith Lynne. (1987). *To Dance Is Human: A Theory of Nonverbal Communication*. Chicago, IL: University of Chicago Press.

Hansen, Dee, Elaine Bernstorf, and Gayle M. Stuber. (2007). *The Music and Literacy Connection*. New York, NY: Rowman & Littlefield Education/National Association for Music Education (NAfME).

Hein, G. and T. Singer. (2008). I feel how you feel but not always: The empathic brain and its modulation. *Current Opinion in Neurobiology, 18*(2), 153–158.

Holewa, Lisa, and Joan Rice. (2008). *What Kindergarten Teachers Know*. New York, NY: Perigee/Penguin Group.

Holst, Gustav. (2009). *The Planets* [London Symphony Orchestra, conducted by Simon Geoffrey]. [CD]. London, UK: Cobra Entertainment, LLC.

Hovhaness, Alan. (1989). *And God Created Great Whales* [Philharmonia Orchestra, conducted by David Amos]. [CD]. Seattle, WA: Crystal Records, Inc.

Jarjisian, C. and J. Kerchner. (1998). *Teaching Music Listening: Selected Principles*. (Unpublished document presented at the International Society for Music Education Conference in South Africa).

Jensen, Eric. (2001). *Arts with the Brain in Mind*. Alexandria, VA: Association for Supervision and Curriculum Development.

Kaa, Keri. (2001). Keynote address delivered at Taonga of the Asia Pacific Rim NZSME and ISME Regional Conference, Auckland, Aotearoa/New Zealand, July 2001.

Kassner, Kirk. (2002, Winter). To be or not to be . . . a reading teacher. *General Music Today, 15*(2), 19–26.

Kassner, Kirk. (2007). *Teaching Math Skills While Teaching Elementary General Music* (Unpublished manuscript available at kassnermusic@info.org/articles).

Katz, Susan A. and Judith A. Thomas. (2004). *The Word in Play* (2nd ed.). Baltimore, MD: Paul H. Brookes Publishing.

Keil, Charles. (2016). *Dance Daily. Dance Early. Dance Now.* http://musekids.org/dancedaily.html

Keil, Charles and Patricia Shehan Campbell. (2015). *Born to Groove*. http://www.borntogroove.com

Kim, Kyung Hee. (2011). The creativity crisis: The decrease in creative thinking scores on the torrance tests of creative thinking. *Creativity Research Journal, 23*(4), 285–295.

Kratus, J. (1985). The use of melodic and rhythmic motives in the original songs of children aged 5 to 13. *Contributions to Music Education, 12,* 1–8.

Kratus, J. (1991). Growing with improvisation. *Music Educators Journal, 78*(4), 35–40.

LaBar, Kevin S. and Roberto Cabeza. (2006). Cognitive neuroscience of emotional memory. *Nature Reviews Neuroscience, 7,* 54–64. http://www.nature.com/nrn/journal/v7/n1/full/nrn1825.html

Lamont, Alexandra M. (2001). Infants' preferences for familiar and unfamiliar music: a socio-cultural study. Paper read at Society for Music Perception and Cognition, August 9, 2001, at Kingston, Ont.

Lazear, D. (1991). *Seven Ways of Knowing*. Tucson, AZ: Zephyr.

Levitin, Daniel J. (2005). *This Is Your Brain on Music: The Science of a Human Obsession*. New York, NY: Penguin.

Levitin, Daniel J. (2008). *The World in Six Songs: How the Musical Brain Created Human Nature*. New York, NY: Penguin.

Luebke, L. (2010). *Elementary General Music Leadership: The Specialist in Communities of Practice* (Unpublished doctoral dissertation). University of Michigan, Ann Arbor, MI.

Mannes, E. (2012). *The Music Instinct: Science and Song* [DVD]. Arlington VA: National Public Broadcasting Company.

Marsh, Kathryn and Susan Young. (2016). Musical play. In G. McPherson (Ed.), *The Child as Musician: A Handbook of Musical Development* (2nd ed.) (pp. 289–310). Oxford, UK: Oxford University Press.

Maslow, Abraham H. (1998). *Toward a Psychology of Being* (3rd ed.). New York, NY: John Wiley & Sons.

McLuhan, Marshall, and Quentin Fiore. (1967). *The Medium Is the Massage: An Inventory of Effects*. London, UK: Penguin.

McPherson, Gary E. (2016). *The Child as Musician: A Handbook of Musical Development* (2nd ed.). New York, NY: Oxford University Press.

Medina, John J. (2008). *Brain Rules*. Seattle, WA: Pear Press.

Meece, Judith, and Denise H. Daniels. (2007). *Child and Adolescent Development for Educators*. New York, NY: McGraw-Hill.

Merriam, Alan P. (1964). *The Anthropology of Music*. Evanston, IL: Northwestern University Press.

Mooney, Carol Garhart. (2000). *Theories of Childhood: An Introduction to Dewey, Montessori, Erikson, Piaget, and Vygotsky*. St. Paul, MN: Redleaf Press.

Music Ace Software [computer software]. (1994). Nekoosa, WI: Harmonic Vision. www.harmonicvision.com

Music Educators National Conference. (1994). *National Standards for Arts Education*. Reston, VA: Rowman and Littlefield.

Nettl, Bruno. (2002). *Encounters in Ethnomusicology: A Memoir*. Warren, MI: Harmonie Park Press.

Newman, Fred. (2004). *Mouth Sounds: How to Whistle, Pop, Boing, and Honk for All Occasions . . . And Then Some*. New York, NY: Workman.

Parker, Steve. (2013). *The Science of Sound: Projects and Experiments with Music and Sound Waves (Tabletop Scientist)*. Mineola, NY: Dover Publications.

Patel, Aniruddh D., Andrew Meltzoff, and Patricia Kuhl. (2004). Cultural differences in rhythm perception: What is the influence of native language? In Scott Lipscomb, Richard Ashley, Robert Gjerdingen, and Peter Webster (Eds.), Proceedings from *The Eighth International Conference on Music Perception and Cognition* (pp. 111–112). Evanston, IL: Northwestern University Press.

Patterson, William. (2015). *Tropical Sweets: Classical Music Video Adventure* [DVD]. Available from www.tropicalsweets.com

Payne, Roger (Ed.). (1991). *Songs of the Humpback Whale* [CD]. Litchfield CT: Earth Music Productions, LLC.

Peretz, Isabelle, Lise Gagnon, Sylvie Hébert, and Joël Macoir. (2004). Singing in the brain: Insights from cognitive neuropsychology. *Music Perception, 21*(3), 383–390.

Phillips, Kenneth H. (1992). *Teaching Kids to Sing*. New York, NY: Oxford University Press.

Pound, Ezra. (1968). *Literary Essays of Ezra Pound*. New York, NY: New Directions Publishing Corporation.

Rasinski, Timothy V. (2003). *The Fluent Reader: Oral & Silent Reading Strategies for Building Fluency, Word Recognition, and Comprehension* (2nd. ed.). New York, NY: Scholastic.

Rasinski, Timothy V., Nancy Padak. (2004). *Effective Reading Strategies: Teaching Children who Find Reading Difficult* (3rd ed.). Columbus, OH: Pearson.

Scott-Kassner, Carol. (1992). Research on music in early childhood. In Richard Colwell (Ed.), *Handbook of Research on Music Teaching and Learning* (pp. 633–650). New York, NY: Schirmer Publishing Company.

Shaw, Gordon. (2000). *Keeping Mozart in Mind* (2nd ed.). San Diego, CA: Academic Press.

Small, Christopher. (1998). *Musicking*. Hanover, NH: Wesleyan University Press.

Standley, Jayne M. (2008). Does music instruction help children learn to read? Evidence of a meta-analysis. *Update: Applications of Research in Music Education, 27*, 17–32.

Steinberg, Laurence. (2016). *Adolescence* (10th ed.). New York: McGraw-Hill.

Subotnick, Morton. (1995). Making Music [computer software]. Irvington, NY: Voyager. Available from http://www.creatingmusic.com

Subotnick, Morton. (1999). Making More Music [computer software]. Irvington, NY: Voyager. Available from http://www.creatingmusic.com

Suzuki, Shinichi. (1969). *Nurtured by Love: A New Approach to Education*. Hicksville, NY: Exposition Press.

Tillman, J. and K. Swanick. (1989). Towards a model of development of children's musical activity. *Canadian Music Educator, 30*(2), 169–174.

Train: The Definitive Visual History. (2014). Washington, DC: DK Smithsonian Publishing.

Trehub, Sandra E. (2003). The development origins of musicality. *Nature Neuroscience, 6*(7), 669–673.

Trottier, Maxine and Annouchka Galouchko (Illus.). (2012). *The Walking Stick*. Markham, ON: Fitzhenry & Whiteside Ltd.

Weikert, Phyllis. (1999). *Teaching Folk Dance: Successful Steps*. Ypsilanti, MI: High/Scope Press.

Welch, Graham F. (2016). Singing and vocal development. In G. McPherson (Ed.), *The Child as Musician: A Handbook of Musical Development* (pp. 311–329). New York, NY: Oxford University Press.

Yopp, Hallie Kay and Ruth Helen Yopp. (1997). *Oopples and Boo-noo-noos: Songs and Activities for Phonemic Awareness*. New York, NY: Harcourt Brace.

Classroom Resources for Children

Books Based on Songs and Chants

Adams, Pam (Illus.). (1973). *There Was an Old Lady Who Swallowed a Fly*. Wiltshire, UK: Child's Play.

Adams, Pam (Illus.). (1975). *Old Macdonald Had a Farm*. Wiltshire, UK: Child's Play.

Aliki (Illus.). (1968). *Hush Little Baby: A Folk Lullaby*. New York, NY: Simon and Schuster.

Bates, Katherine Lee and Wayne Thiebaud (Illus.). (1994). *O Beautiful for Spacious Skies*. San Francisco, CA: Chronicle.

Berry, Holly (Illus.). (1997). *Old MacDonald Had a Farm*. New York, NY: North-South.

Brown, Rick (Illus.). (1994). *Who Built the Ark?* New York, NY: Viking.

Day, Alexandra. (2011). *Frank and Ernest Play Ball*. Seattle, WA: Laughing Elephant.

Dillon, Leo and Diane Dillon. (1998). *To Every Thing There Is a Season*. New York, NY: Blue Sky.

Duke, Kate (Illus.). (1988). *Tingalayo*. New York, NY: Crown Books.

Eagle, Kin and Rob Gilbert (Illus.). (1997). *It's Raining, It's Pouring*. Watertown, MA: Charlesbridge.

Emberley, Barbara and Ed Emberley (Illus.). (1966). *One Wide River to Cross*. Englewood Cliffs, NJ: Prentice-Hall.

Geddes, Anne. (2000). *10 in the Bed*. Riverside, NJ: Andrews McMeel.

Gold, Julie and Jane Ray (Illus.). (1999). *From a Distance*. New York, NY: Dutton.

Goodhart, Pippa and Stephen Lambert (Illus.). (1997). *Row, Row, Row Your Boat*. New York, NY: Knopf.

Greenwood, Lee. (1992). *God Bless the U.S.A. Gift Book*. Gretna, LA: Pelican Publishing.

Hague, Michael (Illus.). (1992). *Twinkle, Twinkle, Little Star*. New York, NY: Morrow Junior Books.

Halpern, Shari. (1995). *What Shall We Do When We All Go Out?* New York, NY: North-South.

Hoberman, Mary Ann and Nadie Bernard Westcott (Illus.). (2004). *Yankee Doodle*. Boston, MA: Little, Brown.

Hurd, Thacher. (1984). *Mama Don't Allow*. New York, NY: Harper Trophy.

Jeffers, Susan. (1974). *All the Pretty Horses*. New York, NY: Atheneum.

Johnson, James Weldon and Bryan Collier (Illus.). (2007). *Lift Every Voice and Sing*. New York, NY: HarperCollins.

Johnson, James Weldon and Jan Spivey Gilchrist (Illus.). (2002). *Lift Ev'ry Voice and Sing*. New York, NY: Scholastic.

Kemp, Moira (Illus.). (1987). *I'm a Little Teapot*. London, UK: Beehive Books.

Langstaff, John and Feodor Rojankovsky (Illus.). (1955). *Frog Went A-Courtin'*. New York, NY: Harcourt Brace.

Lester, Julius and Jerry Pinkney. (Illus.). (1994). *John Henry*. New York, NY: Dial Books.

Long, Sylvia. (1997). *Hush Little Baby*. San Francisco, CA: Chronicle.

Ormerod, Jan. (1996). *Ms. MacDonald Has a Class*. New York, NY: Clarion.

Raffi and David Allender (Illus.). (1987). *Shake My Sillies Out*. New York, NY: Crown Books.

Raschka, Chris. (1998). *Simple Gifts*. New York, NY: Henry Holt.

Ringgold, Faith. (1992). *Aunt Harriet's Underground Railroad in the Sky*. New York, NY: Crown Publishers.

Rosen, Michael and Arthur Robins (Illus.). (1990). *Little Rabbit Foo Foo*. New York, NY: Simon and Schuster.

Seeger, Pete and Michael Hays (Illus.). (1986). *Abiyoyo*. New York, NY: Simon and Schuster.

Sloat, Teri. (1998). *There Was An Old Lady Who Swallowed a Trout!* New York, NY: Henry Holt.

Spier, Peter. (1961). *The Fox Went Out on a Chilly Night*. New York, NY: Doubleday.

Spier, Peter (Illus.). (1973). *The Star-Spangled Banner*. New York, NY: Doubleday.

Staines, Bill and Margot Zemach (Illus.). (1989). *All God's Critters Got a Place in the Choir*. New York, NY: Penguin.

Taback, Simms. (1997). *There Was An Old Lady Who Swallowed A Fly*. New York, NY: Viking.

Taback, Simms. (1999). *Joseph Had a Little Overcoat*. New York, NY: Viking.

Trapani, Iza. (1993). *The Itsy Bitsy Spider*. Boston, MA: Whispering Coyote Press.

Westcott, Nadine Bernard (Illus.). (1990). *There's A Hole in the Bucket*. New York, NY: Scholastic.

Westcott, Nadine Bernard (Illus.). (1987). *Peanut Butter and Jelly: A Play Rhyme*. New York, NY: Puffin.

Whatley, Bruce (Illus.). (2000). *What Will You Wear, Jenny Jenkins?* New York, NY: HarperCollins.

Wickstrom, Sylvie K. (1988). *Wheels on the Bus*. New York, NY: Knopf.

Winter, Jeanette. (1992). *Follow the Drinking Gourd*. New York, NY: Knopf

A45

A46 Classroom Resources for Children

Wolff, Ashley (Illus.). (1990). *Baby Beluga*. New York, NY: Knopf.

Yarrow, Peter, Lenny Lipton, and Eric Puybaret (Illus.). (2007). *Puff, the Magic Dragon*. New York, NY: Sterling.

Zemach, Margot. (1975). *Hush Little Baby*. New York, NY: Dutton.

Books for Sound Play and Soundscapes

Brown, Margaret Wise and Leonard Weisgard (Illus.). (1950). *The Quiet Noisy Book*. New York, NY: Harper Trophy.

Carle, Eric. (1973). *I See A Song*. New York, NY: Crowell.

Carle, Eric. (1990). *The Very Quiet Cricket*. New York, NY: Philomel.

Enderle, Judith Ross and Stephanie Gordon Tessler. (1994). *Six Snowy Sheep*. New York, NY: Puffin.

Evans, Lezlie and Cynthia Jabar (Illus.). (1995). *Rain Song*. Boston, MA: Houghton Mifflin.

Fleming, Denise. (1997). *Barnyard Banter*. New York, NY: Henry Holt.

Fox, Mem and Terry Denton (Illus.). (1989). *Night Noises*. New York, NY: Harcourt Brace.

Heidbreder, Robert, and Bill Slavin and Esperança Melo. (Illus.). (2004). *Drumheller Dinosaur Dance*. Toronto, ON: Kids Can Press.

Lobel, Anita. (2007). *Nini Here and There*. New York, NY: Greenwillow Books.

Lowery, Linda and Pat Dypold. (1995). *Twist with a Burger, Jitter with a Bug*. Boston, MA: Houghton Mifflin.

Martin, Bill, Jr. and John Archambault. (1988). *Listen to the Rain*. New York, NY: Henry Holt.

Martin, Bill, Jr. and Vladimir Radunsky. (1970). *The Maestro Plays*. New York, NY: Henry Holt.

Pfister, Marcus. (1999). *The Rainbow Fish*. New York, NY: North-South.

Pinkney, Brian. (1994). *Max Found Two Sticks*. New York, NY: Simon and Schuster.

Rockwell, Anne. (1991). *Root-A-Toot-Toot*. New York, NY: Simon and Schuster.

Rosen, Michael and Adrien Reynolds (Illus.). (2007). *Bear's Day Out*. London, UK: Bloomsbury.

Scharer, Niko and Joanne Fitzgerald (Illus.). (1990). *Emily's House*. Toronto, ON: Groundwood Books.

Sendak, Maurice. (1963). *Where the Wild Things Are*. New York, NY: Harper & Row.

Seuss, Dr., and Steve Jonhson and Lou Fancher. (Illus.). (1996). *My Many Colored Days*. New York, NY: Knopf.

Shields, Carol Diggory and Scott Nash. (Illus.). (1997). *Saturday Night at the Dinosaur Stomp*. London, UK: Walker Books.

Siebert, Diane and Mike Wimmer (Illus.). (1993). *Train Song*. New York, NY: HarperCollins.

Strickland, Paul and Henrietta Strickland. (1994). *Dinosaur Roar!* New York, NY: Dutton.

Van Laan, Nancy and George Booth (Illus.). (1990). *Possum Come a-Knockin'*. New York, NY: Knopf.

Waddell, Martin and Jill Barton (Illus.). (1991). *The Happy Hedgehog Band*. Somerville, MA: Candlewick Press.

Williams, Linda and Lloyd, M. (1986). *The Little Old Lady Who Was Not Afraid of Anything*. New York, NY: HarperCollins.

Composer Biographies

Krull, Kathleen and Kathryn Hewitt (Illus.). (2013). *Lives of the Musicians: Good Times, Bad Times (and What the Neighbors Thought)*. Boston, MA: HMH Books for Young Readers.

Rachlin, Ann. (dates below). *Famous Children*. Hauppauge, NY: Barron's Educational Series.

> (1992) *Mozart*
>
> (1993) *Tchaikovsky*
>
> (1993) *Brahms*

Venezia, Mike. (dates below). *Getting to Know the World's Greatest Composers*. New York, NY: Children's Press.

> (1995) *Peter Tchaikovsky*
>
> (1995) *George Gershwin*
>
> (1995) *George Handel*

> (1995) *Aaron Copland*
>
> (1996) *Ludwig van Beethoven*
>
> (1996) *Wolfgang Amadeus Mozart*
>
> (1996) *Duke Ellington*
>
> (1997) *The Beatles*
>
> (1997) *Igor Stravinsky*
>
> (1998) *Johann Sebastian Bach*
>
> (1998) *Leonard Bernstein*
>
> (1999) *Johannes Brahms*
>
> (1999) *John Philip Sousa*
>
> (2000) *Frédéric Chopin*

Classroom Resources for Children **A47**

Books About Jazz

Dillon, Leo and Diane Dillon. (2007). *Jazz on a Saturday Night*. New York, NY: Blue Sky.

Ehrhardt, Karen and R. G. Roth (Illus.). (2006). *This Jazz Man*. New York, NY: Harcourt.

Gollub, Matthew and Karen Hanke (Illus.). (2000). *The Jazz Fly*. Santa Rosa, CA: Tortuga Press.

Gray, Libba Moore and Lisa Cohen (Illus.). (1996). *Little Lil and the Swing-Singing Sax*. New York, NY: Simon & Schuster.

Isadora, Rachel. (1979). *Ben's Trumpet*. New York, NY: Mulberry Books.

Igus, Toyomi and Michele Wood (Illus.) (1998). *I See the Rhythm*. New York, NY: Children's Book Press.

Karlins, Mark and Jack E. Davis (Illus.). (1998). *Music Over Manhattan*. New York, NY: Knopf.

London, Jonathan and Henry Cole (Illus.). (2000). *Who Bop?* New York, NY: HarperCollins.

Monceaux, Morgan. (1994). *Jazz: My Music, My People*. New York, NY: Knopf.

Orgill, Roxane and Sean Qualls (Illus.). (2010). *Skit-Scat Raggedy Cat: Ella Fitzgerald*. Somerville, MA: Candlewick.

Pinkney, Andrea Davis and Brian Pinkney (Illus.). (1998). *Duke Ellington: The Piano Prince and His Orchestra*. New York, NY: Hyperion.

Pinkney, Andrea Davis and Brian Pinkney (Illus.). (2002). *Ella Fitzgerald: The Tale of a Vocal Virtuosa*. New York, NY: Hyperion.

Raschka, Chris. (1992). *Charlie Parker Played Be Bop*. London, UK: Orchard Books.

Schroeder, Alan and Floyd Cooper (Illus.). (1996). *Satchmo's Blues*. New York, NY: Doubleday.

Schroeder, Alan and Bernie Fuchs (Illus.). (1995). *Carolina Shout!* New York, NY: Dial Books.

Shange, Ntozake and Romare Bearden (Illus.). (1994). *i live in music*. New York, NY: Welcome Books.

Weatherford, Carol Boston and Sean Qualls (Illus.). (2008). *Before John Was a Jazz Giant: A Song of John Coltrane*. New York, NY: Henry Holt.

Winter, Jonah and Sean Qualls (Illus.). (2006). *Dizzy*. New York, NY: Scholastic.

Weinstein, Muriel Harris and Gregory Christie (Illus.). (2008). *When Louis Armstrong Taught Me Scat*. San Francisco, CA: Chronicle.

Books About Opera

Rosenberg, Jane. (1989). *Sing Me A Story: The Metropolitan Opera's Book of Opera Stories for Children*. New York, NY: Thames & Hudson.

Menotti, Gian Carlo and Michele Lemieux (Illus.). (1986). *Amahl and the Night Visitors*. New York, NY: HarperCollins.

HarperCollins. [Music by Gian Carlo Menotti. Also available on DVD.]

Lesser, Rika and Paul O. Zelinsky (Illus.). (1999). *Hansel and Gretel*. New York, NY: Penguin Group. [Music by Engelbert Humperdink.]

Classical Music Websites

http://kidsmusiccorner.co.uk

End Notes

Chapter 1

1   Levitin, Daniel J. (2005). *This Is Your Brain on Music: The Science of a Human Obsession*. New York, NY: Penguin, 260.

2   Small, Christopher. (1998). *Musicking*. Hanover, NH: Wesleyan University Press.

3   Marsh, Kathryn and Susan Young. (2016). Musical play. In G. McPherson (Ed.), *The Child as Musician: A Handbook of Musical Development* (2nd ed.). (pp. 289–310). Oxford, UK: Oxford University Press.

4   Merriam, Alan P. (1964). *The Anthropology of Music*. Evanston, IL: Northwestern University Press.

5   Keil, Charles and Patricia Shehan Campbell. (2016). *Born to Groove*. Retrieved from http://www.borntogroove.com

6   Trehub, Sandra E. (2003). The development origins of musicality. *Nature Neuroscience, 6*(7), 669–673.

7   Lamont, Alexandra M. (2001). Infants' preferences for familiar and unfamiliar music: A socio-cultural study. Paper read at Society for Music Perception and Cognition, August 9, 2001, at Kingston, OT.

8   Dissanayake, Ellen. (1992). *Homo Aestheticus: Where Art Comes From and Why*. New York, NY: Free Press.

9   Patel, Aniruddh D., Andrew Meltzoff, and Patricia Kuhl. (2004). Cultural differences in rhythm perception: What is the influence of native language? In Scott Lipscomb, Richard Ashley, Robert Gjerdingen, and Peter Webster (Eds.), *Proceedings of the 8th International Conference on Music Perception and Cognition*. (pp. 111–112). Evanston, IL: Northwestern University Press.

10 Shaw, Gordon. (2000). *Keeping Mozart in Mind* (2nd ed.). San Diego, CA: Academic Press.

11 Graziano, Amy B., Matthew Peterson, and Gordon L. Shaw. (1999). Enhanced learning of proportional math through music training and spatial-temporal training. *Neurological Research, 21*, 139–152.

12 Ericsson, K. Anders, Ralf Krampe, and Clemens Tesch-Romer. (1993). The role of deliberate practice in the acquisition of expert performance. *Psychological Review, 100*, 363–406.

13 Hein, G. and T. Singer. (2008). I feel how you feel but not always: The empathic brain and its modulation. *Current Opinion in Neurobiology, 18*(2), 153–158.

14 Jensen, Eric. (2001). *Arts with the Brain in Mind*. Alexandria, VA: Association for Supervision and Curriculum Development.

15 Levitin, Daniel J. (2005). *This Is Your Brain on Music: The Science of a Human Obsession*. New York, NY: Penguin.

16 Gopnik, Alison, Andrew N. Meltzoff, and Patricia K. Kuhl. (2003). *The Scientist in the Crib*. New York, NY: HarperCollins.

17 Levitin, Daniel J. (2008). *The World in Six Songs: How the Musical Brain Created Human Nature*. New York, NY: Penguin.

18 LaBar, Kevin S. and Roberto Cabeza. (2006). Cognitive neuroscience of emotional memory. *Nature Reviews Neuroscience, 7*, 54–64. http://www.nature.com/nrn/journal/v7/n1/full/nrn1825.html

19 Medina, John J. (2014). *Brain Rules*. Seattle, WA: Pear Press.

20 Tomatis, Alfred. (1991). *Pourquoi Mozart? Essai*. Paris, France: Fixot.

21 Gardner, Howard. (1983/2011). *Frames of Mind: A Theory of Multiple Intelligences*. New York, NY: Basic Books.

Chapter 2

1   Drake, Susan M. and Rebecca C. Burns. (2004). *Meeting Standards through Integrated Curriculum*. Alexandria, VA: Association for Supervision and Curriculum Development. Retrieved from http://www.ascd.org/publications/books/103011/chapters/What-Is-Integrated-Curriculum%C2%A2.aspx

2   Polisini, Judith Case and Carol Scott-Kassner, Eds. (1996). *Interconnecting Pathways to Human Experience: Teaching the Arts Across Disciplines*. Tallahassee, FL: Arts for a Complete Education/Florida Alliance for Arts Education.

3   Campbell, L., B. Campbell, and D. Dickinson. (1996). *Teaching and Learning through Multiple Intelligences*. Needham Heights, MA: Allyn & Bacon.

4   Lazear, D. (1991). *Seven Ways of Knowing*. Tucson, AZ: Zephyr.

5   Buehler, Beverly Harding (Program Director). (1999). *Arts Impact Program*. Retrieved from http://www.arts-impact.org/about/

6   Luebke, L. (2010). *Elementary General Music Leadership: The Specialist in Communities of Practice* (Unpublished doctoral dissertation). University of Michigan, Ann Arbor, MI.

7   Catterall, James. (2009). *Doing Well and Doing Good by Doing Art: The Effects of Education in the Visual and Performing Arts on the Achievements and Values of Young Adults*. Los Angeles, CA and London, UK: Imagination Group/I-Group Books.

A50 End Notes

Chapter 3

1 McPherson, Gary E. (2016). *The Child as Musician: A Handbook of Musical Development* (2nd ed.). New York, NY: Oxford University Press, vi.

2 Meece, Judith, and Denise H. Daniels. (2007). *Child and Adolescent Development for Educators*. New York, NY: McGraw-Hill.

3 Holewa, Lisa, and Joan Rice. (2008). *What Kindergarten Teachers Know*. New York, NY: Perigee/Penguin Group.

4 Charlesworth, Rosalind. (2014). *Understanding Child Development* (9th ed.). Belmont, CA: Wadsworth/Cengage.

5 Steinberg, Laurence. (2016). *Adolescence* (10th ed.). New York: McGraw-Hill.

6 Mooney, Carol Garhart. (2000). *Theories of Childhood: An Introduction to Dewey, Montessori, Erikson, Piaget, and Vygotsky*. St. Paul, MN: Redleaf Press.

7 Campbell, Patricia Shehan and Carol Scott-Kassner. (2013). *Music in Childhood* (4th ed.). Boston, MA: Schirmer/Cengage.

Chapter 4

1 Kaa, Keri. (2001). Keynote address delivered at Taonga of the Asia Pacific Rim NZSME and ISME Regional Conference, Auckland, Aotearoa/New Zealand, July 2001.

2 Music Educators National Conference. (1994). *National Standards for Arts Education*. Reston, VA: Rowman and Littlefield.

3 Peretz, Isabelle, Lise Gagnon, Sylvie Hébert, and Joël Macoir. (2004). Singing in the brain: Insights from cognitive neuropsychology. *Music Perception, 21*(3), 383–390.

4 Grape, C., M. Sandgren, L. O. Hansson, M. Ericson, and T. Theorell. (2003). Does singing promote well-being? An empirical study of professional and amateur singers during a singing lesson. *Integrated Physiological Behavior Science, 38*(1), 65–74.

5 Welch, Graham F. (2016). Singing and vocal development. In G. McPherson (Ed.), *The Child as Musician: A Handbook of Musical Development* (pp. 311–329). New York, NY: Oxford University Press.

6 Clift, Stephen, and Ian Morrison. (2011). Group singing fosters mental health and wellbeing: Findings from the East Kent "singing for health" network project. *Mental Health and Social Inclusion, 15*(2), 88–97.

7 Phillips, Kenneth H. (1992). *Teaching Kids to Sing*. New York, NY: Oxford University Press.

8 Hall, Clare. (2005). Gender and boys' singing in early childhood. *British Journal of Music Education, 22*(1), 5–20.

9 Campbell, Patricia Shehan. (2010). *Songs in Their Heads: Music and Its Meaning in Children's Lives* (2nd ed.). New York, NY: Oxford University Press.

Chapter 5

1 Campbell, Patricia Shehan. (2004). *Teaching Music Globally*. New York, NY: Oxford University Press.

2 Scott-Kassner, Carol. (1992). Research on music in early childhood. In Richard Colwell (Ed.), *Handbook of Research on Music Teaching and Learning* (pp. 633–650). New York, NY: Schirmer Publishing Company.

3 Dunning, Brian. (2013, July 9). *The Science of Muzak* [audio podcast]. Retrieved from www.skeptoid.com/episodes/4370

4 Jarjisian, C. and J. Kerchner. (1998). *Teaching Music Listening: Selected Principles*. (Unpublished document presented at the International Society for Music Education Conference in South Africa).

5 Mannes, E. (2012). *The Music Instinct: Science and Song* [DVD]. Arlington VA: National Public Broadcasting Company.

6 Standley, Jayne M. (2008). Does music instruction help children learn to read? Evidence of a meta-analysis. *Update: Applications of Research in Music Education, 27,* 17–32.

7 Dunn, Kenneth and Rita Dunn. (1992a). *Teaching Elementary Students through Their Individual Learning Styles: Practical Approaches for Grades 3–6*. Boston, MA: Allyn & Bacon.

Chapter 6

1 Keil, Charles. (2016). *Dance Daily. Dance Early. Dance Now*. Retrieved from http://musekids.org/dancedaily.html/

2 Hanna, Judith Lynne. (1987). *To Dance Is Human: A Theory of Nonverbal Communication*. Chicago, IL: University of Chicago Press.

3 Campbell, Patricia Shehan. (2010). *Songs in Their Heads: Music and Its Meaning in Children's Lives* (2nd ed.). New York, NY: Oxford University Press.

4 Weikert, Phyllis. (1999). *Teaching Folk Dance: Successful Steps*. Ypsilanti, MI: High Scope Press.

Chapter 7

1 Newman, Fred. (2004). *Mouth Sounds: How to Whistle, Pop, Boing, and Honk for All Occasions . . . And Then Some*. New York, NY: Workman.

Chapter 8

1 Kim, Kyung Hee. (2011). The creativity crisis: The decrease in creative thinking scores on the torrance tests of creative thinking. *Creativity Research Journal, 23*(4), 285–295. https://www.nesacenter.org/uploaded/conferences/SEC/2013/handouts/Kim_Creativity-Crisis_CRJ2011.pdf

2 Campbell, Patricia Shehan. (2010). *Songs in Their Heads: Music and Its Meaning in Children's Lives* (2nd ed.). New York: NY: Oxford University Press.

3 Levitin, Daniel J. (2008). *The World in Six Songs: How the Musical Brain Created Human Nature.* New York, NY: Dutton.

4 Katz, Susan A. and Judith A. Thomas. (2004). *The Word in Play* (2nd ed.). Baltimore, MD: Paul H. Brookes Publishing.

Chapter 9

1 Keil, Charles and Patricia Shehan Campbell. (2016). *Born to Groove* [website]. www.borntogroove.org/

Chapter 10

1 Armstrong, Thomas. (2003). *The Multiple Intelligences of Reading and Writing: Making the Words Come Alive.* Alexandria, VA: Association for Supervision and Curriculum Development.

2 Pound, Ezra. (1968). *Literary Essays of Ezra Pound.* New York, NY: New Directions Publishing Corporation.

3 Kassner, Kirk. (2002, Winter). To be or not to be . . . a reading teacher. *General Music Today, 15*(2), 19–26.

4 Hansen, Dee, Elaine Bernstorf, and Gayle M. Stuber. (2007). *The Music and Literacy Connection.* New York, NY: Rowman & Littlefield Education/National Association for Music Education (NAfME).

5 Eppink, Joseph A. (2008, September 24). Engaged music learning through children's literature. *General Music Today, 22*(2), 19–23.

6 Barkley, Kathy D. and Lynn Walwer. (1992). Linking lyrics and literacy through song picture books. *Young Children, 47*(4), 76–85.

7 Standley, Jayne M. (2008). Does music instruction help children learn to read? Evidence of a meta-analysis. *Update: Applications of Research in Music Education, 27*, 17–32.

8 Yopp, Hallie Kay and Ruth Helen Yopp. (1997). *Oopples and Boo-noo-noos: Songs and Activities for Phonemic Awareness.* New York, NY: Harcourt Brace.

9 Hansen, Dee, Elaine Bernstorf, and Gayle M. Stuber. (2007). *The Music and Literacy Connection.* New York, NY: Rowman & Littlefield Education/National Association for Music Education (NAfME).

10 Rasinski, Timothy V. (2003). *The Fluent Reader: Oral & Silent Reading Strategies for Building Fluency, Word Recognition, and Comprehension* (2nd. ed.). New York, NY: Scholastic.

Chapter 11

1 Nettl, Bruno. (2002). *Encounters in Ethnomusicology: A Memoir.* Warren, MI: Harmonie Park Press.

2 *Culture as Self-Expression.* (2002). New York, NY: American Museum of Natural History. www.amnh.org/content/download/50204/763069/file/sc_u09_selfexp.pdf

3 Chaucer, Geoffrey. (1996). *The Canterbury Tales.* Geraldine McCaughrean (Ed.). London, UK: Puffin Books.

4 *Train: The Definitive Visual History.* (2014). Washington, DC: DK Smithsonian Publishing.

5 Garland, Sherry and Tatsuro Kiuchi (Illus.). (1997). *The Lotus Seed.* Boston, MA: HMH Books for Young Readers.

6 Trottier, Maxine and Annouchka Galouchko (Illus.). (2012). *The Walking Stick.* Markham, ON: Fitzhenry & Whiteside Ltd.

Chapter 12

1 Subotnick, Morton. (1995). Making Music [computer software]. Irvington, NY: Voyager. Available from http://www.creatingmusic.com/

2 Subotnick, Morton. (1999). Making More Music [computer software]. Irvington, NY: Voyager. Available from http://www.creatingmusic.com/

Chapter 13

1 CantOvation Sing and See [computer software]. www.singandsee.com/

2 Payne, Roger (Ed.). (1991). *Songs of the Humpback Whale* [CD]. Litchfield CT: Earth Music Productions, LLC.

3 Hovhaness, Alan. (1989). *And God Created Great Whales* [conducted by David Amos]. [CD]. Camas, WA: Crystal Records, Inc.

4 Crumb, George. (1974). *Vox Balaenae (Voice of the Whale)* [CD]. Los Angeles, CA: Sony Corporation.

5 Holst, Gustav. (2009). *The Planets* [conducted by Simon, Geoffrey, London Symphony Orchestra]. [CD]. London, UK: Cobra Entertainment, LLC.

Chapter 14

1 Maslow, Abraham H. (1998). *Toward a Psychology of Being* (3rd ed.). New York, NY: John Wiley & Sons.

2 Dissanayake, Ellen. (2000). *Art and Intimacy: How the Arts Began.* Seattle, WA: University of Washington Press.

3 McLuhan, Marshall, and Quentin Fiore. (1967). *The Medium Is the Massage: An Inventory of Effects*. London, UK: Penguin.

4 Eisner, Elliot W. (2004). *The Arts and the Creation of Mind*. New Haven, CT: Yale University Press.

5 Goldberg, Merryl. (2006). *Integrating the Arts: An Approach to Teaching and Learning in Multicultural and Multilingual Settings* (3rd ed.). Boston, MA: Allyn & Bacon.

6 Music Educators National Conference. (1994). *National Standards for Arts Education*. (1994). Reston, VA: Rowman and Littlefield.

7 Barrett, Janet R., Claire W. McCoy, and Kari K. Veblen. (1997). *Sound Ways of Knowing: Music in the Interdisciplinary Curriculum*. New York, NY: Schirmer

8 Patterson, William. (2015). *Tropical Sweets: Classical Music Video Adventure* [DVD]. Available from www.tropicalsweets.com

Appendix 1

1 Rothenberg, David. (2002). *Sudden Music: Improvisation, Sound, Nature*. Athens, GA: University of Georgia Press.

2 Music Ace [computer software]. (1994). Nekoosa, WI: Harmonic Vision. www.harmonicvision.com

Appendix 2

1 Jaques-Dalcroze, Émile. (1921). *Rhythm, Music and Education*. (Harold F. Rubinstein, Trans.). New York, NY: Putnam/Knickerbocker Press.

Credits

Photos

Page 2: David Grossman/Alamy Stock Photo; **p. 4**: Billie Judy/Reel Life Productions; **p. 7**: Billie Judy/Reel Life Productions; **p. 12**: Amble Design/Shutterstock; **p. 16**: Billie Judy/Reel Life Productions; **p. 20**: Rawpixel.com/Shutterstock; **p. 24**: Billie Judy/Reel Life Productions; **p. 25**: kali9/Getty Images; **p. 30**: © Susan Snyder; **p. 37**: Billie Judy/Reel Life Productions; **p. 40**: Billie Judy/Reel Life Productions; **p. 42**: Billie Judy/Reel Life Productions; **p. 51**: Jeff Morgan 08/Alamy Stock Photo; **p. 54**: Fh Photo/Shutterstock; **p. 56**: Billie Judy/Reel Life Productions; **p. 58**: Billie Judy/Reel Life Productions; **p. 60**: Designua/Shutterstock; **p. 61**: GEORGES GOBET/AFP/Getty Images; **p. 62**: © Giacomo Pirozzi/Panos Pictures; **p. 65 (top)**: © Elizabeth Crews/The Image Works; **p. 65 (bottom)**: John Prieto/The Denver Post via Getty Images; **p. 74**: Jose Luis Pelaez Inc./agefotostock; **p. 81**: Courtesy of the Cincinnati Symphony Orchestra, photo by Mark Lyons; **p. 82**: Courtesy of Amanda Brotman; **p. 88 (top)**: Courtesy of the Indiana University Jacobs School of Music; **p. 88 (bottom)**: Granger, NYC, all rights reserved; **p. 89**: Keystone/Getty Images; **p. 92**: FatCamera/Getty Images; **p. 95**: Courtesy of Peyton Dirkes; **p. 96**: Courtesy of Aubree Elynck; **p. 103**: Billie Judy/Reel Life Productions; **p. 106**: Henryk T. Kaiser/agefotostock; **p. 107**: Gabe Palmer/Alamy Stock Photo; **p. 109**: Billie Judy/Reel Life Productions; **p. 113**: Billie Judy/Reel Life Productions; **p. 114**: Sergey Novikov/Shutterstock; **p. 119**: JGI/Jamie Grill/agefotostock; **p. 124**: Fh Photo/Shutterstock; **p. 125**: Janet Allison/W. W. Norton; **p. 126 (top)**: Janet Allison/W. W. Norton; **p. 126 (bottom)**: Billie Judy/Reel Life Productions; **p. 127 (top)**: Janet Allison/W. W. Norton; **p. 127 (bottom)**: Gallo Images/Alamy Stock Photo; **p. 128 (top)**: Janet Allison/W. W. Norton; **p. 128 (bottom)**: George Doyle/Getty Images; **p. 129 (top)**: Janet Allison/W. W. Norton; **p. 129 (bottom)**: Billie Judy/Reel Life Productions; **p. 130 (top)**: Janet Allison/W. W. Norton; **p. 130 (bottom)**: Janet Allison/W. W. Norton; **p. 131**: Lebrecht Music and Arts Photo Library/Alamy Stock Photo; **p. 136**: Corbis/agefotostock; **p. 139**: Ghislain & Marie David de Lossy/Getty Images; **p. 146**: © Jerry Gay; **p. 148**: Billie Judy/Reel Life Productions; **p. 149**: Corbis/VCG/Getty Images; **p. 157**: Sketch of a gate in Kiev, one of the "Pictures at an Exhibition" (colour litho), Gartman (Hartmann), Viktor Aleksandrovich (1834–73)/Private collection/Sputnik/Bridgeman Images; **p. 160**: FatCamera/Getty Images; **p. 162**: Billie Judy/Reel Life Productions; **p. 165**: Billie Judy/Reel Life Productions; **p. 169**: kajakiki/Getty Images; **p. 170**: Yooniq Images/Alamy Stock Photo; **p. 173**: Pamela Au/Shutterstock; **p. 176**: Judy Bellah/Alamy Stock Photo; **p. 180**: Andrew F. Kazmierski/Shutterstock; **p. 183**: Blend Images/Alamy Stock Photo; **p. 196**: Janet Allison/W. W. Norton; **p. 201**: ZUMA Press Inc./Alamy Stock Photo; **p. 202**: Photo by Carol Scott-Kassner; **p. 210**: Universal Images Group North America LLC/DeAgostini/Alamy Stock Photo; **p. 212**: Kim Hong-Ji/AFP/Getty Images; **p. 213**: Richard Levine/Alamy Stock Photo; **p. 214 (top)**: Kobby Dogan/Shutterstock; **p. 214 (bottom)**: bpk Bildagentur/Antikensammlung, Staatliche Museen, Berlin, Germany/Art Resource, NY; **p. 215**: Foto Marburg/Art Resource, NY; **p. 217**: Chris Stock/Lebrecht Music & Arts; **p. 219**: A Hardman Peck & Co. player piano, 1907 (silver gelatin print), Byron Company (fl. 1890–1942)/Museum of the City of New York, USA/Bridgeman Images; **p. 220**: Granger, NYC, all rights reserved; **p. 221**: Zoltan Kiraly/Shutterstock; **p. 240**: Sally and Richard Greenhill/Alamy Stock Photo; **p. 242**: Photo by Margaret Portelance; **p. 250**: Melanie Stetson Freeman/The Christian Science Monitor via Getty Images; **p. 261**: wonderlandstock/Alamy Stock Photo; **p. 263**: Romas Photo/Shutterstock; **p. 265**: © Kathy Zagorski; **p. 271**: Konrad Mostert/Shutterstock; **p. 273**: Mark Garlick/Science Source; **p. 276**: Billie Judy/Reel Life Productions; **p. 281**: Billie Judy/Reel Life Productions; **p. 283**: Billie Judy/Reel Life Productions; **p. 286**: IMAGESOURCE/agefotostock; **p. A1**: DAJ/Getty Images; **p. A3**: Antonio da Monza (Italian, active about 1480–1505), decorated initial U, late 15th or early 16th century, Tempera colors, gold leaf, and ink on parchment bound between original wood boards covered with brown leather leaf: 64.1 x 43.5 cm (25 1/4 x 17 1/8 in.), The J. Paul Getty Museum, Los Angeles.

Music and Text

Page 14: From *National Standards for Arts Education.* Copyright © 1994 by MENC: The National Association for Music Education. Used with permission; **Example 8.7**: "Invented notation using abstract symbols," from Rena Upitis, *This Too Is Music* (Portsmouth, NH: Heinemann, 1990), p. 66. Reprinted with permission from the author; **Ex. 8.8**: "Invented notation using letter names of pitches," from Rena Upitis, *This Too is Music* (Portsmouth, NH: Heinemann, 1990), p. 66. Reprinted with permission from the author; **p. 156 (poem)**: "White," from Susan A. Katz and Judith A. Thomas, *The Word in Play* 2nd Ed. (Baltimore, MD: P.H. Brookes Publishing, 2004), p. 17. Reprinted by permission of the authors; **p. 186**: From *National Standards for Arts Education.* Copyright © 1994 by MENC: The National Association for Music Education. Used with permission. "Standards for the English Language Arts," by the International Reading Association and the National Council

A53

of Teachers of English. Copyright © 1996 by the International Reading Association and the National Council of Teachers of English. Reprinted with permission; **Box 10.4**: "Comparative Skills for Reading Text, Music Symbols, and Musical Text," from Dee Hansen, Elaine Bernstorf and Gayle M. Stuber, *The Music and Literary Connection* 2nd Ed. (Lanham, MD: Rowman & Littlefield, 2014). Copyright © 2014 by Dee Hansen, Elain Bernstorf and Gayle M. Stuber. Reprinted by permission of Rowman & Littlefield; **Lesson Plan 11.1**: "Oh Freedom." Arrangement copyright © 2017 by Kirk Kassner. Used by permission. "Follow the Drinking Gourd." Arrangement copyright © 2017 by Kirk Kassner. Used by permission; **Lesson Plan 11.3**: "Sansa Kroma." Arrangement copyright © 2017 by Kirk Kassner. Used by permission. **Lesson Plan 11.5**: "Jo Ashila" from *Roots & Branches* by Patricia Shehan Campbell, Ellen McCullough-Brabson, and Judith Cook Tucker. © 1994 World Music Press/© 2009 Assigned to Plank Road Publishing, Inc. All Rights Reserved.

Used by permission. www.musick8.com; **Lesson Plan 11.6**: "Qua Cau Gio Bay," from *Roots & Branches* by Patricia Shehan Campbell, Ellen McCullough-Brabson, and Judith Cook Tucker. © 1994 World Music Press/© 2009 Assigned to Plank Road Publishing, Inc. All Rights Reserved. Used by permission. www.musick8.com; **Ex. 12.2**: "Five Little Frogs," written by Louise Scott and Lucille Wood. © 1975 EMI Mills Music, Inc. Reprinted by permission of Sony/ATV Music Publishing. **Figure 14.5**: Figure 7.4 from J.R. Barrett, C.W. McCoy, and K.K. Veblen, *Sound Ways of Knowing: Music in the Interdisciplinary Curriculum* (New York: Schirmer Books, 1997), p. 131. Used with permission of the authors; **Fig. 14.6**: Figure 7.5 from J.R. Barrett, C.W. McCoy, and K.K. Veblen, *Sound Ways of Knowing: Music in the Interdisciplinary Curriculum* (New York: Schirmer Books, 1997), p. 131. Used with permission of the authors. **Appendix 4**: From *National Standards for Arts Education*. Copyright © 1994 by MENC: The National Association for Music Education. Used with permission.

Index

Note: Page numbers in *italics* refer to musical examples; page numbers include a *t* indicate a table.

"Abbots Bromley Horn Dance," 216
"Abiyoyo," *194*
Abiyoyo (Seeger), 184, 187, 193, 194
accidentals, A5, *A6*
action songs, 20, 107, 108, 113
ADHD
   adapting instrumental instruction for, 131
   adapting listening for, 80
adolescence
   child development in, 40
   kinesthetic development in, 46, 47*t*
   vocal development in, 45, 62, 64
adults, singing of, 61–62
African American music, 88–90, 144, 175, 176, 177, 221–25
   resources for listening, A24
African drumming patterns, performing, 246–47, *247*
African music, 229–32
agogô bells, 129, *129,* 231, 246–48
"Ala De'lona," 65, 114–15, 212
"A la rueda de San Miguel," 65, 200, 233, *233*
algebra, music and, 258–59
"All Around the Kitchen," 65
allegro, A9
"Alphabet Song, The," 185
alto metallophone, *130,* 222
alto xylophone, *130*
Amahl and the Night Visitors (Menotti), 82
"America (My Country, 'Tis of Thee)," 66, 165, 168
American history, music in, 217–21
   age of discovery, 217–18
   revolutionary period, 218–19
American Sign Language (ASL), 89, 116–17, 173, 200, 202, *202*
"America the Beautiful," 66, 165
amplitude of sound waves, 263
anacrusis, A9
Anastasio, Trey, 89
andante, A9
And God Created Great Whales (Hovhaness), 271
antiphonal choral reading, 205
"Apples and Bananas," 198, *198*
Archambault, John, *Listen to the Rain* (with Martin), 123
arco, A10
"Arirang," 66, 212
Armstrong, Louis, *88,* 88–89
Armstrong, Thomas, *The Multiple Intelligences of Reading and writing,* 183
arranging music, 150. *See also* composing and arranging in National Standards for Music Education
artists' residencies in schools, 28–31, 94
arts community as classroom resources, 31, 93–94, 155
arts connections in National Standards for Music Education, 14
   celebrating holidays and seasons to meet, 169
   creating to meet, 147
   listening to meet, 98
   playing instruments to meet, 122
   reading to meet, 188
   singing songs to meet, 59
   standard for grades 6–8, A36

   standard for grades K–4, A32
   using art to meet, 287
   using movement to meet, 108
   using science to meet, 264
   using social studies to meet, 212
Arts Impact model (Washington State), 33
arts integration
   arts in learning, 279–80
   collaborative planning, 24–25
   community connections, 28–33, 93–94
   designing curricula for, 21–28
   individual planning for, 22
   infusion differentiated from, 22, 23–24
   interdisciplinary approach, 288–90
   models and resources for teacher training in, 33–34, 34*t*
   models of multidisciplinary projects, 25–27, 28
   music in, 276–91
   role of arts, 279
   synthesis activities, 25
   value of, 21–22
assemblies, 32–33
Association for Supervision and Curriculum Development (ASCD), 21
astronomy, music and, 273
attention
   learning implications of, 11
   using music to gain children's, 20
attention-getters, musical, 167
aulos, 214
Auréole, 92–93
"Austrian Went Yodeling, An," 203
autism spectrum disorders
   adapting composition instruction for, 154
   adapting instruction for, 237, 259, 274, 291
   adapting movement instruction for, 117
   adapting vocal instruction for, 69
autoharp, A6, *136,* 222, 226
   played by teacher, 136
   playing, 48
"Autumn's Here," 65

Bach, Johann Sebastian, 219
   Goldberg Variations, 95
   lesson plan on, 83
background music, uses of, 79–80, 166
Baez, Joan, 90
bagpipes, 180, 215
ballet
   listening to, 82, 84–85
   resources for listening, A22
"Bambu," 212
banjo, 220
Barab, Seymour, *Little Red Riding Hood,* 286
Barbe and Swassing's learning modalities theory, 50
"Barb'ry Allen," 65, 69, 202, 218
bars, A8
Bartók, Béla, A14
Basie, Count, 89

A55

bass drum, 129
bass metallophone, *130,* 222
bass staff, A4, *A5*
bass xylophone, *126, 130*
Bateson, Gregory, 51
beat, A6
beatboxing, 145
Beatles, the, 91
bebop, 89
Beethoven, Ludwig van, 219
   lesson plan on, 83
   Rondo in C Major, Op. 51, No. 1, 259
behavior, background music's influence on, 79–80, 166
behavior disorders with externalizing behaviors
   adapting instruction for, 180, 237, 259, 274
   adapting instrumental instruction for, 131
   adapting movement instruction for, 117
   adapting vocal instruction for, 69
behavior disorders with internalizing behaviors
   adapting instruction for, 180, 237, 259, 274
   adapting movement instruction for, 117
   adapting vocal instruction for, 69
behaviorism theory, 50
bells, 170
   playing, 48
Ben-Hur (film), 215
Berrett, Joshua, 79
"B-I-N-G-O," 65
Black History Month, 176–77
blindness
   adapting instruction for, 180, 237, 259, 274, 291
   adapting listening for, 203
   adapting movement for, 117
   adapting vocal instruction for, 69
"Blue Bird, Blue Bird," 211
blues, 88, 220
bodhrán, 180
body percussion, 123–24, 151
   composing with, 142–45
   follow-the-leader games with, 166–67
   learning mathematics with, 255, 256
   raps with, 253, *254*
   telling stories with, 189
Boléro (Ravel), 288
bongo drums, 127, *127*
   playing, 48
Bono, Edward de, 139
"Bounce High, Bounce Low," 65, 200
"Bow Wow Wow," 258
brain-based learning, 10–12
brain research on music, 9–10, 39
   music's effect on brain chemistry, 79
   patterning and, 144
   singing, 60, *60*
brain rules with learning implications, 11*t,* 11–12
brass instruments, 219. *See also specific instruments*
   learning about, 81
   playing, 48
Brecker, Michael, 89
Brecker, Randy, 89
Broca's area, 60
"Brother, Come and Dance with Me" (Humperdinck), 86–87
Bruner, Jerome, 51
bucket brigade percussion, 250, *250*
Buddhist celebrations, 174–75
bugle, 173, 219

button concertina, 220
"Bye Bye Blackbird," 89

cabasa, *125*
call-and-response songs, 175
camp, music at, 168–69
Cano, Nati, 233
Canterbury Tales (Chaucer), 216
CantOvation Sing and See computer program, 270
Carnival, 177
Carnival of the Animals (Saint-Saëns), 81–82, 290
"Carnivorous Chant," *153*
castanets, 215
Cenerentola, La (Rossini), 286
Center for Arts Education (CAE), 31, 34
cha-cha, 116
chants
   building fluency and inflection, 203–5
   counting, 113, 241, 243, 246, 252
   creating, 142–45, 150–53
   integrating rhythmic movement into, 111–12, 133,
      190, 281–82
   nursery, 200
   playground, 65
"Charlie over the Ocean," 65
Chaucer, Geoffrey, *Canterbury Tales,* 216
"Cheki morena," 65
Chevéy system of rhythmic mnemonics, A14
Chicken Little, 193–94
Child, Lydia, 173
child development, 37–52
   age-appropriate activities, 40–41
   artistic-musical growth as critical component of, 37
   creative musical thinking, 49–50, 140
   listening, 48–49, 76–78
   matters of, 39–41
   movement and rhythm, 106–7
   musical skill development, 42–50
   research in, 39
   simple to complex phases of learning, 50–52
   stages of, 41–42
"Children, Go Where I Send Thee," 175, 243, 252
children's literature and music, 187–94
   adding songs to stories, 193–94
   creating soundscapes, 190–91, 192
   illustrated songs and chants, 191–93
   musical play, 187–90
children's songs. *See* songs children sing
Chinese gong, *128*
Chinese New Year, 176, *176*
Chinese opera gong, *128*
Chopin, Fryderyk, Prelude, Op. 28, No. 15, 288
choral reading
   building fluency and inflection with, 203–5
   types of, 205
Christian celebrations, 175
Christmas, 175
Chuseok (Korean harvest festival), 170, *170,* 211
"Cielito lindo," 181
Cinco de Mayo, 180–81
circle games, 113, 174, 177
clarinet, 219
classical music
   concert etiquette, 94
   listening to, 81–88
   resources for listening, A18–A21

classroom, community connections to, 28–33
    bringing artists into schools, 28–31, 93–94, 155
    bringing community into school, 32–33, 93–94
    field trips, 32, 94, 169–70
    larger arts community, 31, 94
    parents as resources, 31, 94
classroom, structuring for musical experiences, 19–21
    camps and, 168–69
    creating music centers, 20–21, 168
    ending the day with music, 166–67
    informal uses of music, 19–20
    language arts integration, 183–209
    musical breaks and transitions between subjects, 167–68
    occasions for music throughout the day, 162–82
    safe movement activities, 109
    signals and attention-getters, 167
    starting the day with music, 165–66
classroom teachers
    becoming attuned to singing, 61
    finding your own musicianship, 19
    instrument playing by, 135–37
    musical importance of, 18–19
    musical signals and attention-getters for, 167
    as music and arts facilitators, 16–35
    remembering childhood games and dances, 108
    song leading by, 66–67
    tips for effective song leading, 67
    training in arts integration, 33–34, 34*t*
claves, 126, *126,* 178
cognitive reasoning, music and, 9, 13
    development in children, 39–41
collaborative planning, 24–25
Coltrane, John, 89
Columbus, Christopher, 217, 218
comet-themed lesson plan, 27
common time, A7
"Complex Piece for Hand Sounds," 143
composing and arranging in National Standards for Music
    Education, 14, 149–50
    celebrating holidays and seasons to meet, 169
    creating to meet, 147
    listening to meet, 98
    playing instruments to meet, 122
    reading to meet, 188
    singing songs to meet, 59
    standard for grades 6–8, A35
    standard for grades K–4, A30
    using art to meet, 287
    using math to meet, 243
    using movement to meet, 108
    using science to meet, 264
    using social studies to meet, 212
composing music in the classroom, 139–59
    chants and raps, 150–53
    creating musical instruments, 145–47
    guidelines, 141
    improvisation and, 147–50
    music for operas and musicals, 155
    music for plays and videos, 154–55
    music representing planets, 283
    poetry and, 154, 155–56
    songs, 153–54
    using body sounds, 142–45
    visual arts and, 156–57
concert etiquette, 94
conch shells, 214

concrete operation stage, 41, 42
conga drum, A10, 127–28, 231
    playing, 48
consonant pitch relationships, 262–63
convergent thinking, differentiated from creative thinking, 49, 142
cool jazz, 89
cooperative learning theory, 50
Copland, Aaron, 82
    Appalachian Spring, 289, 290
    Rodeo, 220
Corea, Chick, 89
"Corn Grinding Song," 234
corpophone (defined), 144. *See also* body percussion
Cortés, Hernán, 217, 218
countermelodies, A5
"Counting Song, The (Uno, dos, y tres)", 243
counting songs and chants, 113, 241, 243, 252
country line dances, 116
cowbells, 129, 178
crash cymbals, 128, *128*
Creative Advantage (Seattle), 34
creative musical thinking, developing, 49–50, 139–59
    convergent thinking differentiated from, 49, 142
creative writing about music, 206
crescendo, A10, A11*t*
Crouching Tiger, Hidden Dragon (film), 96
Crumb, George, *Vox Balaenae,* 271
cuíca, 129
cultural and historical connections in National Standards
    for Music Education, 14
    celebrating holidays and seasons to meet, 169
    creating to meet, 147
    listening to meet, 98
    playing instruments to meet, 122
    reading to meet, 188
    singing songs to meet, 59
    standard for grades 6–8, A36
    standard for grades K–4, A32–A33
    using art to meet, 287
    using math to meet, 243
    using movement to meet, 108
    using science to meet, 264
    using social studies to meet, 212
cultural associations' arts programs, 33
cultural heritage songs, 66, 69
cumulative choral reading, 205
cumulative songs, 202–3
curricula, designing arts-integrated, 21–28
curriculum models
    interdisciplinary, 28
    threaded multidisciplinary, 27–28
    webbed multidisciplinary, 25–27
cut time, A7
cymbals, A10, 128, 215
    playing, 48

Dalcroze Eurhythmics, A12–A13, 107, 281
dance. *See* movement and dance
"Dance a Mambo," *190*
Dancercise, 107
Davis, Miles, 89
deafness
    adapting instruction for, 180, 237, 274
    adapting listening for, 80, 203
    adapting movement for, 117
    adapting vocal instruction for, 69

Debussy, Claude, 220
   La mer, 284
decibels, 263
"De colores," 65
decrescendo, A10, A11*t*
denominator, A9
descriptive writing about music, 206–7
dialogue choral reading, 205
DiFranco, Ani, 90
diminuendo, A10, A11*t*
Dirkes, Peyton, *Variation 20, 95*
discipline development, music and, 9–10
Dissanayake, Ellen, 279
dissonant pitch relationships, 262–63
divergent thinking. *See* creative musical thinking, developing
Diwali (Hindu festival), 173–74
Dixieland bands, 88
djembe drums, A10, 128
Dorian mode, 214
dotted note values, A8
Dowland Consort, 217
drawing in response to listening, 95–96, 283–84
"Draw Me a Bucket of Water," 200
drums, 178, 218. *See also specific drums*
   African, 246–48
   in ancient Greece, 215
   constructing, 145–46
   Korean, 170
   Navajo, 234
   notations for, A10
   playing, 48
Dukas, Paul, *Sorcerer's Apprentice,* 284
"Dúlamán," 180
dulcimer, 215, 220
duple meter, 249, 255
duration, A3
Dylan, Bob, 90
dynamics, A10

"Early One Morning," 218
earth and space sciences, music and, 262, 273
Eid al-Fitr (Muslim holiday), 171–72, 211
eighth grade, National Standards for Music Education,
   A33–A37
eighth note, A7
Einstein, Albert, 261
"El cascabel," 233
electronic keyboards, 130–31
   notations for, A10
   played by teacher, 135
electronic music, 220
Ellington, Duke, 89
"El rey," 233
Elynck, Aubree, *Variation 25, 96*
emotional disorders, adapting instrumental
   instruction for, 131
enactive mode, 51
enculturation, music and, 9, 13
engineering, music and, 262
English language learners (ELL), adapting
   instruction for, 291
Escher, M. C., 284
eurhythmics, 107, 281, A12–A13
evaluating music in National Standards for Music Education, 14
   celebrating holidays and seasons to meet, 169
   creating to meet, 147

   listening to meet, 98
   playing instruments to meet, 122
   reading to meet, 188
   singing songs to meet, 59
   standard for grades 6–8, A36
   standard for grades K–4, A31
   using art to meet, 287
   using math to meet, 243
   using movement to meet, 108
   using science to meet, 264
   using social studies to meet, 212
"Evening Prayer" (Humperdinck), 87
exercise
   learning implications of, 11
   singing as, 60
   using music with, 20
exploration, learning implications of, 12
expository writing about music, 207
eye-hand coordination, music and, 9

facet interdisciplinary model, 289–90
falsetto, A4
"Farmer in the Dell, The," 65, 202
fiddle, 219, 220. *See also* violin
field trips, 32, 93–94, 169–70
fife and drum music, 218, 219
fifth grade
   books recommended for illustrated songs and chants, 193
   books recommended for soundscapes, 192
   child development in, 40
   comfortable singing range in, *64*
   creative development in, 50*t*
   instrument playing developmental sequence, 132*t*
   instrument-playing skill development in, 48
   kinesthetic development in, 46, 47*t*
   listening skills development in, 76–77
   National Standards for Music Education, A33–A37
   rhythmic development in, 107, 110
   songs suitable in, 69–70
   vocal development in, 44*t,* 64
finger cymbals, 128, *128*
finger-snapping, 123, 142–43, 189
first grade
   books recommended for illustrated songs and chants, 193
   books recommended for soundscapes, 192
   child development in, 40
   comfortable singing range in, *63*
   creative development in, 50*t*
   improvising songs, 148
   instrument playing developmental sequence, 132*t*
   instrument-playing skill development in, 48
   kinesthetic development in, 46, 47*t*
   listening skills development in, 76–77
   musical breaks and transitions between subjects, 167
   National Standards for Music Education, A29–A33
   rhythmic development in, 107, 110
   songs suitable in, 67–68
   vocal development in, 43, 44*t,* 63
Fitzgerald, Ella, 89, *89*
"Five Fat Turkeys," 257, *258*
"Five Green and Speckled Frogs," 244, *245,* 246, 252
"Five Little Monkeys," 170, 252
flags, A8
flats, A5
Flohr, J., 50*t*
Florida Alliance for Arts Education (FAAE), 33–34

flutes, 215, 218, 219
folk and American roots music, 220
    listening to, 90–91
    resources for listening, A24–A25
folk dances, 115–16, 281
folk songs, pentatonic, A14
folktales, adding songs to, 193–94
"Follow the Drinking Gourd," 194, 223, *224–25*
follow-the-leader games, 166–67
foreign languages, 176, 200, 232–33, 235–36
form, A3
formal operation stage, 41, 42
forte, A10, A11*t*
fortissimo, A10, A11*t*
Foster, Stephen, 220
found sounds, 123
Fourier analysis, 263
fourth grade
    books recommended for illustrated songs and chants, 193
    books recommended for soundscapes, 192
    comfortable singing range in, *64*
    creative development in, 50*t*
    instrument playing developmental sequence, 132*t*
    instrument-playing skill development in, 48
    kinesthetic development in, 46, 47*t*
    listening skills development in, 76–77
    National Standards for Music Education, A29–A33
    rhythmic development in, 107, 110
    songs suitable in, 69–70*t*
    vocal development in, 44*t*, 63
frame drums, 127, *127*
frequency of sound waves, 263
"Frère Jacques," 253, 254
"Froggie Went A-Courtin'", 65, 200, 202

Gama, Vasco da, 217
gamelan orchestra, 129
Gandhi, Mahatma, 176
Gardner, Howard, 13, 21, 27, 50
Garfunkel, Art, 90
geometry, music and, 258–59
Ghana, music from, 229–32
Ghost Opera (Tan Dun), 91
Glass, Philip, 220
glockenspiel, *130*, 222
"Golden Vanity, The," 218
Goldilocks and the Three Bears, 194
gongs, A10, *128,* 129, 170
"Gong xi-fa cai," 176
"Goodbye, Old Paint," 194
Gottschalk, Louis, 220
gourds, 125, 218
Graceland (Simon album), 91
Grand Canyon Suite (Grofé), 284
grand staff, A3, A4, *A4*
Greece, music in ancient, 214
"Greensleeves," 218
Grieg, Edvard, *In the Hall of the Mountain King,* 185
Grinsteiner, Amy, 95–96
Grofé, Ferde, *Grand Canyon Suite,* 284
"Guadalajara," 233
Guerrero, Francisco, 217
güiro, *126*, 127, 178
    playing, 48
guitar, A6, 181, 220, 222, 226, 233
    notations for, A10

played by teacher, 135–36
    playing, 48
guitarrón, 233
Günther, Dorothee, A15
"Guru ndiani," 212
Guthrie, Sarah Lee, 65–66
Guthrie, Woody, 65–66, 90

haiku, 156
"Hail, Columbia," 219
half note, A7
Halloween, 172
Hamilton (musical), 151
hand-clapping, 123
    songs and chants, 20, 113, 142–43, 151, 250
hand dance for March from *The Nutcracker,* 85*t*
hand drums, 127, *127*
Handel, George Frideric, 219
hand jives, 143–44, *144,* 190
Hansel and Gretel (Humperdinck), 82, 83, *88*
Hansen, Dee, *The Music and Literacy Connection,* 195, 204
Hanukkah (Jewish festival), 174
harmonica, 220
harmony, A2, A5–A6
harp, 147
Harper, Ben, 90
Harrison, George, 91
Hartmann, Victor, *The Hut on Hen's Legs (Baba Yaga),* 284
"Haul Away Joe," 271, *272*
"Hava nagila," 66, 288
"Hava nashira," 114, 172
"Have You Seen the Ghost of John?", 172
Haydn, Franz Joseph, 219
hearing impaired
    adapting instruction for, 180, 237, 259, 274
    adapting listening for, 80, 203
    adapting movement for, 117
    adapting vocal instruction for, 69
"Here Comes Uncle Jesse," 65, 200
hertz, A4, 263
"Hey, Betty Martin," 200, 250, *250*
hierarchy of needs theory, 50
Hindu celebrations, 173–74
hip hop, 150–53
history, illuminating through music and the arts, 213–21
    ancient Greece, 214
    ancient Rome, 214–15
hocketing, 205
"Hokey Pokey, The," 167
Holborne, Anthony, 217
"Hold On," 117
holidays, music and, 169, 170–81
    autumn, 170–73
    calendar, 171*t*
    winter, 173–75
Holst, Gustav, *The Planets,* 273
"Hop, Old Squirrel," 168
hora, 115, 288
horn, 215
hosho, 125, 212
Hovhaness, Alan, *And God Created Great Whales,* 271
Humperdinck, Engelbert, *Hansel and Gretel,* 82, 83, 86–88, *88*
hurdy-gurdy, 215
"Hush, Little Baby," 91, 92–93
Hut on Hen's Legs, The (Baba Yaga) (Hartmann), 284
hydraulis, 214

A60 Index

"I Bought Me a Cat," 170, 203
iconic mode, 51
"I Got Rhythm," 89
"I'm Gonna Sing When the Spirit Says Sing," 114
immersed approach. *See* interdisciplinary approach
  to arts integration
impressionist music and painting, 284
impromptu choral reading, 205
improvising in National Standards for Music Education, 14
  celebrating holidays and seasons to meet, 169
  creating to meet, 147
  listening to meet, 98
  playing instruments to meet, 122
  reading to meet, 188
  singing songs to meet, 59
  standard for grades 6–8, A34
  standard for grades K–4, A30
  using art to meet, 287
  using math to meet, 243
  using movement to meet, 108
  using science to meet, 264
  using social studies to meet, 212
improvising music, 147–50
  Dalcroze approach, A12–A13
  musical conversations and, *148,* 148–49
  Orff approach, A15
  planned improvisations, 149, *150,* 178
Industrial Age, music of the, 219–20
infants
  creative development of, 49, 50*t*
  instrument-playing skill development, 48
  kinesthetic development of, 46, 47*t*
  listening skills development of, 76
  mental stimulation of, 9
  rhythmic development of, 107
  vocal development of, 44*t,* 60, 63
infusion, integration differentiated from, 22, 23–24
inherent musicality of children, 6–7
insect-themed lesson plan, 29
instrument playing
  as chant accompaniment, 133
  developmental sequence, 132*t*
  family-owned instruments, 131
  invented and constructed instruments, 124–25, 145–47,
    250, 267, 268
  motor skill development, 46, 48, 119–38
  occasions for, 133–34
  phonological awareness and, 197
  as song accompaniment, 134, 168
  sound exploration and discovery, 121–22
  sound sources and instrument types, 122–32
  standard classroom, 125–31
  as story reading accompaniment, 134
instrument playing in National Standards for Music Education, 122
  celebrating holidays and seasons to meet, 169
  creating to meet, 147
  listening to meet, 98
  reading to meet, 188
  singing songs to meet, 14, 59
  standard for grades 6–8, A34
  standard for grades K–4, A30
  using art to meet, 287
  using math to meet, 243
  using movement to meet, 108
  using science to meet, 264
  using social studies to meet, 212

instruments, historical, 214–15, 218
intellectual disabilities, adapting instrumental
    instruction for, 131
intensity, A3
interdisciplinary approach to arts integration, 21, 288–90
  project models, 28, 29
International Whaling Commission, 271
In the Hall of the Mountain King (Grieg), 185
invented and constructed instruments, 124–25, 145–47, 250,
    267, 268
Irish holidays, 178, 180
"Itsy Bitsy Spider, The," 184, 187
"I've Been Working on the Railroad," 170, 227, *228*

Jaques-Dalcroze, Émile, A12
jazz, 220
  listening to, 88–90
  print resources on, 89
  resources for listening, A23–A24
Jazz at Lincoln Center, 90
Jenkins, Ella, *65,* 65–66
Jensen, Eric, 22
Jeopardy! theme song, 167
Jewish celebrations, 172, 174
Jewish New Year, 172
jig, 115–16, 180
jingle bells, 129
"Jo ashila," 234, *234–35*
"Johnny Works with One Hammer," 243
Johnson and Johnson's cooperative learning theory, 50
Johnson, James Weldon, 175
Johnson, John Rosamund, 175
Jones, Norah, 91
"Jubilee," 168, 200
jug bands, 270
"Just from the Kitchen," 200

Kaa, Keri, 56
Kandinsky, Wassily, 284
Karenga, Maulana, 175
Katz, Susan A., 156
kazoo, 146
"Keep Your Eyes on the Prize," 117
"Keep Your Hand on that Plow," 117, 177
Keetman, Gunild, A15
Keil, Charles, *Dance Daily. Dance Early. Dance Now,* 103
keyboard accordion, 220
keyboard instruments. *See also specific instruments*
  played by teacher, 135
  playing, 48
key signatures, A5, *A6*
Kim, Kyung Hee, 142
kindergarten
  books recommended for illustrated songs and chants, 193
  books recommended for soundscapes, 192
  child development in, 40
  comfortable singing range in, *63*
  creative development in, 50*t*
  improvising songs, 148
  instrument playing developmental sequence, 132*t*
  instrument-playing skill development in, 48
  kinesthetic development in, 46, 47
  listening skills development in, 76
  musical breaks and transitions between subjects, 167
  National Standards for Music Education, A29–A33
  rhythmic development in, 107, 110

songs suitable in, 67–68
vocal development in, 43, 63
kinesthetic development, 46, 47*t*
King, Martin Luther, Jr., 175–76
Kingston Trio, 90
kithara, 214
Klee, Paul, 283
  Twittering Machine, 284
Knopfler, Mark, 119
Kodály, Zoltán, A13–A14
Kodály method, A13–A14, 63
"Kookaburra," 71, 170
Korean harvest festival (Chuseok), 170, *170,* 211
Kratus, J., 50*t*
Kronos Quartet, 91
"Kwanu'te'", 66, 218, *218*
Kwanzaa (African American celebration), 175
"K'wejina ch'ing ch'ing," 170, 211
Kweskin, Jim, 270
"Kye kye kule," 231–32, *232*

"La Adelita," 233
"La malagueña," 233
language arts
  building fluency and inflection, 203–5
  building reading comprehension, 200–205
  children's literature and music, 187–94
  composing music for plays and videos, 154–55
  developing reading and thinking skills through music, 195
  Greek epic poetry, 214
  improvising on vowels and consonants, 148–49, *149*
  improvising phrases, 198
  learning initial sounds, 196–97
  learning middle vowel sounds, 198
  learning rhyming sounds, 198–200
  music's use in teaching, 183–209
  phonological awareness, 195–200
  relationships with music, 184–85
  spelling with rhythm, 124
  story reading with instrumental accompaniment, 134
  writing about music, 205–8
"La raspa," 66
largo, A9
Lark Ascending (Vaughan William), 284
Lead Belly, 65–66, 90
learning disabilities, adapting listening for, 80, 203
learning modalities theory, 50
learning phase theory, 51
ledger line, A3
left-right differentiation, 166
Leibniz, Gottfried Wilhelm von, 240
"Leila," 65
Lesley University, 34
lesson plans
  Abiyogo, 194
  comets as theme in threaded curriculum model, 27
  Famous Composers from Europe, 83
  "Five Fat Turkeys," 257–58
  insects as theme for interdisciplinary model, 29
  Mexico: ¡Ole! Mariachi, 232–33
  Music from *Hansel and Gretel,* 86–88
  Music from "Hush, Little Baby," 92–93
  music from *The Nutcracker,* 84–85
  Native America: Music the Navajo Way, 234–35
  Northwest Coastal Indian culture, 23–24
  Out of Africa: Rhythm!, 229–32

"Peanut Butter and Jelly" motion song, *201*
  rain as theme om multidisciplinary model, 26
  "Rain Chant," 204
  From Slavery to Freedom, 221–25
  song-based lessons, 71–72
  Spinning a Thread through the Arts, 290
  Transportation and Nation-Building, 226–28
  Vietnam: Traditions and Change, 235–36
  Writing Poetry in Response to Music, 97
  writing skills interdisciplinary model, 29
Levitin, Daniel J.
  This is Your Brain on Music, 4
  The World in Six Songs, 153
life sciences, music and, 262, 270–71
"Lift Ev'ry Voice and Sing" (Johnson), 66, 175
"Linus and Lucy," 89
listening to music, 74–101
  active strategies, 77
  background uses, 79–80, 166
  ballet music, 82, 84–85
  children as listeners, 75
  classical music, 81–88
  concert etiquette, 94
  drawing or painting in response, 95–96
  ending the day with directed, 166
  evolution of, 48–49
  featured composers, compositions, or styles, 80–81
  folk and American roots music, 90–91
  foreground listening, 80–93
  jazz, 88–90
  live performances, 93–95
  occasions for, 78–79
  opera, 82–83, 86–88, 286
  orchestral music, 81–82
  popular music, 90
  preparing children for performances, 94–95
  responses through other arts, 95–98
  skill development, 76–78
  taste and, 80
  visual arts and, 283–84
  word bank for, 78*t*
  world music, 91–93
  writing in response, 96–97
listening to music in National Standards for Music
    Education, 14, 98
  celebrating holidays and seasons to meet, 169
  creating to meet, 147
  playing instruments to meet, 122
  reading to meet, 188
  singing songs to meet, 59
  standard for grades 6–8, A35
  standard for grades K–4, A31
  using art to meet, 287
  using math to meet, 243
  using movement to meet, 108
  using science to meet, 264
  using social studies to meet, 212
literature, music and, 286–87
"Little Cabin in the Woods," 202
"Little Johnny Brown," 65, 250
Little Red Riding Hood (Barab), 286
"Little Sally Walker," 200
Little Train of the Caipira, The (Villa Lobos), 185
"London Bridge Is Falling Down," 200
Louvre online resources, 157
"Low Bridge (Erie Canal Song)", 170, 258

A62   Index

Loy kratong (Thai celebration), 174–75
"Lucy Locket," 200
lute, 215
lyre, 214

Ma, Yo-Yo, 91, 92–93, 96
Magellan, Ferdinand, 217
Magic Flute, The (Mozart), 82, 286
Mahler, Gustav, 220
Making More Music computer program, 259
Making Music computer program, 259
mallets, percussion, A10
Mamas and the Papas, the, 90
mandolin, 220
Maōri people of New Zealand, singing of, 63
maracas, 125, *125,* 231
mariachi bands, 181, 232–33
Mariachi Divas, 233
Mariachi Los Camperos, 233
Mariachi Vargas de Tecalitlán, 233
Martin, Bill, *Listen to the Rain* (with Archambault), 123
Martin Luther King Day, 175–76
"Mary Had a Little Lamb," 168
Maslow, Abraham, 279
Maslow's hierarchy of needs theory, 50
Masters Tech Home, 116
mathematics
    algebra and music, 258–59
    computing fluently, 255–56
    connecting number words and numerals to amounts, 248
    counting with understanding, 243
    estimating strategies, 256, 258
    geometry and music, 258–59
    music's use in teaching, 240–60
    recognizing "how many" in a set, 248–49
    understanding and representing fractions, 249–50
    understanding place value and number order, 243–44
    understanding whole-number addition and
        subtraction, 252–53
    understanding whole-number multiplication and
        division, 253–55
"Mattie Groves," 202, 218
Max Found Two Sticks, 189–90
mbira, 212
McCutcheon, John, 65–66
McFerrin, Bobby, 92–93, 145
McPherson, Gary E., *The Child as Musician,* 37
media arts, music and, 285
medieval Europe, music in, 215–16
Medina, John, 10
melodica, 130–31
melodies, A2
melopoeia, 187–88
memory, repetition and, 11–12
Menotti, Gian-Carlo, *Amahl and the Night Visitors,* 82
Merriam, Alan P., 7–8
metallophones, A10, 130, *130,* 222
metaunderstandings, 25
meter, A3, A6–A7
Metheny, Pat, 89
metronome markings, A6
Metropolitan Museum of Art online resources, 157
Metropolitan Opera (New York), 155, 286
    radio broadcasts, 82
Mexican holidays, 180–81
Mexican music, 232–33

mezzo forte, A10, A11*t*
mezzo piano, A10, A11*t*
"Michael Finnegan," 200
minimalist music, 220
"Miss Mary Mack," 144, *145*
Mitchell, Elizabeth, 65–66
mobility impairments
    adapting composition instruction for, 154
    adapting instruction for, 180, 237, 259, 274
    adapting movement instruction for, 117
    adapting vocal instruction for, 69
modal music, 214
moderato, A9
modes of representation theory, 51
Mondrian, Piet, 283
Monet, Claude, *Water Lilies,* 284
monochord, 268–69
    constructed, 146–47
Morales, Cristobal, 217
"Mos,' mos'!", 212
motor skill development, music and, 9, 13
"Mountain Climbing," 65
"Mouse, Mousie," 200
mouth sounds, 123, 144–45, 151
movement and dance, 103–18
    activities in early childhood, 110
    children, rhythm and, 106–7
    circle dances, 114, 115, 172, 288
    court dances, 217
    early childhood, 110
    elements of dance, 281
    exploring, 107–8
    folk and pattern dances, 115–16
    game songs, 200
    hand jives, 143–44
    integrating with music education, 281–83
    kinesthetic development, 46
    manageable dance experiences, 113–16
    marching, 165, 255
    middle childhood, 111
    in National Standards for Music Education, 108*t*
    Navajo dance, 234–35
    popular dances, 116
    rhythmic components, 109, 165–66
    safe activities, 109
    in song, 112–13
    in speech, 111–12
    teacher's reminiscences, 108
Mozart, Wolfgang Amadeus, 13, 80, 219
    lesson plan on, 83
    The Magic Flute, 82, 286
"Mozart effect," 13, 80
multidisciplinary approach to arts integration, 21
    project models, 25–27
multiple intelligences, theory of, 13, 21, 27, 50, 280
Murphy, Heidi Grant, 92–93
music
    ending the day with, 166–67
    functions of, 7–9, 8*t*
    as part science, part art, 7
    as reward, 79
    science of sound, 262–63
    starting the day with, 165–66
    universal characteristics of, 8–9
    use in teaching language arts, 183–209
    use in teaching mathematics, 240–60

use in teaching other arts, 276–91
use in teaching science, 261–75
use in teaching social studies, 210–39
writing about, 205–8
Music Ace software program, A5
musical elements, A2–A11
"Music Alone Shall Live," 65
musicals, creating, 155, 166, 286
musical skill development, 42–50
    kinesthetic development, 46, 47t
    vocal development, 43–45
musica universalis (music of the spheres), 273
music centers, creating classroom, 20–21, 168
Music Educators National Conference (MENC), A28–A37, 14.
        See also National Association for Music Education
        (NAfME)
music in school, value of, 7, 12–14
musicking (defined), 6
music word bank, 78t
Muslim celebrations, 171–72
Musorgsky, Modest, *Pictures at an Exhibition,* 95, 156–57, 284
mutes, instrumental, A10
"My Dog Rags," 167
"My Grandfather's Clock," 220

narrative writing about music, 206
National Association for Music Education (NAfME), A28–A37, 14
National Council for the Social Studies (NCSS), 161, 211, 227
National Council of Teachers of English and the International
        Reading Association (NCTE/IRA), 161
National Council of Teachers of Mathematics (NCTM), 161
    basic goals, 242
    computing and estimating as goal, 255–58
    understanding meanings of operations as goal, 251–55
    understanding numbers and relationships as goal, 243–51
National Endowment for the Arts (NEA), 28
National Science Teachers Association (NSTA), 161, 262
National Standards for Arts Education, 280
National Standards for Music Education, A28–A37, 14, 221, 226
    celebrating holidays and seasons to meet, 168
    creating to meet, 147
    integrating with language arts, 185–87
    integrating with other arts, 280–87
    playing instruments to meet, 122
    singing requirements, 59t
    using art to meet, 287
    using listening to meet, 98
    using math to meet, 243
    using movement to meet, 98
    using reading to meet, 188
    using science to meet, 264
    using social studies to meet, 212
National Standards for Social Studies, 221, 226
National Standards for the English Language Arts, 186, 200, 203
Native Americans, 218, 234–35
naturals, A5
Navajo-language songs, 234–35
Nettl, Bruno, 210
neumes, A2, *A3*
New Horizons for Learning, 34
New York City, Center for Arts Education, 34
Nguyên Lê, 89
Nightingale, Earl, 139
nongak (Korean farmer's dance), 170, *170*
non-Western songs, 69
Northwest Coastal Indian Culture lesson plan, 23–24

notation, musical, A2
    of intensity, A10–A11, *A11*
    invented, 150, *151, 152*
    of pitch, A3–A6, A15
    reading, 63
    of timbre, A10
    of time, A6–A10, A15
note reading development, 48
note values, A7–A8, A8t
Nova (TV show), 273
Nutcracker, The (Tchaikovsky), 82, 284

ocarinas, 218
octave, A3, A5
Odetta, 90
"Oh Freedom," *222–23*
"Oh My Darling, Clementine," 168, 194
"Oh! Susanna," 194
"Old MacDonald," 203
"One, Two, Three Alary," 200, 252
"One Little Elephant," 243
onomatopoetic words, 189–90, 286–87
opera
    creating, 155, 166, 286
    listening to, 82–83, 86–88, 286
    resources for listening, A22
oral transmission, 90
Orff, Carl, A15, 130
Orff Schulwerk, A14–A16, 107, 111–12, 130
organ, 215
Organization of American Kodály Educators (OAKE), A14
orthographic or graphophonemic awareness, 196
"Oru kallu," 174
oscilloscope, 263, *263*
ostinatos, A5
"Over the River and through the Wood," 173, 211
overtones, A3, 263

"Paddling Song, The," 23–24, 200
painting in response to listening, 95–96, 283–84
panpipes, 214, 269
Parents as Arts Partners (PAAP), 31
parents as classroom resources, 31
parent-teacher associations, 32–33
Parker, Charlie, 89
partner songs, A5
patriotic songs, 66, 69, 165
    resources for listening, A23
pattern dances, 115–16
Patterson, Bill, 290
Paz, Suni, 65–66
"Peanut Butter and Jelly," 200, 201, *201*
pentatonic folk songs, A14
percussion instruments. *See also specific instruments*
    invented and constructed, 145–46, 250, 267, 268
    Korean, 170
    learning about, 81
    notations for, A10
    performing African drumming patterns, 246–48
    played by teacher, 137
    playing, 48
    unpitched, 125–29, 268
persuasive writing about music, 207
Peter, Paul, and Mary, 90
Peter and the Wolf (Prokofiev), 95, 185, 286
Petrushka (Stravinsky), 220

A64 Index

Pfister, Marcus, *The Rainbow Fish,* 290
Phish, 89
phonemic awareness concept, 111
phonological (phonemic) awareness, 195–200
photography, music and, 285
phrases, A2
Phrygian mode, 214
physical disabilities, adapting instruction for, 291
physical sciences, music and, 262–70
Piaget, Jean, 41
pianissimo, A10, A11*t*
piano, 130–31
   notations for, A10
   played by teacher, 135
piano (dynamic), A10, A11*t*
pick-up notes, A9
Pictures at an Exhibition (Musorgsky), 95, 156–57, 284
pitch, musical, A2, 268–70
   notation of, A3–A6
pizzicato, A10
Planets, The (Holst), 273
planets of the solar system, 273
Plato, 214
player piano, *219, 220*
playground songs and games, 65, 143–44, 151
playing. *See* instrument playing
poetry, composing music for, 154, 155–56
polyrhythms, 109
popular dances, 116, 281
popular music, 220
   listening to, 90
   resources for listening, A25
popular songs, 66, 202, 219–20
Prelude, Op. 28, No. 15 (Chopin), 288
preoperational stage, 41–42
preschool. *See* toddlers and preschool
Presidents' Day, 178
"Presidents for Their Time," 178, *179*
presto, A10
Price, Leontyne, 175
program music, 81–82, 284
   listening to, 286
Prokofiev, Sergei, *Peter and the Wolf,* 95, 185, 286
psaltery, 215
puberty, boys' voices in, 64
p'ung mul (Korean percussion ensemble), 170, *170*
Pythagoras, A3, A5, 262–63
Pythian Games, 214

"Qua Cầu Gió Bay," 202, 236, *236*
quadruple meter, A7, 249
quarter note, A7
"Quien es ese pajarito?", 69

"Rain Chant," 204
rainstick, constructing, 146
rain-themed lesson plan, 26
"Ramadan el sana di," 172, 211
range of children's voices, 45*t*, 62, 63, *63*
ranges of adult voices, 62
raps
   epic Greek poetry and, 214
   inventing, 150–53
   on multiplication tables, 253, *254*
rasps, 129
   constructing, 146

rattle drums, *127*
rattles, 125, *125,* 246–48
   constructing, 145
   playing, 48
Rauscher, Frances, 80
Ravel, Maurice, *Boléro,* 288
reading and notating music in National Standards for Music
      Education
   celebrating holidays and seasons to meet, 169
   creating to meet, 147
   listening to meet, 98
   playing instruments to meet, 122
   reading to meet, 188
   singing songs to meet, 14, 59
   standard for grades 6–8, A35
   standard for grades K–4, A31
   using art to meet, 287
   using math to meet, 243
   using movement to meet, 108
   using science to meet, 264
   using social studies to meet, 212
reading skills
   building comprehension, 200–205
   building fluency and inflection, 203–5
   developing through music, 195, 286–87
   singing and, 60–61
rebab, 215
rebec, 215
recorders, 215, *217,* 222
   fingering chart, *137*
   played by teacher, 136
   playing, 48
Reflections PTA arts program, 33
Reggio Emilia schools, 34
Reich, Steve, 220
resonance, 266–68
rhythm, A3, A7–A8, *A9*
   in African music, 229–32
   beat subdivisions and extensions, 253*t*
   exercises for, A8–A9
   hand jives and, 143–44, 190
   improvising, 178
   meter and, 249
   movement and, 106–7, 109–13, 165
   performing African drumming patterns, 246–47
   playing patterns with instruments, 133
   spelling skills and, 124
"Rhythm Complexes with Subdivisions of the Beat," 250, *251*
rhythmicking, 109
rhythm sticks, 125–26, *126,* 178, 246–48
   constructing, 146
"Rig-a-Jig-Jig," 200
Riley, Richard W., 276
"Ring Around the Rosie," 200
"Rocky Mountain," 170
"Roda pião," 177, 212
Rodeo (Copland), 220
Rome, music in ancient, 214–15
Rondo in C Major, Op. 51, No. 1 (Beethoven), 259
Rosenberg, Jane, *Sing Me a Story,* 83
Rosh Hashanah, 172
Rossini, Gioachino
   La Cenerentola, 286
   William Tell Overture, 284
Rothenberg, David, A1
rototoms, 128, *131*

Index **A65**

rounds, A5, 172, 253–54
"Row, Row, Row Your Boat," 200, 253–54
Rowling, J. K., 162

sackbut, 215
Saint-Saëns, Camille, *Carnival of the Animals,* 81–82, 290
"Sakura," 66
"Sally Sells Seashells," 197, *197*
salsa, 116
samulnori (Korean percussion ensemble), 170, *212*
sand blocks, 126, *126,* 178
    playing, 48
"Sansa kroma," 212, 229, *230–31*
"San Sereni," 200
"Savalivalah," 69
saxophone, 219
scale, A3
scat singing, 89
Schoenberg, Arnold, *Verklärte Nacht,* 220, 284
Schuller, Gunther, *Twittering Machine,* 284
science, music's use in teaching, 261–75
"Scotland's Burning," 258
scratching, 151
sea shanties, 271, *272*
seasonal celebrations, music and, 169, 170–81
    autumn occasions, 170–73
    calendar, 171*t*
    winter, 173–75
second grade
    books recommended for illustrated songs and chants, 193
    books recommended for soundscapes, 192
    child development in, 40
    comfortable singing range in, *63*
    creative development in, 50*t*
    improvising songs, 148
    instrument playing developmental sequence, 132*t*
    instrument-playing skill development in, 48
    kinesthetic development in, 46, 47*t*
    listening skills development in, 76–77
    musical breaks and transitions between subjects, 167
    National Standards for Music Education, A29–A33
    rhythmic development in, 107, 110
    songs suitable in, 67–68
    vocal development in, 44*t,* 63
Seeger, Pete, 65–66, 90
    Abiyoyo, 184, 187, 193, 194
Sendak, Maurice, *Where the Wild Things Are,* 191
sensorimotor stage, 41
sensory integration, learning implications of, 12, 13
sequencing songs, 202–3
seventh grade, National Standards for Music Education, A33–A37
sforzando, A11
Shankar, Anoushka, 91
Shankar, Ravi, 91
sharps, A5
Shaw, Gordon, 80
shekere, 125, *125,* 231
"She'll Be Comin' 'Round the Mountain," 167, 203
"Ship's Carpenter, The," 65
shofar, 172
"Shortnin' Bread," 65
sight identification, 196
signals, musical, 167
Signing Savvy, 116
Silk Road Ensemble, 91, 93
Simon, Paul, 90, 91

"Simple Gifts," 289, *289*
"Simple Piece for Hand Sounds," 143
"Singabahambayo," 69, 72
singing, 57–72. *See also* vocal development of children
    adult voice, 61–62
    becoming attuned to, 61
    a cappella, 145
    child voice, 62–64
    as core activity, 58–59
    cultural differences in, 62–63
    as healthy endeavor, 60
    inherent need for, 153
    National Standards for, 59
    vocal development of children, 43–45
    voice as personal instrument, 60–64
    to young children, importance of, 9
singing games, 20, 40, 108, 113, 257
    African, 229–32
    Mexican, 232–33
    movement with, 104, 107, 200, 281–82
singing in National Standards for Music Education, 14, 59*t*
    celebrating holidays and seasons to meet, 169
    creating to meet, 147
    listening to meet, 98
    playing instruments to meet, 122
    reading to meet, 188
    standard for grades 6–8, A33–A34
    standard for grades K–4, A29
    using art to meet, 287
    using math to meet, 243
    using movement to meet, 108
    using science to meet, 264
    using social studies to meet, 212
"Sing Together," 168
"Si nos dejan," 233
sixteenth note, A7
sixth grade
    books recommended for illustrated songs and chants, 193
    books recommended for soundscapes, 192
    comfortable singing range in, *64*
    creative development in, 50*t*
    instrument playing developmental sequence, 132*t*
    instrument-playing skill development in, 48
    kinesthetic development in, 46, 47*t*
    listening skills development in, 76–77
    National Standards for Music Education, A33–A37
    rhythmic development in, 107, 110
    vocal development in, 43, 44*t,* 64
Skinner's behaviorism theory, 50
"Skip to My Lou," 114, 198–200, *199*
"Skye Boat Song," 66, 200
slapstick, 129
sleep, learning implications of, 12
slit drums, 126–27
    constructing, 146
Smith, John, 218
Smithsonian Folkways Recordings, 65–66, 90–91
social interactions, music and, 10, 13–14, 20
socialization theory, 50
social studies
    American history, 221–36
    illuminating history through music and the arts, 213–21
    musical connections to time and place, 213
    music's use in teaching, 210–39
    sample lesson plans, 221–36
    valuing culture through music and the arts, 227–36

A66 Index

Society for Research in Child Development, 39
"Soldier, Soldier, Will You Marry Me?", 219
solfège, A12–A13, A14
song leading, tips for, 66–67, 67t
songs children sing, 64–66
    accompaniment for, A5–A6
    composing, 153–54
    cultural songs, 66
    ending the day with, 166
    instrumental accompaniment for, 134
    patriotic songs, 66
    popular songs, 66
    sequencing and cumulative, 202–3
    song-based lessons, 70–72
    songs by children, 64–65
    songs for children, 65–66
    starting the day with, 165
    structures of, 258–59
    suitable for intermediate grades, 69–70
    suitable for young children, 67–68
Songs of the Humpback Whale (recording), 271
soprano metallophone, *130*
soprano xylophone, *130*
Sorcerer's Apprentice (Dukas), 284
sound effects, 191
soundscapes, creating, 190–91
    books recommended for, 192
sound sources. *See also* instrument playing
    body sounds, 123–24
    found sounds, 123
sound waves, 263
    vibrations, 263–65
Sound Ways of Knowing: Music in the Interdisciplinary
        Classroom, 288–89
Spanish-language songs, 180–81, 232–33
special needs children
    adapting composition instruction for, 154
    adapting instruction for, 180, 203, 237, 259, 274, 291
    adapting instrumental instruction for, 131
    adapting listening for, 80
    adapting movement for, 117
    adapting vocal instruction for, 69
speech, integrating rhythmic movement into, 111–12, 133
spelling skills, rhythm and, 124
spirituals, 88
square dance, 115, 116
St. Patrick's Day, 178, 180, *180*
Standley, Jayne, 195
Stars and Stripes Forever, The, 255
"Star-Spangled Banner, The," 66, 165, 168
stems, A8
step dancing, 107
Still, William Grant, Symphony No. 1 (*Afro-American*), 284
Stockhausen, Karlheinz, 220
Stravinsky, Igor, 82
    Petrushka, 220
stress, learning implications of, 12
string instruments. *See also specific instruments*
    invented and constructed, 146–47
    learning about, 81
    notations for, A10
    playing, 48
"Sumer is icumen in," 216, *216*
survival, learning implications of, 11
suspended cymbal, *126, 128*
Suzuki violin study, 48

Swanick, K., 50t
Sweet Honey in the Rock, 65–66
swing music, 89
syllabification concept, 111
symbolic mode, 51
Symphony No. 1 (*Afro-American*) (Still), 284
symphony orchestra, *81*
synthesizers, 263

taiko drum, 129, *129*
Take 6, 175
"Take the 'A' Train," 89
talent, myth of innate, 10
tambourine, 129, *129,* 215
    constructing, 146
    playing, 48
Tan Dun
    Ghost Opera, 91
    theme music from *Crouching Tiger, Hidden Dragon,* 96
"Taps," 117, 173, 219
Taylor, James, 90
Tchaikovsky, Pyotr Il'yich, *The Nutcracker,* 82, 84–85, 284
teachers. *See* classroom teachers
technical writing about music, 207–8
technology, music and, 220–21, 262
"Teddy Bear, Teddy Bear," 196–97, *197*
temple blocks, 126
tempo, A6, A9–A10
"Ten in the Bed," 252
"Ten Little Alligators," 244, *245,* 246
Tennessee Arts Academy, 33
tessellations, 242
tessitura of adult voices, 62
tessitura of children's voices, 45t, 62
Thai moon festival (Loy Kratong), 174–75
Thanksgiving, 173, 211
"That's a Mighty Pretty Motion," 71
theater, music and, 285–86
third grade
    books recommended for illustrated songs and chants, 193
    books recommended for soundscapes, 192
    child development in, 40
    comfortable singing range in, *63*
    composing independently in, 150
    creative development in, 50t
    instrument playing developmental sequence, 132t
    instrument-playing skill development in, 48
    kinesthetic development in, 46, 47t
    listening skills development in, 76–77
    National Standards for Music Education, A29–A33
    rhythmic development in, 107, 110
    songs suitable in, 69–70
    vocal development in, 44t, 64
thirty-second note, A7
"This Land is Your Land," 69, 165, 170
"This Old Man," 200, 243–44, *244,* 252
Thomas, Judith A., 156
threaded curriculum model, 27–28
"Three Blind Mice," 253, 254
tie, A8
Tillman, J., 50t
timbre, A3, A10
time estimation, music and, 167–68
time signature, A7, *A7*
timpani, 130
    playing, 48

"Tingalayo," 134, *135*
Tobey, Mark, 284
toddlers and preschoolers
    books recommended for illustrated songs and chants, 193
    books recommended for soundscapes, 192
    creative development of, 49, 50*t*
    improvising songs, 148
    instrument playing developmental sequence, 132*t*
    instrument-playing skill development, 48
    kinesthetic development of, 46, 47*t*
    listening skills development of, 76
    rhythmic development of, 107, 110
    songs suitable for, 67–68
    vocal development of, 43, 44*t*, 63
Total Learning Institute, 34
transdisciplinary approach to arts integration, 21
transportation-themed lesson plan, 226–28
treble staff, A4, *A5*
triangle, A10, *128,* 128–29
    playing, 48
triple meter, A7, 249
triplets, A9
trumpet, 173, 214, 215, 219, 233
tuba, 219
"Twelve Days of Christmas, The," 203
twentieth-century music, 220–21
"Twinkle, Twinkle, Little Star," A3, 168, 192, 249, 258
Twist with a Burger, Jitter with a Bug, 190
Twittering Machine (Klee), 284
Twittering Machine (Schuller), 284

ukulele, 222, 226
    playing, 48

Vagin, Vladimir, *The Nutcracker Ballet,* 82
Valentine's Day, 177
"Valentine's Day Greeting" rhyme, 177, *178*
Varèse, Edgard, 220
Vaughan, Sarah, 89
Vaughan Williams, Ralph, *Lark Ascending,* 284
Verklärte Nacht (Schoenberg), 220, 284
verse-chorus song structures, 258
Veteran's Day, 173
vibraslap, 129
Vietnamese-language songs, 235–36
vihuela, 217
Villa Lobos, Heitor, *The Little Train of the Caipira,* 185
violin, 233. *See also* fiddle
viols, 219
visual arts
    composing and, 156–57
    elements of, 283
    integrating with music education, 283–85
    in response to listening, 95–96
visual impairments
    adapting instruction for, 180, 237, 259, 274, 291
    adapting listening for, 203
    adapting movement for, 117
    adapting vocal instruction for, 69
Vittoria, Tomás Luís de, 217
vocal development of children, 43–45
    cultural differences, 62–63
    physical, 62

    range and tessitura, 45*t*
    voice changes in adolescence, 45, 64
voice types, A10
"Volver volver," 233
Vox Balaenae (Crumb), 271
Vygotsky's socialization theory, 50

"Wabash Cannonball," 192, 226, *227*
Wagogo people of eastern Africa, singing of, 63
Waldorf schools, 34
Washington, Booker T., 175
Washington (state)
    Arts Impact model, 33
    Creative Advantage (Seattle program), 34
Weavers, The, 90
webbed curriculum model, 25–27
"Weevily Wheat," 200
Welch, Gillian, 90
We're Going on a Bear Hunt, 188–89
Wernicke's area, 60
"We Shall Not Be Moved," 176
"We Shall Overcome," 117, 168, 170, 176, 200, 202
whale communication, 270–71
"What a Wonderful World," 89
"When I First Came to This Land," 219
"When Johnny Comes Marching Home," 69, 170, 250
Where the Wild Things Are (Sendak), 191
whip, 129
"Who Built the Ark?", 170, 192, 202
whole note, A7
wiggle songs, 167
Williams Syndrome, 13
William Tell Overture (Rossini), 284
wind instruments. *See also specific instruments*
    invented and constructed, 146
    learning about, 81
    notations for, A10
    playing, 48
Women of the Calabash, 175
Wonder, Stevie, 175
wood blocks, 126, *126,* 170, 178
word banks, generating, 78*t*, 287
world music, 220
    listening to, 91–93
    resources for listening, A26
writing
    about music, 205–8
    in response to listening, 96–97
writing skills interdisciplinary model, 29

xylophones, A10, 130, *130*
    constructing, 146
    Orff, A14
    playing, 48

"Yankee Doodle," 194, 219
Yo! Hungry Wolf: A Nursery Rap, 194
Yopp, Hallie Kay, 200
Yopp, Ruth Helen, 200

Zumba, 107
"Zum gali gali," 69